GIFTS TO THE
TSARS

ѺБРАЗ ВЕЛИКАГО
ГДРА ЦРА ИВЕЛИКАГО
КНЗА · АЛЕѮѢА МІХАЙЛОВІ́ЧА
ВСЕА ВЕЛІКІА ІМАЛЬА
ІБѢЛЬА РОСІІ САМОДЕ́РЦА ·

GIFTS TO THE
TSARS

1500 – 1700

TREASURES
from the KREMLIN

Barry Shifman and Guy Walton, General Editors

HARRY N. ABRAMS, INC., PUBLISHERS,
IN ASSOCIATION WITH THE INDIANAPOLIS MUSEUM OF ART
AND THE STATE HISTORICAL-CULTURAL MUSEUM PRESERVE, MOSCOW KREMLIN

Published on the occasion of the exhibition "Gifts to the Tsars: 1500–1700, Treasures from the Kremlin," organized by the Indianapolis Museum of Art in conjunction with The State Historical-Cultural Museum Preserve, Moscow Kremlin, held in Indianapolis from September 23, 2001, through January 13, 2002.

The publication of the catalogue was made possible by the generous support of the Alliance of the Indianapolis Museum of Art.

THE STATE HISTORICAL-CULTURAL MUSEUM
PRESERVE, MOSCOW KREMLIN
Elena Y. Gagarina, Director-General
Dr. Nonna Sergeyevna Vladimirskaya, Museum Deputy Director
Dr. Aleksey Konstantinovich Levykin, Director of Science
Galina Anatolievna Markova, Deputy Director, Western European Metalwork Department
Elena Anatolievna Morshakova, Deputy Director, Ancient Russian Metalwork Department
Dr. Inna Isidorovna Visnevskaya, Deputy Director, Textiles Department

EXHIBITION CURATORS:
Dr. Irina Akimovna Bobrovnitskaya, Curator, Ancient Russian 12th Century Metalwork and Russian State Regalia
Natalia Viktorovna Bushueva, Curator, Patriarch's Palace Museum
Irina Alexandrovna Zagorodnyaya, Curator, Western European Metalwork Department
Liubov Pavlovna Kirillova, Curator, Carriages and Stable Treasury
Anzhella Gennadievna Kudriavtseva, Curator, Western European Metalwork Department
Marina Vasilievna Martynova, Curator, Ancient Russian 12th–15th Century Metalwork
Dr. Olga Borisovna Melnikova, Curator, Stable Treasury Collection
Asya Ivanovna Romanenko, Research Associate
Valentina Georgievna Chubinskaya, Curator, Paintings Collection
Elena Alexandrovna Yablonskaya, Curator, Western European Firearms
Sergei Pavlovich Orlenko, Research Associate

CATALOGUE CONTRIBUTORS:
Dr. Nonna Sergeyevna Vladimirskaya, Senior Catalogue Editor
Elena Anatolievna Morshakova, Irina Alexandrovna Zagorodnyaya, Compilation

AUTHORS: Dr. Irina Akimovna Bobrovnitskaya (IAB); Natalia Viktorovna Bushueva (NVB); Valentina Georgievna Chubinskaya (VGC); Liubov Pavlovna Kirillova (LPK); Anzhella Gennadievna Kudriavtseva (AGK); Dr. Aleksey Konstantinovich Levykin (AKL); Marina Vasilievna Martynova (MVM); Dr. Olga Borisovna Melnikova (OBM); Eleana Anatolievna Morshakova (EAM); Asta Ivanovna Romenenko (AIR); Barry Shifman (BS); Dr. Inna Isidorovna Vishnevskaya (IIV); Guy Walton (GW); Elena Alexandrovna Yablonskaya (EAY); Irina Alexandrovna Zagorodnyaya (IAZ)

EDITORS OF THE RUSSIAN TEXT: Tatiana Nikolaevna Kuleshova; Mata Nikolaevna Larchenko; Irina Alexeyevna Pantykina; Natalia Vasilievna Rashkovan

COMPILER OF BIOGRAPHIES: Guy Walton

PHOTOGRAPHS (unless otherwise credited): Viktor Nikolaevich Seregin

PHOTOGRAPH EDITOR: Barry Shifman

HARRY N. ABRAMS, INC.
EDITOR: Barbara Burn
DESIGNER: Lindgren/Fuller Design

Library of Congress Cataloging-in-Publication Data
Shifman, Barry.
   Gifts to the Tsars, 1500–1700 : treasures of the Kremlin / Barry Shifman and Guy Walton.
      p. cm.
   Published in connection with an exhibition at the Indianapolis Museum of Art.
      Includes bibliographical references and index.
      ISBN 0-8109-0600-7 — ISBN 0-936260-75-0 (pbk.)
      1. Decorative arts—Exhibitions. 2. Romanov, House of—Art collections—Exhibitions. 3. Art objects—Russia (Federation)—Moscow—Exhibitions. 4. Gosudarstvennaël Oruzheænaël palata (Russia)—Exhibitions. I. Walton, Guy. II. Indianapolis Museum of Art. III. Title.
NK512.I53 S54 2001
745'.094'0744731—dc21   2001022185

Harry N. Abrams, Inc.
100 Fifth Avenue
New York, N.Y. 10011
www.abramsbooks.com

FRONTISPIECE: Anonymous, *Tsar Alexei Mikhailovich*, 1670s. State Historical-Cultural Museum Preserve, Moscow Kremlin (cat. no. 21)

CONTENTS

In May of 1999, when I set foot for the first time in the galleries of the Armory Museum of the Moscow Kremlin, I stood in amazement as I gazed upon the treasures exhibited there. Although I had studied these remarkable objects in photographs and reproductions, I nevertheless was unprepared for the splendor I encountered when my colleagues and I entered the galleries at the head of the museum's grand stairway.

In towering cases, on tiered platforms covered in velvet, were arrayed row upon row of precious objects of silver and gold studded with gemstones and pearls. Together with jeweled church objects (crucifixes, censers, gospel covers) these magnificent pieces conveyed a vivid idea of the brilliance of the ceremonial life of the tsars of old Russia. The display continued in an adjacent chamber where we discovered an important group of vessels associated with the dining of the tsars. Notable among these was the jeweled drinking cup of Tsar Mikhail Romanov. A selection of these works, many of which were fabricated in the Kremlin workshops, comprise the first section of the exhibition *Gifts to the Tsars*, the occasion for publication of this catalogue.

As we continued our progress through this unique museum, my colleagues and I discovered in subsequent galleries extraordinary objects from the Ottoman Empire (Turkey), Safavid Persia, and the rulers of major European powers. With these splendid works of art we come to the central theme of this book and the exhibition it documents: *Gifts to the Tsars*. Many of the treasures preserved in the Armory Museum came to Russia in the hands of diplomats seeking treaties or merchants seeking trading privileges.

In the museum's last and largest gallery one finds breathtaking displays of silver and gilded silver objects in the form of enormous standing cups, ewers, basins, table ornaments in the form of animal and figural sculp-

tures and other extravagant objects—literally hundreds of diplomatic and ambassadorial gifts to the tsars. Whole cases are devoted to the display of gifts from Poland, Holland, England, Denmark and Sweden. Gifts from Austria and other German-speaking lands are arranged to show sixteenth and seventeenth-century silver from the great goldsmithing centers of Nuremberg, Hamburg, and Augsburg—surely the finest collection of this material in the world. Most of the objects illustrated in this book and included in the exhibition were drawn directly from these display cases. It is our hope that these superb works of art will give a sense of the impact of a visit to this unique museum in Moscow.

Our exhibition is *of*, but not exclusively *about* precious objects. For the treasures shown here also are historical documents that speak eloquently of the often turbulent relations among rulers and nations at the time. The list of recipients and donors is studded with names that resonate in world history: Russian tsars Ivan the Terrible, Boris Godunov, Mikhail Romanov, Peter the Great; English monarchs James I, Charles II; Queen Christina of Sweden; Shah Abbas II of Persia; Ottoman Sultan Murād IV; John III Sobieski, hero king of Poland; Emperor Leopold I of Austria; Christian IV of Denmark. This truly is an exhibition of "history written in silver and gold."

We share with our friends at the State Historical-Cultural Museum Preserve, Moscow Kremlin the hope, eloquently expressed by the Director-General of that multifaceted institution Elena Y. Gagarina, that this publication and the exhibition it was prepared to accompany will make a "beautiful contribution" to relations between the United States and Russia. On behalf of the Indianapolis Museum of Art, its governing board, trustees and staff, I express our gratitude to Elena Gagarina and her colleagues at the Kremlin Museums for their cooperation and their excellent work in preparing the objects for this exhibition and the essays and catalogue entries for this publication. In particular, I wish to thank for their special efforts Dr. Aleksey Levykin, Director of Science, Armory Museum, and Elena Morshakova, Deputy Director, Ancient Russian Metalwork Department. For the exhibition concept I am pleased to acknowledge the help of Galina Markova, Deputy Director, Western European Metalwork Department. I also wish to thank Irina M. Rodimtseva, the Kremlin Museums' former director-general, for her support of this project in its initial stages.

I thank the authors of the catalogue essays, the introductory essays that preface each section of the catalogue, and the catalogue entries. Their contributions have enhanced the experience of visitors to the exhibition and have made this book a significant contribution to understanding the practice of diplomatic gift giving and its role in international politics. I also am pleased to acknowledge the hard work and wise counsel of my colleague Ellen Lee, Deputy Director and Chief Curator of the Indianapolis Museum of Art.

We are also appreciative of the work it took to plan and implement the exhibition "Gifts to the Tsars" at the Indianapolis Museum of Art. Numerous staff members need to be thanked for their efforts: Sue Ellen Paxson, Director of Exhibitions; Sherman O'Hara, Chief Designer; Vanessa Burkhart, Registrar; Hélène Gillette-Woodard, Senior Conservator of Objects; A. Michael Bir, Mount Builder, Conservation; Kathy Lang; Director of Marketing and Communications; Susan Long-henry, Director of Education; Rosie May, Manager of Public Educational Program; Stan Blevins, Foundation Relations Coordinator; and Judy Grimes, Coordinator of the Alliance Museum Shop.

We are grateful as well to the generous individuals, foundations, corporations and other organizations that have given financial support to the ambitious enterprise of bringing this exhibition to Indianapolis. A particular thanks to the Alliance of the Indianapolis Museum of Art for their support of this publication. I also wish to thank Harry N. Abrams, Inc., publishers of this volume, and their able editor Barbara Burn who guided its creation.

Many, many scholars, friends and colleagues from Russia, the United States, and elsewhere have generously given of their time and expertise to help with our exhibition and this publication. I beg their forgiveness for not mentioning each here by name.

Finally, I am pleased to acknowledge and applaud the ambition, insight and effective efforts of my colleague Barry Shifman, curator of the exhibition and general editor of this book together with co-editor Professor Guy Walton of New York University. Mr. Shifman and Professor Walton together have guided this project from its inception to conclusion with invaluable contributions from the distinguished catalogue authors and the able assistance of the staff of the Indianapolis Museum of Art. I join them in thanking all whose contributions have helped make this undertaking a success.

Bret Waller, Director
Indianapolis Museum of Art

For millions of people throughout the world, their knowledge of Russia, its history and culture, begins with the ancient Moscow Kremlin, which served for centuries as the residence for Muscovite rulers, first the grand dukes and then, from the mid-sixteenth century on, the Russian tsars. In the early eighteenth century, Tsar Peter I (the Great) moved the capital to his newly built city on the Neva, St. Petersburg, but Moscow remained the "original" capital in the eighteenth and nineteenth centuries. This is where all the Russian emperors were crowned, and in 1918 it regained its status as the capital. Even today the Kremlin is the residence of Russia's head of state.

This lofty status of the Kremlin—an ancient fortress with magnificent churches and palaces—determined its history. In the fourteenth century, the grand duke's court already possessed a rich treasury of ancestral relics and treasures. Handed down from generation to generation, from father to son, lovingly preserved and added to, the treasury remains the richest Kremlin treasure house and Moscow's oldest museum—the Armory.

The high artistic quality of the Armory's collections is not all that makes this museum unique. The collection mirrors the life of the capital and the most fascinating pages in Russia's history. Between the late fifteenth and the seventeenth century, as its power grew and was consolidated, Russia's role in the international arena became increasingly visible and important. This was the period when Russian diplomacy took shape through the activities of the first Russian diplomats and when one of the most colorful and sumptuous court rituals was defined— the ceremonial reception of foreign ambassadors. The central event in this ceremony was the sovereign's reception of the envoys and the formal presentation of the ambassadorial gifts. The richness and diversity of these gifts can be judged from surviving documents: exotic animals and splendid horses, clever mechanical devices and weapons, precious fabrics and the ravishing work of goldsmiths. These rare works of art decorated the halls of the tsar's palace, while the fabrics were used to create magnificent court dress.

Precious gifts went into the sovereign's treasury, where they remained until they later became the core of the Armory collection. Today the gifts from Eastern and Western rulers brought to the Russian tsars stun visitors to the Kremlin museums with the fantastic diversity of their forms, the sumptuous grandeur of their decoration, and the elegance and virtuosity of their execution.

In sixteenth- and seventeenth-century Russian court culture, side by side with these imported foreign exotica, were creations by Russian artists and jewelers that were remarkable for their uniqueness and perfection of execution. This magnificent juxtaposition was the visible embodiment of diplomatic and political alliances and cultural interchange.

We can only hope that this exhibition at the Indianapolis Museum of Art will not only be a vivid symbol of this kind of cultural interchange between Russia and the United States but will also make its own small yet beautiful contribution to relations between our countries.

Elena Y. Gagarina, Director-General
State Historical-Cultural Museum Preserve,
Moscow Kremlin

A C K N O W L E D G M E N T S

Much of the credit for the exhibition and this catalogue should be given to Bret Waller, Director of the Indianapolis Museum of Art, whose involvement, enthusiastic support, and hard work have proved indispensable. The help of Ellen Lee, the museum's Deputy Director and Chief Curator, must also be acknowledged, as she has been involved in the exhibition project in many ways from the very beginning. The concept of the exhibition was developed in close consultation with the administration and staff of The State Historical-Cultural Museum Preserve, Moscow Kremlin. Galina Markova refined and articulated the exhibition concept. Elena Morshakova and Dr. Aleksey Levykin also played a fundamental role. Our editor at Harry N. Abrams, Inc., Barbara Burn, has done a superb job in crafting this catalogue; we are grateful to her for her constant support.

We thank both Marian Schwartz and Nadia Zlatanova Strenk for their superb translations of the Russian texts published here. Other important translation work was done both in Moscow and in Indianapolis by Dr. Maria Pavlovszky and George Fowler, Associate Professor of Slavic Languages, Indiana University. Both Dr. Pavlovszky and Mr. Fowler have from the very beginning provided enormous help on numerous aspects of the catalogue and exhibition project, for which we are grateful. Donald Reindl furnished translations of some German material.

The editors have imposed on various colleagues to read sections of the catalogue manuscript and have incorporated many of their suggestions. Edward L. Keenan, Director, Dumbarton Oaks, Harvard University, made corrections and insightful comments. The comments of other specialists were also very welcome: Donald LaRocca, Curator, Department of Arts and Armor, The Metropolitan Museum of Art, New York; Dorothy Sites Alig, Senior Conservator of Textiles,

Indianapolis Museum of Art; and Dr. Thomas Lentz, Director of International Art Museums Division, Smithsonian Institution.

Other colleagues have offered their help in various ways: Dr. Bernhard Appenzeller, Librarian, Ulm Stadtbibliothek; Dr. Beatrix Basics, Head of the Historical Gallery, Hungarian National Museum, Budapest; Edward Kasinec, Chief Librarian, Slavic and Baltic Division, New York Public Library; Robert Davis, Jr., Librarian, Slavic and Baltic Division, New York Public Library; Philippa Glanville; Tamara Igoumnova, Deputy Director, State Historical Museum, Moscow; Dieter Lohmeier, Librarian, Schleswig-Holsteinische Landesbibliothek; Dr. Mikhail Petrovich Lukichev, Director of the Russian State Archive of Ancient Documents, Moscow; Dr. Lorenz Seelig, Curator of Metalwork, Bayerisches Nationalmuseum, Munich; and Dr. David Sarkisyan, Director, A.V. Shchusev State Museum of Architecture, Moscow. Others to be thanked for their assistance are Katya Kurakayeva, Julia Shklyar, Priscilla Soucek, Gleb Uspensky, Mary Jane Vogelsang, and Carola Walton. Myrna Nisenbaum, Administrative Assistant, Indianapolis Museum of Art, has worked closely with the catalogue and exhibition project.

We are grateful to members of the staff of various museums, libraries, and cultural institutions who helped in the finding and acquisition of photographs for this publication: Dr. Filiz Çagman, Director, Topkapi Palace Museum, Istanbul; Jennifer Day; Dr. Brigitte Holl, Head of the Museum Department, Heeresgeschichtliches Museum im Arsenal, Vienna; Peter Kristiansen, Curator, The Royal Danish Collections; Elisabeth Reicher, Kunsthistorisches Museum, Vienna; Dr. Ursula Sjöberg, Curator of Textiles, The Swedish Royal Collections; Sussi Wesström, Nationalmuseum, Stockholm.

Barry Shifman and Guy Walton

1

THE PROJECTION
AND CELEBRATION OF POWER

JAMES H. BILLINGTON

From the sixteenth to the eighteenth century, the Russians created something far more imposing and awesome than a mere nation-state in the eastern half of Europe. In effect, they combined an empire on the scale of Genghis Khan and the spiritual authority of a Byzantine emperor. At one level, this rise of Russia as a great power can be seen as a typical European phenomenon of the time. Russia replaced first Poland and then Sweden as the dominant power in northeastern Europe, much as Prussia replaced Austria in central Europe and France supplanted Spain in southwestern Europe. Like Prussia, Russia was essentially a military state; like France, Russia embodied its power in a megalomaniac architecture.

Yet the great palaces of St. Petersburg were much more than a mere multiplication of Versailles. Although Russian courtiers adopted the French language, as those in Prussia did, the Russian monarch had—and retained—even more control over his subjects than Louis XIV had wielded over his. And the place in which the tsars of Russia first concentrated and exercised that power, the Moscow Kremlin, created an aura of absolutism

FIG. 1. The Moscow Kremlin (photo courtesy the State Historical-Cultural Museum Preserve, Moscow, Kremlin)

that was more Asian than European and has lasted to this day.

In the period covered by this catalogue, Russia went from being basically a principality (Muscovy) bearing the name of a city to becoming the first and most enduring of the modern European empires. Its expanse covered much the same territory as the Mongol Empire, which had overrun and subjugated the earlier Kievan state of the Orthodox Eastern Slavs in the thirteenth century. Moscow had slowly risen to dominate the scattered principalities of Kievan Rus, largely on the strength of its special relationship with the Mongols, first as the collecting agent for paying tribute, then as the organizing force for the armed resistance that led to the end of the Mongol yoke in 1480.

But the danger to a resurgent Russia did not end (in some ways it actually increased) in the sixteenth and early seventeenth centuries. A number of the successor states (Tatar khanates) of the Mongol Empire came together under the leadership of the khan of Crimea and, with periodic support from the powerful Ottoman emperor, intermittently invaded and ravaged Muscovy from the south. Russia was faced with perpetual insecurity in what they then called the "wild field," the open steppe of southern Russia and Ukraine (fig. 2).[1] Both the Tatar raiders and the Cossacks brought in to fight them divided and often switched their allegiances between their rival Christian overlords, Russia and Poland, who were in turn often more at war with each other than either was with the Muslim Tatars, who were not fully subjugated by Russia until the late eighteenth century.

Tsar Alexei Mikhailovich definitively bested the Poles after a century of intermittent warfare, and he turned eastern Ukraine into "Little Russia" in the mid-seventeenth century. His son, Peter I (the Great), finally defeated the Swedish rivals of the Poles early in the

eighteenth century, after the Swedes also tried to ally with the steppe people to the south against Russia.

In the process of building the largest army in the world, early modern Russia enserfed its peasantry and violently suppressed political and religious dissent. In the space of less than a century and a half, a landlocked principality had extended its imperial reach to the shores of the Baltic, Black, and Caspian Seas and to the Pacific Ocean. The authoritarian claims of the Russian tsars had grown accordingly—and become as arbitrary and absolute as those of the Tatar khans, whose domains they were rapidly and systematically absorbing. The oriental presumption of prostration (in Russian *chelobit-nya*, "beating the forehead") before the tsar was so well established that the window in the Kremlin palace built by Tsar Alexei for receiving his subjects' petitions was

FIG. 2. Claes Jansz. Visscher after Hessel Gerritsz, *Map of Russia with Plan of Moscow*, 1651. Copper engraving on paper, hand colored, 16³/₄ x 21 in. (43 x 54 cm). Amsterdam University Library, Map Collection

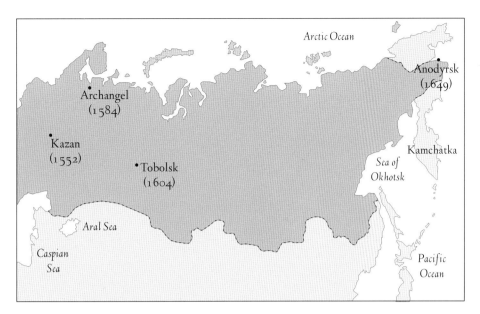

FIG. 3. *The Russian East*, c. 1700 (map drawn by Varnau Creative Group, Inc., Indianapolis). Dates indicate when cities were established or conquered.

called the *chelobitnoe* window. And the throne on which he sat was designed in Persia, the most absolute monarchy with which Russians were then in direct contact.

The Russian movement eastward was, of course, part of the general expansion of a Europe that had lost its historic Mediterranean links with the Middle East once the Muslim Ottoman Empire had conquered Christian Constantinople in 1453. England and Holland, whose explorers sought a northwest passage through North America to Asia, also sought a northeast passage around Russia. The Western European desire for Russian resources developed rapidly, and nearly all the major countries in Europe, which was in the final throes of religious wars between Catholics and Protestants, became interested in the possibility of alliance with a large and expanding Orthodox country that did not seem clearly committed to either side of the western religious divide.

But the Russia that the rest of Europe was discovering diplomatically during this period linked power with religion in its expansion more intimately than any other European nation, except those of the distant Iberian Peninsula. The Moscow Kremlin was not merely the center of power; it was the ultimate walled citadel, where the final defense could be made of an empire that had no protective natural boundaries. The Kremlin was

also the center and source of sanctification for the entire imperial enterprise. Architects had come from Renaissance Italy to thrust up three glorious white-stoned churches inside the Kremlin in the late fifteenth century: one for the baptism of the tsar (in honor of the Annunciation), another for burial (in honor of the Archangel Michael), and the grandest of all for marriages and coronations (in honor of the Assumption) (fig. 4).[2] These architects had also raised up a mighty bell tower, which was thought to radiate sanctity as far out into the gray, wooden world of Muscovy as the sound of the largest bell could be heard.

All of this took place under the grand duke of Russia, Ivan III (r. 1462–1505), who was the first to adopt the title of tsar (the Russian version of Caesar) and the first ruler of Russia later to be called "the Great." By marrying the niece of the last emperor to rule the Eastern Christian Empire in Constantinople (the "Second Rome"), Ivan created an aura that soon led a monk to suggest that although ancient Rome had fallen to the barbarians in the fifth century and the Second Rome to the Muslims in the fifteenth, Moscow was now the Third Rome—in effect the locus of the final millennial realm on earth.[3]

This exalted claim seemed to be vindicated not just by the rapid expansion of Russian power, but also by a concurrent contraction in the power of the only other credible claimant to the Roman imperial heritage: the Holy Roman Empire. By the time of Peter the Great, this venerable institution was already well on the way toward

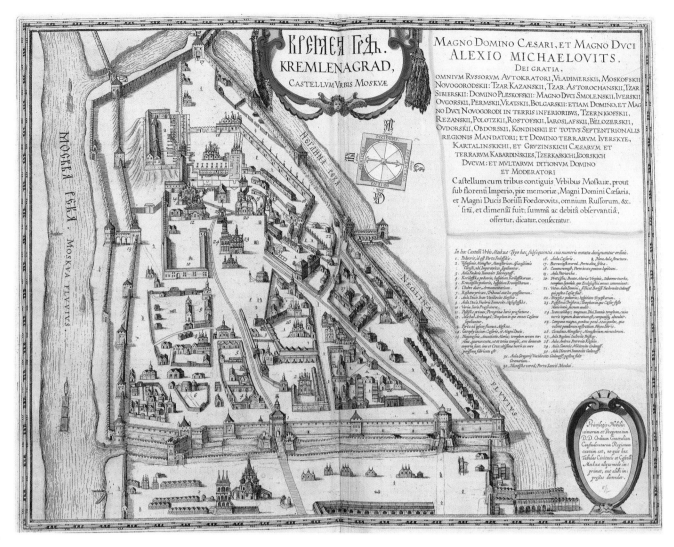

its celebrated fate of becoming neither holy, nor Roman, nor much of an empire. Ivan III had adopted the seal of the two-headed eagle, which both the Byzantine and the Holy Roman Empire had used; in 1547 Ivan IV (the Terrible) was the first to be formally crowned tsar in the Kremlin with full regalia; and in 1696 Peter the Great assumed the Latin title of Imperator and named his new imperial city of the Baltic St. Petersburg, not after himself (as is often assumed) but after the Apostle Peter. The implication seemed to be that by the eighteenth century the Russian Empire had in some sense superseded Rome as well as Constantinople in Christian preeminence. And Peter drove the point home by using the venerated remains of Alexander Nevsky, a medieval warrior who

had fought the Catholic West rather than the pagan Mongols, to sanctify the new city.

The Moscow Kremlin remained the place where tsars were crowned and power sanctified even after the capital was formally transferred to St. Petersburg in 1712. The Kremlin became once again the functioning center of power after the Bolshevik Revolution, the Third International having replaced the Third Rome as the mythic source of sanctification; and it has remained the center of power since the fall of communism. From the late medieval period to the post-modern era, the Moscow Kremlin has had as its main place of entry the Gate of Salvation (fig. 5) and as its principal open-air display items the largest bell in the world and the cannon with the largest bore-to-length ratio in military history. Known from time immemorial as Tsar-Kolokol (fig. 6) and Tsar-Pushka, respectively, these mighty metal monuments illustrate the megalomania

FIG. 5. Gate of Salvation from Red Square, Moscow Kremlin (photo courtesy The State Historical-Cultural Museum Preserve, Moscow Kremlin)

of both the spiritual pretensions and the military menace with which Russia has so often confronted the outside world.[4]

How would a resurgent Russia with exalted religious pretensions relate to a divided Europe wearied from long years of its own religious wars? The Russians brought to their increasing diplomatic encounters with the West two predispositions formed during their long period of conflict with the Tatars and other hostile steppe peoples. First and foremost was the tendency to assume that diplomatic missions were merely masks for military intelligence. Russia's Tatar enemies had generally lacked artillery and depended on surrounding and starving out key Russian cities. An enemy who got a negotiating mission inside the walled Kremlin could assess the personnel and provisions and calculate more accurately the prospects for a siege. Russians, therefore, became extremely reluctant to let foreigners into their inner citadels, and they tended to let diplomats approach Moscow itself only in carefully controlled stages and

always accompanied by a Russian watchdog (called a *pristav*, or bailiff, the lineal ancestor of the Soviet era *stukach*, or "wiretapper").

Secondly, Russian diplomats took over from their experience with steppe politics a belief in what early German observers called *Gegengrenzlichkeit*, "the law of opposite boundaries." According to this "law," a people with many potential attackers and no natural barriers for defense must learn to treat the lesser enemy on the opposite border of an adjacent enemy as a tactical ally. Thus, when Poland was Russia's nearest foe, first the German Empire and then Sweden became a tactical friend; then, as Sweden became the leading threat, Denmark became a target for dynastic marriages. Protestant England and Holland were consistent if distant friends so long as Catholicism in Poland, Lithuania, and western Ukraine seemed to pose a major threat on the immediate borders of Orthodox Russia.

Nearly continuous fighting on one front or another combined with frequent changes in the allegiance of military units, as well as of presumed allies, to induce a certain paranoia within the Russian Kremlin. Alliances were regarded as temporary and friendships as provisional. Particular importance was attached by Moscow to the responsibility of provincial governors (*voevodas*) to delay and report on embassies as they crossed the border into Russia, so that Moscow could obtain at least as much intelligence about the foreigners as they were going to glean about Russia. The tsar's entourage also wanted to prevent peripheral regions from identifying with their immediate neighbors to the west rather than with their distant Kremlin overlords. But Moscow was also careful to treat all major embassies that reached the Kremlin, even those of hostile powers, with elaborate courtesy, since today's foe might be tomorrow's friend.

There was no Ministry of Foreign Affairs in Muscovy and only a few approximations of permanent foreign embassies by the early 1630s (from France and the Protestant countries of northern Europe).[5] Important foreign relations were conducted largely by elaborate delegations that traveled to and from Moscow, generally for a specific purpose (to negotiate a treaty, conclude a

FIG. 6. The Tsar Bell, Moscow Kremlin. The bell was cast in 1733–35 in the Kremlin by Ivan Motorin and his son, Mikhail (photo courtesy The State Historical-Cultural Museum Preserve, Moscow Kremlin)

trade agreement, or arrange a dynastic marriage), which often required a lengthy stay (see Chapter 3). Records were kept in the Posol'skiy Prikaz (a chancery literally for "Emissary Orders"), but relations with regions previously under Mongol control were generally administered from separate offices (such as the Kazan and Siberian Prikazy), and the khan of Crimea conducted his contentious affairs through his own permanent representative in Moscow, who dealt with a separate Crimean Prikaz in the Kremlin. Much international business was conducted by the dominant figures in the various foreign quarters of Moscow who dealt directly with whomever they were closest to in the tsar's entourage.

When eastern Ukraine and Belorussia were brought under Tsar Alexei's sovereignty, they were administered under a Little Russian Prikaz and a White Russian Prikaz, respectively. The title of the sovereign (*gosudar*) was expanded to encompass "Great, Little, and White Rus"; but the chanceries of government (*gosudarstvo*) treated these regions more like foreign nations than domestic

provinces. Russia's rapidly expanding empire was not yet fully consolidated, and its capital was swarming with foreign mercenaries and traders who often had their own contacts at the court. Because of the chaotic nature of diplomacy and the multiple channels of communication, the tsars tended to rely increasingly on more disciplined inner circles for the most important international matters (the famed *oprichnina*, or "separate estate," under Ivan IV, the Tainy [secret] Prikaz under Alexei). Keeping the Kremlin itself inaccessible and lifting the tsar to an ever more exalted level above the fray became important tools of state for making the raw new empire secure at home and respected abroad.

Both the many-staged processional approach to the Kremlin that visiting embassies were required to take and the lengthy ceremonies that awaited them within were deeply influenced by the religious rituals of the Russian Orthodox Church. Increased contact with the West had triggered a nationalistic reaction and a desire to reassert Russia's Orthodox Christian identity and to extend the reach of church rituals out into Russian society. As the expanding empire began absorbing more non-Slavic peoples, Orthodoxy became the glue that held the tsar's domain together. The church's authority was strengthened by the creation of a Moscow patriarchate, which lasted from the late sixteenth to the early eighteenth century (fig. 7). The patriarch was the featured performer at great public spectacles in Red Square on Epiphany and Palm Sunday; and the blend of military and religious processions became almost complete in the great parades that took place on that vast open plaza facing the Kremlin and its Gate of Salvation.

The religious revival began when Patriarch Germogen starved to death inside the Moscow Kremlin in 1612, in protest against the apostasy to Catholicism that seemed implicit in the Polish occupation of Moscow during the Time of Troubles (1605–13). The national uprising against the occupiers that Germogen had called for led to the installation of the new Romanov dynasty in 1613, but the new Tsar Mikhail was in many ways controlled by his father, Patriarch Filaret. Mikhail's successor, Tsar Alexei, was under the spell of the even stronger Patriarch Nikon, until the latter was exiled in 1667 and the way was prepared for the abolition of the patriarchal office and the formal installation of state control over the church under Peter the Great.

Both Filaret and Nikon shared the imperial title of Great Sovereign (*Veliky Gosudar*) with the tsar and received their own steady flow of gift-bearing embassies, not just from Greece and Constantinople, but also from the other historic sees of Orthodoxy, such as Antioch in Syria and Jerusalem in Palestine. The Russian Church sent emissaries to the ancient churches of the Caucasus in Georgia and Armenia—and subtly incorporated into its own regalia and terminology some elements from Persia, which had supplied Russia with its bejeweled throne (see Chapter 5, fig. 2).

Embassies from Orthodox (and sometimes other Christian) lands were often housed in Moscow monasteries while awaiting their reception in the Kremlin. All embassies were provided with lavish meals and accommodations for what was often a very long stay. All had to dismount and remove their hats upon first meeting the tsar's emissaries on the outskirts of Moscow before being allowed to enter the city and be escorted to their local host. If subsequent discussions and negotiations proceeded satisfactorily, the visitors were eventually invited to the Kremlin, which they approached in an ornate procession. They then dismounted and entered in silence for a series of three successive formal greetings as they proceeded slowly toward their audience with the tsar in the Palace of Facets. The entire serpentine approach path to the throne room was lined with colorfully dressed guards and grandees, none of whom made any sound or evinced any sign of recognition of the approaching guests.

When a foreign ambassador finally emerged from the shadowy hallways into the royal presence, he was initially dazzled by the enormous diamonds and myriad jewels that glittered from the tsar's heavy robe and from the giant orb in his left hand, which required a special stand to enable the ruler to hold it up (fig. 8). The secretary to the English embassy of 1663 reported that the people "coming suddainly out of the dark are dazled with the brightness of the Sun.... The Tzar like a sparkling sun darted forth most sumptuous rays."[6]

FIG. 7. The Tsar Cannon, in front of the Church of the Twelve Apostles, the patriarch's domestic church, built in the mid-17th century. The bronze cannon was cast in Moscow by Andrei Chokhov in 1586 (photo courtesy The State Historical-Cultural Museum Preserve, Moscow Kremlin)

The imperial orb, surmounted by a cross, symbolized the sovereignty of Christianity over the world; the scepter in the tsar's right hand was an emblem of sovereignty over the governance of his realm (fig. 9). Foreigners were expected to prostrate themselves before presenting their gifts, but they were eventually allowed to approach the throne and to kiss the tsar's hand if they were Christians. The tsar then washed his hands to erase alien impurities and went on to the reception hall of the Palace of Facets for the festive banquet.

Only the tsar and his son sat at the raised central table; everyone else was seated in order of status, beginning with the "great table" to the ruler's right followed by the "curved table" to his left. The table for the visiting embassy was sometimes paired with the table reserved for the Church hierarchy, as if to guard against alien influence within the Kremlin. Everyone received bread at the beginning as a sign of the tsar's favor, but only selected people received salt as a sign of his love.

FIG. 8. Scepter and Orb of Tsar Alexei Mikhailovich. Turkey (Constantinople). Scepter: 1658; gold, enamel, precious stones; l. 34¼ in. (87.7 cm). Orb: mid-17th century; gold, diamonds, emeralds, rubies, enamel; h. 11⅜ in. (29.2 cm), circ. 15 in. (38.5 cm). The State Historical-Cultural Museum Preserve, Moscow Kremlin (P-16, P-19)

Food and wine were then served to guests in the perceived order of their station in society. A special sign of favor was to be served food from the tsar's separate serving table (covered with a resplendent tablecloth, which like the throne came from Persia). And the highest honor of all was to be given food that the tsar himself had already partially eaten (see Chapter 7, fig. 13).

The feast usually lasted five or six hours and ended with a protracted series of toasts, which Russians of all stations continue to tack onto meals even today. Everyone had to stand and bow to the recipient of each toast, which provided a certain amount of calisthenic relief from all the gluttony. Russians faced the added obligation of having to stand up and remove their hats at every mention of the tsar's name. The meal would usually end with mead or some other sweet drink. On occasion, the foreign embassy would stay at the table after the feast had ended to conclude or modify their negotiations in the solemn environs (though no longer the presence) of the tsar.

Gifts from the East tended to be ornamental textiles and precious stones, materials used to enhance the majesty of the court. Gifts from the West tended to be richly decorated silver and gold objects, such as goblets and platters that had some practical use and served to demonstrate the superior craftsmanship and wealth of Western nations (cat. no. 54). Gifts from the Ottoman Empire often included ornate weapons, a subtle reminder of the fighting ability of the Turks. Since the tsar's entourage tended to judge the seriousness of a foreign embassy by the opulence of its gift, the Kremlin rapidly acquired the richest repository of precious foreign objects in Russia (cat. no. 38). Russia imported craftsmen from Armenia, Holland, and other foreign lands to work inside the Kremlin in order to imitate the crafts represented in the foreign gifts. By the late seventeenth century, foreign artists were producing there large numbers of icons in the ornate and naturalistic manner of Western paintings.

Under Peter the Great, Russia became part of, rather than an interlocutor with, the Western world. He wrested from the Turks a window on the Black Sea at Azov in 1696 and opened up a "window to the West" on the Baltic Sea by founding St. Petersburg in 1703. Although he was crowned in the Kremlin, Peter made his day-long military processions rather than religious coronations "the defining ceremony of the realm,"[7] and he replaced Greek with Latin for learning and the Mother of God with Minerva in his symbolism of authority. Far from making Western diplomats kowtow to him, Peter became the first Russian ruler to travel abroad in order to learn from the West. He brought increased order and uniformity into diplomacy by creating a collegium for foreign affairs based on the Swedish model. When the capital moved from Moscow to St. Petersburg, a new era began, one in which Romanov Russia in some ways came to resemble Hapsburg Austria and Hohenzollern Prussia more than its own Muscovite past.

FIG. 9. Ivan Vereschchagin, et al., *The Transfer of the Regalia to the Dormition Cathedral on July 11, 1613, Palace of Facets, Moscow Kremlin,* plate in *Book On the Selection to the Most High Throne of the Great Russian Realm of the Great Sovereign, Tsar and Grand Prince Mikhail Fyodorovich, Autocrat of All Russia* (Moscow, 1672–73). From left to right: Treasury Palace, Annunciation Cathedral with porch and gallery, Golden Chamber with the roof of the Dining Court behind it, the Palace of Facets with the red porch (ambassadorial staircase), the Dormition Cathedral, the multitude of Kremlin churches. The State Historical-Cultural Museum Preserve, Moscow Kremlin

But the vast peasant interior of Russia changed very little. Coronations were still held in the Moscow Kremlin's Cathedral of the Assumption, and foreign gifts continued to pour into the Kremlin Armory. When Moscow again became the capital early in the twentieth century and the Kremlin began to be opened up, leading to the recent renovation of the Armory, it became possible to see the range of tribute that an often mystified outside world had paid to an empire that once spanned half of both Europe and Asia.

NOTES

1. This relatively little known story is recounted somewhat melodramatically, but with good documentation, by Kargalov 1998, "Na Stepnoi Granitse," pp. 164–328.

2. The rich literature on the imperial transformation of the Kremlin during this period is summarized in Bondarenko 1997, pp. 26–51.

3. This theory was set forth in a letter from the Pskovian monk Filofei to Grand Prince Vasily III in 1510. Malinin, 1901, appendix, p. 55. For the relationship between religious and secular ideology in this period, see Skrynnikov 1991.

4. See Billington 1970, pp. 37–43. See, more recently, Williams 1985; Portnov 1990; and Bondarenko 1998.

5. For the formal organization and conduct of Russian diplomacy during this period, see Potemkin 1959, vol. I, pp. 130–45, 261–68, 291–318, 355–72. For the court ceremonies used to receive embassies in the Kremlin, see Zabelin 1915–18. For subsequent changes in these rituals beginning with Peter the Great, see Wortman 1995. The initial fear of foreigners was so great that Ivan III received the first ambassador from the Holy Roman Emperor privately with no ceremony at all in 1486. Only after he sent his own embassy abroad in 1489 and heard how lavishly he had been received by the emperor did he begin the elaborate public ritual that became characteristic of Russian tsars. Potemkin 1959, vol. I, pp. 261, 363.

6. Cited from the report of the British embassy to Tsar Alexei Mikhailovich by the secretary to the earl of Carlisle (1663–64) in Zabelin 1915–18, vol. II, p. 364. A second effect of sudden dazzlement was later created in the reception hall by the shelves full of gold and silver service items that surrounded the enormous column in the middle of the room.

7. Wortman 1995, p. 44.

Atlantic Ocean

NORWAY

SWEDEN

Barents Sea

White
Sea

• Archangel

FINLAND

North Sea

Stockholm
•

Lake
Ladoga

RUSSIA

DENMARK

Gulf of Finland

St. Petersburg
(1703)

SCHLESWIG-
HOLSTEIN

Baltic Sea

Copenhagen
•

Narva
•

ESTONIA

• Novgorod

Gottorp

LIVONIA

DUTCH
REPUBLIC

Riga
•

ENGLAND

POMERANIA

• Moscow

• Kazan

Gdansk
•

LITHUANIA

PRUSSIA

BELORUSSIA

Smolensk
⚔

FRANCE

GERMAN
STATES

Warsaw
•

• Minsk

POLAND

River Volga

Vienna
•

• Voronezh

AUSTRIA AND
IMPERIAL TERRITORIES

Kiev
•

Poltava
•

KHANATE
OF
CRIMEA

Gurgev
•

Azov
⚔

OTTOMAN
EMPIRE

Sea of
Azov

• Astrakhan

Bakhchisaray
•

Black Sea

Caspian Sea

Mount
Athos
•

Constantinople (Istanbul)
•

Turkey

Mediterranean
Sea

PERSIAN
EMPIRE

Legend:
- Russia
- Ottoman Empire
- Poland
- Sweden
- Denmark
- England
- Dutch Republic
- Khanate of Crimea
- Persian Empire
- Prussia
- Schleswig-Holstein

2

RUSSIAN FOREIGN RELATIONS AND DIPLOMACY

IRINA A. ZAGORODNYAYA

Beginning in the fifteenth century, European diplomatic practice was to send individuals of exalted rank as ambassadors to discuss important political, military, and economic issues with the ruler and his government in Moscow. In Russia these were known as Great Ambassadors, and their embassies were called Great Embassies. Diplomatic missions were also carried out by other, lesser diplomats and merchants traveling abroad. Merchants often attached their convoys to official ambassadorial missions, especially those from eastern Europe. The merging of international political communication and trade was so common that the distinction between them was not always clear.

During the seventeenth century, ambassadors and merchants also delivered gifts—refined works of art that were both fashionable and of great value. Especially striking, in both quality and quantity, were the gifts presented by the rulers and ambassadors of Russia's neighbors and rivals, the Polish-Lithuanian Commonwealth and the Ottoman Empire. Gifts from sovereigns in Western Europe (England, Holland, Sweden, Denmark, and the Holy Roman Empire) were invariably of

FIG. 1. Russia, Europe, and the Near East in 1700

greater interest and value than those given by the envoys and merchants who delivered them.

At the first and most formal presentation by ambassadors at the Kremlin Palace, gifts were divided into two categories: *pominki* (mementos) from rulers and *chelobitia* (from a Russian term meaning a low bow and the giving of thanks), which were the personal gifts of foreign diplomats (fig. 2).[1] At the end of the audience, the gifts were taken into safekeeping by the staff of the various palace departments. Precious silver and gold objects, furniture, jewelry, weapons, and ceremonial horse trappings first went to the tsar's treasury.[2] Gifts that were considered especially pleasing might be sent directly to the tsar's palace, bypassing the treasury altogether. Treasury staff, with the help of local artists and merchants, then appraised the gifts and provided them with labels, although a preliminary evaluation of the gifts had already preceded the ambassadors' first visit to the Kremlin. Inscriptions were engraved on silver or gold objects, indicating who gave the piece and when, how much it weighed, and how much it was worth. Furniture was subsequently moved to the interiors of the palace or state institutions, weapons to the Armory,[3] and horse trappings to the storehouse of the Stable

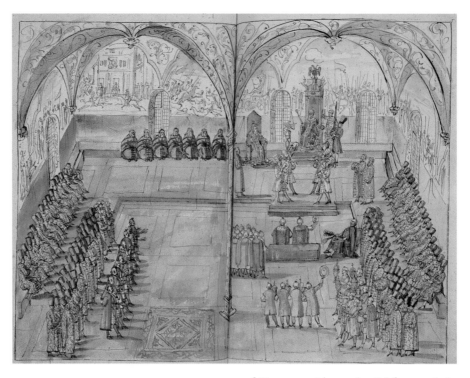

FIG. 2. Anonymous, *A Tsar Receiving a Delegation in the Reception Hall of the Palace of Facets at the Moscow Kremlin*, early 17th century. Pen, ink, and watercolor on paper, 14⁷/₈ x 22³/₈ in. (38 x 57.4 cm). Herzog August Bibliothek, Wolfenbüttel, Germany

Office. (Horses and carriages were, for practical reasons, taken to the stables shortly after evaluation.)[4] Aside from the principal storehouses for royal property, there were other rooms in the Kremlin in which precious objects and jewelry were kept. Narrowly specialized court workshops such as the embroidery workshop and the Northern Chamber were used for these purposes, as was the Armory. At the end of their stay in Moscow, diplomats visited the sovereign one more time, and during the departure ceremony, substantial gifts, often of fur, were presented to them by representatives of the court.

The task of separating the diplomatic gifts from the many imported works of art in the Armory's collection and of assessing their political and artistic importance has long been subject to considerable study. Publications by the leading Russian historians of the eighteenth and nineteenth centuries—M. M. Shcherbatov, N. M. Karamzin, S. M. Solovev, and V. O. Kliuchevsky—include lists of gifts that they linked with Russia's foreign policy and descriptions of ambassadors' visits. A formal publication, which appeared at the time of the Kremlin Armory Museum's founding in 1806 by decree

of Emperor Alexander I,[5] featured descriptions of individual works of art in the tsar's treasury, including gifts. In 1844 A. F. Veltman studied a wide range of documents in order to determine how several diplomatic gifts came to be in the treasury.[6] Similar research was also done some years later by the authors of a remarkable multivolume history of the state treasury.[7]

The Armory collection was first studied as a whole beginning in the 1850s, after it was installed in its own museum building designed by Konstantin Ton as an adjunct to the Grand Kremlin Palace, which had opened in 1851. At that time, a group of scholars, including D. Filimonov and L. P. Yakovlev, made a detailed and systematic inventory of the Armory; it was published between 1884 and 1893 and retains its scholarly significance to this day.[8] On the basis of this publication, as well as information from Swedish and Danish archives, Fredrik Robert Martin was able to reconstruct in general outline the groups of diplomatic gifts sent in the seventeenth century from Stockholm[9] and Copenhagen.[10] His books, published in German at the turn of the twentieth century, enjoyed a substantial circulation in Europe. Subsequently, the gifts were studied and exhibited as separate collections.[11] The German art historian O. Pelka discussed important seventeenth-century gifts of amber from Brandenburg.[12]

An extremely important step in the study of the history of the Kremlin treasury and its collections was the publication of a group of essays by museum associates in 1954.[13] In it, M. N. Denisova's essay on ceremonial horse trappings and T. Goldberg's catalogue of English silver contain solid historical information about how many of the objects arrived in Moscow. G. L. Malitsky's essay is wholly devoted to a history of the treasury.

Objects made by English silversmiths, including many diplomatic gifts, were later studied by the English art historian Charles Oman,[14] and in 1991 a remarkable exhibition of English metalwork took place in London at Sotheby's.[15] Gifts representing diplomatic ties with Poland were studied for the first time as a special group and then catalogued and exhibited in 1998.[16] The catalogue and exhibition of Swedish gifts of silver, held in 1997 at the Stockholm Armory, included important additional material.[17]

The present exhibition "Gifts to the Tsars, 1500–1700," by showing diplomatic gifts from many countries during the seventeenth century, sheds important light on the relations between Russia and the world of that time. It also reveals something of the culture of Old Russia represented by the tsar's court as it existed at the Moscow Kremlin before Tsar Peter I (the Great) moved Russia's capital to St. Petersburg.

The Early Years of Tsar Mikhail Romanov (1613–33)

In 1613, the seventeen-year-old Tsar Mikhail Fyodorovich ascended the throne. This began a period of national reconciliation in the country, which had been seriously disrupted during the Time of Troubles (1605–13) and the Polish-Swedish invasion following the death of Tsar Boris Godunov in 1605. The new monarch's principal foreign-policy objective during the first years of his reign was to achieve international recognition of his status as tsar. This was no simple task, given the ongoing wars with Poland and Sweden. In this complex situation, the Moscow government undertook a major diplomatic action: it sent missions to report that the Time of Troubles had ended and that a legitimate monarch had been accepted by a Russian parliament.

New alliances were proposed with Turkey, Persia, the Crimean Tatars, Austria, Denmark, England, and Holland. Soon afterward, John Merrick arrived in Moscow from London with an offer from the English king to act as intermediary in the peace negotiations with Sweden. Baltic trade was vital for England, which had an interest in the Russian market, where it had enjoyed trade privileges since the times of Ivan IV, and England was concerned that Sweden would acquire overwhelming strength in this region. By acting as intermediary in settling Russian-Swedish relations, the English counted on gaining control over the Russians but also on the prospect of establishing their own trade with Persia via Russia.

Ambassador John Merrick was received in the Golden Chamber on January 1, 1615. The many gifts he brought to the tsar were of two types: silver and textiles.[18] English silver was not popular on the Continent, but textiles were a very important item of English trade with Russia. These two parts of the gift reflected the embassy's dual purpose: to make a favorable impression on the new tsar by presenting gifts according to accepted diplomatic practice and to offer high-quality works of art that had good prospects for the Russian market.[19] The silver plate in the group was quite diverse and included, among other objects, flagons (cat. no. 57), tall tankards, perfume pots, and eleven standing cups. This type of object, in which gold coins were frequently offered, began to appear among diplomatic gifts in the mid-sixteenth century and, by the first half of the seventeenth, was the most commonly presented gift from monarchs, ambassadors, and members of their entourages.[20] Also in Merrick's gift were variously shaped chafing dishes, which seem to have resembled deep skillets with open-work lids and wooden handles. They are known from many diplomatic visits, but the most striking example was sent to Moscow in 1664 (fig. 3).

For one year, until February 1617, John Merrick served as mediator in Russian-Swedish peace negotiations. According to the treaty reached in the village of Stolbovo, Russia regained Novgorod but gave up strategically important fortresses on the Baltic coast. Sweden, in turn, gained control over the mouth of the Narva

FIG. 3. Attributed to John Noye, *Perfuming Pot and Cover, Stand, and Liner.* England (London; maker's mark IN), 1663. Silver, gilding; overall h. 17¹/₂ in. (45 cm); overall w. of stand: 11⁵/8 in. (29.8 cm). Offered to Tsar Alexei Mikhailovich in 1664 by King Charles II of England. The State Historical-Cultural Museum Preserve, Moscow Kremlin (MZ-695/1-4)

River and as a result was able to seal up Russian access to the Baltic. For the tsar this signified the loss of northern lands, but it also meant that trade now could pass only through the merchants of the Swedish town Revel (now Tallin) and that Russian merchants could not trade on Swedish territory.[21] Although Russia made attempts to change these borders more than once during the seventeenth century, for the most part the treaty remained in effect for that time. Only in 1703, as a result of its victory in the Northern War (1700–1721), did Russia gain direct access once again to the Baltic Sea.

John Merrick left Russia in July 1617, half a year after the Peace of Stolbovo. Unlike most diplomats who visited the Muscovite court in the seventeenth century, he was presented with a gift of silver platters from the tsar's table at the time of his departure. Merrick was also invited to a formal dinner in the Golden Chamber,

where he was given very expensive presents by the tsar that were not at all commensurate with the gifts he had given the monarch and clearly represented Moscow's expression of gratitude for Merrick's role in the mediation with Sweden. The total value of the tsar's gifts to Merrick exceeded 2,000 rubles, half of which was the value of the clothes he received, including formal court dress made of precious Persian silk lined in sable and embroidered with pearls and gemstones, together with a tall fur cap. Merrick also received sumptuous textiles from the Near East and Siberian furs, a silver drinking ladle, and a gold chain with a portrait of Tsar Mikhail Fyodorovich on a medallion.[22]

Merrick made one more visit to Moscow in 1620–21, officially to congratulate the tsar on the end of his war with Poland in 1618 and the freeing of Patriarch Filaret, Mikhail Romanov's father, from Polish captivity in 1619. England's real concern, however, was the problem of trading with Persia through Russia. Raw silk was exported from Persia to Europe through Ottoman Turkey, which benefited economically from the stiff duties they charged for this material so essential to European weaving. In 1614, the English had mounted their first sea expedition to the Persian Gulf, and the shah of Persia was intrigued by the idea of establishing sea trade with Europe through their mediation, although a route across Russia still appeared desirable at the time.

On December 15, 1620, in the presence of fifteen individuals, John Merrick was received by Tsar Mikhail Fyodorovich and Patriarch Filaret in the Golden Chamber. The embassy had brought a respectable quantity of royal gifts for the tsar (worth more than 1,000 rubles) and for the patriarch (worth a little more than 370 rubles), as well as personal gifts from Merrick and offerings for the tsar from members of the English nobility.[23] The choice of gifts was unusual for England. They fell into the same categories as earlier gifts—stately objects made of precious materials and textiles—but among them were works of art not previously encountered: a crystal salt, a jasper cup with gold mounts, silver sculptures shaped like a lion, a unicorn, and an ostrich. Objects like these had never figured among the gifts from the English crown, nor would they after this visit. Silver and textiles were also included in the gift, as well as animals for the tsar's menagerie—a pair of parrots and an antelope.

Unfortunately, as with Sweden, the war with the Polish state ended on terms unfavorable for Russia. In 1618 Polish troops led by the king's son, Wladislaw (later King Wladislaw IV), were quartered in Tushino, next to Moscow, and so the Russian delegation was forced to agree to significant concessions to end the war. Under the Treaty of Deulino, therefore, the lands of Smolensk, Chernihiv, and Novgorod-Severskaya were ceded to Poland.[24] Moscow's relations with its closest neighbor remained tense until the Treaty of Andrusovo in 1667.

In 1621, three years after the beginning of the Thirty Years' War (1618–48), a Russian embassy was sent to Germany, France, and England to gather information on the situation in Europe and to search for allies. No allies were found among those distant countries, but the embassy did return to Moscow with a report that gave the tsar and his circle knowledge of the anti-Hapsburg coalition, which consisted primarily of the Protestant states Sweden, Holland, and England. The Russian government adopted a specific line of support, and in 1628, after many diplomatic visits, Sweden received the right to purchase grain in Archangel, duty-free. This was wheat intended for the victorious army of King Gustavus Adolphus, who had fought Poland, a Hapsburg ally, but the grain actually went to Europe's principal grain market, Holland,[25] where it was resold at a high price. The profit went into the Swedish treasury and so represented a different sort of aid to Sweden than the tsar had envisioned.[26] All these trade operations were carried out by a group of Dutch merchants, including Carl Desmoulins (see cat. nos. 67-68).

The Dutch trade diaspora, those merchant residents in Moscow, Archangel, and so on, became the largest in Russia at this time, and its dealings were the most active in the Russian market.[27] A confirmation of the special status of the Dutch is to be found in the way they were treated by the tsars. For example, after ascending the throne in 1645, Alexei Mikhailovich received many foreign subjects, including Dutch merchants, who visited the court in the hope of continuing to do business under the new monarch. Each visit brought

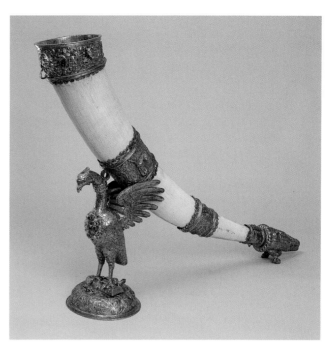

FIG. 4. Jacob Mores the Elder, *Drinking Horn*. Germany (Hamburg), 1597–1609. Silver, gilding, ivory, precious stones, pearls; overall h. 14 in. (36 cm), overall l. 24⅝ in. (63 cm). Offered to Tsar Alexei Mikhailovich by the Dutch merchant Peter Deladall in 1645. The State Historical-Cultural Museum Preserve, Moscow Kremlin (DK-206)

with it lavish gifts. The large Deladall family was one of the select few who traded in grain in the 1620s and 1630s and later successfully continued to operate in the Russian market (fig. 4).[28]

In the 1620s, Turkey was at war with its principal rival, Persia.[29] It was crucial for the Ottomans that they prevent a parallel conflict with its Christian neighbors to the west, Austria and Poland. Shah Abbas I had been looking to Moscow for military assistance against the sultan since the middle of 1614. A mission led by Mohammed Qasim in the guise of a merchant caravan offered textiles, rugs, and a Damascus knife of rare beauty to the tsar[30]; the mission had been sent primarily to obtain information and to reach an agreement with Moscow "about the Russian state ensuring the security of Persia's northern borders during the impending war between the shah and the Ottoman sultan."[31]

Of all the Christian powers, only Poland—which was oriented toward Austria, the Ottoman Empire's longtime opponent—was any cause for concern in Constantinople, since the Hapsburgs themselves were occupied in the Thirty Years' War. The sultan's government wanted

FIG. 5. *Church Vestment* (sakkos) *of Patriarch Nikon.* Textile: Turkey, first half of 17th century; embroidery: Russia (Moscow, Kremlin Workshops), 1653. Silk, pearls, jewels, metallic threads; l. 54¹/₄ in. (139 cm). The State Historical-Cultural Museum Preserve, Moscow Kremlin (TK-14)

to exclude the possibility of a Russian-Polish alliance, and the Muscovite government in turn not only wished to obtain military assistance from Constantinople against Poland, but also counted on using the sultan's authority in the Crimea to shield from ruin the southern territories of Russia at risk from military forays by Crimean Tatars.[32]

The issue of an anti-Polish union made up of Russia, Turkey, Transylvania, and Sweden was discussed between 1627 and 1630, but ultimately Russia began

the War of Smolensk against the Poles in August 1632 without the support of the Ottomans or Sweden, and the war ended with Russia's defeat in 1634. The Treaty of Polianovka, signed when Russia realized that it must give in, was a considerable gain for Poland, but King Wladislaw IV did acknowledge Mikhail Fyodorovich's title as tsar and agreed not to make further claims on the Muscovite throne.[33]

During the process of Russian-Ottoman reconciliation, which coincided with the Polish war, there was a strengthening of "political ties between the Russian government and the Eastern patriarchs and various representatives of the elites of the Greek community."[34] The policy of Patriarch Cyril I Lucaris of Constantinople was aimed at rapprochement with Protestantism,[35] which coincided with the favorable position of the Muscovite government regarding the anti-Hapsburg Protestant states.

Representatives of the Greek aristocracy and the Christian clergy participated in six embassies that visited Russia between 1621 and 1636. The missions in 1621, 1627, 1630, and 1632 were led by Thomas Cantacuzenus, scion of a distinguished Greek family who represented the trade and financial elite of Constantinople that played an important role in Russian-Turkish relations. The Cantacuzenus family was engaged in trade with Russia; Thomas's grandfather had been given a monopoly on the Russian fur trade by the sultan.[36] There was no more suitable person in the sultan's court for the dialogue with Moscow.

As a result of the diplomatic visits from Constantinople between 1621 and 1644 from representatives both of the patriarch and of the sultan, the Kremlin treasury accumulated a group of Ottoman works from the late sixteenth and seventeenth centuries that were unusually splendid. The Armory has in its possession extremely rare textiles, ceremonial weapons, precious horse trappings, sumptuous practical objects, jewelry, and ceremonial vessels made of semiprecious stones with gold mounts. It should be pointed out that the sultan's gifts were significantly more modest in value than the offerings of the Ottoman Christians, which can be explained by the fundamental difference between the Islamic secular authority's attitude toward alliance with Russia and the attitude of the Patriarch of Constantinople and the Christian Greek merchant class.

With rare exceptions, the primary gifts from the sultan, as well as the ambassadorial offering if the ambassador was a Muslim, were luxurious textiles or garments made from them. These included brocades and satins woven with impressive amounts of gold thread, the demand for which was tremendous at the Muscovite court. The fabrics were used to decorate palace interiors, to make clothing for members of the tsar's family, garments for the church hierarchs, and court uniforms worn by ranking officials (fig. 5). At formal events, in the quarters of the tsar's palace or in the patriarch's chambers at ambassadorial audiences, boyars (the high-

FIG. 6. *Ceremonial Mace* (pernat). Turkey (Constantinople), first third of 17th century. Rock crystal, rubies, emeralds, gold, enamel, wood; l. 29¹/₄ in. (75 cm). Offered to Tsar Mikhail Fyodorovich by Ambassador Thomas Cantacuzenus in 1630. The State Historical-Cultural Museum Preserve, Moscow Kremlin (OR-186)

est-ranking government officials), *okolnichy* (a social group second in status to the boyars), and merchants wore clothing made exclusively of these golden fabrics.[37]

Personal gifts from ambassadors, merchants, and the Christian clergy included splendid textiles as well, but their diplomatic offerings were much more varied. The crystal and nephrite vessels, mirrors, fans, enameled inkwells and ceremonial weapons (fig. 6), velvet and silk rugs with gold threads, and jewelry such as studs, buttons, and rings did not linger in the treasury but were quickly moved into the private quarters of the tsar's family and to the court workshops. This is not at all surprising, since the style of the works by Ottoman jewelers and silversmiths fitted perfectly with seventeenth-century Russian court taste. As a rule, these types of objects were given high appraisals in the tsar's treasury, especially when the visitor was useful to the

Muscovite government and conveyed information on events in Turkey and the disposition of the sultan's troops and other military intelligence. All Christians were given a reward at least double the usual amount in furs, as a form of encouragement and support.

A large group of clergy took part in the 1631–32 mission from Constantinople. They did not attend the secular reception, but their offerings figure among the embassy's gifts. Archimandrite Amphilogios, had visited Moscow several times with diplomatic missions, often as a translator, and brought gifts from Patriarch Cyril I Lucaris of Constantinople. The head of the Russian church received a vestment made of satin woven with gold with pearl embroidery; the tsarevich was given a fan with a precious handle and the tsar a crystal tankard mounted with rubies and emeralds (cat. no. 22). For the tankard and fan, Cyril I Lucaris was sent twice the usual amount of sables and for the church vestment, triple. At the end of 1632, Thomas Cantacuzenus visited Moscow for the fourth time in the capacity of ambassador, bringing horse trappings, jewelry, and precious silver and gold plate to the tsar and the patriarch.[38]

The Later Years of Tsar Mikhail Romanov (1634–45)

After the Treaty of Polianovka was concluded in 1634 between Russia and Poland, the sultan's interest in Russia as a potential ally dropped off considerably. To continue pursuing the war against Persia successfully, however, the Ottomans needed the Russian government to stop encouraging the Cossacks, since they drew off some of the Crimean forces needed by the sultan. This matter was discussed in the negotiations with Ambassador Musly Aghā in the years 1634 to 1636. Accompanying the ambassador at the audience of October 24, 1634, was an unprecedented number of twelve Christian merchants.[39] Archimandrite Amphilogios came with a mission on one more occasion, this time accompanied by the Greek clergy. Representatives of the Greek community offered the Russian sovereign precious textiles and garments, weapons, crystal, jewelry, and a significant number of ceremonial horse trappings.

Russia's defeat by the Polish in the battle of Smolensk (1633) had drained the treasury, and the government found itself in acute need of money. For this reason, ambassadors from the German duchy of Schleswig-Holstein, Philip Crusius and Otto Brügmann, were received favorably in Moscow in 1634. The purpose of their mission was to reach an agreement on conducting trade with Persia across Russian territory, and they were able to reach an agreement with the Muscovite government in return for substantial material compensation. Under this agreement, beginning in 1639, the tsar's treasury could count on regular financial contributions for ten years. Presents given in connection with these negotiations include unique ceremonial horse trappings (cat. nos. 95a,b). The Holstein duke later refused to meet the terms of the agreement, when Shah Safi would not negotiate with him, and the tsar's treasury suffered a loss as a result.

The idea of regaining the Baltic lands retained by Sweden in 1617 under the Peace of Stolbovo frequently preoccupied the Russian rulers. In the first half of the 1640s, the Kremlin saw an opportunity to alter Russia's position on the Baltic with the help of a dynastic marriage between Tsarevna Irina Mikhailovna and Count Valdemar, the natural son of King Christian IV of Denmark and Kirsten Munk. Denmark and Sweden were age-old rivals, and Christian IV was at this time contemplating an anti-Swedish alliance with the Holy Roman Empire and Poland. A 1643–44 embassy from Denmark was received with unprecedented ceremony and with several divergences from the usual ambassadorial protocol, thanks to the participation of the tsar's future son-in-law. The gifts from the king, the presents from Count Valdemar, and the offerings of the ambassadors were unusually extensive and unique.[40]

In 1643, the Swedish army suddenly attacked Denmark, and they were victorious.[41] Moscow was worried about spoiling relations with Stockholm, bearing in mind the instability on its southern border. Count Valdemar, who had been in Moscow since the end of 1643, did not learn of events in the Baltic immediately, but his previously favorable situation had changed. Debates at court about Orthodoxy and the Protestant faith became intense, although these may have been a pretext for drag-ging out the negotiations and ultimately rejecting the marriage.[42] Valdemar finally became a virtual prisoner, but after the sudden death of Tsar Mikhail Fyodoro-vich on his forth-ninth birthday, the Danish count was released by the new tsar, Alexei Mikhailovich, and some of his gifts adorn the Armory to this day.

Valdemar had brought gifts for the entire distaff side of Mikhail Fyodorovich's family. His wife and daughter received precious miniature works of silver plate meant for their own personal sideboards, as well as jewelry—necklaces, earrings, and bracelets. The gift for the future bride had been chosen with special care. Valdemar knew that the stone most highly prized in Russia after diamonds was the sapphire, and so Tsarevna Irina received objects decorated with sapphires and diamonds. For his future relative by marriage, Tsarevich Alexei, Valdemar brought a type of object never before seen in Moscow—headgear then very fashionable in Europe embellished with gold elements, pendants, and feathers decorated with eighty-four diamonds. Inasmuch as these precious items do not figure among those received by the treasury, we can assume that they were sent immediately to private quarters or to the court workshops.

The Danish king's gifts were addressed only to the tsar and included royal silver—standing cups, fruit dishes with stands, ewers and basins, flagons and tankards, and exotic items in natural materials with sil-ver mounts. They also made up the bulk of the gifts from Valdemar to his future father-in-law: there were twenty of them. Such a large assortment of cups was because of the impending wedding, since in European countries the standing cup was then the most common wedding gift. As head of the embassy, Valdemar brought gifts from his father and himself, together with those of the second ambassador and his suite, and altogether these included seventy-nine standing cups, jewelry, a ewer-and-basin set, and ewers in the form of a deer (cat. no. 93) and a giraffe.[43] During the 1640s, this type of object was still a novelty, but by the second half of the century, ewers and basins had become an inevitable part of the gift-giving, although ewer-and-basin sets

FIG. 7. Jürgen Richels, *Ewer*. Germany (Hamburg), 1671–73. Silver, gilding; h: 18³/₄ in. (48 cm). The State Historical-Cultural Museum Preserve, Moscow Kremlin (MZ-249/1-2)

were sometimes made by different masters and in dif-ferent places (fig. 7).

During the reception for Count Valdemar, immedi-ately after the ewers and basins, genuine rarities were carried past the tsar's throne—shell and porcelain objects made into standing cups. Christian IV had sent three Nuremberg silver-mounted nautiluses to Moscow. Two of them were identically decorated with the fig-ure of a siren on the stem and the most delicate open-work carving on the shell itself (fig. 8); the bowl of the third rested on a gilded-silver figure of Hercules bat-tling the Hydra and covered with a lid depicting An-dromeda's rescue by Perseus (fig. 9). The last of these

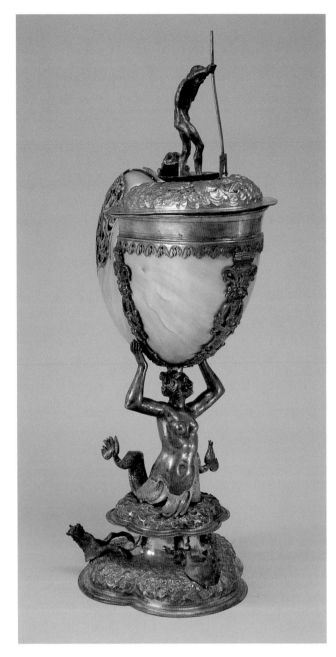

FIG. 8. Dietrich Thor Moye, *Nautilus Cup and Cover*. Germany (Hamburg), 1633–44. Silver, gilding, nautilus shell; h. 16³/₈ in. (42 cm). Offered to Tsar Mikhail Fyodorovich by King Christian IV of Denmark and Norway in 1644. The State Historical-Cultural Museum Preserve, Moscow Kremlin (MZ-179/1-2)

FIG. 9. Johannes Claus, *Nautilus Cup and Cover*. Germany (Nuremberg), 1628–43. Silver, gilding, nautilus shell, enamel; h. 19⁵/₈ in. (49 cm). Offered to Tsar Mikhail Fyodorovich by King Christian IV of Denmark and Norway in 1644. The State Historical-Cultural Museum Preserve, Moscow Kremlin (DK-178/1-2)

FIG. 10. Hieronymous Bang, *Goblet*. Germany (Nuremberg), 1630. Porcelain (Chinese), coral, silver, gilding; h. 11⁷/₈ in. (28 cm). Offered to Tsar Mikhail Fyodorovich by King Christian IV of Denmark and Norway in 1644. The State Historical-Cultural Museum Preserve, Moscow Kremlin (F-119)

"natural" gifts was a unique standing cup with a porcelain bowl on a coral stem and a silver base decorated with miniature figures. Originally, this piece had a silver lid topped by a small Cupid (fig. 10). There were no such large-scale gifts of royal plate to the Moscow treasury again until 1699, with the great gift of the Swedish King Charles XII.

The Reign of Tsar Alexei Mikhailovich (1645–76)

During the latter half of the 1640s the new tsar, Alexei Mikhailovich, became active in foreign policy, above all in his continuation of the dialogue with the Polish king, Wladislaw IV, concerning an anti-Crimean alliance to assure Poland's eastern borders. Alexei's interest in a Polish alliance resulted in part from the fact that relations between Moscow and Crimea and the Ottoman Empire had become significantly strained. Crimea was then a high priority in Moscow's foreign policy in the Near East, where the southern frontiers of Russia were defended only by the Cossacks,[44] but on the whole Russia was still not ready for war with the Ottoman Sultan Ibrahim. The Ottomans actually professed peaceful intentions at the time. During a visit to Moscow in 1644 the Ottoman ambassador, Asan Aghā, confirmed the sultan's desire to live in friendship with the tsar. Nonetheless, in 1645, since the sultan was distracted by war with Venice, and unlikely to render help to the Crimeans, Moscow regarded this as a propitious moment to go to war with the Crimeans and Ottomans.[45]

Later, in 1646–47, the Polish ambassador Adam Kisiel arrived in Moscow with a plan for a Russian-Polish alliance against both the Ottomans and Crimeans, and these proposals were later confirmed by a visit from representatives of Lithuania, a state attached at the time to Poland.[46] There are many more gifts from this Polish mission in the Armory collection than there were from other Warsaw embassies.[47] Wladislaw IV's gifts were presented to Tsar Alexei Mikhailovich in the Palace of Facets on October 24, 1647, by Kazimierz Pac a representative of the Grand Duchy of Lithuania acting for Poland. In European fashion, the king sent ewers with basins, cups, and covers, among which were

FIG. 11. *Covered Cup.* Western Europe (Poland?), 1620. Silver, gilding; h. 41 in. (105 cm). Offered to Tsar Alexei Mikhailovich by King Wladislaw IV of Poland in 1647. The State Historical-Cultural Museum Preserve, Moscow Kremlin (MZ-151/1-2)

works of previous decades, including a giant gilded-silver cup (fig. 11).

Tsar Alexei was visited by two other embassies in 1647, one from Sweden and one from Holland, each with the purpose of congratulating the tsar on his ascending the Russian throne. Thus, in the mid-1640s, after a prolonged lull, there was a reaffirmation of Russian-Swedish friendship.[48] The 1647–48 Swedish mission was the first in the seventeenth century to bring royal gifts. Led by Erik Gyllenstierna, who had already been to Russia in 1634, and Hans Wrangel, the mission took place after Sweden's victories in Germany during the Thirty Years' War, which had left the Stockholm royal treasury substantially richer. The gifts of Queen Christina of Sweden consisted primarily of German silver; ambassadors Gyllenstierna's and Wrangel's personal gift included three small

FIG. 12. Johann Baptist Weinhold I, *Table Fountain*. Germany (Augsburg), 1640–45. Silver, gilding; h. 14⁵/₈ in. (37.7 cm), diam. 13³/₄ in. (35.3 cm). Offered to Tsar Alexei Mikhailovich by Ambassador Hans Wrangel of Sweden in 1647. The State Historical-Cultural Museum Preserve, Moscow Kremlin (MZ-327)

cups and table fountains, one of which is still in the Armory (fig. 12), and a pair of pistols.

In the second half of the 1640s, the Russian government approved a number of decisions that affected the development of trade and stimulated diplomatic activity among its old trading partners. By this time, domestic trade was increasing, and the Russian merchants were now strong enough to have become aware of their own interests. At the same time, foreign traders, especially the Dutch and English, enjoyed special privileges in the Russian market, which were not advantageous to Russian merchants. The situation finally reached a breaking point, and in 1646 and 1649 the merchants asked the tsar for help, reiterating their demands in speeches at the 1648–49 session of Russia's Assembly of the Land.[49] The tsar met the merchants halfway and undertook a number of measures to limit the activities of foreign merchants in the country. First of all, the privileges of the English Muscovy Company, which had bought and sold duty-free all over Russia for more than a hundred years, were rescinded and their merchants could now trade only in Archangel. The rules for levying customs duties changed as well.[50]

These undertakings on behalf of the Russian merchants evoked an immediate reaction from the Dutch government. On June 20, 1647, Ambassador Koenraad Burgh was received in the Golden Chamber bearing many substantial gifts. These can be divided into the three groups that were characteristic of Dutch gifts before and after this mission: silver plate; Asian furniture with Japanese lacquer decorations made of exotic woods; textiles, primarily heavy cloth, a product of which the Dutch were proud; and spices, which Dutch merchants had successfully imported to Russia. Through the Ambassadorial Office, the Dutch ambassador asked for 120 men to move the presents.[51] Most of the silver presented was unusual and purely Dutch in form, unlike anything encountered in the gifts from other countries, although a few objects had been made in England, such as a flagon and a gilded-silver cup (fig. 13). All the Dutch silver was embellished with Russia's coat of arms, which suggests that they were ordered especially for this embassy.[52]

An embassy from Warsaw arrived in 1651, bearing decorative silver plate with semiprecious stones from King John II Casimir.[53] The gifts presented to the tsar in the Palace of Facets on April 11 were extremely rare works by German and Flemish silversmiths, including a painted glass tankard; an Antwerp ewer made of shells, a masterpiece of the Armory museum's collection of naturalia (fig. 14), as well as a gilded-silver table fountain in the form of a celestial globe. When the 1651 Polish embassy did not accomplish its assigned goals, it left Moscow, apparently in a huff; the ambassadors refused to accept the tsars' gifts and the sables they had been given were returned to the tsar's treasury damaged, perhaps intended as an insult.

Russia made a number of important foreign-policy moves on its southwestern frontier during the mid-seventeenth century. As a result of the uprising in Ukraine

FIG. 13. *Standing Cup.* England (London; maker's mark with "K"), 1589–90. Silver, gilding; h. 14 3/8 in. (37 cm), diam. of base 4 5/8 in. (12 cm). Offered to Tsar Alexei Mikhailovich by the States General of the Dutch Republic in 1648. The State Historical-Cultural Museum Preserve, Moscow Kremlin (MZ-636)

(1648–54) under the command of Bogdan Khmelnitsky, as well as the decisions reached in January 1654 by the Council of Pereyaslav (the Assembly of Representatives of the Ukrainian people) when they joined the Ukrainian and Belorussian lands to Russia, the tsar finally decided to go to war with Poland.[54]

After the meeting of the Russian Council of the Land, the war with Poland was ready to begin. Missions were sent to Austria, France, Sweden, Denmark, Holland, Venice, and the Crimea asking these lands to join the anti-Polish alliance. Not one of these governments, however, was willing to affirm the tsar's acquisition of parts of Ukraine resulting from Khmelnitsky's change of allegiance; Crimea expressed outright displeasure with Khmelnitsky's behavior, categorically refusing to

fight the Poles. Russia then began a war with both Poland and Crimea. The ensuing Thirteen Years' War did not end until January 1667 with the signing of the Truce of Andrusovo. Russia came out of it with Smolensk and Novgorod-Seversky, as well as eastern Ukraine and the city of Kiev and its suburbs (although for only two and a half years). Western Ukraine and all of Belorussia remained part of the Commonwealth. However, the treaty did produce a fundamental change in the disposition of Russia's military forces, and the treaty that concluded it laid the groundwork for Russian-Polish rapprochement.[55]

The Truce of Andrusovo brought gifts to Moscow that included works made by silversmiths from Gdańsk and rare examples of amber carving.[56] Amber objects are a distinguishing feature of a number of Polish gifts of the period (cat. no. 45), although there were also significant presents of amber from Brandenburg as well (fig. 15). At an audience in the Palace of Facets on October 20, 1667, ambassadors Stanislaw Kazimierz Bieniewski and Cyprian Pawel Brzotovski, who had come to confirm the truce, brought the tsar gifts that represented a huge investment for Poland. The horses and a carved gilded carriage were sent to the stables, but the large silver ewer and basin went into the treasury (cat. no. 48a,b).

The most important decision taken at Andrusovo was to formulate the broad outlines of a Russian-Polish alliance. In Europe there was still a conflict between the Hapsburg bloc, and the anti-Hapsburg alliance of England, Sweden, and France. But changes in Polish internal politics gradually resulted in the alliance of a large number of Europe's Christian powers, some of them previously enemies, and Europe slowly moved toward a widely based anti-Ottoman alliance.

As for Russian-English relations, the 1660s brought a rapprochement after a break between Tsar Alexei and the English Commonwealth of the 1650s. Charles II

FIG. 15. *Cup.* Germany, 1630–49. Amber, gold, ivory; h. 12¹/₂ in. (32 cm). Offered to Tsar Alexei Mikhailovich by Frederick William, Elector of Brandenburg in 1650. The State Historical-Cultural Museum Preserve, Moscow Kremlin (DK-1166/1-2)

was crowned in London in 1660, and one of the steps taken as a result was an embassy to Russia led by a high-ranking intimate of the king, Charles Howard, earl of Carlisle. The ambassador was supposed to make the official announcement of the restoration of the legitimate heir to the British throne, and he sought to recover trading privileges for English merchants in the Russian market, which the tsar had canceled after the Parliament's execution of King Charles I. The ambassador was received in the Palace of Facets on February 18, 1664.[57]

The English gifts had been carefully chosen (see introduction to English section, pp. 231–33).[58] The list of offerings opened with a memorial object—the rifle of Charles I, which, according to the ambassador, was no longer shiny but was priceless in its value to the son of its original owner, now the ruler of the kingdom of Great Britain.[59] The silver gifts were preceded by a French ewer and basin (cat. no. 66a,b) that had

FIG. 14. *Ewer.* Netherlands (Antwerp), mid-16th century. Silver, gilding, nautilus shell, gold, diamonds, rubies, pearls; h. 14 in. (36 cm). Offered to Tsar Alexei Mikhailovich by King John II Casimir of Poland in 1651. The State Historical-Cultural Museum Preserve, Moscow Kremlin (DK-187)

once belonged to Queen Henrietta Maria, daughter of the French king Henri IV, wife of King Charles I, and mother of Charles II.[60] In addition to the silver and textiles, Charles II sent six brass cannons to Russia. The early 1660s was a difficult time for the Russian army, which was fighting Poland in the Ukraine and Belorussia, and the cannons in the royal gift may have been included as an indication of English readiness to render concrete assistance.

The ambassador himself also offered silver to the tsar,[61] and his gift has been noted in the official documentation.[62] The ambassador had not succeeded in his commercial objectives, and he left the country in the summer of 1664. In December the visit of a representative of the Dutch States, England's primary competitor in the Russian market, was met with greater success. The chief topic of Russian-Dutch negotiations was trade and the status of Dutch merchants in Russia, which was compared to the former status of the English. The Dutch asked to be allowed to trade duty-free in Russia for as many years as the English merchants had—about a century. They also demanded that Russia recognize the sovereignty of the Dutch States General and the inclusion of the appropriate designations in the title mentioned in the diplomatic documents. The tsar, however, resisted these requests.

On January 23, Ambassador Jacob Boreel visited the tsar and was received in the dining room of the tsar's palace, an unusual place for a diplomatic reception. The tsar was dressed not in his ceremonial outfit but in his court uniform, a long caftan with slit armholes and false sleeves. All the other requirements of protocol were observed, however. The gifts from the Dutch government consisted of fashionable furniture with tortoise-shell inlay, exotic Eastern objects—Chinese porcelain vases, Japanese lacquered bowls, elephant tusks with drawings, and a Persian horn with a gold cover (fig. 16)—spices in sacks and boxes, expensive textiles, and massive silver.[63] The ambassador was unusually well rewarded, thanks to the rich gifts that had been received by Russian ambassadors in the Netherlands in 1662,[64] gold chains and enamel portraits of the Prince of Orange, the stadtholder. At first Boreel was rewarded with

just double the value of his offerings, but remembering the unusually generous reward for the Russian ambassadors, he appealed to the tsar through the Ambassadorial Office and received far more.

Moscow received its richest group of gifts from the Dutch government in 1675, when specific military and political problems were discussed in addition to the usual issues of trading conditions for merchants, Russia's new trade regulations, and the transit trade with Persia across Russian territory. About 2,500 rubles' worth of goods are estimated to have entered Muscovy's treasury and the Stable Office.

On January 17, 1676, Ambassador Koenraad van Klenck, an experienced diplomat who had lived in Russia for a long time and who, like his father before him, had a personal interest in trade contacts with the tsar's treasury, was received by Tsar Alexei Mikhailovich, also in the dining room of the tsar's palace. He presented gifts from the Dutch States General and the Prince of Orange, the last diplomatic gift the tsar ever received. He fell ill and died soon after, and the embassy's farewell audience was performed according to the mourning protocol by his son and heir, Tsar Fyodor Alexeyevich, in the spring of 1676.[65]

Among the Dutch gifts were horses fitted with ceremonial trappings bearing the coats of arms of the stadtholder, the Prince of Orange, as well as a gilded carriage drawn by six horses.[66] Such presents came fairly often from Poland, but they were absolutely atypical for Holland. Following these was French wine in multicolored bottles mounted in silver, and then groups of presents traditional for Holland, including a tremendous quantity of fabrics, such as velvets, satins, and Italian brocades. The most original pieces of silver were probably the so-called horns of war, or military bugles, and there were also silver table pieces. The ambassador's gifts were very respectable and included, in addition to the carriage and horses, a crystal chandelier and a ewer-and-basin set then fashionable in Holland (cat. no. 76). The accepted explanation for such generosity is that Koenraad van Klenck was seeking permission to explore the route across Siberia to Persia or China.[67]

During Tsar Alexei's last years, a matter of priority for Russia was the question of Russia's western frontier, which had not been fully determined. Immediately after the Truce of Andrusovo with Poland was ratified, the Ambassadorial Office sent representatives to all the countries with which Russia maintained diplomatic relations. For Moscow, it was important to begin with Poland, since the terms of their truce required outside mediation if by 1669 Russia and Poland had not come to a peaceful agreement. As a result, the Holy Roman Empire, France, England, Sweden, Denmark, and Brandenburg agreed to help.[68] The Austrian Hapsburgs had a strong interest in a Russian-Polish peace, since the combined forces of Russia and Poland counterbalanced Ottoman power, which by this time had set its sights on the Hapsburg possessions in Hungary and even the Austrian capital city of Vienna. The sultan had not recognized the terms of the Truce of Andrusovo.

At the next negotiations with the Polish mission in Moscow in December 1667, a defensive alliance was decided upon in the event of an attack on Ukraine by the Ottomans. The talks continued in Moscow in 1671 with the Polish ambassadors Jan Gmiński and Cyprian Pawel Brzostowski from King Michael Wisniowiecki. Russia held on to Kiev but on the whole, Moscow agreed to the Polish conditions. The tsar agreed to demonstrate his military power on his borders with the Crimea and Turkey.[69]

Mementos from this diplomatic visit are a wood table with a silver cover and a unique work of German silver sculpture by famous Augsburg artists—a heraldic eagle from King Michael Wisniowiecki (cat. no. 50). The monetary appraisal of the royal gifts was small compared to other embassies. The tsar's wife also received gifts from the Polish queen and all the ambassadors,

FIG. 16. *Drinking Horn.* Persia, first quarter of 17th century. Buffalo horn, gold, rubies, tourmalines, turquoise, glass; max l, 16 in. (41 cm). Offered to Tsar Alexei Mikhailovich by the States General of the Dutch Republic in 1665. The State Historical-Cultural Museum Preserve, Moscow Kremlin (DK-263)

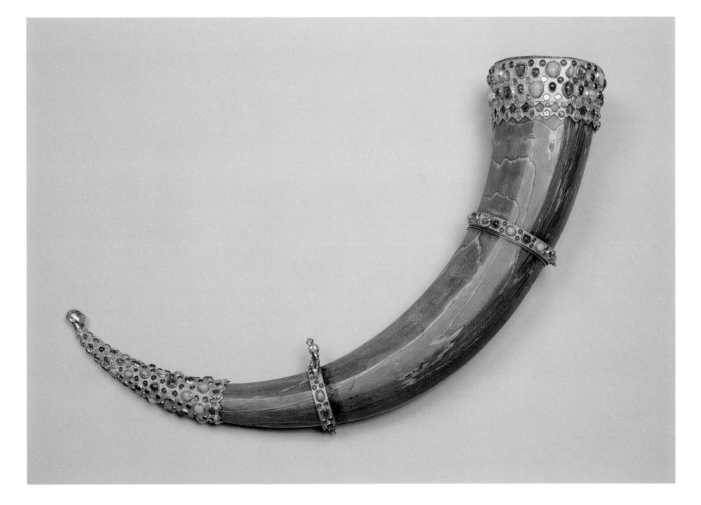

including ewers and basins and a gold watch, or small clock.[70]

In the summer of 1672, the Ottoman army inflicted a serious defeat on Polish troops, and in October Poland signed a treaty with Constantinople under very harsh terms. The Ottoman Empire became even more formidable, and five years later, in August 1677, the Ottomans laid siege to the Ukrainian city of Chyhyryn. In 1681, Moscow and Constantinople concluded an armistice in Bakhchisarai that further weakened the position of the Poles.[71] Central Europe was thus at risk at the time of Alexei's death and during the short reign of Tsar Fyodor III (1676–82).

The Regency of Sofia (1682–89)

The sultan took advantage of European weakness to move his troops north. The Austrian emperor Leopold I fled his capital, which was besieged in June 1683. Only the victory of Polish troops under John Sobieski at the siege outside Vienna on September 12, 1683, saved the capital of the German Holy Roman Empire. During these momentous years, it was widely perceived that Russia had an important role to play, although the country only had two very young rulers, Tsars Peter I and Ivan V. Embassies came nonetheless and found Tsar Alexei's daughter, the regent Sofia, a competent ruler. Negotiations continued to sort out the role of Russia in Europe. Swedish diplomats were received in Moscow on May 2, 1684 bearing important gifts from King Charles XI addressed jointly to the new co-tsars and lesser gifts separately to the regent.[72] Her gifts included feminine accessories with filigree decoration, writing implements, multicolored stockings embroidered with silver threads and tiny precious stones, and leather gloves embroidered with silver and silk. As with the gifts from other countries of this period, the silver included a multitiered centerpiece (fig. 17), as well as three ewers and basins, with ewers made in the form of figures.

Two weeks later, the tsars were visited by ambassadors from the Holy Roman Empire, Christof Baron von Zyrova Zyrovsky and Sebastian Reichs-Freiherr von Blumberg, who were received on May 16. The gifts

FIG. 17. Hans Jacob Baur II, *Table Centerpiece*. Germany (Augsburg), 1675–79. Silver; h. 38 5/8 in. (98.9 cm), w. 27 3/8 in. (70 cm). Offered to Tsars Ivan V and Peter I by King Charles XI of Sweden in 1684. The State Historical-Cultural Museum Preserve, Moscow Kremlin (MZ-532/1-3)

from the emperor and ambassadors, consisting of silver plate and decorations for interiors of the palace, were initially divided between Tsars Ivan and Peter and presented to them individually.[73] Each tsar received a large ewer-and-basin set; the set given to twelve-year-old Peter included images of the recent events of the siege of Vienna (cat. nos. 54, 55).

The rout of the Ottomans at Vienna did not mean the end of the war. Russia was in a position to draw off some of the Ottoman and Crimean forces to the east and thus help the European powers. Poland finally persuaded Russia to do just that, and in 1686 she became a de facto member of a Holy League that had been formed to protect Europe and to defeat the Muslim Ottomans.

(Russia's membership was not formalized until 1697.) Poland paid a high price for this alliance and definitively relinquished the eastern Ukraine and Zaporozhye to Russia.[74]

To ratify a 1686 treaty related to membership in the League, five diplomats arrived at the court of Tsars Ivan and Peter led by the Poznan commander Krzystof Grzimultowski and Chancellor Marcjan Oginski of the Grand Duchy of Lithuania. The tsar's treasury received gifts not only from the Polish king but also from his ambassadors and participants in the audience held in the Palace of Facets on February 11.[75] The Polish king John III Sobieski, sent silver objects to Moscow, of which the most outstanding were a multitiered centerpiece and a pair of fashionable vases with decorative motifs related to the 1683 victory over the Turks outside Vienna, for which he had been responsible (cat. no. 51). The gifts were appraised at an unusually high figure by the treasury. The ambassadorial gifts, which were more than four times the value of the Polish state's gifts, consisted of silver presented by the first ambassador and horses in ceremonial trappings presented by the other four diplomats.

The Reign of Peter I from 1689

After joining the Holy League, Russia's principal foreign-policy aim was to gain access to the Sea of Azov and the Black Sea. In 1696 Tsar Peter I, in his first important military victory, captured the Turkish fort of Azov. Even so, the sea was still far away, and by this date the Holy League, which might have strengthened his hand, was disintegrating. The tsar's attempt to reactivate anti-Ottoman sentiment and revive the Holy League was one of the tasks of his famous Great Embassy across Europe in 1697–98, in which he himself, now the sole ruler, participated incognito, though of course standing six feet seven inches tall and of an unusually dark complexion, Peter was recognized everywhere and he demanded special treatment. At that time, the tsar and his country gained recognition throughout Europe as potential major players in European politics.

In 1699, Peter I began to look toward the Baltic, and Russia, Poland, Saxony, and Denmark united against Sweden, whose holdings along the Baltic Sea had effectively closed off Russia's easiest access to Western Europe. Since 1697, Sweden had been ruled by a very young and inexperienced king, Charles XII, and that was the year the last major embassy from Stockholm visited Moscow. The mission arrived with an enormous quantity of gifts for Tsar Peter, and a sizeable number of gifts were given to him by the ambassadors. The embassy, led by Baron Johan Bergenhielm, had ostensibly come to confirm several of the seventeenth-century peace treaties between Russia and Sweden following the death in 1696 of Peter I's older brother and co-tsar, Ivan, although it was clearly a fact-finding mission.

The Swedish ambassadors found a changed Russian court at the Kremlin. An audience was held on October 12 in the Palace of Facets, but with important changes in protocol.[76] The tsar was dressed not in ceremonial costume but in a heavy cloth caftan whose sole adornment was its gold loops. He was not wearing a crown, nor were the tsar's bodyguards present. The costumes of the court were simple: instead of gold textiles, fur coats, and light silk tunics, they wore heavy cloth caftans. Although the parade of silver before the throne was lengthy, it was not as formal as before: while the gifts were being presented, the tsar conversed amiably with the ambassadors. The future Emperor of Russia was transforming his court.

The gifts from King Charles XII—diverse items made of silver—weighed nearly 270 pounds (123 kilograms) and were appraised by the treasury.[77] Sweden had never made such a grand gesture before, and the gift certainly reflects an attempt to preserve the peace. Simple beakers (cat. no. 86) and remarkable works of Swedish silver that were fashionable in Stockholm court circles headed the list of gifts. They were followed by ten ewer-and-basin sets, most of which consisted of ewers in the form of various figures or animals (cat. no. 85). At the end of the long list of gifts are the works of filigree (fig. 18). It is interesting that the treasury employees considered these unusual items highly attractive, for they began appraising and describing the

gifts with them. When the embassy left Moscow in December 1699, Russia had already begun preparations for the Great Northern War, the next step in Peter's move to establish Russia's presence once again along the shores of the Baltic Sea.

FIG. 18. Ferdinand Sehl the Elder, *Toilette Box*. Sweden (Stockholm), 1691. Silver, gilding; h. 2³/₄ in. (7 cm), diam. 4¹/₄ in. (10.8 cm). Offered to Tsar Peter I by King Charles XII of Sweden in 1699. The State Historical-Cultural Museum Preserve, Moscow Kremlin (MZ-576/1-2)

NOTES

1. On the Ambassadorial Office, see Belokurov 1906; Bondrenko 1916, pp. 98–107; Alpatov 1966, pp. 88–89; *Oko vsei velikoi Rossii . . .* 1989; Rogozhin 1994.
2. Leontev 1961, pp. 43–59.
3. Malitsky 1954, pp. 507–60; Levykin 1992, pp. 10–20; Levykin 1998, pp. 240–54.
4. Leontev 1961, pp. 64–69; Melnikova 1992, pp. 21–30.
5. *Istoricheskoe opisanie* 1807.
6. Veltman 1844, pp. 125–28, 135–39, 144, 146.
7. *Drevnosti* 1849–53.
8. Inventory 1884–93. On the course of the work on the inventory, see Tutova 1997, p. 14.
9. Martin 1900/1.
10. Martin 1900/2.
11. Bencard and Markova 1988; *Silverskatter* 1997.
12. Pelka 1920.
13. *Gosudarstvennaia Oruzheinaia palata* 1954.
14. Oman 1961.
15. *English Silver Treasures* 1991, pp. 115-98.
16. *Skarby Kremla* 1998.

17. *Silverskatter* 1997.
18. Ambassadorial Book 1614–17, fols. 57–58v; see Kologrivov 1911, pp. 20–21 (the name given for the ambassador here is wrong).
19. On Russian-English trade, see Liubimenko 1912; Liubimenko 1923; Liubimenko 1933; Arel 1995. On silver services among the gifts of English diplomats, see Goldberg 1954, pp. 438, 442–65.
20. Cups and covers were so popular that in 1632 even the Turkish ambassador, Ahmed Aghā, attempting to follow European fashion, gave Tsar Mikhail Fyodorovich, in addition to fabrics, a gilded-silver cup with rich enamel design (Ambassadorial Affairs 1631–32, fols. 287, 358; Book of Receipts 1631–32, fols. 39v–40). We also know of one instance of European plate being given by a Turkish diplomat: in 1649, when cups with covers began gradually to replace ewer-and-basin sets, Ambassador Mustafa Cheush presented Tsar Alexei Mikhailovich with a small ewer and basin set (Ambassadorial Affairs 1649, fols. 190–91).
21. Shaskolsky 1964.
22. This is the only piece of information we have about the presence in Russia at that time of works of miniature painting

(Ambassadorial Book 1614–17, fols. 469–70; Ambassadorial Book 1620–21, fol. 565); see Solovev 1990, bk. 5, vols. 9–10, p. 90.

23. Ambassadorial Book 1620–21, fols. 168–174v, 567–571v, 573–575; see Kologrivov 1911, pp. 48–57.

24. Savich 1939.

25. Here and henceforth, "Holland" is used to refer to all the United Provinces.

26. Porshnev 1945, pp. 319–40; Porshnev 1976, pp. 202–9; Ekholm 1974, pp. 57–103.

27. Demkin 1994, no. 1, p. 5, no. 2, pp. 34–36, 67–81; *Gollandtsy i russkie* 1989, pp. 27, 49–54.

28. Demkin 1994, no. 2, p. 71. On the presentation of the drinking horn to Tsar Mikhail Fyodorovich in 1645 from Peter Deladall (Book of Receipts, 1645–46, fol. 141v). The horn was appraised highly—at 35 rubles.

29. Floria in press.

30. Bushev 1987, p. 138.

31. Ibid. p. 140. .

32. Floria 1990, p. 20.

33. Porshnev 1964, pp. 513–24.

34. Floria 1992, p. 111.

35. On Cyril I Lucaris and his political views, see Hering 1968.

36. Floria in press.

37. Fabrics or entire garments, including those cut Turkish fashion, were sent by sultans and brought to Moscow by their representatives. In 1621 and 1624, the sultan's gifts to the tsar and patriarch consisted of precious garments (Book of Receipts 1621, fol. 99; Ambassadorial Book 1624, no. 1, fol. 38, pp. 116–17). Sultan Murād sent golden satins to Moscow in 1627, 1633, and 1634 (Ambassadorial Book 1627, fols. 110–111, 157v; Ambassadorial Book 1633, fols. 260, 305; Ambassadorial Affairs 1634–36, fols. 33, 37), and Sultan Ibrahim and his vizier sent various fabrics in 1644 (Ambassadorial Affairs 1644, fols. 194–195, 353–356). There were often fabrics among the gifts of Greek traders and Moldavian envoys (Book of Receipts 1644–45, fols. 177–178v). On Eastern fabrics at the Russian court, see Levinson-Nechaeva 1954; Vishnevskaya 1993; Vishnevskaya 1996/1; Vishnevskaya 1999.

38. Ambassadorial Affairs 1631–32, fols. 244–248, 393–399, 402–414.

39. Ambassadorial Affairs 1632, fols. 31–41a.

40. Ambassadorial Affairs 1644, fols. 94–100; Book of Receipts 1643–44, fols. 133–158; see Kologrivov 1911, pp. 113–22; Bencard and Markova 1988, pp. 51–54, 67, 68–71.

41. *Istoriia Shvetsky* 1974, p. 191.

42. Golubtsov 1891.

43. Ambassadorial Book 1641, fols. 229v–234v, 252–252v, 374v–377.

44. Novoselskii 1948, pp. 204–22.

45. Smirnov 1946, p. 90.

46. Floria 1989, pp. 126–33.

47. *Skarby Kremla* 1998, pp. 23–25, no. 18–22.

48. Shaskolsky 1998, pp. 86–96.

49. Bazilevich 1932; Shaskolsky 1998, pp. 87–88.

50. Bazilevich 1940, pp. 10–11.

51. Ambassadorial Book 1647–48/1, fols. 164–167, 172v, 180–181, 228–229; Book of Receipts 1647–48, fols. 119v–126.

52. Markova 1990, p. 6.

53. *Skarby Kremla* 1998, pp. 24–26, nos. 23–25.

54. *Istoriia vneshnei politiki* 1999, pp. 277–80, 282–83.

55. On various assessments of the Truce of Andrusovo, see Sanin 1979, p. 276; Galaktionov, 1960, p. 99; Wójcik 1968, pp. 7, 11, 13, 25, 28; Apanovych 1961, p. 207.

56. *Skarby Kremla* 1998, p. 26, nos. 26–30.

57. Ambassadorial Book 1663–64, fols. 274v–278, 445–456.

58. Ibid., fols. 201v–202v, 283v–286v. In the Treasury Office, the silver was appraised somewhat higher than usual for the 1660s.

59. Blackmore 1985, p. 31.

60. We are grateful to Michèle Bimbenet-Privat, chief curator of the Archives Nationales in Paris, for her written report on locating the corresponding document in the Bibliothèque Nationale de Paris.

61. Ambassadorial Book 1663–64, fols. 202v–203v.

62. Ibid., fols. 784v–786v.

63. Ambassadorial Book 1664–65, fols. 88v–92, 97v–99, 140–143v, 315v–316.

64. Ibid., fols. 319–322v.

65. Ambassadorial Book 1675–76, fols. 510v–533.

66. Ibid., fols. 224v–226, 236–288, 504–523v.

67. Ibid., fols. 476–492; see *Gollandtsy i russkie* 1989, p. 61.

68. *Istoriia vneshnei politiki* 1999, p. 326.

69. Sanin 1979, p. 284.

70. *Skarby Kremla* 1998, p. 27, nos. 31–33.

71. Kostomarov 1989, pp. 223, 290–96.

72. Ambassadorial Book 1683–84/1, fols. 352v–356, 369–378, 389–392.

73. Ambassadorial Book 1683–84/2, fols. 467v–470v, 595v–597v; *Pamiatniki diplomaticheskikh snoshenii* 1862, pp. 502–3, 691–93.

74. *Istoriia vneshnei politiki* 1999, p. 340.

75. *Skarby Kremla* 1998, pp. 29–30, nos. 35–38, 53–58.

76. Ambassadorial Affairs 1699, fols. 459, 461.

77. Ibid., fols. 418–421, 427–434, 537–542.

3

AMBASSADORIAL CEREMONY
AT THE TSAR'S COURT

ANZHELLA G. KUDRIAVTSEVA

THE ROOTS OF MUCH Russian diplomatic ceremony extend deep into antiquity, to early Kievan Rus of the tenth century.[1] With the arrival in Russia of Princess Sofia Paleologue, niece of the last Byzantine emperor, who became the wife of Grand Duke Ivan III in the fifteenth century, the Moscow court acquired new brilliance and imperial grandeur. This must have been the time when the ancient Russian custom of receiving foreign ambassadors was established. Three centuries later, this ceremony would become codified when the College of Foreign Affairs, in 1744, drew up the "Plan of the Ceremony for Ambassadors from Foreign Sovereigns at the Imperial All-Russian Court," which incorporated contemporary diplomacy into ancient tradition.

The Ambassadorial Office

The guardian of ritual in the reception of foreign guests was a special body of professional diplomats—the Ambassadorial Office—which was created as a separate

FIG. 1. Matthiae Beckeri?, *Reception of the Dutch Ambassadors by Tsar Ivan IV (the Terrible) on August 21, 1578*. Plate 2 in Jacob Ulfeldt, *Hodoeporicon Ruthenicum* (Frankfurt, 1608). Rare Books Division, The New York Public Library, Astor, Lenox and Tilden Foundations

department in 1549. All aspects of Russia's foreign policy were the purview of the Ambassadorial Office, whose business was conducted by officials known as *dyaks* (secretaries) and their assistants, clerks, and interpreters. In the late fifteenth and early sixteenth centuries, Ambassadorial Office *dyaks* were engaged in the affairs of the embassies from Eastern and Islamic states, and another group, the palace *dyaks*, were involved with those of Europe. Eventually, all countries came under the supervision of the Ambassadorial Office, and in its heyday during the seventeenth century, the authority and obligations of the office had expanded to include monitoring the mail, adjudicating lawsuits, and collecting customs duties. The office resolved border disputes and appointed military commanders and local officials; it also controlled other institutions that played an important role by supplementing the office's income and being responsible for matters of foreign trade.

The expansion of Moscow's international ties, especially beginning in the middle of the seventeenth century, and the rise of professionalism in world diplomacy made it necessary to increase the staff of the Ambassadorial Office. With time, the affairs of individual countries were organized by regions assigned to specific groups of

FIG. 2. Historical reconstruction of a room in the 17th-century Ambassadorial Office, Moscow. At the center is a portrait of the Russian nobleman and diplomat Prince Potemkin in the attire of a great ambassador (photo courtesy The State Historical-Cultural Museum Preserve, Moscow Kremlin)

dyaks and *stolniks* (courtiers ranking below boyars, the highest council of the realm) who knew several foreign languages and had traveled to other countries as representatives of the tsar's government. In the 1680s, the Ambassadorial Office consisted of five sections, three European and two Eastern.[2] Beginning in the 1660s, some official work began to be done in foreign languages. The Ambassadorial Office employed fifteen translators and forty-five interpreters engaged primarily in spoken translation. Among these were employees who knew Latin, Polish, Tatar, Georgian, German, Swedish, Dutch, Greek, Arabic, English, Turkish, and Romanian.

Surprisingly the Ambassadorial Office also employed artists, who were used to illuminate the tsar's documents by painting the edges of the pages and the first words in gold. One of the most usual but important documents was the letter of credence. This "writing and oath" precisely stated the titles of the monarchs as well as the ambassador's name and rank and was followed at the end by "a request to 'give credence': that he [the ambassador] shall undertake to tell you, and that you would believe him, that is, our speeches."[3] "Friendly" documents confirmed amicable relations between countries and contained a request to render assistance to the embassy and to let it pass without detention. "Decree" documents were also issued to the embassy's escort and "bore instructions for local commanders to provide an ambassador en route with food or means of transport."[4] In the seventeenth century the Ambassadorial Office had its own seal, which it used to confirm the authenticity of a document. From earliest times in Russia, seals in either green or red had been affixed to the cord around the documents being sent to foreign rulers.

When it was first established, the Ambassadorial Office carried out the decisions of the Boyar Council. Jerome Horsey, a merchant from England, described the activities of the office in a memoir of his 1571–91 sojourn in Moscow.[5] In this office, apparently, the tsar was regularly trying to "combine . . . the professional competence and diligence of the non-noble, simple officials, the clerks, with the nobility, high birth, and prestige of the boyars."[6] Between 1549 and 1553, the head of the Ambassadorial Office was Ivan Mikhailovich Viskovaty, the ambassadorial *dyak*, and a member of the Boyar Council whom most foreign diplomats referred to as chancellor. Viskovaty possessed not only the talent of a diplomat and extensive knowledge but also a position in the Ambassadorial Office equal in importance to chancellors in European countries.[7] Under his direction, regular diplomatic relations were established first with the Crimean khan and later with the pope.

By the middle of the seventeenth century, Tsar Alexei Mikhailovich raised the status of the director of the Ambassadorial Office, enabling him to defend his independent point of view in the Boyar Council on matters of foreign policy and trade. During the second half of the century, the director was often a member of the council, and between 1643 and 1699, many of the country's most celebrated figures served as directors of the Ambassadorial Office. At first they served only briefly, but by the end of the century the career of the head of the Ambassadorial Office might last a decade. The best-known director of the Ambassadorial Office was probably the boyar Afanasy Lavrentievich Ordin-Nashchokin. Under his administration, the Ambassadorial Office reached its acme.

The office's functions concerning embassies were to extend a welcome, provide an escort, lodge, feed, protect, and attend to the needs of the embassy while it was on Russian territory. The normal sequence of the reception was strictly observed: the meeting at the border, the escort to the capital, the choice of lodging for the embassy and its guard, the serving of its meals, its reception by the sovereign, and the escort that accompanied the embassy back to the border. Before the reception of each embassy, the *dyaks* were asked by the tsar to study all the details of the previous reception of diplomats from that country, as well as the recent receptions of similar missions from other countries, and to follow reasonable approximations of these. Variations were possible, but the meeting at the border was mandatory and proceeded almost identically for all embassies.

The Crossing of the Border

The crossing of the border was the beginning of the reception ceremony. As a rule, the crossing took place on the second or third day after the embassy reached the border, after all the formalities that had been stipulated with the tsar's representative had been observed, and all disagreements on procedure resolved. Russian guards arranged themselves formally along the route as the ambassadors made their symbolic crossing. In 1674, at the welcoming of the Swedish embassy from King Charles XI, the ceremony was particularly magnificent because a royal carriage had been sent from Sweden as a mark of respect for the tsar (fig. 3). Each country's representatives kept a close eye on every detail, for any deviation from established etiquette could be regarded as an insult to the honor of the ambassador's sovereign and

FIG. 3 Erik Palmquist, *The Ambassadors Reach the Swedish-Russian Border at Moravena. The Swedes, in wide-brimmed hats are about to cross a plank bridge where Russian troops, in fur caps, shoulder arms.* Drawing from Palmquist, *Some Observations of Russia* . . . (Stockholm, 1674). The Swedish National Archives, Stockholm (photo: Kurt Eriksson)

country. Issues such as who removed his hat or dismounted from his horse first, or whether the first meeting would take place in the middle of the road—all this was important and often took a long time to resolve while the embassy's progress was halted. The formalities were performed with special care when meeting a Great Embassy, one with an ambassador of particularly distinguished birth and with a large entourage. In this case, a similarly large number of dignitaries were dispatched to Russia's border and often the tsar sent his own carriage (or sleigh).

Greeting foreign ambassadors at the border and escorting the embassy through Russia to the capital was the responsibility of the tsar's bailiff. According to the definition of Austrian diplomat Prince Daniel von Buchau, the bailiff was a kind of master of ceremonies in charge of the special welcoming group.[8] As the first official person to present himself to the foreigners before they crossed the border, the tsar's bailiff was supposed to greet the embassy according to custom: first he would introduce himself, politely ask the traditional questions about the purpose of the visit, inquire about the health of the monarch and ambassador, and also hear other requests and wishes. Then, if the necessity arose, he would provide the embassy with more comfortable quarters before it officially crossed the border.

The bailiff was accompanied by an interpreter in order to avoid any possible misunderstanding. "The sovereign ordered [the embassy] be provisioned abundantly... with carts and victuals [food] in full."[9] To ensure the embassy's safety and to show respect, a special guard consisting of ten to twenty Streltsy Guards was assigned to it. These were the tsars' own guards from the Moscow Kremlin. The number of escorts increased gradually as the embassy advanced deeper into the country.

A courier set out immediately for the capital with news of the diplomats' arrival and to receive instructions concerning the route and schedule for the ambassadors and whether any of the documents the ambassador had brought needed to be delivered to the tsar urgently. "In Muscovy... thanks to the couriers travel speed and frequent changing their tired horses (for there are everywhere standing at the ready fresh and healthy horses), they bring the news extraordinarily quickly."[10]

Preparations in Moscow

From the moment the news of an embassy's arrival at the border was received in Moscow, preparations for its reception began. The road the diplomats were to take was checked and, if necessary, repaired. (The sovereign himself issued instructions to offer money and assign men to repair bridges and level the road itself, and the governor-general saw to it that the instructions were carried out.) Then their stopping places en route were determined. In the capital, by special decree of the tsar, an equerry readied a residence for the ambassador, either in Moscow or somewhere nearby; the quarters set aside for the ambassador were repaired, painted, and supplied with everything he might need for his visit. Seven formal residences and two modest wood houses were allocated for the 1684 embassy from Sweden. Each of the three most important officials in the embassy was presented with two residences apiece, and all those accompanying them were lodged in quarters downstairs. According to tradition, not only were all expenses to be inventoried, but so were the textiles, rugs, taffeta, and damask used to upholster the interior rooms where the embassy was quartered, to say nothing of the guard's weapons.[11] It was also determined which of the tsar's courtiers and employees of the Ambassadorial Office would greet and receive the ambassadors, and who would participate in the negotiations, audiences, dinners, and so on. For employees of the Ambassadorial Office, the slightest mistake might also result in severe punishment. A *dyak* who incorrectly wrote or pronounced the tsar's title while greeting diplomats would be beaten with cudgels. Russian ambassadors departing on analogous missions abroad received strict instruction to behave themselves.

It is a commonly held belief that Tsar Peter I broke with all such traditions, but in fact, for greeting the 1699 Great Embassy from Sweden, he ordered that

FIG. 4. Johann Rudolph Storn, *The Camp of the Mission near the Monastery at the Lake Il'men' (and crossing)*. Plate 22 from Augustin von Meyerberg, *Al'bom Meierberga: vidy i bytovyia kartiny Rossii XVII vieka* [Album, View, and Everyday Life Pictures from Russia of the 17th Century] (Moscow: repr. ed., 1903). The State Historical-Cultural Museum Preserve, Moscow Kremlin

everything be arranged as it was "of old," following the model of the embassy of Conrad Gyllenstierna from Sweden in 1684, with some modifications. Finally a place was selected for the embassy's residence, "not on Pokrovka in the palaces of the Ambassadorial Office but in the higher clergy's…residences, where the Great Cross Hall was set aside for meetings between the ambassadors and *dyaks* (instead of another hall of the Ambassadorial Office in the Kremlin). The sentries were not Streltsy Guards, as previously in similar instances, but soldiers from the new regiments.[12] A most colorful mix of new and old was manifested in the arming of the honor guard. The Armory issued "silver-gilt maces, staffs…ceremonial Damask sabers with silver and gold covers decorated with precious stones and pearls of Circassian and Polish make; broadswords…made of fine and burnished steel; polished Damask steel cuffs…bow covers and quivers decorated with gold and colors,…black arrows with an eagle feather; Turkish bow covers embroidered in spun gold with brass covers…banners on poles, gilded pistols with holsters, carbines with buckskin crossbelts; and even…spears, with snakes and without."[13] The guard was dressed in a mix of velvet and heavy cloth.

Passage Across Russia

Some ambassadors perceived the protection of the Ambassadorial Office with mistrust and dissatisfaction: "Neither ambassadors nor merchants of other nations who have arrived in Muscovy with [the grand duke's] permission are permitted free passage throughout the country, and for as long as they are in Muscovy they are held under a manner of honorable arrest. Special men are assigned to watch what they are doing and those with whom they speak."[14] Diplomats were mostly regarded by princes as potential or real spies. After the embassy entered Russian territory, it was expected to follow the "ambassadorial road." The northern (summer) route lay through Archangel. From there each embassy might stop in towns such as Novgorod the Great, Pskov, Vologda, Rostov, Torzhok, Tver, Dubna, and Mozhaisk (fig. 4). An ambassadorial caravan traveled two to six miles in a day during daylight hours, its speed depending on the embassy's numbers, the weather, epidemics, and sometimes civil and military unrest.

"The grand duke gives very many villages freedom from some taxes that weigh heavy upon some on condition that they always have horses at the ready…. Therefore, anyone who is traveling on official business is allowed for the sake of speed to take new horses at these places. Places of this kind are separated from one another by nearly six miles."[15] For example, in the ambassadorial caravan from Sweden in 1674, which Erik Palmquist reports about in his atlas, there were 440 horses readied at every station. The horses were "shorter than average, strong, and fast-going," as the Venetian ambassador Marco Foscarini wrote.[16] His fellow countryman, the diplomat Giovanni Paolo Compagni, reported of frequent nights spent in the open air in tents and remarked about the shortage of inns.[17]

More often than not, embassies reached the borders of Russia and traveled across its territory in the winter. The English ambassador Anthony Jenkinson explained the choice of season this way: "In the wintertime…the road is firm and smooth from the snow; all the waters and rivers freeze, and one horse harnessed to a sleigh can take a man as much as 400 miles in three days; but in the summertime the roads are covered in deep mud and traveling is very hard."[18] The important embassy personnel were conveyed by richly furnished sleighs, the bottom of which were frequently spread with a white bearskin decorated around the edge with marten hides and sable tails. The horses, as a rule, were fitted out with many fox and wolf tails around their necks.[19]

The burden of meeting the ambassadorial caravan and finding lodgings for it was traditionally that of the monasteries. There was a certain logic to this: embassies of different faiths were lodged in isolated cloisters (built like well-fortified fortresses, with double walls) and were thus in no danger of inflicting harm on the Orthodox population; the monks might even "purify" and "permeate" the visitors with the spirit of the true faith before their meeting with the tsar. After the 1580s, ambassadors were received more often by prominent royal officials at their residences, particularly as they approached Moscow. An embassy from the Hanseatic

FIG. 5. Johann Rudolph Storn, *The Arrival of the Austrian Mission at Moscow on May 25, 1661* [Russian regiments meeting and accompanying the ambassadorial convoy, the carriage of the great ambassadors]. Plate 53 in Augustin von Meyerberg, *Al'bom Meierberga: vidy i bytovyia kartiny Rossii XVII vieka* [Album, View, and Everyday Life Pictures from Russia of the 17th century] (Moscow, repr. ed., 1903). The State Historical-Cultural Museum Preserve, Moscow Kremlin

League to Tsar Boris Godunov reached Moscow and stopped at the residence of "a certain distinguished boyar not far from the palace where we took up quarters, having received, thank God, all manner of victuals [food] in abundance."[20]

Arrival Outside Moscow

According to tradition, a mile before the capital the embassy was again greeted ceremoniously by one or several important dignitaries in the name of the tsar: "In brocade caftans and silver fox hats they first shook hands with each of us and then the eldest of them . . . a nobleman who had formerly been a commander in Siberia, bared his head . . . and began his speech."[21] In the 1630s, the ambassadors were often met by the tsar's equerry. One of the most sumptuous formal welcomes was given to the Austrian embassy of Emperor Leopold I on May 25, 1661 (fig. 5). In a field outside the city (as a rule at that time the welcome was set outside the Tver gates), there was a procession "in the front [of which] went two cavalry standards." Behind a court regiment came another infantry troop in purple dress with ten banners of white nankeen with black, who were followed by other prestigious soldiers dressed in

FIG. 6. Isaac Massa, Map of Moscow (said to show Siege of Moscow in 1605), from *Album amicorum*, 1618. Pen and ink, heightened with watercolor on off-white paper, 7 x 5½ in. (18 x 14 cm). National Library of the Netherlands, The Hague, Netherlands

various colors. After literally thousands of such troops there rode a *dyak* of the Boyar Council... wearing a formless marten cap and brocade dress, on a richly fitted horse. Behind him came the state 'chamberlains,' that is, those brought in [to serve] in the private rooms; Behind them... rode the ambassadors... two were in the tsar's carriage, which was lined with red velvet... in front of them were two of the tsar's *pristavs* (bailiffs). Behind the carriage rode other members of the embassy, as many as twenty men, two by two, and they were dressed in red livery made of... heavy cloth with sky-blue trouser stripes and white silk stripes. Behind them, last, came [their] road carriages."[22]

As the embassy approached Moscow, it made a stop, either in the city itself, in outlying monasteries, or in nearby suburbs, where it was presented with the Muscovite *pristav* different from the bailiffs who had escorted the ambassador from the border (fig. 6). His

first order of business was to report to the tsar that the embassy had safely arrived and was awaiting an audience. In the sixteenth century, this waiting period often took several months, which was part of an established etiquette. Some obstacles to the speedy reception of the embassy by the tsar could be any of the many Orthodox holidays or the traditional regular events of Russian court life. By the middle of the seventeenth century, however, a specific rule was worked out that an embassy should spend no more than one or two weeks in the capital before meeting the tsar. This was in fact the minimum time necessary to familiarize the party with the protocol of the reception and to make an inventory of the ambassadorial gifts. The process went more rapidly at the end of the seventeenth century, when an ambassador might be received on the day of his arrival or the day after.

Awaiting the First Audience

No one in the embassy could complain about inattention to the guests. The tsar's bailiffs visited the embassy daily and listened to their requests or complaints, often resolving them on the spot. For instance, when in 1602 those accompanying Duke Hans of Schleswig-Holstein, a Danish prince who was seeking the hand of Tsar Boris Godunov's daughter, did not have enough space in the residences set aside for the embassy, "the tsar immediately ordered several new buildings constructed in the large courtyard,"[23] so that each member of the embassy could be given housing in accordance with his status. Provisions and all other essentials were sent regularly to the ambassadors.

What were these temporary residences for an embassy like? In the 1630s, they were usually preexisting foreign residences, such as the Lithuanian, Nagai, English, and, for especially extravagant receptions, the Persian establishments. Embassies might also be lodged in the houses of foreign merchants residing in Moscow. By the end of the seventeenth century, however, new houses were often built, especially on Khodynka Meadow or in the capital itself. For the diplomats who visited in the early seventeenth century, spacious wood residences

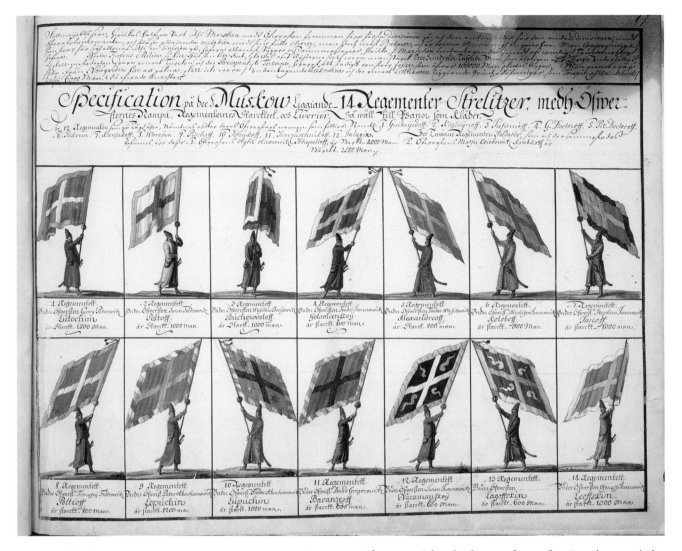

FIG. 7. Erik Palmquist, *Ambassadorial Flag Bearers*. Drawing from Palmquist's *Some Observations of Russia* . . . (Stockholm, 1674). Pen, ink, and watercolor on paper. The Swedish National Archives, Stockholm (photo: Kurt Eriksson)

were constructed. The rooms were usually empty, containing only wood tables and benches, and the sole decorations were tile stoves, but by the 1670s it had become customary to decorate the ambassadors' quarters according to their presumed taste. Thus, for the reception of Polish diplomats in 1678, "in one of the rooms presented to the prince-ambassador, which was luxuriously furnished, a platform had been readied with an expensive canopy under which there was a portrait of the Polish king; beneath it was an armchair intended for the prince-ambassador."[24] When the ambassador received important guests at his residence, "rugs sewn with gold" were issued to adorn his rooms. The windows in the rooms in all the buildings so used were covered

with grates "the thickness of a . . . fist," and around the residence there was a guard posted, "in order to thwart, as [the Russians] said, any attempts by robbers and thieves."[25] By the middle of the seventeenth century, some foreign countries had established permanent diplomatic representation—England (1585), Denmark (1627), France (1629), Holland (1631), Sweden (1631), and Poland (1673)—and diplomats sometimes preferred to stay in these residences.[26]

The First Audience with the Tsar

At some point, the Muscovite bailiffs and interpreters announced to the embassy the day of their reception by the tsar. The scenario for the ceremonial entry of the ambassadors into the Kremlin was worked out in advance by the *dyaks* of the Ambassadorial Office and was explained to the embassy. That same day or the next, the bailiffs and their suite would arrive to escort the ambassadors to the Kremlin: "The *pristavs* were dressed in royal, gold-embroidered, brocade caftans (not covered with pearls and precious stones); their tall black fox hats elicited our amazement. *Streltsy* appeared with arms at their sides, four to a row, 148 men, in order to carry the gifts; everyone in green dress.... When the hour of the reception came, the tsar's equerry arrived with sleighs for the ambassador and white horses for his suite. The first horse, which I [Nicolaas Witsen] mounted, was snowy white and magnificently adorned with an embroidered saddle and silver bridle and harness.... The secretary [of the embassy] rode first, holding aloft the letters of credence wrapped in a silver cloth."[27]

Following the white horses and their riders was the carriage of the head of the mission accompanied by his suite; the most important figures in the embassy rode in other carriages or sleighs, while several members of the party rode richly fitted horses. Five hundred to several thousand Streltsy Guards might participate; other regiments wearing different-colored uniforms in green, white, or crimson either marched along with the embassy procession or else presented themselves as a living wall of troops along the procession's route. "Along the left side there were 24 regiments of infantry with 200 weapons, and on the right, cavalry. Before each company stood trumpeters and musicians with tambourines and pipes, which produced . . . a dreadful racket."[28]

Slowly, in ceremonial step, the embassies entered the capital, sometimes long after an early morning departure. Along its route, the ambassadorial procession was watched by several thousand people. Traditionally, the population—the boyars, noblemen, merchants, and people of Moscow—assembled to welcome the embassy in response to the tsar's decree, but many were also drawn by curiosity: to see both the guests themselves and the gifts, which were displayed in the procession, and which could also include rare animals. Heinrich von Staden describes how during the reign of Ivan IV the gifts from Queen Elizabeth I of England included a lion and lioness.[29] In the Kremlin itself, and in front of it on both sides of the road, stood Muscovite "riflemen numbering four thousand with long rifles; for the most important embassies they rang the big bells in all the Kremlin churches."[30] This bell-ringing was so loud that it was said to make the earth shake. The ambassadorial caravan entered the Kremlin through the Savior Gate, then crossed the Ivan and Cathedral squares, went "down a long street [on which] to the right and left . . . in a long and thick row of soldiers,"[31] the tsar's guard was arrayed. Before entering Cathedral Square, they passed "200 cannon . . . facing barrel to barrel; some had as many as three openings [muzzles], they were decorated in various manners and surrounded by numerous sentries."[32]

At the Tsar's Palace

The route to the audience hall for ambassadors from Christian countries went either through the front parvis of Annunciation Cathedral or else through the Red Porch of the Palace of Facets (fig. 8). A special part of the diplomatic ceremony took place at this stage. "On the porch, directly in front of the grand duke's rooms, the presents . . . were set out on pillows so that they could be carried."[33] Later, "upon our mounting the porch the sentries ordered us to remove our weapons and led everyone into the palace unarmed."[34] By custom, the ambassadors were met two or three times during that procession, in a "lesser," "middle," and "great" encounter, each of them conducted by a *stolnik* and a *dyak*. The first meeting took place at the Red Porch, where the ambassadors were greeted, their health was inquired about, and they were escorted to the doors of the Golden Chamber. Here the embassy was greeted once again and met by a *stolnik* and an ambassadorial *dyak*, but of a rank higher and more distinguished than the first. They led the procession into the specific palace hall that had been selected for the reception of the particular embassy, at the doors of which they were again met by yet another *stolnik* as well as the chief *dyak* of the Ambassadorial Office, who were to present them to the tsar. Often the last of the *stolniks* to greet the ambassadors was a distinguished boyar who held an important post at court, and sometimes it was the head of the Ambassadorial Office, who might be known to the foreign ambassador, since he had often been the Great Ambassador on a mission from Russia to the foreign ambassador's ruler. The last of the welcoming *dyaks* was also an important individual and was the person in charge of the affairs of the visiting embassy.

After the rather noisy ceremony on the streets of Moscow and Cathedral Square, the guests were startled by the silence in the reception halls, despite the number of people present, 150 to 300 in each of the reception halls. "The silence of the official receptions . . . for the sake of ceremony . . . when the ambassadors pass by, for which all the doors are open, no one moves from their spot and everywhere there reigns a silence such that you think the hall is empty. This is how ambassadors are supposed to be received here."[35] This unusual conduct on the part of those present in the palace amazed the ambassadors: "The bodyguards and sentries at [the tsar's] court stand like voiceless, immobile statues. In his palace, all is so quiet, it is as if no one lived there."[36]

The ambassadors and their suite of courtiers would finally be met by one of the tsar's close advisors, a distinguished prince, or *boyar-okolnichy*, who conducted the reception ceremony in the throne hall, acting as its master of ceremonies and intermediary between the sovereign and the ambassadors. When they finally reached this large chamber, the diplomats noted details of the furnishings, even though they did not always appreciate their significance. The walls were painted, as a rule, with Biblical scenes in bright, festive tones and gold, and for this reason one of the reception halls was called the Golden Chamber. The floors and benches were spread with rugs. A tiered buffet was set up in a prominent place for gilded silver objects from the tsar's treasury. The reception hall was well lit in the Palace of Facets, in the daytime by many large and small windows, and at night by several sumptuously decorated chandeliers (fig. 9). During the reign of Ivan IV, receptions were held in a hall that has not survived, but it was described by a contemporary: "The palace is so great that from its doors you can barely distinguish what is going on at the other end of it. It is built in the

form of a gallery or church nave and . . . is very long; its vaults are supported at regular intervals by forty gilded wood columns decorated with carving in the form of large leaves and other ornaments; the thickness of the column is such that two men can barely encircle it."[37] Like the central column in the reception room of the Palace of Facets, these columns divided the space of the hall into separate sections, where each had its own purpose.

Thus, according to ancient Russian tradition, the sovereign's dias was in the "red corner" (the word "red" also means beautiful in old Russian) under the icons, among which were depicted the faces of Christ, Mary the Mother of God, and saints, always including Saint Nicholas. In Russia great emphasis was placed on the sovereign's piety and closeness to God, and as he sat beneath the saintly images during the audience, the Russian sovereign was literally "under oath" and "supposed to watch vigilantly to ensure that no word tore from his tongue that was not filled with the five . . . virtues. Let him appear to those who saw and heard him like mercy, fidelity, directness, humanity, and piety, especially piety itself."[38] For when a sovereign truly prays, his nation and state pray with him. All court life in the sixteenth and especially the early seventeenth century passed, if it can be expressed this way, according to "Orthodox time." The audience for ambassadors was usually scheduled for a day or hour that was not connected with any religious ceremony in which the tsar had to participate, and, beginning in the mid-seventeenth century, a special decree was issued that forbade the reception of foreigners on Sundays.[39]

The Ceremony of Greeting

The tsar usually received ambassadors seated on his throne. No specific throne was used for receiving an embassy in the Kremlin, so the choice of one of the three

FIG. 8. Palace of Facets, Moscow Kremlin (photo courtesy The State Historical-Cultural Museum Preserve, Moscow Kremlin)

FIG. 9. Reception Hall of the Palace of Facets, Moscow Kremlin (photo courtesy The State Historical-Cultural Museum Preserve, Moscow Kremlin)

or four was determined by the rank of the diplomatic mission, the importance of the day of the reception in the court schedule, and the desires of the sovereign himself. Thus, in the reign of Tsar Alexei Mikhailovich a gold throne was most often used, but in the 1680s it was a double silver throne created especially for Tsars Ivan and Peter. Each of the thrones was a unique work of art with precious adornments that always included the Russian coat of arms and that of Moscow, as well as the symbols of the tsar's power—the lion—and of the purity of his intentions—the unicorn. A canopy was above the throne: "Silver-plated columns with a canopy [either carved wood or metal] on which there were three or four turrets such as those we have on organs, but also silver-plated."[40] In the late seventeenth century, a velvet canopy was installed above Tsar Peter I's throne.

The tsar's throne was elevated three or four steps, which were covered with plaques of silver. On the window closest to the throne or, later, on a special stand, lay the orb. "To his right at an equal height with the throne, placed on a special pyramid, was the orb, which was made of embossed gold and crowned with a cross. The tsar turned toward it slightly each time he had to speak, making the sign of the cross over himself as he did so."[41] During the joint reign of Tsars Ivan and Peter, a triangular silver stand with two orbs stood before each of them, but each of the young sovereigns had his own set of regalia. The orb in the mid-seventeenth century had a symbolic role, being equal to the crown and scepter, one of the three principal objects of the tsar's regalia (see Chapter 1, fig. 8). To the right of the throne was a "handsome . . . basin and ewer, a hand-washing set, which the sovereign used more than once that day."[42] Numerous testimonials have suggested that in the fifteenth and sixteenth centuries the sovereign performed a ceremonial hand washing in front of the ambassadors in order to emphasize the purity of his intentions. The later presence in the reception hall of a hand-washing set and special towel, as well a separate servant standing alongside them, was also related to ancient custom. The Gospels lay in a special place and played a role in diplomacy since they were used for swearing the oath on the book when treaties were concluded or ratified.

As they approached the spot where the sovereign sat, the ambassadors noted that to his right on long benches placed along the walls in three or four rows were the Moscow patriarch and the ecclesiastical authorities, and to his left the most distinguished of the boyars, those who belonged to the Council: "500 courtiers dressed in brocade, sable or marten, and caps with stones,"[43] all those present "sat ... on a rise, but so that the grand duke himself sat much higher than they."[44] The ambassadors would be meeting with several boyars later while negotiating and reaching agreements.

The patriarch's presence at the ceremony where the ambassadors were presented became traditional starting in the early seventeenth century, during the reign of Tsar Mikhail Fyodorovich, whose father, Patriarch Filaret, was in fact the power behind the throne. Later the patriarch was invited only in the case of a reception for ambassadors from Christian monarchs and rulers, and by the end of the seventeenth century this occurred more and more rarely. But then the patriarch could invite an ambassador or all the members of an embassy to visit him at his own palace for a discussion or a dinner. During the reign of Peter the Great at the end of the seventeenth century, neither the patriarch nor the higher clerical Orthodox dignitaries received ambassadors independently, and they were almost never present at ambassadorial audiences. Only envoys from spiritual leaders of the Orthodox world might be received by the Moscow patriarch in the sovereign's absence, if the purpose of the visit pertained to church matters.

The Ceremony of Presentation

The actual presentation of ambassadors to the tsar began with the master of ceremonies leading the chief ambassador toward the sovereign, stopping a short distance from the throne. Nicolaas Witsen wrote: "The tsar [Alexei Mikhailovich] ordered it to be announced that he desires noblemen and senior officers [of the embassy] to approach his hand. My turn was first. Still standing in place, I

bowed very low to him, took three or four steps, bowed once again and again for a third time before his throne, then he stretched out his right hand, which was supported by Prince Yakov [Ya. K. Cherkassky], and in this manner I kissed it. . . . There is no doubt that if the tsar had not stretched his hand farther, and I my neck, I would have fallen in his lap. Having accomplished this, I moved backward to my place repeating the former ceremonies and bows."[45] On either side of the throne stood the tsar's bodyguards, the *ryndas*, four young men, two each to the left and right of the throne, wearing white velvet or brocade uniforms with crossing gold chains and tall white fur caps. Each guard held a large sharp silver axe on his shoulder, blade up (see cat. no. 8); "they stood like statues, without stirring,"[46] "and their look suggested that they were ready to hack anyone who dared come too close"[47] (see page 269).

The tsar and patriarch were lavishly dressed. When receiving an embassy, the tsar wore attire from the Great Treasury, "a cross ... scepter, and orb; a state robe ... shoes of white morocco [embroidered with pearls]; an embossed staff."[48] On his head the tsar wore a crown, and his costume consisted of at least six different garments layered over each other, all of them painstakingly selected to match. Garments were lined with precious furs, such as sable, ermine, and marten. Only from the very few seventeenth-century portraits and one of the rarest icons of that period (cat. no. 15) can we form an impression of the tsar's costume, whose bulk nearly prevented him from fitting into the large throne. Different attire was used on days of mourning and funerals, when the sovereign, his guard, and those close to him were dressed in crimson. When the patriarch was present at the ceremony, he sat on a gilded chair and was dressed in a church vestment—a precious *sakkos* (cat. no. 20) with a cross and a *panagiia*, or pendant, on his chest (cat. no. 19). In his hands he held a staff (cat. no. 26), and "he wore a gold miter adorned with a cross."[49]

In Russia special attention had always been paid not only to the way the Russians dressed but also to the way those in the embassy dressed. In the sixteenth century and even into the late seventeenth century, diplomats visiting the Russian court from both East and West remarked with admiration on the Russian garments scattered with precious stones and lined with furs that they had received from the tsar as gifts. These were preferred for court receptions, because of the novelty of the garments and out of a desire to please the tsar.

During the reign of Ivan IV, the heir or heirs of the tsar were already attending some ceremonies, and in the reign of Alexei Mikhailovich, the heirs were placed to the left of the sovereign's throne, on a smaller throne. When the tsar held the scepter, his heir could hold either a smaller scepter or a staff. His clothing was equally formal and precious: "The tsarevich [Fyodor Borisovich, the son of Tsar Boris Godunov] wore garments embroidered in gold and pearls. His crown [cap], scepter, and needlework shone with the brilliance of the marvelous diamonds and other precious stones that adorned them . . . his staff is similar to the monarch's and finishes on top with the likeness of a cross. . . . A tall cap made of dark red fox woven with gold and with studs of precious stones and the traditional fur trim, was on the heir's head."[50] He did not take part in the ceremony, merely observing it, as a rule, and the ambassador could not address him. The heir usually had the right to attend ambassadorial audiences from the age of twelve. If the tsarevich happened to be ill, his invisible presence at the ceremony of greeting was symbolically marked by a "gold pyramid with a crown" that stood to the left of the tsar. The sovereign's brother, who sat "two yards" away, could also attend an ambassadorial reception.

The Presentation of Credentials, Letters, and Other Documents

For more than fifty years during the middle of the seventeenth century, a significant distance was maintained in court ceremony between the tsar and the ambassadors, which was supposed to underscore the greatness of the Russian tsar. The most important part of the ambassadorial ceremony was the handing over of the documents and letters from the foreign ambassador's monarch by the tsar's courtiers or his master of ceremonies. Beginning in the mid-seventeenth century, the sovereign's presence at the ceremony was largely sym-

bolic. Diplomats were forbidden to address the tsar personally and might sit through the entire reception without speaking or moving. Being permitted to hand documents directly to the sovereign himself was considered a special honor, even a triumph, for the ambassador.

Each ambassador spoke his own language, and two interpreters were present. One was provided by the Ambassadorial Office; the other, as a rule, was one of the embassy's participants. If any of those present spoke too softly or indistinctly, the master of ceremonies would reprimand him. While repeating the title of the Russian sovereign or his own master's, the ambassador would bow several times to the tsar. Sometimes in the presence of the embassy, a message from a monarch addressed to the tsar would be read aloud (if it was not confidential). Then, according to the protocol instituted in the sixteenth century, the sovereign would stand and inquire about the monarch's health and the ambassadors' health. (In the mid-seventeenth century this formula was pronounced either by the *dyak* in charge of the embassy's business or else by the master of ceremonies). Traditionally the ambassador was also asked questions about whom he represented and his purpose in coming to Russia. At the end of the conversation, ambassadors were allowed to kiss the sovereign's hand, and sometimes this honor was bestowed upon several members of the embassy.

The Presentation of Gifts

Then came the presentation of the gifts, which symbolized both the presence of the monarch who had sent the embassy and the high esteem in which he held the tsar (figs. 10, 11). The presentation was conducted by the master of ceremonies, who bared his head and announced to the tsar what the gifts were and from whom they had been received. They might be accepted or not, depending on the political message the tsar wished to convey.

After the traditional presentation of gifts and exchange of compliments, the ambassador received permission to sit on a bench that had been specially prepared for him, facing the throne and covered with a rug

FIG. 11. Johann Rudolph Storn, *The Reception of the Austrian Mission (the presentation of the gifts) in the Chamber of Tsar Alexei Mikhailovich in the Terem Palace at the Kremlin on April 24, 1662*. Plate 77 in Augustin von Meyerberg, *Al'bom Meierberga vidy i bytovyia kartiny Rossii XVII vieka* [Album, View, and Everyday Life Pictures from Russia of the 17th century] (Moscow, repr. ed. 1903). The State Historical-Cultural Museum Preserve, Moscow Kremlin

(see Chapter 2, fig. 2). The other members of the embassy were seated at a greater distance from the throne or stood throughout the ceremony. The length of the embassy's reception and its exchanges with the tsar might be either short or very long. This was determined by the embassy's status or the sovereign's interest, if he and the ambassador engaged in conversation.

Usually an audience would be cut off at two or three hours. Then the ambassadors left the hall behind the *dyak* in charge of that embassy's business and retreated into a free hall of the palace. The halls where the ambassadors were kept waiting were as opulently decorated as the audience hall with displays of rare items, which could be examined to help pass the time. "In the middle of the hall where we were sitting stood a great four-sided pillar under the vaults; around it on all sides was a broad table, and that table was the width on each side of two good boards; and was a

cubit and a half from the ground. On this table around the pillar mentioned was a display of gilded silver objects of great magnificence and value; it reached higher than half the height of the pillar, and rose shelf upon shelf (see Chapter 4, figs. 9–12) Furthermore, in the vestibules adjoining the hall there were also shelves beginning at a cubit and a half from the floor and reaching higher than halfway up the walls; these were filled all around the walls and on all sides and even above the entrance and exit doors with nothing but large and small silver bowls."[51] Often, after an interval, the embassy was invited, either by the tsar himself or in his name by an *okolnichy*, to be seated at the tsar's table, that is, to have a meal in the palace. Then the ambassadors returned from the palace to the Ambassadorial Court where they were staying and remained there until time came for the formal dinner with the sovereign, which usually began at six o'clock and took place to the light of many candles.

The Tsar's Ambassadorial Banquet

These formal dinners were organized according to the traditions of Muscovite hospitality. This occasion was an invariable part of receptions in the sixteenth century, but in the early seventeenth, during the reign of Tsar

Mikhail Fyodorovich, it was virtually dropped from the ambassadorial reception ceremony altogether. During the reign of Mikhail's son, Alexei Mikhailovich, the dinners were gradually restored and used as a way to show special favor. The sovereign appeared in the feasting hall having changed his robes: "On the 19th day of November Foreigners were with the Sovereign in the Dining Pavilion. And the Sovereign wore a splendid fur coat."[52] Formal meals in the presence of the tsar were usually held in either the dining hall or the reception hall of the Palace of Facets. The protocol would have been discussed in advance, before the tsar's meeting with the embassy. Several tables were usually set around the dining hall. Aside from the tsar's table, which stood separately and on a platform, a table was set for the ambassadors (usually referred to as "curved," that is, semicircular, so that all the places at it were equally prestigious). There was also the boyars' table, and if there were clergy present, a patriarch's table. At the beginning of the dinner, each person was supposed to sit where a place had been assigned him beforehand, but after the tsar's departure, it was possible to circulate.

The Meal

The master of ceremonies appointed for this banquet was the tsar's carver—a distinguished courtier or a prince—and a *stolnik* was assigned to assist him. Each table was presided over by a prince and his assistant (a nobleman). They "watched the tables . . . the Great . . . the Curved."[53] The ambassadors sat at the same table with their Muscovite *pristavs*. The guests, in accordance with Russian custom, were supposed to be "regaled." This position was filled by yet another courtier, also a prince, one with the rank of *stolnik*. Ambassadors might also be invited to the tsar's table for a period, at which time one of the *stolniks* "would go to invite ambassadors in the Sovereign's name."

According to sixteenth-century Russian tradition, tables were not set beforehand, so the guests found themselves before empty tables spread with "the cleanest of tablecloths."[54] The exception was the salt con-

tainer (cat. no. 59), which was placed before the most distinguished and honored guest, such as the Great Ambassador. Stands were set up in the hall with precious drinking utensils: "On low stepped shelves stood innumerable large platters and livery pots made of good gold . . . several silver loving cups [see cat. no. 11] and bowls, which no one man could wield by himself, to say nothing of using them as vessels for drinking. Generally speaking, there was everything in abundance except for plates, because they are not used at all by Muscovites or even the grand duke himself."[55] Food in sixteenth-century Russia was not eaten from plates but served to the ambassador from a platter; sometimes the serving platter was placed in front of him. In the late seventeenth century, however, a dinner plate was placed in front of each guest.[56]

Boyars and *okolnichy* were assigned to watch the buffets, and "palace men" watched after the *stolniks* to make sure food and drink were served at the tables at the right time. The dishes served were those prescribed by custom: swan meat, roast quail, pies, and so forth. "The food is put on the table not all at once but rather, first they eat one dish, then another, and a third, until the last."[57]

It was considered a special honor to receive a dish sent personally from the tsar to one or another member of the embassy. When this happened, the recipient's name was pronounced loudly, and the boyar watching the tables sent a servant to him. While the proffered food was being passed, the recipient made bows to the four corners of the earth. The same thing happened with drink; whoever was singled out to receive it had to stand up and bow in four directions (an ambassador might rise as many as sixty-five times during a meal). In the seventeenth century, unrestricted conversations with the tsar were not allowed, and all topics were strictly determined in advance, such as the health of the absent monarch and so on. The dinner proceeded decorously and slowly until the tsar's departure, after which a boyar especially chosen for the occasion would continue the affair. Most travelers remarked that the concluding portion of the meal was livelier and relieved by pleasant and less official conversations.

The Negotiations

A period of time would pass following the first audience, from a few days to a couple of weeks, and then the tsar would call the ambassadors in for a second important audience. The ambassadors' second entrance into the Kremlin area was almost as splendid as the first. The ceremony might take place in the same hall, but there were significantly fewer people present and the dress, even for the tsar, was more modest. At this ceremony the ambassadors were not permitted to ask the tsar any questions whatsoever but were merely expected to thank him for his kindness and for the "tsar's table" and to leave. The sovereign, or an *okolnichy* in his name, would inform the diplomats that the monarch had familiarized himself with their documents and assigned boyars to respond, that is, to conduct the actual negotiations.

Meetings between the participants in the negotiations were held fairly often, every two to four days. On these occasions, a special place in the Kremlin was set aside for the ambassadors to meet—sometimes in the Northern Chamber. In the negotiations, the partic-

ipants diligently followed each point proposed for a future treaty: all points were discussed, the translations painstakingly checked, and the discrepancies clarified. The results of the negotiations were "response folios," letters from the sovereign to the monarch—be he king, shah, or sultan—and, if an agreement acceptable to everyone had been reached, "treaty deeds."

Upon acceptance of a treaty in Moscow, it was customary for the tsar to kiss the cross. This ceremony took place in the presence of the visiting ambassadors and the tsar's advisors: "The Sovereign...[reciting a prayer] kissed the life-giving Cross on the peace resolution. The tsar's cap was removed from the Sovereign and held by the Prince Ivan Borisovich Cherkassky. The scepter was taken from the Sovereign.... The Cross on the lectern was offered by the boyar Prince Andrei Vasilievich Khilkov."[58] While kissing the cross, the tsar bowed to the ground in all four directions. An oath on the cross was considered unbreakable and sincere, which is why it was called "truth."

The Daily Life of the Ambassadors

After the presentation and between audiences with the tsar, life for the ambassadors and their entourages livened up. In Moscow they might be invited to take

FIG. 12. Anonymous 17th-century German engraver, *Solemn Procession of Tsar Mikhail Fyodorovich*. Plate 67 in *Tsarstvuiuschchy dom Romanovykh 1613–1913* [The Ruling House of the Romanovs, 1613–1913] (Moscow, 1913). The State Historical-Cultural Museum Preserve, Moscow Kremlin

part in religious ceremonies, to review the troops or see the Kremlin arsenal, or to visit the tsar's treasury. Ambassadors might see the patriach and the sovereign often and sometimes even speak with them (fig. 12). Some would take part in funerals or periods of mourning when the entire court dressed in black and crimson. It was also possible to get a glimpse of the ceremonies connected with the public appearance of the tsar's family—considered quite a coup.

Ambassadors were invited to visit their colleagues, the Russian diplomats, which is when they got to know the daily life of Moscow. Moreover, diplomats from the various countries made an effort to associate with one another in Moscow, despite the fact that the embassy's guard and *pristav* made an effort to prevent this kind of contact. Nonetheless, even in the mid-seventeenth century, the least propitious period for this, ambassadors and especially the soldiers and merchants who made up the mission did visit one another; they arranged dinners and suppers and traded impressions and secrets learned, such as whether or not the tsar had a personal library. Often diplomats acquired essential political and economic information from fellow countrymen who had entered into the service of the tsar.

Final Audience with the Tsar

Its business done in Moscow, the embassy was given a final audience with the sovereign—its "release." The ambassadors were received sumptuously this time, as well. As a rule, all those who had participated in the first ceremony were present. The sovereign again wore a costume from the Great Treasury, but somewhat different from the first: "a cross; the second diadem; a *friaskaya* cap; a scepter; a state robe."[59] The ambassadors were then given reciprocal gifts and documents to carry to their rulers. If an ambassador had been polite and his mission had ended to everyone's mutual satisfaction, he might also receive a personal gift from the tsar: a silver standing cup and cover, ceremonial horse trappings, or—most desirable and precious of all—wonderful Russian furs. The ambassadors' release might conclude with an invitation to the tsar's table or a parcel with

refreshments from the sovereign's *stolknik* to the ambassadorial court.

The Return Journey

The tsar's *pristav* had an interest in the embassy's leaving both the capital and the country's borders as quickly as possible, whereas some ambassadors searched for reasons or an excuse to delay, particularly if they had been sent to gather intelligence. In the towns through which the embassy passed, its affairs and problems were once again the business of the military commander. Many diplomats complained of inattention and a reduction in the funds allocated for their return trip. On the return journey, diplomats were rarely allowed to visit the towns themselves, but some semblance of a departure ceremony for embassies was arranged in Novgorod the Great: "Everything came to pass just as it had upon our entry: from the court to the landing soldiers stood 'at arms,' though now they were many fewer. For departures they brought in fitted horses; but no one escorted the ambassador except the interpreter....Feed was provided but irregularly."[60]

The rituals of the border crossings when leaving the tsar's lands were often simpler and shorter than those that had marked the embassy's arrival. This was not taken as an insult to the dignity of the ambassador and his sovereign but rather as desirable, since the return home was an important part of the diplomatic transaction. The returning ambassador inevitably carried with him important documents, which in most instances were ceremoniously presented upon his return to his ruler.

The ambassador was frequently received at a public audience with his ruler or representatives of the government. He then handed over a packet containing a combination of personal greetings (ruler to ruler, as well as to the ruler's close family) and drafts (often carrying great seals) of the agreements and treaties that had been negotiated. Those from the Russian tsar were generally beautifully written by scribes and decorated at the workshops of the Ambassadorial Office at the Kremlin.

The reception on the ambassador's return might take place before notables of the ambassador's sovereign's court, including members of the royal family, and in the presence of the resident diplomatic corps and even ambassadors from abroad. Sometimes reciprocal gifts from the tsar were presented by the ambassador to his ruler. The ambassador was thanked or congratulated in public and, if things had gone well, rewarded either financially or with honors.

Private consultations with rulers, government ministers, and others directly concerned with the issues discussed during the embassy either preceded or followed the public ceremony, and in the case of special agreements, decisions were made promptly as to whether the return of the countersigned documents required a full embassy or only a carrier.

A final, full written report by the ambassador was often filed. This could contain an enormous amount of information, both about the specifics of the particular embassy and about the situation of the court and the conditions in Russia of the time. These diplomatic documents make an important contribution to our knowledge of Russia in those distant times.

NOTES

1. For more detail, see Sakharov 1991; Adelung 1846, p. 101. See also Diplomatic Section 1744.
2. See Rogozhin and Chistiakova 1988, p. 115.
3. Ibid., p. 119.
4. Ambassadorial Office, no earlier than 1615; Ambassadorial Office 1673; Ambassadorial Office, second half of the 17th century.
5. Horsey 1991, p. 97.
6. Pokhlebkin 1992, p. 161.
7. Kerner 1991, p. 49. See Grala 1994.
8. See *TsGADA Guide* 1991, 1: 249.
9. Ambassadorial Office 1683, d. 61.
10. Litvin 1991, p. 94.
11. Ambassadorial Office, early 17th century, d. 1; Stolbtsy 1699, d. 3.
12. Stolbtsy 1699, d. 1.
13. Stolbtsy, late 17th century, fols. 1–3.
14. Compagni 1991, p. 87.
15. Buchau 1991, p. 83.
16. Foscarini 1991, p. 55.
17. Compagni 1991, p. 87.
18. Jenkinson 1991, p. 47.
19. Bussow 1991, p. 194; Gyldenstjerne 1991, p. 141.
20. Brambach 1991, p. 159.
21. Burgh 1991, p. 311.
22. Obuchowicz 1991, p. 339.
23. Gyldenstjerne 1991, p. 142.
24. Tanner 1991, p. 388.
25. Ibid., p. 388–89.
26. For more detail, see Pokhlebkin 1992, pp. 201–4.
27. Witsen 1996, pp. 93–94.
28. Shubinsky 1995, p. 11.
29. See Staden 1991, p. 72.
30. Heuss 1991, p. 134.
31. Shubinsky 1995, pp. 11–12.
32. Tanner 1991, p. 388.
33. Heuss 1991, p. 134.
34. Tanner 1991, p. 388.
35. Bartenev 1916, p. 139.
36. Collins 1991, p. 331.
37. Juan of Persia 1991, p. 139.
38. Machiavelli 1990, p. 53.
39. Ambassadorial Office 1684.
40. Witsen 1996, p. 95
41. Litvin 1991, p. 166.
42. Ibid.
43. Witsen 1996, p. 142.
44. Chancellor 1991, p. 29.
45. Witsen 1996, p. 98.
46. Ibid, p. 96.
47. Brambach 1991, p. 160.
48. *Vykhody Gosudarei* 1844, p. 5.
49. Burgh 1991, p. 312.
50. Witsen 1996, p. 142.
51. Gyldenstjerne 1991, p. 142.
52. *Vykhody Gosudarei* 1844, p. 4.
53. *Povsiadnevnykh zapisok*, 1769, p. 106.
54. Adams 1991, p. 39
55. Heuss 1991, p. 136.
56. Margaret 1991, p. 181.
57. Maskiewicz 1991, p. 259.
58. *Povsiadnevnykh zapisok* 1769, p. 103.
59. *Vykhody Gosudarei* 1844, p. 27.
60. Witsen 1996, p. 205.

ЦРЬ İ ВЕЛИКİ КИ̃ЗЬ.
МИХАİЛЪ ѲЕО̃ДОРО
ВİЧЬ В̃ СЕѦ ВЕЛИКİѦ
РОСİİ САМ О
ДЕРЖЕЦЪ

4

ENVOYS AND TREASURES:
ILLUSTRATIONS FOR THE TSARS

EDWARD KASINEC AND ROBERT H. DAVIS, JR.

THE ARMORY OF THE Moscow Kremlin is a treasure house of exquisite gold and silver decorative objects, arms and armor, and textiles given to the Muscovite tsars. As with many museum exhibits, however, these works of art can only be seen in an artificial physical setting, arranged in modern display cases that were installed in buildings constructed long after the works were created. The purpose of this essay is to introduce the reader to some of the rare illustrated publications that place the objects that were given between the six-teenth and eighteenth centuries, the years covered by this catalogue, and to the personalities who gave and received them, within their original context. We have focused on materials available at the New York Public Library, as it is one of the largest collections of its kind in the United States and the most publicly accessible.[1]

The surviving examples of these extraordinary works are marked by considerable chronological breadth, ranging from the sixteenth through the early twentieth century, and exist in a variety of formats.[2] Many are

FIG. 1. Anonymous, *Portrait of Mikhail Fyodorovich Romanov*, no. 31 in *Portrety, gerby i pechati Bol'shoi gosudarstvennoi knigi* (Moscow, 1672 St. Petersburg, repr. 1903). Slavic and Baltic Division, The New York Public Library, Astor, Lenox and Tilden Foundations

splendidly illustrated and designed and may be consid-ered works of art in their own right; all of them are basic sources for the study of this period of Russian his-tory and its architecture and artifacts. Of the publica-tions that appeared during the lives of the Muscovite tsars, the most relevant to this catalogue are the numer-ous accounts by travelers and diplomats to and from Russia during the sixteenth and seventeenth centuries. These rare images are invaluable records of the events, sites, customs, and objects that caught the eyes of for-eign observers on the eve of Russia's dramatic transition from the insular Muscovy to the outward-looking Russ-ian Empire of Peter I (the Great).

Also of interest in the context of this catalogue are the richly engraved and colored lithographic depictions of the coronations of Peter the Great's eighteenth- and nineteenth-century successors.[3] Although chronologically and aesthetically distant from historical Muscovy, the prints contain illustrations of rooms and objects—such as the vast central pier of the reception hall in the Palace of Facets, ringed with silver and gold given by foreign ambassadors—as they appeared during the reigns of the Riurikid descendants and their successors, the early Romanovs. In the nineteenth-century albums, particularly

FIG. 2. Matthiae Beckeri, *Foreign Ambassadors Being Received at the Court of Ivan IV (the Terrible) in 1578*. Untitled plate 3 in Jacob Ulfeldt, *Hodoeporicon Ruthenicum* (Frankfurt, 1608). Rare Books Division, The New York Public Library, Astor, Lenox and Tilden Foundations

638 accounts in Latin or Western European languages produced between 1486 and 1700.[4] Many such books appeared in print during the lives of the travelers (and of the tsars in whose court they were received); others were published much later, even as late as the twentieth century, transcribed from archival documents.[5]

By contrast, the printing of secular and religious travel literature within the territories of Muscovy tsardom and later the Russian Empire was not popular until the late eighteenth century.[6] Interest on the part of native Russian historians and bibliographers in the accounts of foreign travelers emerged during the first half of the nineteenth century with the reign of Tsar Nicholas I, when they were collected comprehensively and retrospectively—forming the so-called Rossica Collection of the Imperial Public Library in St. Petersburg.[7] By 1900 Russian publishers, bibliophiles, and collectors began to reprint—or in some cases, to print for the first time in Russian—some of the more important writings of earlier travelers to Moscow. Given the appalling lack of indigenous Russian printed sources (and, for that matter, archival documents) for the Muscovite period, the importance of foreigners' accounts as primary sources for historians cannot be overemphasized.[8] Unfortunately, very few of the original travel books contain woodcuts or engravings depicting the topography or flora and fauna of Muscovy, let alone the personages and protocols of the royal and patriarchal courts and their respective treasures. However, two firsthand accounts in the collection of the New York Public Library do contain such illustrations, and it is to these that we now turn.

those of Tsar Alexander III and his son Tsar Nicholas II, nostalgia for the seventeenth-century roots of the Romanov dynasty is reflected in the use of traditional Muscovite design motifs, costumes, and ceremonies. We have also included several nineteenth- and early-twentieth-century collections of engravings and chromolithographs that describe, among other things, the court, protocols, and treasures of the tsars of Muscovy from Ivan III to the accession of Peter the Great in 1689.

The literature of travel description (broadly called *Reiseliteratur*) became a staple in the repertory of European printing houses beginning in the sixteenth century. In fact, the historiography and bibliography of travel accounts are so vast as to constitute a separate discipline; a recent bibliography of the genre cites more than

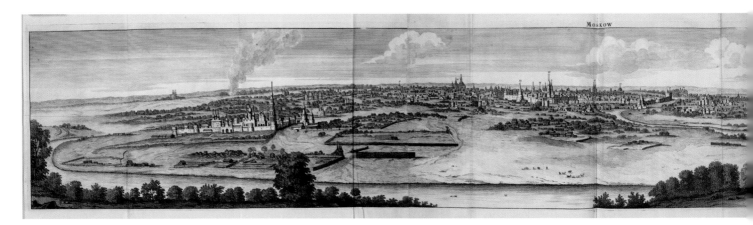

A particularly interesting illustrated account is that of Jacob Ulfeldt, who visited Muscovite Russia in 1578 as the Danish ambassador to the court of Ivan the Terrible. Ulfeldt's journey was not especially pleasant or even productive from a diplomatic point of view. He proceeded no further than the royal *oprichnina* at Alexandrovskaia Sloboda, then about sixty miles northeast of Moscow.[9] There he was "feted," perhaps ridiculed, by Ivan and his courtiers, who were in the midst of a power struggle with the boyars (nobles), and may have wanted to sabotage the mission. Ulfeldt's artist provides one of the very few contemporary woodcut depictions of the Muscovite court and of the ceremony and protocols governing the manner in which foreign ambassadors were received and entertained (fig. 2). Another brilliant visual source from a somewhat later period (1661–63) is the suite of drawings made on the spot by Johann Rudolph Storn, who accompanied the Holy Roman Emperor's envoy August von Meyerberg to Muscovy during the reign of Tsar Alexei Mikhailovich. The text describing Meyerberg's embassy was first printed in Leiden in 1688; the illustrations, however, were reproduced for the first time only in 1903 (see Chapter 3, fig. 11).[10]

Like many other travelers of their day, the Duke of Holstein's envoy Adam Olearius, who made many visits to Muscovite Russia between 1634 and 1643, and the Dutchman Cornelis de Bruyn, who visited between 1701 and 1703, were fascinated by the architecture and the peoples of Muscovy.[11] Both Olearius and de Bruyn include a number of broad panoramas, as well as maps that are more than cartographic representations of the geography

FIG. 3 Anonymous, *Map of Moscow*, from Adam Olearius, *Voyages très curieux & très renommez, faits en Moscovie, Tartarie, et Perse* (Leiden, 1719). Slavic and Baltic Division, The New York Public Library, Astor, Lenox and Tilden Foundations

and travel routes of Muscovite Russia (figs. 3, 4). With their miniature people and animals, architectural sites, and ruins, such maps are a veritable tableau of how the Western European mind imagined Muscovite Russia. The sumptuous engravings of the Kremlin (fig. 5) and of the religious buildings of mid-seventeenth-century Muscovy that appear in the 1719 Leiden edition of Olearius (fig. 6) are among the best of their kind and form an impressive visual backdrop to the distinguished diplomat's narrative.

Generally speaking, the texts of those who visited the tsar's court are far better known and studied than the writings of Russians who traveled to Western and Central Europe, the Middle East, and the Far East in the service of the tsar during this period. This is unfortunate, as these accounts provide a degree of perspective to Western perceptions of Russia. The account of German-born Evert Ysbrants Ides, Tsar Peter I's ambassador to the Chinese court of the Ching emperor in 1692–94 is a fitting counterpart to contemporary Western European descriptions of journeys

FIG. 4. Anonymous, *Panorama of Moscow*, from Cornelis de Bruyn, *Reizen over Moskovie, door Persie en Indie* . . . (Amsterdam, 1714). Slavic and Baltic Division, The New York Public Library, Astor, Lenox and Tilden Foundations

FIG. 5. Anonymous, *Procession Before the Moscow Kremlin on Palm Sunday*, from Adam Olearius, *Voyages très curieux & très renommez, faits en Moscovie, Tartarie, et Perse* (Leiden, 1719). Slavic and Baltic Division, The New York Public Library, Astor, Lenox and Tilden Foundations

FIG. 6. Anonymous, *Audience of Ambassadors in the Muscovite Court*, from Adam Olearius, *Voyages très curieux & très renommez, faits en Moscovie, Tartarie, et Perse* (Leiden, 1719). Slavic and Baltic Division, The New York Public Library, Astor, Lenox and Tilden Foundations

to the Muscovite court. His verbal description of the exotic peoples and fauna encountered along the arduous land route to the court of the Chinese emperor is enhanced by graphic illustrations of the Russian embassy's formal reception into the inner courts of the Forbidden City (fig. 7).

By the beginning of the nineteenth century, thanks in part to private support and imperial benefaction, Russian printing houses had at last established a reputation for producing illustrated volumes of high quality. Two categories of such publications are of particular relevance here: first, Russian imperial coronation albums of the eighteenth and nineteenth centuries, and second, nineteenth-century illustrated folio (i.e., oversize) volumes, some of which commemorated specific events and anniversaries and some of which were the result of projects documenting the institutions and cultural wealth of Russia. These complementary types of iconographic publications are valuable supplements to the limited number of images in seventeenth-century travel literature.

The Embassadors Introduction into the Audience hall

FIG. 7. Evert Ysbrants Ides, *The Embassadors* [sic] *Introduction into the Audience Hall*, from his *Three Years Travels from Moscow . . .* (London, 1706). Rare Books Division, The New York Public Library, Astor, Lenox and Tilden Foundations

Beginning in 1726, during the reign of Catherine I, the imperial court issued irregularly (and not always simultaneously with the event) impressive bound volumes and collections of loose plates devoted to imperial coronations. In the case of bound coronation albums, which included text as well as plates, editions were usually published in Russian and in one other European language—either German or French. These albums served to document and validate the monarch's accession to the throne and to suggest the glory and significance of the attendant events.[12] The subjects depicted in the eighteenth and nineteenth centuries are often the same as those in sixteenth- and seventeenth-century foreign views of Muscovy. For example, the buildings and open spaces of the Moscow Kremlin—such as Cathedral Square, the Cathedral of the Dormition, and the Bell Tower of Ivan the Great—appear in virtually every coronation album, symbolic of the antiquity and power of the Russian state. This repetition of images is

brilliantly illustrated in one of the rarest of the albums, that of Tsar Nicholas I and his consort, Alexandra Fyodorovna (the First), in 1826 (fig. 8).

The reception hall in the Kremlin's fifteenth-century Palace of Facets appears in many of the coronation albums, as it was the favored venue for imperial feasts

RETOUR DE LEURS MAJESTES AU PALAIS DES ANCIENS TSARS.

FIG. 8. V. Adam (artist) and L. Courlin (draftsman), *Return of Their Majesties from the Palace of the Early Tsars*, plate 9 in Henry Graf, *Vues des cérémonies les plus intéressantes du couronnement de Leurs Majestés Impériales L'Empereur Nicholas Ier et L'Impératrice Alexandra, à Moscou* (Paris, 1828). Slavic and Baltic Division, The New York Public Library, Astor, Lenox and Tilden Foundations

FIG. 9. Ivan Alekseevich Sokolov (engraver), *Interior Perspective of the Reception Hall, Palace of Facets*, plate 31 in *Obstoiatel'noe opisanie . . . Koronovaniia . . . Imperatritsy Elizavety Petrovny* (St. Petersburg, 1744). Slavic and Baltic Division, The New York Public Library, Astor, Lenox and Tilden Foundations

FIG. 10. Jean Louis de Veilly, *Coronation Feast, Reception Hall, Palace of Facets*, from *Risunki prinadlezhashchie k Opisaniiu koronovaniia imperatritsy Ekateriny II* (St. Petersburg, 185?). Slavic and Baltic Division, The New York Public Library, Astor, Lenox and Tilden Foundations

FIG. 11. Vasily Fyodorovich Timm, *Coronation Feast, Reception Hall, Palace of Facets*. Plate in *Opisanie s sviashchenneishogo koronovaniia . . . Aleksandra Vtorogo . . .* (St. Petersburg, 1856). Slavic and Baltic Division, The New York Public Library, Astor, Lenox and Tilden Foundations

FIG. 12. Konstantin Egorovich Makovsky, *Coronation Feast, Reception Hall, Palace of Facets*, from *Opisanie sviashchennogo koronovaniia imperatora Aleksandra Tret'ego . . .* (St. Petersburg, 1883). Slavic and Baltic Division, The New York Public Library, Astor, Lenox and Tilden Foundations

and for the reception and entertainment of dignitaries. On these state occasions, silver and gold objects presented by foreign rulers to the Muscovite treasury during the sixteenth and seventeenth centuries—some of which appear in this catalogue—were displayed on shelves circling one of the central piers that support the hall's vaulted ceiling. The views of the reception hall presented here are from the coronations of the Empresses Elizabeth (1744) and Catherine II (1762) and the Emperors Alexander II (1856) and his son Alexander III (1882) (figs. 9–12). In 1856, the Synodal Typography[13] reproduced seventeenth-century

drawings from the archives of the Ministry of Foreign Affairs of the events surrounding the 1613 coronation of Mikhail Fyodorovich as the first Romanov tsar. This was the first time these images had appeared in print.

These and other depictions of treasures in the reception hall were clearly intended to emphasize the historicity, wealth, and power of the Russian Empire and its geopolitical stature in relation to neighboring powers. The images are similar to those found in earlier travel accounts, and yet the message and intent are decidedly different. Western travelers attempted merely to document places and events, and only secondarily to illustrate the more exotic elements of their experience. In these eighteenth- and nineteenth-century Russian publications, however, one encounters depictions of contemporary events taking place in surroundings that emphasize the continuity of the imperial present with the reflected luster of its venerable Muscovite patrimony.

Bound sets of engravings and chromolithographs produced during the nineteenth and early twentieth centuries, such as the coronation albums, served the dual function of documenting events, personalities, and objects and exalting them.[14] Many collections of illustrations were printed with the approbation of the tsar's court and its high functionaries,[15] in limited editions and in the presses of government or quasi-governmental institutions such as the Publishing House for State Papers or the Academy of Sciences Printing House. In some instances, even the private sponsors, or "publishers," of these publications were well-connected government officials or members of the aristocracy.[16] All titles published in the empire were subjected to pre-publication review by state censors, which virtually guaranteed some degree of official oversight. Imperial sponsorship allowed the compilers of such works unlimited access to some of Russia's most remarkable manuscript collections and treasure houses and guaranteed the financial support to produce volumes that were themselves works of art.

A number of illustrated collections of loose plates issued during the nineteenth and early twentieth centuries were based on unique drawings of seventeenth-century events that had never been published. For example, a description of the 1626 wedding celebration of Tsar Mikhail Romanov to Evdokiia Luk'ianov, printed in Moscow in 1810, reproduces seventeenth-century drawings of ceremonies surrounding the nuptials (fig. 13). The reception hall of the Palace of Facets is shown at the time of the wedding feast, featuring a table laden with gifts from foreign well-wishers. Once again, the image is contemporary with the event, but it did not appear in print until 1810. A publication of 1903 reproduced—for the first time—seventeenth-century portraits of rulers of the East Slavic

FIG. 13. Anonymous, *Palace of Facets, Ceremonial Table set with Various Foreign Gifts*, from *Opisanie v litsakh torzhestva, proiskhodivshogo v 1626 godu . . . brakosochetanii . . . Mikhaila Feodorovicha . . .* (Moscow, 1810). Slavic and Baltic Division, The New York Public Library, Astor, Lenox and Tilden Foundations

lands, from the time of Riurik to the reign of Tsar Alexei along with important patriarchs of the seventeenth century (see pages 307–14). This volume of portraits, armorials, and seals was based on the so-called *Great Book of State* of 1672, a manuscript prepared during the reign of Tsar Alexei (see cat. no. 21).

The first description of some of the Kremlin Armory's most spectacular treasures was prepared by Alexei Fyodorovich Malinovsky and published in 1807, but his book was later superseded and vastly supplemented by the multivolume work by Fyodor Grigorevich Solntsev printed between 1849 and 1853 and containing detailed, accurate color lithographs of Armory objects (figs. 14, 15).[17] Other publications, including a collection of lithographs assembled by Fyodor Fyodorovich Rikhter, illustrated in considerable detail surviving examples of Muscovite architecture and ornament, such as the doorway of the palace's reception hall (fig. 16). This intense documentation of the historical roots of the Romanov Dynasty reached a crescendo in 1913, on the occasion of its three-hundredth anniversary. Books such as *The Annalistic and Personal Anthology of the House of Romanov* reproduced images relating to the dynasty's Muscovite and imperial past and present, including the Romanov coat of arms as it appeared in its earliest known variant (fig. 17).

FIG. 14. Fyodor Grigorevich Solntsev, *Crystal Ewer Encrusted with Precious Stones, Sent to Alexei Mikhailovich by the German Emperor Leopold*, plate 49 in Fyodor Grigorevich Solntsev, *Drevnosti Rossiiskogo gosudarstva*, vol. 5 (Moscow, 1849–53). Slavic and Baltic Division, The New York Public Library, Astor, Lenox and Tilden Foundations

FIG. 15. Fyodor Grigorevich Solntsev, *Vases Sent to Peter Alekseyevich by Emperor Leopold in 1684*, plate 55 in Fyodor Grigorevich Solntsev, *Drevnosti Rossiiskogo gosudarstva*, vol. 5 (Moscow, 1849–53). These vases were, in fact, given to the co-tsars Ivan V and Peter I by King John III Sobieski of Poland (cat. no. 51a,b) in 1686. Slavic and Baltic Division, The New York Public Library, Astor, Lenox and Tilden Foundations

One final but important example of a publication devoted to documenting the Muscovite past is Sergei Petrovich Bartenev's two-volume work on the history of the Moscow Kremlin, which was published in Moscow in 1916. While not a great bibliographic rarity, this book collects an enormous amount of information—both textual and visual—on the history of the Kremlin and on those who visited and worked there during the Muscovite period. In addition to providing late prerevolutionary views of some of the important interior spaces, such as the Palace of Facets's reception hall (fig. 18), Bartenev also reproduces illustrations from earlier manuscripts prepared by foreign embassies but not widely circulated, as well as pictures from published accounts. Reproduced elsewhere in Bartenev's book are the reception of Swedish envoy Count Gustaf Oxenstierna in the Golden Chamber of the Kremlin Palace, as it appeared in the manuscript diary of Swedish military engineer Erik Palmquist (see page 269), the reception of the 1675 Dutch Embassy in the same room, based on the engravings in Koenraad van Klenck (see Chapter 3, fig. 10), and the entry into Moscow of Ambassador Johann Georg Korb, who represented Emperor Leopold I of the Holy Roman Empire in 1698 (see page 224).

In spite of their inherent differences of perspective and purpose, books and visual material published in the Russian Empire in the eighteenth and nineteenth centuries constitute an important iconographic complement to the largely textual sixteenth- and seventeenth-century European accounts of Muscovy.[18]

In the 1920s, a number of the religious buildings of the Kremlin, including the Miracles (Chudov) Monastery and the Assumption (Voznesensky) Female Monastery, as well as a portion of the contents of these and other institutions, became targets of the Soviet government's policy of "reconstructing" the ancient capital and expropriating (and, in some cases, selling for hard currency) works of art, rare books, and manuscripts belonging to the imperial regime. Indeed, with some rare exceptions, most of the books cited above and in the Bibliography were acquired by the New York Public Library during the 1920s and 1930s through the Soviet antiquarian export agency International Book. Some may,

FIG. 17. Anonymous, *Romanov Arms*, plate IV in *Letopisnyi i litsevoi izbornik doma Romanovykh* (Moscow, 1913). Slavic and Baltic Division, The New York Public Library, Astor, Lenox and Tilden Foundations

FIG. 16. Fyodor Fyodorovich Rikhter (lithographer), *Doorway of the Reception Hall of the Palace of Facets*, plate 30 in his *Pamiatniki drevniogo russkogo zodchestva* (Moscow, 1850). Slavic and Baltic Division, The New York Public Library, Astor, Lenox and Tilden Foundations

in fact, have been taken from collections within the Moscow Kremlin—certainly many came from the personal and palace libraries of the Romanovs in St. Petersburg.[19]

Even the Diamond Fund and the Armory were not spared.[20] It is unlikely that the motivation for these sales was solely an economic one. The institutions of the Kremlin, the contents of these institutions, and their depictions in the albums of the eighteenth through the twentieth century were also physical reminders of some of the more significant cultural, spiritual, and political attainments of the Muscovy and the Russian Empire. This may explain in part why the imperial regalia, foreign diplomatic silver objects, and rare books and albums from the Romanov collections were so eagerly included in the officially sponsored Soviet government sales of the 1920s and 1930s. Fortunately for Russian Soviet cultural institutions, several of these sales were unconsummated, but a sufficient number enabled libraries in the West to acquire some of the important printed depictions of the tsars of Muscovy, their envoys, and their treasures.

NOTES

1. The greater number of these printed works are considered bibliographical rarities, found primarily in the important research libraries of North America, among them the Newberry in Chicago, the Lilly in Bloomington, Indiana, the Morgan in New York City, the Huntington in San Marino, California, the Library of Congress, the Harvard University

FIG. 18. Anonymous, 1916 photographic view of the Palace of Facets, showing interior decoration, elements of which date from the reign of Tsar Fyodor Ioannovich, no. 254 in vol. II of Sergei Petrovich Bartenev, *Moskovskii Kreml' v starinu i teper'* (Moscow, 1916). Slavic and Baltic Division, The New York Public Library, Astor, Lenox and Tilden Foundations

Libraries, and of course the New York Public Library (NYPL), to name but a few of the more prominent repositories.

The travel literature holdings of the NYPL are notable not only for their size and linguistic diversity, with more than a hundred texts from the fifteenth through seventeenth century, but also for the range of classic publishers represented (Aldus Manutius, Plantin, Elzevir, et al.), as well as the provenance of the accounts themselves. For example, NYPL's copy of the first edition of Antonio Possevino is from the library of Eugene Schuyler, the nineteenth-century American diplomat and traveler to Russia. (A portion of his library was given to the NYPL by his widow, Gertrude King Schuyler, in 1901.) Several of the texts come from the library of the Counts Shuvalov.

2. For simplicity's sake, we are concentrating here on print sources, thereby excluding from consideration here the vast historical archives and manuscript collections in both Eastern Europe (especially Russia, of course) and the countries from which the diplomatic and ambassadorial gifts were sent (Middle East, Scandinavia, Western Europe, and so on).

3. See Kasinec and Wortman 1992, pp. 77–100.

4. Poe 1995. On the substance of foreign descriptions of Muscovy during various historical periods, see, for example: Sergei Mikhailovich Seredonin, *Izvestiia inostrantsev o vooruzhennykh silakh Moskovskogo gosudarstva v kontse XVI vieka* [Foreign Reports Concerning the Armed Forces of the Muscovite State at the End of the 16th Century] (St. Petersburg: Izd. red. zhurnala "Bibliograf," 1891), or his *Sochinenie Dzhil'sa Fletchera "Of the Russe Common Wealth" kak istoricheskii istochnik* [Giles Fletcher's "Of the Russe Commonwealth" as a Historical Source] (St. Petersburg: Tip. I.N. Skorokhodova, 1891); A.I. Malein's translations of Albert Schlichting (fl. 16th cent.), *Novoe izvestie o Rossii vremeni Ivana Groznogo; "Skazanie" Al'berta Shlikhtinga* [New Information Concerning Russia in the Time of Ivan the Terrible: The "Tales" of Albert Schlichting] (Leningrad: Izd-vo Akademy nauk SSSR, 1934), and Johann Georg Korb's *Diarium itineris in Moscoviam, Dnevnik puteshestviia v Moskoviiu* (1698 i 1699 gg.) [Korb's Memoir of Travel in Muscovy] (St. Petersburg: Izd. A. S. Suvorina, 1906).

5. See, for example, the accounts of Heinrich von Staden (fl. 16th cent.), his "Moscowiter Land und Regierung," translated and edited by Thomas Esper in Esper 1967, and some of the other *oprichniki* (i.e., supporters of Tsar Ivan IV during the *Oprichnina* period; see note 13).

6. Vasily Grigorovich-Barsky's (1701/2–1747) posthumous *Puteshestvie k sviatym miestam, v Evropie, Azii i Afrikie nakhodiashchimsia, predpriiatoe v 1723, i okonchannoe v 1747 godu* [Travel to Holy Places in Europe, Asia and Africa Begun in 1723 and Concluding in 1747] (St. Petersburg: Imperatorskaia Akademiia nauk, 1778), was apparently the first printed travel account written by a Russian. See Stavrou and Weisensel 1986.

7. The Rossica Collection was begun at Nicholas's behest and implemented by the "imperial" public librarian, Baron Modest Andreevich Korff (1800–1876).

Compiled by K.F. Fetterlein (1836–1902), the *Catalogue de la section des Russica, ou écrits sur la Russie en langues étrangères*, 2 vols. (St. Petersburg, 1873) was the first published documentation for this rich collection, now part of the Russian National Library in St. Petersburg. This catalogue has been reprinted in Amsterdam (P. Schippers, 1964), and New York (Da Capo Press, 1970). Systematic development of the Russian National Library's Rossica Collection ceased in 1930. To our own day, the catalogue of this collection remains (along with some modern-day derivative works) a basic guide to the printed literature of travelers' and observers' accounts of Old Rus', Muscovy, and the Russian Empire. For a recent English-language compilation, see Poe 1995.

Earlier bibliographies include Friedrich von Adelung, *Kritisch-literärische Übersicht der Reisenden in Russland bis 1700*, 2 vols. (St. Petersburg, 1846); and V. Kordt, *Chuhzozemni podorozhni po skhidnii Evropi do 1700*. [Foreign Travelers from Europe to 1700] (Kiev, 1926 in *Zbirnyk Istorychno-filolichnoho viddliu* [Miscellany of the Historical-Philological Faculty], p. 38.

As of this writing, the single best brief overview of the Rossica Collection remains A.L. Gol'dberg's "Kollektsiia 'Rossika' Gosudarstvennoi Publichnoi biblioteki im. M.E. Saltykova-Shchedrina" ["'Rossica' Collection of the Saltykov-Shchedrin State Public Library"] *Istoriia SSSR*, 6 (1964), pp. 92–[102]. His detailed work has been published, with entries in chronological order, as *Dorevoliutsionnye izdaniia po istorii SSSR v inostrannom fonde Gosudarstvennoi publichnoi biblioteki im. M.E. Saltykova-Shchedrina: sistematicheskii ukazatel'* [Prerevolutionary publications on the History of the USSR in the Foreign Language Collection of the Saltykov-Shchedrin State Public Library: A Systematic Index] (Leningrad/St. Petersburg: Gosudarstvennaia publichnaia biblioteka im. M.E. Saltykova-Shchedrina, 1982–93). Thus far, volumes 1–4 have been issued.

8. Accounts of diplomatic travels by representatives of Muscovy, for example, were limited to the archival "ambassadorial books" intended for consumption at only the highest levels of officialdom. On these books, see Rogozhin 1994, and the collection of excerpts from ambassadorial observations found in *Puteshestviia russkikh* 1954.

9. The term *Oprichnina* refers to the period between 1565 and 72, during which Ivan the Terrible created an independent principality within Muscovite Russia.

10. See Meyerberg 1903. The originals, formerly in Dresden at the Sächsische Landesbibliothek, were taken to Moscow by the Soviet Army in 1945 and are today in the Museum of the History and Reconstruction of Moscow, in central Moscow. See Poe, 1995, p. 170.

11. Particularly with those they termed "Tatars," namely the Turkic peoples incorporated into Muscovy during the sixteenth century. See, for example, *Russia seu Moscovia itemque Tartaria commentario topographico atque politico illustratae* (Lugd.

Batavorum, 1630); or the works of Nicolaas Witsen, *Noord en oost Tartarye* (Amsterdam, 1705); John Perry *The State of Russia Under the Present Czar* (London, 1716); of Jan Struys, *Les Voiages de Jean Struys, en Moscovie, en Tartarie, en Perse . . .* (Amsterdam, 1681), all held by the NYPL.

12. For a detailed study of the uses of such ceremony and tradition in imperial rule (i.e., from the time of Peter I onward), see Wortman's two-volume *Scenarios of Power* (Wortman 1995, 2000). For the Muscovite court, see especially Crummey 1985, pp. [130]–58.

13. The Synodal Typography was a sophisticated, specialized printing house in both Moscow and St. Petersburg under the jurisdiction of the governing body of the Russian Orthodox Church from the eighteenth through the twentieth century.

14. Many such works are included in a checklist prepared by Benjamin E. Goldsmith (Goldsmith 1992).

15. Among them, the eminent bibliophile, collector, and scholar of works on paper, and public prosecutor of the city of Moscow, Dmitry Rovinsky (1824–1895).

16. The most prominent was Rovinsky. Earlier in the century, Platon Beketov (1761–1836) was also a notable sponsor of sumptuous collections of iconography.

17. On academician Solntsev and this compilation, see Vzdornov 1986, pp. 43–46.

18. In addition to NYPL's important holdings of travel literature, coronation albums, and illustrated folio books documenting the gifts of foreign countries to the Muscovite court, the library's collections are among the richest in North America of books prepared and printed in Muscovy during the sixteenth and seventeenth centuries. These include several Slavonic illuminated manuscripts and some of the most notable books of this period, including the *Tetro Evangelie* of Radishevsky printed in Moscow in 1606, containing four full-page illuminated woodcuts and possibly of patriarchial provenance and finally, the first "secular" book ever to appear in Muscovy, *Uchenie i khitrost' ratnogo stroeniia pekhotnykh liudei*, a translation of *Kreigskunst zu Fuss* of Wallhausen and published in Moscow in 1647, containing thirty-five double copper engravings.

19. On the question of Romanov books sold to North American collections during the 1920s and 1930s, see Davis and Kasinec 2000. In winter 1997–98 the NYPL exhibited a selection of its Romanov library holdings entitled "The Romanovs: Their Empire, Their Books. The Political, Religious, Cultural, and Social Life of Russia's Imperial House." See also the essay by Marc Raeff (Raeff 1997), pp. 42–75, accompanied by a checklist of items included in the exhibition, pp. 76–153.

20. See Davis and Kasinec 1991, pp. 53–59.

5

DIPLOMATIC AND AMBASSADORIAL
GIFTS OF THE SIXTEENTH AND
SEVENTEENTH CENTURIES

❧

GUY WALTON

WHILE IT IS WIDELY recognized that the reception by rulers of ambassadors at court must be counted among the major events of diplomatic history, relatively little attention has been paid to the subject of the enormously expensive, often spectacular gifts that were considered a major component of these rituals.[1] Large numbers of splendid objects were displayed at these receptions and were formally presented to the host ruler as he sat enthroned in the presence of important state officials garbed in gala dress for the occasion. The host would accept diplomatic gifts from the ruler who had sent the embassy, as well as gifts from members of the ambassadorial party. On the departure of an ambassador, the host would present reciprocal gifts during the final interview, not only to the ruler who had sent the embassy but also to the ambassador himself and sometimes to members of his party. The reciprocal gifts to rulers were generally of a similar value and quality as those received by the host, but the gifts

to ambassadors were often worth more than those the ambassador had given, in order to provide partial reimbursement for expenses incurred during the trip.

It may be argued that these diplomatic and ambassadorial gifts played a role as significant as that of the written greeting from the donor, since their number and value conveyed important coded messages about the esteem in which the recipient was held by the donor who sought his ear. The status of the ambassador's prince and that of the ambassador himself were likewise expressed in the gifts they received in return.

Certain types of princely gifts, often those of the most spectacular sort, were meant to demonstrate a sense of the superior position of the donor, a tradition that dates back to antiquity and gained particular momentum during the Middle Ages. For example, in the year 1001, Stephen, son of Prince Géza and later the patron saint of Hungary, received the crown (now lost) for his coronation as the first king of Hungary from Pope Sylvester II and the Holy Roman Emperor Otto III, who undoubtedly intended to suggest that they were bestowing upon Stephen the right to rule.[2]

Byzantine emperors also seem to have presented crowns implying the bestowal of rank. King Andrew I

FIG. 1. *Crown.* Byzantium (Constantinople), c. 1042–50. Gold, enamel; h. 4¹/₂ in. (11.5 cm). Inscribed: Constantine IX Monomachus. The emperor is shown with his empresses, Zoe and Theodora, and figures representing Justice and Humility. Hungarian National Museum, Budapest

FIG. 2. *Throne of Tsar Boris Godunov*. Persia (Isfahan), late 16th century. Wood frame covered with gold sheeting, turquoises, rubies; h. 35 in. (90 cm). Upholstery: French velvet, 18th century. The State Historical-Cultural Museum Preserve, Moscow Kremlin (P-28)

of Hungary is said to have received a gold crown from the Emperor Constantine IX Monomachus of Constantinople, probably between 1046 and 1052 (fig. 1).[3] A surviving gold crown of the eleventh century, incorrectly called the crown of Saint Stephen, part of the present regalia of the Hungarian state, contains enameled gold elements that were given for a coronation (probably of a Hungarian queen) by the Byzantine emperor Michael VII Ducas (r. 1067–68, 1071–78).[4]

In 1605 the Austrian Holy Roman Emperor Rudolf II sent regalia to Tsar Boris Godunov that included a crown, a scepter, and an orb, a gift regarded by the Moscow government as confirmation of Boris's status as "emperor and king."[5] In the same year the Turkish Sultan Ahmet sent a golden crown to Stephen Bocskay, king of Transylvania, as a symbol of Turkish overlordship of his kingdom.[6] It should be noted that in diplomatic salutations Turkish sultans traditionally included the following phrase: "I am the Sultan of Sultans . . . the distributor of crowns to monarchs [Chrosroes] of the

world. . . ."[7] In this same tradition was the throne that Shah Abbas I of Persia had given to Boris Godunov in 1604 (fig. 2).[8]

In 1687 Louis XIV of France sent a gold crown "à fleurons enrichie de diamants, rubis, emeraudes et perles," along with other splendid gifts, including globes and clocks, to the king of Siam, not to bestow rank but to intimidate the ruler of a country that he was planning to invade in order to make it a French protectorate.[9] (The result of the invasion was not favorable to the French, however, and provoked a coup d'état that closed Siam to foreigners for more than a century.)

Exactly the opposite message, that of an inferior relationship, was conveyed by gifts of tribute. Princes defeated in war and lesser rulers or officials gave gifts to their conquerors or to more powerful states, some on demand and some voluntarily with the intention of winning favor. The importance of such gift offerings was considerable, often because of their actual value (so that they served as a kind of tax paid) or because they were symbolic of the power of the recipient. During the sixteenth century, the most interesting and impressive gifts made specifically for tribute were giant mechanical clocks; these also functioned as scientific instruments and occasionally resembled mechanical toys. The clocks were specifically demanded by the sultans of the Ottoman Empire from the Austrian emperor under the terms of peace treaties signed, after the defeat of Austria, by Süleyman the Magnificent and his successors. The first such gift, "a machine of silver which combined a clock with a planetarium," was given in 1541 to Süleyman after Austria lost Hungary to the Ottomans. A 1694 engraving by Andreas Thelott depicts a scene in which an envoy of the Holy Roman Emperor Rudolf II presents a clock to Sultan Murād III.[10] Although only small objects of this nature survive today, most of these gifts to the sultans stood about six feet high and were accompanied on their journey by clockmakers who stood ready to make any repairs required after the trip.[11]

The idea of gifts as a form of tribute was often central to the meaning of many presentations, even when not clearly identified as such. Typically, rulers accepting ambassadorial gifts tended to treat them as some kind of tribute, whether or not this was the case. Certainly, gifts received by Eastern rulers (the emperors of China, sultans of Turkey, and the shahs of Persia) from Western courts were regarded as tribute, regardless of the donor's status, since Easterners invariably believed their foreign counterparts to be inferior in rank.

However, the vast majority of gifts exchanged by monarchs in a diplomatic context were intended to please fellow princes, "dear cousins," or even "dear brothers," as rulers often addressed each other in diplomatic correspondence. This rubric of amity also occurred in decidedly unfriendly situations, when the giver might actually be preparing to go to war even as negotiations continued.[12] Many gifts were intended to please individual recipients. Resident diplomats were often asked to indicate what objects were likely to find favor with a particular prince, and a special effort would be made to find such.[13]

During the seventeenth century, when European monarchs sought to develop luxury industries in their kingdoms, gifts were occasionally used to promote these enterprises, and by the eighteenth century objects produced by the royal porcelain factories came to predominate the tradition of gift giving.[14] Henry IV and Louis XIII of France, who strived during the first half of the seventeenth century to establish tapestry manufactories in competition with those of Flanders, were determined to demonstrate the quality of French tapestries by placing them in significant collections throughout Europe.[15]

The arms and armor presented by the Dutch government to Tsar Mikhail Romanov in 1630–31 may have been intended to suggest the availability of such equipment to Russia, in spite of a public policy forbidding arms sales abroad. Many gifts from England and Holland were offered as a means of proposing trade possibilities.[16] A classic example of such a promotional gift is the set of two tablecloths sent by Christian IV, king of Denmark and Norway, to the tsar in 1622, through Russia's ambassador to Denmark, Grand Duke Alexei Mikhailovich L'vov (cat. no. 89).[17] Christian had upgraded a cloth factory established in 1605 and founded new cloth and silk factories in 1620 and

1621, having brought in Karel Thijssen, an established master from the Netherlands, to improve the quality of the products. Large silk damask cloths decorated with figural motifs and inscriptions, one in blue and white and another in yellow and red (Denmark's royal colors), were probably presented to the tsar in order to inspire an order from the Moscow court. (Such orders were not forthcoming from Moscow or anywhere else, however, and King Christian's factory closed in 1626.)

Assembling the Gifts

From antiquity onward, it was widely understood that gifts presented at the reception of ambassadors should be numerous and impressive, since tradition called for the objects to be displayed by a procession of diplomats and servants before the prince, the court, other ambassadors, and even the general public, as can be seen in a seventeenth-century engraving of such an event in Moscow (see Chapter 3, fig. 10).

The task of assembling a large group of sufficiently impressive gifts was a constant problem for courts, exacerbated by the demands of diplomatic urgency, which frequently required that important gifts be gathered within a period of about three months to accompany an embassy. Any delay might be considered impolite in embassies of congratulation, and political negotiations often called for rapid action. Furthermore, courts usually needed to send more than one embassy at a time to different courts, which would require the accumulation of several groups of gifts simultaneously. The usual procedure in the sixteenth and seventeenth centuries was to commission a number of gifts from local craftsmen or from the prince's own palace workshops. So great were the demands in terms of quantity that this procedure rarely sufficed, and inquiries were frequently sent to agents across the continents requesting suitable objects of high quality. In the case of European metalwork or ceremonial arms, objects from major centers with impressive reputations, such as Nuremberg, Augsburg, and Hamburg, were in great demand. Near Eastern rulers in similar situations turned to craftsmen from Isfahan, Constantinople, and Jerusalem. Armenian merchants seem

FIG. 3. *Caftan*. Persia (Isfahan), probably 1630s. Brocaded velvet with silk and metallic thread; collar to seam, 49³/₈ in. (126.5 cm). Royal Armory, Stockholm (photo © The Royal Armory, Sweden/Göran Schmidt)

to have played a major role in locating objects for gifts from Near Eastern rulers to Russia.[*]

Rulers were sometimes obliged to empty the shelves of their own personal collections and treasuries in order to achieve an adequate offering. It is logical to assume that beyond a nucleus of carefully selected gifts, most courts were forced to amass rapidly a variety of objects of a character suitable to any royal recipient.[18] The marvelous Persian caftan (fig. 3) sent by Tsar Alexei Mikhailovich to Queen Christina of Sweden before 1645 was undoubtedly a gift of this type,[19] and Christina herself later sent four huge silver standing cups to Russia

that had been documented fifteen years earlier in the Swedish royal collection (see cat. no. 79).

There may not have been a formal international consensus on what constituted a worthy group of ambassadorial gifts, but clearly there were established levels of value, to judge by the reaction in France to a group of about 2,500 objects presented to Louis XIV by three ambassadors of Phra Narai, the king of Siam, on September 1, 1686. The gifts were put on display in the Salon de la Guerre at the end of the Hall of Mirrors at Versailles after the Siamese ambassadors had concluded their audience with the king. Although graciously received by the king, who was renowned for his exquisite manners, the gifts were less well received by the court.[20]

The Marquis de Sourches disdained them, saying, "The presents which the king [of Siam]...sent to the King and to Monsieur the Dauphin...consisted of a large number of rather ugly porcelains, of some attractive Chinese cabinets and screens, and some mediocre vases of gold and others of tambac."[21] The Marquis de Louvois, who was at the time both Minister of the Army and in charge of the arts at Versailles, made the essential point in addressing the Abbé de Choisy, a French envoy who had traveled with the Siamese: "Is it not correct that all these things you brought back are not worth more than 1500 pistols?"[22] The main problem was that the porcelain, though rare, lacked intrinsic value, and even if the gold-colored tambac vases shone more brightly than real gold, they too departed from a standard that measured proper respect by the weighed value of gems, silver and gold.[23] (An earlier notorious failure was the small jeweled watch given by King Francis I of France to the Turkish sultan in 1583. As a court official put it, "The Sultan was ill-pleased with him [the ambassador] and his king on the occasion [of the circumcision of the sultan's heir]. While all other princes had made suitable presents, the king of France who claimed to be so great had sent a watch only...."[24])

Whatever the doubts of the French court about the value of the Siamese gifts, there was a very high level of public interest in them, one that resulted in the unprecedented publication of accurately drawn images of a substantial number of ambassadorial gifts. The large calendar

---

[*] For further information see Steinmann 1986; and McCabe c. 1999.

almanac engraving of the Siamese presentation ceremony at Versailles, made for the New Year of 1687, not only shows a quantity of gifts but actually identifies them as well (fig. 4).[25] The selection of objects for the almanac clearly reflects the attitude of the Marquis de Sourches, for the huge collection of porcelain was passed over by the almanac's publisher, although the lacquer cabinets and screens that had pleased him were also omitted. Most of the identified objets d'art chosen for depiction are of gold, along with caskets containing jewels and a pair of cannons with silver ornaments,[26] suggesting that the focus was on weapons and gifts of the highest possible intrinsic value.

The Siamese ambassadorial visit to France clearly constituted a "Great Embassy" of the most prestigious sort. A description of it was published in three special volumes by the *Mercure Galant*, the newspaper that recorded court events.[27] Such a plethora of gifts was unusual. Foreign ministries probably sought to determine from previous experience appropriate levels of extravagance in gifts, linked to each occasion. Gifts for different types of embassies, such as those of congratulations and nuptial negotiations, and for discussions of frontiers, military affairs, and trade agreements, were certainly differentiated. These standards remain difficult to establish, however, and an understanding of them awaits the systematic study of the numerous lists of gifts in the archives of many foreign ministries.

Another issue was the quantity, type, and value of the gifts given to and by ambassadors themselves, often alongside the royal gifts.[28] Gold chains and miniature portraits of rulers, sometimes enriched with jewels, were commonly given to ambassadors—chains from the earliest times and portraits after the sixteenth century, and still later in Russia.[29] Other important gifts frequently accompanied these items, and tapestries, furnishings, and other fine objects are still to be found in the great houses of the European nobility whose ancestors served as ambassadors.[30]

The Role of Religion in Gift Giving

In the Near East, the sacred book of Islam, the Koran, was always regarded as the most important gift for

FIG. 4. F. Jollain, *King Louis XIV Receives the Siamese Ambassador.* France (Paris), 1686. Engraving with etching, 32 x 20^{1}/4 in. (82 x 52 cm). Many inscriptions, including numbers within the image and a key for identifying the gifts. Musée du Louvre, Paris, E. Rothschild Collection (photo R.M.N.—J.G. Berizzi)

fellow Muslim rulers, and depictions of presentation ceremonies generally show two to four Korans as the first gifts being offered. A sense of the types of gifts received and the manner in which they were presented to the sultan is conveyed in the illustrations by the painter Nakkaş Osman in the chronicles of the Ottomans, including the reception of a Safavid ambassador from Persia in 1567 (fig. 5).[31] The ambassador, Shahquiis, is being held for security by two chamberlains, while members of his party, having already received gifts of clothing, are garbed in Ottoman robes of honor. Korans are being presented, along with parts of tents, which are suggestive of military activity (round tent

FIG. 5. Nakkaş Osman, *Presentation of Gifts by the Safavid Ambassador Shahquli to Selim at Edirne, early in* 1567. Turkey (Istanbul), 1581. Watercolor with gold leaf on paper, from vol. 2 of Loqmān, *Şehnâme-i-Selim Hân*; each page 11 3/4 x 7 in (30 x 18 cm). Library, Topkapi Saray Museum, Istanbul

tops are recognizable). Contemporary documents describe carpets so heavy that it took seven men to carry them and report that 19,000 pack animals were required to carry the embassy's baggage and the gifts. Pope Clement VIII seems to have understood the place of religious books in such Islamic presentations. He sent three gospel manuscripts in Persian with his embassy of 1604 to Shah Abbas I.[32]

Muslim rulers, as defenders of their faith—and in the case of the sultans, protectors of the Holy Shrine of Mecca—were not supposed to receive embassies from nonbelievers, since that might have suggested an impossible equality. Western embassies to the Ottoman sultan were generally received by the grand vizier, and in Izmir rather than in the "Sublime Porte" of Constantin-

ople, although there were many exceptions.[33] The role of intermediaries was also fundamental to these exchanges between Christians and Muslims. A number of gifts from Persia to the tsars, even the most extravagant among them, such as the diamond-studded throne of Tsar Mikhail, were presented by Armenian Christian merchants, rather than by the Islamic rulers, probably for this reason.[34] At one point the sultan partly avoided this problem by frequently appointing his subject Thomas Cantacuzenus, a Byzantine Christian, to act as ambassador to Moscow between 1621 and 1636. Greek Orthodox prelates from Constantinople seem to have also served occasionally as intermediaries with Christian rulers, particularly with the Russians.[35]

The Orthodox patriarch of Constantinople wore two hats, that of a Turkish subject and that of the head of the Greek Orthodox church. The patriarchate conducted its own limited diplomacy and was responsible for one of the most prestigious diplomatic gifts ever offered, the Codex Alexandrinus, among the two or three earliest texts of the Christian Gospels, which was sent to King Charles I of England and is now in the British Museum. Sir Thomas Roe, a resident ambassador in Constantinople in 1627, was given the codex by Cyril Lucaris, patriarch of Constantinople. Lucaris had previously been patriarch of Alexandria, the place where the manuscript may have originated, and the codex may have been a personal possession.[36] This gift indicates that the patriarch saw the manuscript as appropriate for a Christian king, since a Muslim ruler would have expected to receive a Koran from a prince of his own faith. (Some gifts from the patriarchs of Constantinople to the Russian patriarchs are included in this catalogue.)

The issue of diplomatic gifts to and from the Vatican was a complicated one. Although the Roman pontiff was the head of the Catholic church, he was also regarded as a secular prince of the Papal States, and over the centuries popes had assumed many of the dignities of the Holy Roman Emperor, part of a tradition related to the so-called Donation of the Emperor Constantine, a forged document giving lands to the popes that was alleged to convey the status of secular prince to the head of the Catholic church. In any event, popes were ranked first among the princes of Europe. Although the presentation rituals of ambassadorial letters of accreditation to the Vatican were among the most lavish, the popes do not seem to have been the givers and receivers of the numerous valuable gifts, as was the custom during this time.[37] Perhaps because a papal gift was considered an honor conveying a special blessing, popes usually sent only a few objects—although these could be very splendid.[38] Not surprisingly, religious relics figured prominently among them.

Papal gifts were most often triggered by very old traditions, the best known of which was the presentation of a golden rose to a worthy person, usually a woman, or to a city. The rose was first used as a part of annual ceremonies at Santa Croce in Gerusaleme in Rome. Many of these roses, some centuries old, still survive today.[39] Popes presented swords to leaders of military action against the infidel Turks, a famous surviving example being the sword given by Julius II in

1509 to the Hungarian King Wladislaw II that is now preserved at the National Museum in Budapest. The presentation of a sword and jeweled hat at Christmas to a prominent person, such as the king of Castille or the grand duke of the Tyrol, occurred with some regularity after the fourteenth century.[40] There were other exceptional moments when papal gifts were expected, as in the tradition that the pope should send swaddling clothes to the French king on the birth of his heir, the dauphin.[41]

It was the papal nuncios, ambassadors of the church, who tended to receive the traditional, lavish diplomatic presents during the seventeenth century, especially when they were members of important princely families and as cardinals enjoyed a real possibility of eventual election to the papacy. A famous example of such largesse was the gift (now in Philadelphia) of a series of French tapestries designed by Peter Paul Rubens and given to Cardinal Francesco Barberini by Louis XIII of France, truly a princely gift and indirectly a fine present to the pope through this nephew.[42] Ten tapestries depicting episodes from the legend of Rinaldo and Armida, woven after designs of Simon Vouet by Raphael de la Planche in Paris about 1635 (now at the Flint Art Museum in Michigan), are also alleged to have been a part of this gift, which, if this is true, was definitely extravagant. Fabio Chigi (later Pope Alexander VII) received a splendid amber standing cup decorated with the Hapsburg eagle for his work as nuncio at the Congress of Westphalia, which ended the Thirty Years' War (1618–48). The gift, though precious, was far more modest than the French royal gifts mentioned above.[43]

Gifts to the Tsars

The gifts given to and received by the Moscow tsars during the sixteenth and seventeenth centuries formed a unique group astride the traditions of East and West. Located between the great capitals of the Near East—Isfahan and Constantinople—and Western Europe, between Muslim and Christian worlds, and as the last imperial capital professing the Orthodox faith, Moscow

FIG. 6. Szymon Boguszowicz (attributed), *A Tsar Receiving a Delegation in the Reception Hall of the Palace of Facets at the Moscow Kremlin*, early 17th century. Oil on wood panel, 17 x 25 in. (43.5 x 64 cm). Hungarian National Museum, Budapest

was a world unto itself in many respects. The tsars' conduct toward Catholic emissaries was deeply resented by the Vatican legate Antonio Possevino, according to his account of his Russian journeys (1586) and by later European ambassadors, Protestants as well as Catholics, who objected to the Orthodox prince's washing his hands after receiving them. Muslims were led in by a special door, avoiding the Kremlin churches, and they too must also have sensed a deliberate distancing.[44] But the tsars' religious condescension toward the Turks was modified by their belief that in the entire world only the sultan (as the descendant of the Byzantine emperors) occupied a throne equal to that of the tsar.

As far as gifts were concerned, the tsars were open to receiving many objects traditionally given by both Muslim and European courts. Adam Olearius, traveling in the 1630s to Moscow with an embassy of the duke

of Schleswig-Holstein, mentions that both the floors and the walls of the reception hall of the Kremlin's Palace of Facets were covered with "lovely rugs," many of which may be presumed to have been received as gifts (fig. 6).[45] Bolts of precious Persian and Turkish textiles frequently accompanied the rugs as gifts. Splendid European textiles were also often included with gifts of textiles from the Near East. These fabrics were usually finished in Moscow, either as boyar robes (garments of the court nobility) or as church vestments. Today some of these examples are preserved among the church vestments in the Kremlin Armory collection.

From Western Europe came quantities of royal plate, sometimes gold, but more often gilded silver. This was a particularly welcome gift in Moscow after the 1605–13 Time of Troubles, when much of the silver in the Kremlin palaces was allegedly stolen or melted down for coin. So appreciated were these gifts of silver that the tsar undertook to purchase additional plate himself, most notably from the Danes and the English.[46]

FIG. 7. *Cup* (bratina). Russia (Moscow), 1630s. Gold, enamel, niello, rubies, sapphires, emeralds, pearls; h. 10¹/₂ in. (27 cm). This cup was a gift from Tsar Mikhail Fyodorovich to King Wladislaw IV of Poland in 1637. Kunsthistorisches Museum, Vienna

The tsars only rarely gave away the metalwork that they were so anxious to receive. However, one important Russian piece, which passed through the neighboring Polish court and is now in Austria, is a well-known exception (fig. 7).[47] In his study of English silver at the Moscow Armory, Oman argues that the tsars knew the foreign diplomats were unlikely to appreciate works in the Near Eastern or Byzantine styles prevalent at the Russian court,[48] but cups were regularly offered and on one occasion a hundred golden plates (with food) were given to the Danish ambassador and his party.[49]

For the most part, the remarkable collections amassed by the tsars included objects and animals that were standard, even old-fashioned, gifts at the time in Europe. Many of the Turkish and Persian arms were

of only ceremonial interest, and the gifts the tsars received of jeweled objects and precious metals were of the sort that had been exchanged in Europe and the Near East for centuries. Nevertheless, it is possible to trace a gradual change in the character of certain gifts, particularly during the seventeeth century. The embassy from Holstein in 1634, for example, brought two technically advanced German clocks, as well as a modern apothecary apparatus (though one with gold elements).[50] And the gift of twelve cannons brought by an earlier Holstein mission, in 1632, suggests that Russia, seeking to modernize her military, was particularly interested in weaponry, a concern that produced the remarkable gift of three hundred cannons from Charles XI of Sweden in 1697.[51]

A broader interest in Western European culture and technology characterized the later years of Tsar Alexei Mikhailovich's reign, especially during the 1670s, although relatively few objects in this category showed up as gifts, since European princes continued to view Alexei as a strong traditionalist. A bit later,

FIG. 8. Anonymous, *Presentation of the Gifts to the Pasha of Ofen at Buda,* from a series of eleven gouaches of Ambassador Count Ludwig von Kuefstein's Austrian embassy to Sultan Murād IV, September 29, 1628. Austrian, after 1628. Gouache on parchment; $15^{5}/_{8}$ x $10^{1}/_{4}$ in. (40 x 26 cm). Museum Pechtoldsdorf im Wehrturm, Pechtoldsdorf, Germany

Western European rulers could have had no doubt of the technological and scientific bent of Alexei's son Tsar Peter I, particularly after his "Great Embassy" to Europe in 1697, and they responded with important gifts, particularly of scientific instruments and tools.[52] In any case, the great Swedish gifts presented to Peter by the embassy of 1699 demonstrate that the European concept of what was acceptable to the tsars actually changed slowly, since they still included giant sculpted gilded-silver basins from Augsburg, ewers of gilded silver in the form of animals, and so on.[53] It is possible that some understanding of Peter's uniquely informal lifestyle is reflected in a few of the Swedish objects, such as candlesticks (cat. no. 87).[54] The image of Muscovy abroad, even in Peter's time, was still primarily related to a traditional perception of the culture of the old Kremlin court. This situation would not change until the removal of the government to the new capital at St. Petersburg at the beginning of the eighteenth century.

Types of Gifts Exchanged

The majority of diplomatic and ambassadorial gifts were chosen for the visual impact they would make while being paraded from an ambassador's temporary residence through the streets of the city and into the palace, where they would be presented to the ruler. As a consequence, most gifts were impressive in size and breathtaking in their materials and craftsmanship. Gifts varied widely, however, since many of the most important ones were intended to suggest that special attention had been paid to the particular tastes of the recipients and to the situation that had precipitated the embassy. Some of the types of gifts given frequently during the sixteenth and seventeenth centuries are described below.

REGALIA. Although they were a standard part of the repertory of diplomatic gifts, crowns, scepters, and orbs were sent only in very special circumstances. In the sixteenth and seventeenth centuries, the primary donors of such items were the Austrian Holy Roman emperor and the Ottoman sultan. These rulers asserted the right to bestow kingdoms on other princes who were thought to occupy less prestigious thrones feudally subservient to them. Although the pope probably reserved the right to bestow regalia as the first prince of western Christendom, he rarely exercised it during this period. The emperor, on the other hand, continued the feudal medieval tradition by sending regalia to Boris Godunov, while the Ottoman sultan asserted his rights in this respect by sending a crown to Transylvania, since he was the occupant of the imperial throne of Constantinople.[55]

ROYAL PLATE. Standing cups of gilded silver, often more than eighteen inches tall, were perhaps the most frequent European diplomatic gifts, especially to the tsar, to judge by several surviving drawings and prints. These objects were often presented with large ewers and basins, which were useful for ceremonial hand washing at both religious and secular functions. Tazzas, table decorations, wine fountains, tiered confectionary trays, candlesticks, wall brackets, and even chandeliers were often added to these groups of table silver, joining the massive displays of royal plate in princely residences. The shapes of these silver objects were often striking and of a sculptural character that hid their true function, as in the case of a ewer in the form of a rearing lion (cat. no. 85).

Silver, however, was not always welcome. Saxony, for example, received very little, because its mines provided most of the silver used at Augsburg, Nuremberg, and even Hamburg, all centers where large amounts of plate were crafted. Although Islamic countries accepted silver for ceremonial presentations, they generally melted it down after reception, since many Muslims believed that the use of such silver for dining was forbidden in the Koran (fig. 8).[56]

ANIMALS. During this period, well-bred horses were greatly valued, and fine stallions were often among the

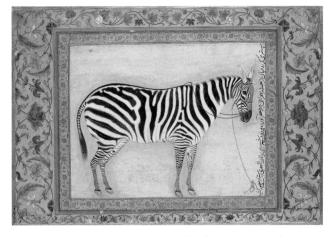

FIG. 9. Master Mansur, *Zebra*. India (Agra or Delhi), 1621. Double-page book illustration: tempera and gold on vellum; each page 7 1/4 x 9 3/8 in. (18.3 x 24.1 cm). Victoria and Albert Museum, London (photo courtesy of the Trustees of the Museum)

most esteemed gifts, particularly the highly prized Arabs of North Africa and the Near East.[57] Horse trappings from the Near East and Europe were also particularly appreciated (see cat. no. 31). Equally grand as a gesture were wild animals suitable for display in royal menageries. Lions obtained from Africa, which were appropriate for heraldic reasons, were often sent as gifts along with elephants, zebras, rhinoceros, and many exotic species of birds. The famous picture of a zebra by the Mughal painter Mansur commemorates one such gift (fig. 9), which was received from the Ottomans by Jahangir, the Mughal emperor of India, who mentions the gift in his memoirs. "As it was a rarity it was (later) included among the royal gifts sent to my brother [the Persian] Shah Abbas." Among the most popular animal gifts were birds of prey, especially falcons, for use in hunting. Tsar Alexei, an enthusiastic hunter, received hunting birds from the rulers of Turkey, Poland, England, and Denmark and gave many as gifts.[58]

STATE COACHES. The celebrated state coach ordered by Elizabeth I of England for Tsar Boris Godunov was sent by her heir, James I, in 1604 after her death. A relief carving in wood showing Boris as a "golden armored, garland-crowned, chariot-borne Roman Emperor" served as the front panel of the coach and reflected the imperial pretensions of the Moscow tsars (fig. 10).[59] Several

Another kind of present ubiquitous in international exchanges included tapestries and bolts of precious textiles from both Europe and the East, particularly those made of silk and large amounts of gold thread. These textiles suggest that the patrons either had special access to important trade routes or owned factories. Textiles were especially welcome since after they were received as gifts they could play a role at court, and they were often given in turn by princes to their courtiers.[60]

Gift textiles were also used for the decoration of palaces. The most important example of such use during the seventeenth century was at Gottorp Castle in Germany, where gold and striped-silk cloth from Persia was used throughout the castle for many purposes, including a table canopy above a throne and the decoration of nine state beds. There were sixteen Persian table carpets (nine of which were of cloth-of-gold and silver), and two of the rooms had elaborate Persian wall coverings. Along with silk and satin textiles were rich Persian velvets elegantly figured with floral and figural patterns, some of these embellished with birds (fig. 12). Thirteen long panels of velvet survive (with numerous other fragments) in the Danish royal collections in Copenhagen. These textiles were the gift of

FIG. 10. *Carriage.* England, completed 1603. Carved oak, painting, gilding, forged iron; max. h. 8 ft. 4 in. (250 cm), max. l. 19 ft. 9 in. (608 cm). Italian velvet added c. 1630 (photo courtesy The State Historical-Cultural Museum Preserve, Moscow Kremlin)

other coaches were sent from Poland to Moscow during the seventeenth century. Gifts related to ceremonial transport were not restricted to the Europeans, however. A seventeenth-century silver elephant saddle and a silver palanquin are preserved at the Merangahr Fort at Jodhpur in India, a gift of the Mughal emperor Shah Jahan to the maharani of Jodhpur, Sasmant Singh.

FURS AND TEXTILES. Bundles of furs, often including black sable, from the great northern forests (fig. 11), usually offered in packs of forty pelts, were sent by the Russian tsars; because of the rarity of these furs outside Russia, they were the most appreciated of all Russian gifts.

FIG. 11. Michael Peterle, *Russian Ambassadorial Party at the Austrian Court of Emperor Maximilian II.* Germany, 1576. Color woodcut on paper; 59⅞ x 16¾ in. (153.5 x 43 cm). Victoria and Albert Museum, London (photo courtesy of the Trustees of the Museum)

Shah Safi to the duke of Holstein, either given in return for those presented to the shah by the duke's embassy of 1636–38 or else brought to Holstein by the shah's ambassador, who returned via Moscow with the Holstein party in 1639.[61]

ARMS AND ARMOR. Rare firearms from famous armories have been documented as gifts in many European collections. An exceptional garniture of a wheellock carbine and a pair of holster pistols in a uniquely advanced design was given by the Venetian Senate to Louis XIII of France in 1638, and probably passed along by Anne of Austria, queen of France, to Queen Christina of Sweden.[62] Dutch and German firearms were given in substantial quantities, and several fine examples are represented in this exhibition (cat. nos. 67, 68).

The arms and armor sent as diplomatic gifts often included parade armor, such as jeweled ceremonial maces, shields, bow cases and quivers (cat. no. 27), and helmets, which became part of the symbolic presentation of royal power at court. Such gifts to the tsars were common from the Turkish sultans and Persian shahs, as well as other rulers.

HARDSTONES AND JADE. Many hardstone (semiprecious) vessels of ancient Roman, Byzantine, or even contemporary origin were also used as gifts. Almost all such objects were mounted on silver or gold bases and decorated with jewels.[63] The Asian equivalent of these Western gifts were spectacular jade carvings, usually

FIG. 12. *Textile from Gottorp Castle* (detail showing pattern of serrated leaves). Persia (Isfahan), c. 1620s. Silk velvet with metallic thread; 94 x 27³⁄₈ in. (241 x 70 cm). Rosenborg Castle, Copenhagen

bowls or vessels, but occasionally of small figure sculptures. When such jades found their way to the West, they were often treated as the equivalent of antique hardstone vessels. A jade bowl sent by the king of Siam to Louis XIV may be seen today at the Prado in Madrid among the "Gems of the Dauphin," the objects that

FIG. 13. *Chest.* Japan, 1580–1600. Cedarwood, lacquer, mother-of-pearl; h. 25³/₈ (65 cm), w. 51¹/₈ in. (131 cm). This chest belonged to Gustavus Adolphus, king of Sweden. The Swedish Royal Collections, Gripsholm Castle (photo by Mariefred © Kungl. Husgerädskammaren, The Royal Collections, Stockholm)

Philip V of Spain inherited from his father, the Grand Dauphin of France, who had received three jade bowls from Louis XIV.[64] Tabletops inlaid with brightly colored hardstones were frequent and popular gifts from Florence and Rome during the sixteenth and seventeenth centuries.[65] Objects made of amber were frequently sent from countries along the Baltic Sea (see cat. no. 45).

JEWELRY. Jewelry of various kinds, such as notable gems, necklaces, collars, and pendants, some with interesting provenance, were included among the gifts of nearly every embassy. Jeweled and enameled gold collars frequently conveyed membership in exclusive orders of chivalry such as the orders of the Golden Fleece (Austria) or the Garter (England).

EXOTICA. A message of exclusivity was exemplified by the many lacquer pieces given by the Dutch state during the seventeenth century, especially Japanese lacquered chests. The most famous surviving example is a chest at Gripsholm Castle in Sweden, made of lacquer and inlaid mother-of-pearl, which was presented by the Dutch States General to the Swedish King Gustavus Adolphus in 1616 (fig. 13).[66] This gift reflected both

the value of the remarkable Dutch shipping routes to the East (Spice Islands) and also the routes to the Baltic, where the Dutch obtained wheat and timber. Other gifts that demonstrated the widespread power of far-flung empires must have been numerous. One example is the ivory casket of 1545 in the treasury of the Munich Residenz. Its carved reliefs, commissioned by the ruler of Ceylon (Sri Lanka) as a gift to King John III of Portugal, represent the recognition by the Portuguese king of Dhampala as heir to the Ceylonese throne.[67] Another such gift is the great South American emerald cluster obtained by the Emperor Charles V as ruler over Hispanic America.[68] Before the Europeans discovered how to make porcelain, vases and plates of this material were often used as gifts, both by Asian rulers and by countries that were, like the Dutch, engaged in the luxury import trade. As I noted above, however, porcelains were occasionally dismissed as merely decorative, unworthy as royal gifts.

HEIRLOOMS. In a world where power was tightly linked to royal bloodlines, an object that had belonged to a well-known relative was usually appreciated by the recipient. The Austrian emperor Leopold I presented Louis XIV of France with the treasure of King Childeric, a Frankish king from whom Louis was directly descended. The treasure included Childeric's sword, a breastplate in the form of a bull's head, and ninety-four small bees, which had once decorated a horse harness, among other objects. The breastplate, the sword handle, and the bees were made of enameled gold, and the group dates from about A.D. 480. Shortly after receiving the gift in 1666, Louis commissioned the great *ébéniste* Pierre Gole to make a lacquer cabinet in the form of a mausoleum to contain the treasure.[69] Another important example of such a gift is the gold drinking cup (*kovsch*) believed to have been presented to the Elector Augustus of Saxony, king of Poland, by Peter the Great during a visit by the tsar to Dresden in 1709. Ivan IV (the Terrible) commissioned the cup, which is inscribed: "The sovereign commanded this bowl to be made of Polatskian gold when he conquered his inheritance, the city of Polatsk on February 15, 1563"

FIG. 14. *Drinking Cup* (kovsch). Russia (Moscow), after 1563. Gold, niello, sapphires, rubies, pearls; l. 9 in. (23 cm). This cup belonged to Tsar Ivan IV. Staatliche Kunstsammlungen, Dresden

(fig. 14).[70] In addition to those who may have had family ties, many recipients simply appreciated objects with interesting histories and connections to famous people.[71]

RELICS. Religious relics were also frequent royal gifts in the Catholic, Orthodox, and even Muslim and Buddhist worlds. Among the most famous of these were the thorns of Christ's crown, which were scattered across Europe during the thirteenth century to relatives and friends by Saint Louis IX, king of France, who obtained the crown relic from Emperor Baldwin II of Constantinople.[72] Such gifts were usually presented in jeweled reliquaries, which increased their suitability as gifts worthy of their royal recipients. Although relics

as prestigious as Christ's crown were rarely available, other objects from the passion of Christ and the bones of saints housed in jeweled reliquaries appear frequently among gifts.[73]

Antiquity, family connections, religious interest, and even a royal workman figure in an extraordinary gift that is today at El Escorial in Spain: a reliquary containing a bone of Saint Blas (fig. 15). King Wenseslas III of Poland himself hammered a gold covering for the bone in 1306, and in the sixteenth century the object was sent by his descendant, the Holy Roman Emperor Maximilian II, to the Spanish King Philip II, his cousin, for Philip's celebrated collection of relics.[74]

PAINTINGS AND SCULPTURE. The high value placed on the unique achievements of Renaissance painters caused a major innovation during the late fifteenth century in diplomatic gifts: the presentation of works by living

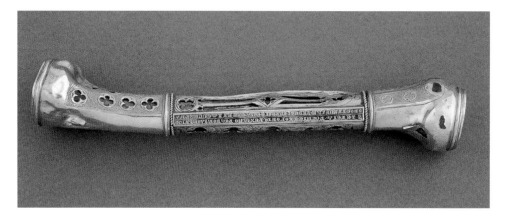

FIG. 15. King Wenseslas III et al., *Reliquary for a Bone of Saint Blas.* Poland (Cracow?), 1306. Silver, gold, enamel; l. 10³/8 in. (26.5 cm). Inscribed: [This bone of Saint Basil, decorated by Wenseslas III, king of Poland and Bohemia (1306)]. Patrimonio Nacional, El Escorial, Madrid (photo © Patrimonio Nacional, Madrid)

artists who were largely or exclusively attached to one patron, a tradition that began with Lorenzo de' Medici.[75] Cecil Gould has discussed the substitution of a studio copy for *The Virgin of the Rocks* by Leonardo da Vinci, so that the duke of Milan could send the original (fig. 16) as a wedding present to the duchess of Tyrol.[76] Popes Leo X and Clement VII (Medici) used access to their artists a few years later as a factor in their negotiations with certain European princes. Francis I of France was a particular beneficiary of this diplomatic strategy.[77] Gifts of Northern European painting were made as well,[78] and sculpture also figured among diplomatic gifts. The Russian tsars appear to have been uninterested in gifts of Western European painting and sculpture during this period.

The most famous gift of paintings of the seventeenth century was the Dutch gift, which included both Italian Renaissance and contemporary works, to Charles II of England after his restoration to the throne in 1660.[79] Joachim von Sandrart mentions the gift in his art-historical treatise *Teutsche Academie* of 1679. The Venetian ambassador to the English court informed his government at the time of the gift that its presentation had been something of an event and that "the king appreciated the present highly." The works were put on display in the banqueting hall at Whitehall Palace. The Dutch States General had seized the opportunity to buy much of the most prestigious collection of Italian art in Holland, including twenty-four paintings and twelve sculptures from the collection of Gerrit and Jan Reynast, who had assembled most of it while living in Venice. In addition, the government had persuaded the painter Gerrit Dou to add one of his own works, along with two other works that he owned, one by Saenredam and the other by the esteemed German painter Adam Elsheimer. Additional works of art were included in this large gift, which was intended to offset the sale of Charles's father's great collection during the Puritan Revolution.

At the end of the sixteenth century, the Tuscan grand dukes realized that small bronze replicas of sculptural masterpieces would be well received at many courts. The Tuscan workshops, which employed Giambologna and subsequently Tacca and Susini, provided reproductions of both ancient and Renaissance masterpieces, as well as original compositions made for the bronze format, well into the seventeenth century. Such gifts were numerous and highly sought-after as bronzes became de rigueur in royal collections.[80] Some bronzes, which may be Venetian in origin, were included in the Dutch gift to Charles II described above.

FESTIVAL BOOKS, ENGRAVINGS, MANUSCRIPTS. Engravings of court celebrations, often bound in portfolios, were frequently given to returning ambassadors, first and foremost those received by the Grand Dukes of Tuscany, and later, on an even more lavish scale, by Louis XIV, who added to the festival engravings images of his famous gardens of Versailles and the new east facade of the Louvre.[81] Gifts of engravings of the grand decorations that were erected for rulers lying in state before burials were given as well, although not typically at embassies. These were most often presented by resident diplomats at private interviews.[82]

Manuscripts such as gospels, books of hours, and breviaries, though perhaps more commonly given during the late Middle Ages, make sporadic appearances among the gifts of the sixteenth and even seventeenth centuries. Louis XIV maintained a workshop for the production of hand-decorated church service books until after 1700, but more often than not old books, venerable because of connections to royal or church figures, were preferred as gifts. A great illustrated thirteenth-century Old Testament from the scriptorium of the French king, Saint Louis IX, was presented in 1604 by a papal embassy to Shah Abbas I of Persia, a holy book that had belonged to a saint.[83] In one extraordinary instance, an ambassador, Don Francesco de Rojas, altered a book made for his own use in the Netherlands and gave it to Queen Isabella of Spain while he was involved in complicated marriage negotiations as Spain's resident envoy at the Austrian court of Emperor Maximilian I.[84]

NATURAL RARITIES AND SCIENTIFIC INSTRUMENTS. The Renaissance in Europe gave birth to the idea of the enlightened, broadly educated monarch, an idea that found its ultimate material statement in the European royal *kunst- und wunderkammer*. (Many Asian rulers had demonstrated the same taste for centuries.) This tradition, which began with a room or two in the palace and grew to museum proportions in such places as Innsbruck and Prague and later Peter the Great's museum in St. Petersburg, added substantially to the repertoire of possible princely gifts.

Natural rarities and oddities, including especially remarkable giant gemstones, as well as elaborately decorated scientific instruments, mechanical toys, minerals, preserved animals, skeletons, and the like, were often given.[85] Although the possibility of employing such objects as diplomatic gifts was generally limited to recipients who happened to have a scholarly bent,

FIG. 16. Leonardo da Vinci, *The Virgin of the Rocks*. Italy, c. 1495. Oil on wood (transferred to canvas), 78 x 48 in. (199 x 122 cm). Musée du Louvre, Paris (photo R.M.N.–Gérard Blatt Jean Schormans)

nautilus shells, elaborately carved ivory objects and coconut shells, and flawless rock-crystal balls combined natural interest and aesthetic quality and had a wider potential circulation, as in the case of crystal balls given to Louis XIII of France and to the Elector of Saxony.[86] Unicorn horns (usually the horns of narwhals, a species of marine mammal), when fashioned into cups, were believed to prevent poisoning and were widely esteemed, even by those with no interest in the natural sciences.[87] Such specimens were sometimes lavishly mounted in gilded silver by master goldsmiths and thus made an impressive gift when presented by diplomats at ambassadorial receptions.

Commissioned Dipolmatic Gifts

During the sixteenth and seventeenth centuries, orders for diplomatic gifts were not the most important activity for artists and artisans, most of whose production was intended for use by their patrons. Important rulers sought out renowned masters and created and supported workshops that could meet the continual demands of their courts. Illustrated in this book are a number of works made for the tsars at the Kremlin workshops (cat. no. 9), of which at least one was a gift to a foreign ruler.

The sources of objects used for diplomatic exchange varied considerably from one embassy to another, but many were produced specifically as gifts, some in court workshops. Those decorated with coats of arms and initials of the recipients appear to have been particularly appreciated. Several European examples in this catalogue feature the coats of arms of Russian tsars and may be presumed to have been commissioned. While it is difficult to calculate exactly how many of these objects were specifically commissioned as gifts, surviving lists suggest that one-third to one-half were commissioned rather than purchased on the market.

Commissions for diplomatic gifts were nonetheless significant, and the objects produced for use as gifts were often major works of art made of unusually expensive materials, such as gilded silver and precious jewels, which were used decoratively in extravagant quantities, especially for metalwork, embroidered textiles, and horse trappings. The artists usually counted these gifts among their most important creations, and many of them must be considered masterpieces of applied art. These gift commissions often contributed to the financial stability of the workshops; not only were the artists well compensated for their work, but the gifts served an important role in providing exposure that guaranteed future orders, not only from the patrons whose reputations were at stake but also from the recipients.[88] This promotional aspect was especially important for workshops that were not directly supported by rulers, such as those in city-states that depended on orders from abroad.[89] The recognition of an artist's achievement by a shah, sultan, emperor, tsar, king, queen, or prince was as essential as it was gratifying.

Diplomatic gifts functioned in the context of an opulent court life, where elegance and novelty were the norm. For this reason, these objects were often very stylish, and today many of them are among the finest examples of the styles of different periods. As the works discussed and illustrated in this book should make abundantly clear, diplomatic gifts deserve an important place in the history of Islamic, Renaissance, and Baroque art.

NOTES

1. Diplomatic and ambassadorial gifts and their presentation are virtually omitted from the standard histories of diplomacy, such as Hill 1905–14, Renouvin and Dunoselle 1997, and Nicolson 1954. One specialized volume is a notable exception: Arnold 2000. A book-length study of an unusual and important gift from the king of Portugal to Pope Leo X should also be noted: Bedini 2000.
2. Kovács and Lovag 1980, p. 8.
3. Fülep 1988, p. 12, no. 11 (colorplate). An inscription gives the name of Constantine IX Monomachus and his empresses.
4. Kovács and Lovag 1980, pp. 18–58.
5. See Polynina and Rakhmanov 1994, p. 42.
6. The Transylvanian crown is illustrated in Fillitz 1964, fig. 133.
7. See Kurz 1969, p. 249.
8. An amber throne was given to Emperor Leopold I in 1677, this by the Elector of Brandenburg for Leopold's twentieth jubilee. Parts are in the Kunsthistorisches Museum, Vienna. See Ottillinger 1988, p. 14.
9. Van der Cruysse 1991, p. 400.
10. Kurz 1975, p. 30. Kurz mentions numerous gifts of clocks to sultans and argues that European monarchs, French and English as well as Austrian, frequently included extravagant clocks, at first of gilded silver and, at the end of the sixteenth century, heavily jeweled. Thelott's engraving of 1694 is reproduced in Kurz.
11. Few automata or mechanical toys can be identified as diplomatic gifts, although the small shooting bear in the Munich Schatzkammer (F. 891) by Hans Ment II of c. 1570–75 and its counterpart in Vienna would seem to have been gifts. See Seelig 1989, p. 118, fig. 17. Kurz 1975, p. 30, mentions a probable copy retained in Austria, an elephant clock surmounted by a tower topped with a Turkish crescent. See Maurice 1968, fig. 37.
12. cat. nos. 84, 85, gifts from King Charles XII of Sweden to Tsar Peter I.
13. The gift of twelve horses from Louis XIV to Charles XI of Sweden is a case in point. See Conforti and Walton 1988, p. 164.
14. On the history of European porcelain gifts that postdate the period under consideration, see Jedding 1990, pp. 142–73; Brulon 1993, pp. 184–87; also Von Sanssouci 1994.
15. See Weigert 1962, p. 98; Coural 1967; Denis and Saunier 1996, pp. 31–39. A serious study of the use of tapestries as

diplomatic gifts over several centuries is Brassat 1989. Chapter 2 contains long lists of gifts, although even these are incomplete. My thanks to Elisabeth Mikosch for this reference.

16. See Abramova 1998, p. 62. Dutch ambassadors Burgh and van Feltril list two cuirasses among their gifts to the tsar.

17. See Kondrikova 1996, pp. 262–65; Bencard and Markova 1988, p. 90., no. 3; and Martin 1900/2, p. 13.

18. See Bencard and Markova 1988; the authors, have gathered information throughout their catalogue on the gifts given by King Christian IV of Denmark to the tsars over the years. Oman 1961, p. 29, adds another, while Olearius 1967, pp. 60–61, lists gifts given to the tsar by the Schleswig-Holstein embassy in 1634. Olearius visited Moscow on three occasions with the embassy: in August–December 1634; in March–June 1636 on the way to Persia; and in January–March 1639 on the way back from Persia. He published the first edition of his chronicle in 1647, a revised edition in 1656, and there were numerous later editions. Thanks to Dr. Dieter Lohmeier of the Schleswig-Holsteinsische Landesbibliothek for this information. Martin's works on Danish and Swedish silver in the Kremlin likewise include references to groups of gifts; see Martin 1900/1 and 1900/2. For Louis XIV's 1686 embassy from Siam, see Van der Cruysse 1991, pp. 392, 400.

19. Sandin 1998, pp. 40–41, cat. no. 6. The garment is in Stockholm's Royal Armory, inv. no. 6195. Its identification as a gift is from an inscription attached to the garment; Alexei may have received the garment from the shah of Persia via the Persian embassy to the duke of Holstein in 1639.

20. See Van der Cruysse 1991, p. 392.

21. Ibid., p. 393.

22. Abbé Choisy replied, "Je n'en sais rien, monsieur, lui dis-je le plus haut que je pus, à fin qu'on m'entendit; mais je sais fort bien qu'il y a pour plus de vingt mille écus d'or pesant . . . [I do not know about that, sir, I said as loudly as I could so that he could hear me. I know full well that the value is more than the weight of twenty thousand gold écus . . .]," ibid.

23. There is a certain irony in the disrespect shown for Asian porcelain, since Louis XIV himself, with the decor of his Trianon de Porcelaine, was responsible for influencing the taste for Chinese porcelain in Europe. On the afterlife of the Siamese porcelains, particularly those given by Louis XIV to the Grand Dauphin, see Watson and Whitehead 1991, pp. 13–52. The dauphin's valuation of the porcelain gifts was certainly different from those of Sourches and Louvois. See Castelluccio 2000/1.

24. See Kurz 1975, p. 25.

25. Published by Préaud 1995, pp. 85–87, cat. no. 26.

26. The cannons were kept at the Garde-Meuble Royale in Paris and used by the mob at the storming of the Bastille in 1789. Jacq-Hergoualc'h 1985, pp. 317–34.

27. See Hedin 1992, pp. 149–72.

28. See Silverskatter 1997, an important recent study of diplomatic gifts. The Augsburg gilded-silver table fountain by Johann Baptist Weinhold I was presented to Tsar Alexei

Mikhailovich by Hans Wrangel, a member of Queen Christina's embassy on September 3, 1647 (pp. 74, 187, cat. no. 6; entry by Galina Markova). See Chapter 2, fig. 12.

29. The frequent giving of bejeweled miniature portrait gifts came rather late to Russia with Peter the Great, although John Merrick received one on a gold chain in 1617. See Seling 1991, p. 212, cat. no. 75. A recent work, by Nikitina 1995, makes no special mention of early gifts of orders or portraits to ambassadors.

30. Examples include the furniture by Pierre Gole at Boughton House in England, the French ebony cabinet at Skokloster in Sweden, and the Bielke bed now at the Stockholm Nationalmuseum, gifts of Louis XIV.

31. My thanks to Filiz Çağman, Director, Topkapi Palace Museum, for her help with research there in 1990 and for more recent aid. She published my fig. 5 in Rogers 1986, p. 211. Further thanks are due to Lale Uluç for information about gift books at Topkapi. See also Uluç 1987–88, pp. 85–107.

32. The remarkable story of this embassy (which crossed Russia en route from Rome to Persia in the Time of Troubles) is told by Sydney C. Cockerell in the introduction to Cockerell 1927. When the embassy stopped for a long time in Poland, Cardinal Maciejewski added a magnificent book to the gifts, one made in Paris in the thirteenth century in the royal workshops, illustrating scenes from the Old Testament (Pierpont Morgan Library). The embassy reached Isfahan at the end of 1607.

33. The story of the treatment of foreign embassies by the Sublime Porte was outlined in an exhibition in Holland and Istanbul about Dutch-Turkish relations. See Slot 1990. A more extensive catalogue was published in Dutch in 1988 by the Museum voor Volkenkunde, Rotterdam. (Rotterdam: Trustees of the Museum, n.d.). Cockerell 1927, p. 11, indicates that Christians were allowed to kiss the hand of Shah Abbas of Persia, while Moslems kissed his feet.

34. The throne made in Isfahan in 1659 was presented to Tsar Alexei Mikhailovich by the Armenian merchant Zacharias Sarandarov as a gift from the New Julfa Armenian Trade Company in 1660. Kondrikova 1996, pp. 203–5, and Polynina and Rakhmanov 1994, pp. 84–85.

35. The patriarchs of Antioch and Alexandria attended Patriarch Nikon's Russian Church council of 1667.

36. Barber 1979, p. 54. It is not known whether Lucaris fully understood the importance of his gift.

37. A sense of the lavishness of an ambassadorial reception at the Vatican is conveyed in Bessone 1993, pp. 78–88. Coaches for this embassy of the Marquês de Fontes to Pope Clement XI (1716) are preserved at the National Coach Museum. See also Bessone 1996.

38. A great coffer, a gift to Francis I of France, is illustrated in Chapter 6, fig. 7. Such coffers seem to have been sent regularly by the popes to queen consorts as wedding gifts and were occasionally put into service as reliquaries. Some examples are in the reliquary collection of the convent of Las Descalzas Reales in Madrid.

39. See the Ph.D. thesis of Elisabeth Cornides (Cornides 1967). Some examples: The rose by Simone da Firenze given to the

city of Siena by Pius II in 1458, and a rose given to the same city by Pope Alexander VII (seventeenth century), both now at the Palazzo Comunale, Siena. See also Bedini 2000, pp. 66–68.

40. Cornides 1967, passim. Kurz 1969, p. 258, believes he has identified such a hat in the Urbino portrait of Federico da Montefeltro seated in his study (by Joos van Ghent or Beruguete). An older study is Modern 1901, pp. 127–68. The most sensational surviving example of such a gift was sent by Pope Pius V in 1582 and is today in the Vienna Waffensammlung, inv. no. A989.

41. Drawing inscribed "designs for the swaddling bands for the King of France," attributed to Johann Paul Schor, is possibly related to the Dauphin's swaddling cloths of 1660. See Walker and Hammond 1999, p. 176, cat. no. 45; also Fusconi 1986, pp. 42, 43.

42. Dubon 1964 has devoted a monograph to both Louis XIII's Rubens tapestries and also the later series commissioned by the Barberini in Rome by Pietro da Cortona completing the history of Constantine.

43. The object, made in the 1640s, is preserved today at Wetzlar with its leather carrying case. See Reineking von Bock 1981, p. 92, who states that a similar cup exists in the Kremlin Armory.

44. Olearius says, "We were conducted . . . past a beautiful church. . . . We were conducted past the church because we were Christians. Turks, Tartars, and Persians are not brought this way. . . ." (Olearius 1967, p. 61). "The Tsar permits only Christians and not Turks, Persians or Tartars to kiss his hand. Possevino, who was very displeased with this handwashing, wrote 'He washes his hands as if to cleanse a sin.'" (p. 63).

45. See also Oman 1961, ill. opposite p. 15.

46. These facts are related in a number of studies of the Kremlin silver. See Bencard and Markova 1988, passim. Most notable were the purchases of 1629 at Archangel on the White Sea.

47. Leithe-Jasper and Distelberger 1982, p. 120.

48. Oman 1961, p. 2.

49. Bencard and Markova 1988, pp. 22–26.

50. See Olearius 1967, p. 60.

51. Baron 1967 wrote in the introduction to Olearius 1967: "It was no doubt understood that Mikhail could continue to count upon Holstein (in 1634) for munitions, soldiers and skilled technicians" (p. 8). A gift from the Dutch of a breastplate at a later date has recently been interpreted as a sign that they too were willing to contribute arms (perhaps selling them) to Tsar Alexei. See Abramova 1998, p. 62.

52. Some are still to be seen in Tsar Peter's Museum in St. Petersburg, the former Kunstkammer on Vasilievskii Island. A globe of silver and brass with the initials and crown of George I of England is in the Monplaisir Palace at Peterhof.

53. Silverskatter 1997, cat. nos. 34–50, 59–61, 64–68. This sampling of the large gift was shown in Stockholm in 1997. Fredrik Robert Martin attempted to identify all the surviving pieces of the 1699 gift. In Martin 1900/1, pp. 22–25, pls. 40–51.

54. This was argued in Walton 1992, p. 208.

55. See p. 76 above.

56. Seelig 1999, pp. 166–79, gives a comprehensive account of silver gifts for the table. He reproduces (in figure 4, our figure 8), which illustrates German silver gifts (in Neo-Islamic style!), and he suggests that such may have been regularly produced for use in the East.

57. See Chapter 6 for a discussion of one of the most sensational European gifts of the seventeenth century, a gift of twelve horses and their trappings and arms. The archives of the French ministry of foreign affairs contains a note that the gift was so immensely rich that no value could be given. See Conforti and Walton 1988, pp. 164–71.

58. A Moroccan embassy sent King Charles II of England two lions and thirty ostriches. See Roosen 1976, p. 118. Albrecht Dürer's famous 1515 woodcut of a rhinoceros (Bartsch 136) was drawn on the basis of a description (now lost) made when the animal, a present from the king of Portugal to Pope Leo X (see Bedini 2000, passim), was in Portugal, before it was lost at sea. A drawing by Dürer is in the British Museum (L. 257). Tsar Alexei sent many birds; see documents published in Sviazi 1990.

The Mughal emperor Jahangir commissioned a painting of the zebra, which he refers to in his memoirs as "exceedingly strange." Jahangir 1909, p. 201. See Welch 1978, fig. 27.

An elephant given to Emperor Maximilian I survived stuffed in the natural history museum in Munich until World War II; for illustration, see Seelig 1989, p. 126.

59. Kondrikova 1996, pp 158–65. The relief is reproduced in color over two full pages. My quote is from Duncan 1968, pp 84–85.

60. Studies on the use of textiles (some of them probably gifts) to differentiate rank at court include Starevisier 1982 and Piponnier 1970. On gifts of fur, see Sviozi 1990, where it is also indicated that fur was used to pay the expenses of Russian embassies abroad.

61. Bier and Bencard 1995, pp. 61–75. See also note 19.

62. On the Venetian guns, see Conforti and Walton 1988, p. 121. My thanks to Dr. Johannes Ramharter for his comments on gifts of arms.

63. See Chapter 6, fig. 5.

64. Castelluccio 2000/1, pp. 68–69. See also Castelluccio 2000/2, p. 41.

65. See Chapter 6, fig. 8.

66. Inv. no. HGK 406. See Vahlne 1986, pp 26–29.

67. Munich Residenz Treasury, no. 1241.

68. In the Green Vault, Dresden. See Chapter 6, fig. 4.

69. Scheurleer 1980, p. 389. On the treasure, see Babelon 1924.

70. Reproduced by Habsburg 1997, p. 73, and Menzhausen 1968, p. 36.

71. The 1602 reliquary inscribed as made for Tsar Boris Godunov, given by King Sigismund III of Poland to William V of Bavaria in 1614, was almost certainly taken by the Poles when they captured Moscow and was doubly interesting for its connection with a ruler and with the Polish victory over Moscow during the Time of Troubles. Munich Residenz Treasury, inv. no. 65.

DIPLOMATIC AND AMBASSADORIAL GIFTS OF THE SIXTEENTH AND SEVENTEENTH CENTURIES

72. Two of the thorns in fourteenth-century reliquaries survive, one at the Swiss Abbey of Saint-Maurice-d'Augaun, another in the Treasury of the Basilica of St. Francis at Assisi. See Hertline 1965, pp. 54-70; Morello and Kanter 1999, no. 49, p. 170.

73. The receipt of a piece of fabric advertised as "Christ's robe" by Patriarch Filaret of Moscow from the Persian Shah Abbas I is an example. See Keenan 1991, pp. 142-49 for a summary by Daniel C. Waugh of writings on the relic.

74. The Royal Collections in Madrid kindly provided me with this information orally and from a database.

75. See Elam 1988, pp. 813-26.

76. Gould 1994, pp. 215-22.

77. Cox-Rearick 1994, pp. 239-58. Italian paintings given as gifts to French kings and queens include Sebastiano del Piombo, *Visitation* (Louvre); Raphael, *Saint Michael* (Louvre); Raphael, *Holy Family* (Louvre); Raphael, *Saint Margaret* (Louvre); Giulio Romano, *Giovanna d'Aragona* (Louvre); Rosso Fiorentino, *Moses and the Daughters of Jethro* (Uffizi). Bronzino's *Allegory of Venus* (London, National Gallery), was a later gift from Florence.

78. An example is the gift from the Elector Christian II to Emperor Rudolf II of Albrecht Dürer's *Adoration of the Magi* from Wittenberg. Ottillinger 1988, p. 11. The gift of a Dürer self-portrait of 1498 from the city of Nuremberg to King Charles I of England through his ambassador the duke of Arundel is noteworthy. See Jaffé 1996, p. 24.

79. See Mahon 1949-50, pp. 303-5, and Mahon 1950, pp. 249-50. For a recent discussion of the gift, see Brantl 1998.

80. The prestige of such objects is suggested in the recent Louvre exhibition catalogue (Louvre 1999). The idea that Louis XIV received bronzes as diplomatic gifts is definitively refuted here, although gifts of bronzes are preserved in Vienna and in several splendid examples at the Dresden Green Vault. A copy of Gianbologna's *Mercury* was given to Emperor Maximilian II by the Tuscan Grand Duke Cosimo when he visited Vienna. See Ottillinger 1988, p. 9.

81. Bertela and Tofani 1969. On the issues of the *Mercure Galant*, with both descriptions and lavish engraved illustrations, presented to the Siamese, see Hedin 1992, pp 149-72.

82. An example is the presentation of Pierre Le Pautre's engraving of the catafalque of Queen Ulrika Eleonora the Elder of Sweden to the French court by Daniel Cronström, the Swedish resident. Weigert and Hernmarck 1964, pp. 230 ff.

On the engravings, see Snickare 1999, pp. 191-94, cat. nos. 24-42.

83. See Cockerell 1927, introduction.

84. Barber 1979, p. 23. The manuscript is in the British Library.

85. Typical would be the iron sculpture *Charles II as St. George Defeats the Dragon of the Revolution* by Gottfried Christian Leygebe (Dresden Green Vault, inv. no. IX, 2), presented by Elector Frederick William I of Brandenburg to Elector John George II of Saxony. Joachim von Sandrart 1675-79 explains that it was carved from iron, then an impossible feat; see vol. II, bk. 3, p. 86. The piece actually consists of pieces of cast iron riveted together; see Menzhausen 1968, pl. 93.

86. Crystal Balls at the Dresden Green Vault (inv. no. V-174) and at the Jardin des Plantes Trésoire du Musée in Paris. The French sphere (inv. no. 7.57) was not a normal diplomatic gift but rather a part of an important gift from Cardinal Richelieu to Louis XIII. See Morel 1988 and handbooks of the Musée Nationale d'Histoire Naturelle, Galerie de Minéralogie, and Jardin des Plantes, Paris. Schubnel 1993, p. 18. The Dresden ball was given by Duke Emanuel Philibert of Savoy to Elector Augustus of Saxony and was included in the Kunstkammer inventory of 1587. Emanuel Philibert died in 1580. My thanks to Jutta Koppel for indicating the donor and recipient. See Menzhausen 1977, p. 182. I am grateful to the author for indicating the existence of this gift.

87. Greenland was the source of narwal tusks, often confused with unicorn horns and used to make numerous precious cups, many of which served as gifts. Mogens Bencard, writing on seventeenth-century works at Rosenborg Palace, in Bencard 1990, discusses the type of object but not an actual diplomatic gift.

88. The Swedish envoy to Moscow from 1645 to 1687, Johan Gabriel Sparfvenfeld, appears to have commissioned a masterpiece of the guncraft made by the Kremlin Armory to take home with him (along with the gifts he received from the tsar). The rifle was presented by him to Crown Prince Charles (later King Charles XII) in 1687. It is decorated with the initial "C" and with other appropriate symbols. Drejholt 1996, vol. 1, pp. 206-10.

89. Seelig has discussed the energetic search for clients by the goldsmiths' guild of the German city of Augsburg. Seelig 1994, vol. I, pp. 32-56.

6

EUROPEAN DECORATIVE ARTS
AS DIPLOMATIC GIFTS

BARRY SHIFMAN

THE ARMORY MUSEUM in the Moscow Kremlin has the largest collection of diplomatic gifts in the world. Many of these objects reflect an extraordinarily high level of craftsmanship, and some of them are the finest examples made by the most important artists of their time. This unique collection provides the visitor with a rare opportunity to experience the overwhelming effect these masterpieces must have had on those who witnessed the original presentation of gifts. In addition to pieces of exceptional quality, these objects often included such rarities as ivories, amber, hardstones, and precious gems and were extremely valuable in monetary terms, an important consideration as recipients were obligated to return gifts of approximately equal value.[1] These gift-giving rituals were widespread throughout Europe and the Near East, but unfortunately most royal collections of diplomatic gifts outside Russia have not been preserved or documented as successfully as the group in the Kremlin Armory. Nevertheless, spectacular objects were exchanged, especially in Western Europe of the sixteenth and seventeenth

centuries, and in this essay I have chosen to discuss a few of them to help place the Armory objects in the context of diplomatic gift-gifting of the time. Although many of the original gifts outside Russia have been lost or destroyed or cannot be associated with specific embassies, the few fine examples that do exist serve to demonstrate how very exceptional and important are the holdings of the Kremlin Armory in the history of the decorative arts. In gathering large and impressive groups of gifts, rulers and their ambassadors frequently commissioned new objects specifically for the purpose. If there was not sufficient time to order new works of art, however, donors were sometimes also required to offer objects already in their possession, such as unique heirlooms from their own treasuries.

The Russian tsars had a strong interest in preserving diplomatic gifts and documenting their history; they were a tangible sign of the tsars' wealth and power, and they impressed foreign visitors. Western European rulers, however, did not view the diplomatic gifts they received in the same way. They seem to have given many away or melted them down for the value of the materials. When the need arose, gifts were sold for ready cash, and many have simply disappeared without

FIG. 1. Benvenuto Cellini, *Salt Cellar*. France (Paris), 1540–43. Gold, enamel, h. 10¹/8 in. (26 cm), l. 13 in. (33.5 cm). Kunsthistorisches Museum, Vienna

documentation. That the group of diplomatic gifts at the Moscow Armory should have remained virtually intact—not counting the losses over the centuries to fire or theft—is critical to our understanding of the unique nature of the Armory collection.

There are, of course, other important collections of European diplomatic gifts, but these are limited and do not contain the enormous amount of identifiable gifts as in the Armory holdings. For example, magnificent diplomatic gifts presented over several centuries to the Hapsburg rulers can be found in the Kunsthistorisches Museum in Vienna, some of them clearly documented as such, although others cannot be precisely identified. The Swedish royal collection includes objects presented to the kings and queens of Sweden, but the overall number is relatively small. The Green Vault (Das Grüne Gewölbe) in Dresden, the Tower of London, and the Residenz in Munich, among other collections, possess some objects that were originally presented to rulers as diplomatic gifts; in rare instances, these gifts are documented and their histories carefully recorded.

As in Russia, a large proportion of princely gifts presented as part of diplomatic protocol in Europe was of superb quality. Some are considered the finest examples of European decorative arts, because they were usually made of precious materials, were very costly, and were technically superior, having been made by distinguished masters. For the purpose of this essay, only objects made in Europe in the following categories are examined: gold, silver, gems and semiprecious hardstones, wood, horse trappings, guns, tapestries, and carpets.

Objects made of gold have always been considered the most prestigious, because this valuable metal has long been the preferred material for lavish works of art. Emperors and kings routinely dined from gold dishes and commissioned special gold vessels designed by such major artists as Raphael, Holbein, and Dürer.[2] Excellent goldsmiths were essential when rulers wanted to raise the international visibility of their courts. During the sixteenth century, for instance, when King Erik XIV of Sweden wished to improve the image of the Swedish monarchy, he brought German goldsmiths of great ability to the far north. It was not uncommon for skilled goldsmiths to travel throughout Europe to work at various courts during their careers.

Sumptuous Renaissance gold objects were presented by King Charles IX of France in 1570 to Archduke Ferdinand II of the Tirol, who served as a proxy for Charles at his marriage to Elizabeth of Austria, the daughter of Ferdinand's brother Emperor Maximilian II. A great art collector in the Hapsburg tradition, Ferdinand received many gifts for his efforts in arranging this political marriage, especially objects that were intended to appeal to his collecting impulse. Charles's gifts were not commissioned as such but were simply taken from the French royal treasury, and among them were some great masterpieces.

The most celebrated of this group is a gold-and-enamel salt cellar, which was made by Benvenuto Cellini in Paris between 1540 and 1543 for Charles IX's grandfather, King Francis I of France (fig. 1).[3] This unique salt cellar is one of the best-known examples of Renaissance gold in the world, and the artist was sufficiently proud of his creation to include a description of it in his autobiography. The container for salt is fashioned in the shape of a ship, by which sits Neptune, god of the sea, facing Tellus, goddess of the earth. Beside Tellus is a small triumphal arch that was designed to contain spices and pepper. Cellini originally received the commission for the salt cellar in Rome in 1539 from Cardinal Ippolito d'Este, for whom the artist made a model, but after he was summoned to France in 1540 to serve Francis I, Cellini was immediately instructed by the king to make a final version. Considered a great treasure in the French royal collection at the time, the salt cellar is a rare piece that was not melted down and the only extant gold object by Cellini. It is also unquestionably the greatest surviving diplomatic gift made of gold. Another Cellini masterpiece that served as a diplomatic gift was a crucifix that he carved in 1562 of Carrara marble for his own tomb. Grand Duke Francesco I de' Medici persuaded Cellini to sell him the sculpture, which he then presented to King Philip II of Spain in 1576. The work is now in the basilica of the monastery of El Escorial near Madrid.

Another gift to Archduke Ferdinand from Charles IX is a gold cup decorated with jewels, a striking Flemish piece renowned for its rarity, design, and superb quality (fig. 2). Surmounted by a figure of Saint Michael vanquishing the Devil—a reference to the royal Order of Saint Michael created by Louis XI of France in 1469—the cup is decorated with colored enamels and includes eighty-eight diamonds, two emeralds, twenty-seven rubies, and one hundred twenty-three pearls.[4] Like the Cellini salt cellar, the cup was not new when it was offered to Archduke Ferdinand in 1570. It had been made either in the Antwerp workshop of Josse Vezeler, a major dealer of international reputation at this time who supplied objects to the French court, or in a studio under his direction.[5] The cup was delivered to Francis I at Boulogne in 1532, on the occasion of a meeting between the king and Henry VIII of England, when the two rulers signed a military pact against the Turks called the Treaty of Calais. A reflection of the prestige of French culture and the Valois dynasty, the cup appeared in a 1537 inventory of precious works of art owned by the king. It was also listed in the 1561 inventory of the French crown jewels and the king's cabinet at Fontainebleau, where it was considered one of the highlights of the royal collection.

Imposing cups of this kind were made to be displayed on sideboards in order to demonstrate the wealth and power of their owners. The Vatican has a related cup of gilded silver, which was made by Vezeler between 1530 and 1531 and may have been commissioned by Francis I as a diplomatic gift to Pope Clement VII.[6]

Charles IX of France was very generous to offer such masterpieces in gold to Archduke Ferdinand, for these royal gifts are of unusual quality, even among official gifts. In weight alone, the objects are very impressive. The marriage of a French king to a daughter of the Holy Roman Emperor, however, was a significant event, and politics and matters of protocol played a decisive role in the selection of objects. Undoubtedly, Archduke Ferdinand appreciated these well-chosen gifts, not just for their value but also for their historical connection to

FIG. 2. Josse Vezeler, *Covered Cup.* Netherlands (Antwerp), c. 1532. Gold, diamonds, emeralds, rubies, pearls, enamel, h. 20¹/8 in. (51.7 cm). Kunsthistorisches Museum, Vienna

Francis I, the great rival of his uncle, Emperor Charles V. These unique and spectacular works of art also reflect Ferdinand's interest in genealogy and his connoisseurship as a serious art collector. While he was in the Tirol, the archduke installed his collection in Ambras Castle near Innsbruck, in what is today considered the first European museum. After his death in 1595, Ferdinand's possessions at Ambras remained in the care of the Tirolean Hapsburgs until the line died out in 1663, at which time everything reverted to the imperial branch of the family. By 1805, the best of the Ambras collection had been transferred to Vienna, and most of Archduke Ferdinand's treasures were incorporated into the imperial collections, where many are now on view at the Kunsthistorisches Museum and at the imperial treasury.

Extraordinary silver objects made by master silversmiths have always been favored as royal gifts. As with other materials, including gold, it was not crucial that the pieces be in the latest fashion and design, but they had to be magnificent so that they could be presented at an ambassadorial audience with appropriate pomp and circumstance.[7] The audience chambers of royal palaces were decorated with many shelves filled with massive displays of silver fashioned into large and complicated works of art. These objects were often gilded to imitate the appearance of gold in order to enhance the impression they made on visitors.

Some of the finest European silver objects were made at three major cities in Germany—Augsburg, Hamburg, and Nuremberg. The celebrated goldsmith Wenzel Jamnitzer contributed to the establishment of Nuremberg as a center of design and production of silver during the Renaissance. Like Cellini, Jamnitzer enjoyed the patronage of powerful and cultured individuals and also received commissions from four Holy Roman emperors in succession—Charles V, Ferdinand I, Maximilian II, and Rudolf II. Jamnitzer's most distinguished extant work is a gilded-silver and enamel table decoration (known as the Merkel centerpiece), which was commissioned by the Nuremberg City Council and delivered in 1549 (see Chapter 7, fig. 8). The piece was intended as a diplomatic gift for either Emperor Charles V or his son, King Philip II of Spain, on the occasion of a planned visit to the city, but because the ruler never arrived, the table decoration remained city property until 1806.[8] After passing through various distinguished private collections, it was acquired by the Rijksmuseum in Amsterdam. Another splendid work by Jamnitzer is a gilded-silver cup made between about 1565 and 1570 and probably given by the Nuremberg City Council to Emperor Maximilian II on the occasion of his entry into the city in 1570 (fig. 3).[9] This cup is one of the most important examples of German silver-

FIG. 3. Wenzel Jamnitzer, *Covered Cup*. Germany (Nuremberg), c. 1565–70. Silver, gilding, h. 26⅞ in. (69 cm); h. of figures on lid: 3⅜ in. (8.6 cm). Kunstgewerbemuseum, Berlin

smithing, because of its artistic merit and historical significance. It was clearly designed to honor the emperor (whose figure is mounted on its cover), but the decoration also conveyed a specific political motive. Below the figure of the emperor are those of three ecclesiastical princes and one secular prince, members of the Landsberg Alliance, a group of neighboring imperial estates formed in 1556 by both Catholic and Evangelical powers to preserve peace and order within the empire. Although the Nuremberg City Council and the emperor wished to restrict membership in the alliance

FIG. 4. Balthasar Permoser (figure), Johann Melchior Dinglinger (jewels), Martin Schnell (lacquer), *Moor*. Germany (Dresden), c. 1724. Pearwood, silver, gilding, emerald crystals, rubies, sapphires, topaz, garnets, tortoiseshell, h. 24 7/8 in. (63.8 cm). Staatliche Kunstsammlungen, Dresden

to those represented on the cup, the Catholic members, led by the Bavarian duke, sought to expand and strengthen their role.

Over a century later, Louis XIV of France is also known to have presented magnificent gifts of silver, although none have survived in spite of their legendary character. In 1666 he offered silver furniture, including a large mirror, a chandelier, and a table with two candlestands, to the Electress of Brandenburg; some of these

spectacular pieces may not have been made especially for the electress but came from the French royal collection.[10] The king himself lived with many pieces of silver furniture at the Château of Versailles, an indication of his appreciation for this type of object. In 1670 he sent a gilded-silver dressing service to the new queen of Poland,[11] and in 1676 she also received from him silver furnishings, including a chandelier, a mirror, a table, two candlestands, firedogs, and a brazier, all made by the little-known Parisian silversmith Pierre Marcade.[12] Louis XIV's daybooks list silver dressing services purchased by the king and offered to ambassadors or visiting foreign dignitaries.[13]

Unmounted gemstones of great value were given to foreign dignitaries and appear regularly on lists of gifts, and of course costly objects decorated with precious gems, such as diamonds, rubies, and emeralds, were frequently offered to rulers. Coffers filled with gems were also presented by ambassadors to powerful monarchs. One of the best-known objects in the Dresden Green Vault is a sculpture of a Moor, made of lacquered pearwood, holding a cluster of uncut emerald crystals (fig. 4).[14] The rulers of Saxony had a long tradition of purchasing large and rare gemstones, especially diamonds and emeralds, which their rich mines did not produce. Originally made up of sixteen crystals, this cluster of emeralds had been mined in Colombia, South America, and may have originally been given to Emperor Charles V as a demonstration of the riches of the New World. In 1581, when Elector Augustus of Saxony visited Emperor Rudolf II in Prague, he received this mineral specifically as a gift, and it was immediately placed in Saxony's cabinet of curiosities. The stones were so treasured by the elector that he ordered them preserved for eternity in memory of his electoral house and lineage, and his descendant Elector Frederick Augustus I (known as Augustus the Strong) of Saxony in about 1724 commissioned the jeweler Johann Melchior Dinglinger and the sculptor Balthasar Permoser to make a figure to hold the emeralds.

Works of art made of semiprecious hardstones (*pietre dure*), such as rock crystal, onyx, lapis lazuli, and malachite, were often given as tokens of esteem. Some

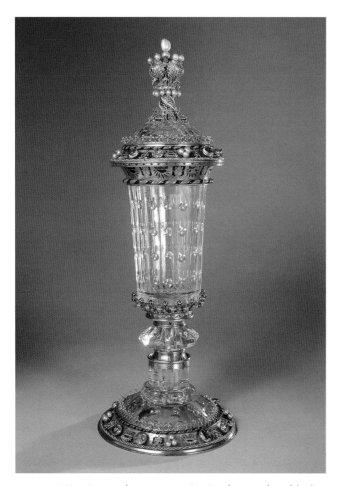

FIG. 5. *Goblet*. Burgundy, c. 1453–67. Rock crystal, gold, diamonds, rubies, pearls, enamel, h. 18 in. (46 cm). Kunsthistorisches Museum, Vienna

FIG. 6. Richard Toutain, *Ewer*. France (Paris), c. 1560–70. Onyx, gold, enamel, diamonds, emeralds, rubies, h. 10½ in. (27.1 cm). Kunsthistorisches Museum, Vienna

of these exotic materials, mounted in gold, silver, or gilded silver and decorated with precious jewels, were made into luxury objects by accomplished craftsmen in Milan, Florence, and Prague. In 1684 Louis XIV gave three carved rock-crystal cabinets to the ambassadors of the king of Siam, and to the king himself he presented a large rock-crystal cabinet.[15]

Two masterpieces of carved hardstone were part of the gift Charles IX gave to Archduke Ferdinand along with the Cellini salt cellar and the Saint Michael cup described above. One of these, a rare rock-crystal goblet made in Burgundy between 1453 and 1467, was first owned by Philip the Good, duke of Burgundy, whose emblems are on the gold mounts (fig. 5).[16] This court goblet is among the most precious late-medieval hardstone carvings from the treasury of the dukes of Burgundy. The second piece is an onyx ewer made by the royal goldsmith Richard Toutain in Paris between

1560 and 1570 (fig. 6).[17] Mounted in gold and set with diamonds, emeralds, and pearls, the ewer is a rare surviving example of French gem-carving. The style of the mounts, with their white strapwork on a black-enamel ground, is typical of the artist's work. Like the Cellini salt cellar, Toutain's ewer was originally part of the French royal treasury.

In 1530 Pope Clement VII (Medici) commissioned a superb coffer mounted in gilded silver and ornamented with rock-crystal panels engraved with scenes from the life of Christ (fig. 7).[18] The coffer was presented by the pope to King Francis I of France in 1533 as a wedding gift for the marriage of the king's son, the future Henry II, to Clement's niece Catherine de' Medici.[19] Valerio Belli, a goldsmith and one of the greatest engravers of crystal in the early sixteenth century, received many orders from the pope, but these panels are his masterpiece.[20] Because of the brilliant engraving

FIG. 7. Valerio Belli, *Coffer.* Italy (Vicenza), 1532. Rock crystal, silver, enamels, gilding, h. 5³/₄ in. (15 cm), l. 10³/₈ in. (26.7 cm), w. 5⁵/₈ in. (14.5 cm). Museo degli Argenti, Florence (photo courtesy Ministero per i Beni e le Attivita' Culturali)

of the rock crystal, this is considered one of the finest coffers made in the early sixteenth century and the most celebrated of the king's sacred objects at Fontainebleau. After Francis's death, the coffer was inherited by his widow, who bequeathed it to her favorite granddaughter, Christine of Lorraine. In 1589 Christine took it to Florence at the time of her marriage to Grand Duke Ferdinando I de' Medici.

The celebrated Medici family had a long history of commissioning hardstone objects, which were made at the Grand Ducal workshop (Galleria dei Lavori) that Ferdinando had established in Florence in 1588. The workshop devoted part of its production to making refined objects to be given away as diplomatic gifts. Ferdinando knew of Emperor Rudolf II's passion for hardstones, and one of the first objects commissioned from the new workshop was an extraordinary table-

top, which Ferdinando presented to the emperor at the time of his marriage to Christine in 1589.[21] The Venetian ambassador to Prague described the tabletop as "made of crystal and other stones, of admirable and exceptional workmanship and great value . . . very much to the liking of his imperial majesty, who addressed the ambassador in the most affectionate terms, concluding that he accepted the gift with great pleasure, since it was sent to his majesty in order that he have something by which to remember the marriage of his highness."[22]

Another marvelous tabletop, composed of black marble inlaid with a variety of semiprecious hardstones including jasper, agate, chalcedony, and lapis lazuli, was made in the late seventeenth century in the same Grand Ducal workshop (fig. 8).[23] The tabletop was presented by Grand Duke Cosimo III de' Medici to the Elector of Saxony, Frederick Augustus I, during the latter's visit to Florence in 1689. The grand duke also gave a hardstone tabletop to the king of Denmark in 1720.[24]

Amber, a natural resin found in the region of the Baltic Sea, was used to create many gifts, including

FIG. 8. Grand Ducal Workshop, *Tabletop*. Italy (Florence), late 17th century. Black marble, semiprecious hardstones, including jasper, agate, chalcedony, lapis lazuli, l. 40³/₈ in. (103.5 cm), w. 34¹/₂ in. (88.5 cm). Staatliche Kunstsammlungen, Dresden

tankards such as the example in cat. no 45. In 1677 Frederick William of Brandenburg, the Great Elector, commissioned a magnificent amber throne as a gift for the Hapsburg emperor Leopold I.[25] This throne, made to celebrate the twentieth year of the emperor's reign, represents an early example of monumental amber furniture. One of the most famous diplomatic gifts of all time is the celebrated Amber Room (fig. 9), which the Great Elector's son, Frederick I, ordered in 1701 for his palace in Berlin to celebrate his coronation that year as the first king of Prussia.[26] The original plans for the Amber Room have been attributed to Andreas Schluter, chief architect of the Prussian royal palace. Schluter invited Gottfried Wolfram, court amber master of the Danish king Frederick IV, to work on this

room, which is said to have been made of 100,000 pieces of amber with floral patterns, royal symbols, and profiles in a unique technique that allowed the fusion of small pieces set into panels, which must have been a dazzling sight.

In 1716 Frederick I's son King Frederick William I and Tsar Peter I (Peter the Great) signed a Russo-Prussian alliance against Sweden. To commemorate this important political event, the king offered the Amber Room to the tsar, who later transferred it to St. Petersburg. Using elements from the original room, the tsar's daughter, Empress Elizabeth, created a new Amber Room in 1745 for her Winter Palace in St. Petersburg. Ten years later, she ordered the architect Francesco Bartolemeo Rastrelli to take apart the Amber Room in the Winter Palace and, using the original elements, created yet another Amber Hall in the Catherine Palace at Tsarskoe Selo, where it remained until 1941, when German troops moved it to the castle in Kaliningrad (old Königsberg). Today the whereabouts of the Amber Room are unknown, and it has become the subject of a major dispute between the Russian and German governments. An original amber mosaic resurfaced in 1997, and artists and craftsmen are now re-creating the Amber Room at Tsarskoe Selo, where it is scheduled for completion in April 2003.

Splendid examples of furniture with rich surface decoration were occasionally presented as gifts to ambassadors. According to family tradition, a desk made in Paris about 1672 by Pierre Gole, now at Boughton House in England, was a gift from Louis XIV of France to Ralph, first duke of Montagu, four times ambassador to France between 1666 and 1678.[27] In the collection at Knole in England are two wood candlestands and a wood table carved in Paris by Matthieu Lespagnandelle, each with a marquetry top of engraved brass on pewter by Gole. These were all presented by Louis XIV in 1672 to Charles Sackville, later sixth earl of

FIG. 9. *Amber Room.* Germany, c. 1700. Amber. Whereabouts unknown (photo from Grimaldi 1996, p. 187)

Dorset, who was ambassador to Paris in 1669 and 1670.[28] Other objects in wood that may have been diplomatic gifts include five important carved and inlaid doors and frames made in Augsburg (now at El Escorial near Madrid), possibly presented by Emperor Maximilian II to his cousin and brother-in-law, King Philip II of Spain, in 1567, although there is no documentation to prove this assumption.[29] Tradition has it that everything made in Germany at El Escorial was a gift from Philip's sister, the Empress Maria, or her husband, Maximilian II. In this case, the gift was justified not only by the quality of the work but also by the appropriateness of the gift to a king, a close relative, who was decorating his new residence. However, the doors and frames could have been purchased by Philip himself, as it is known that he had acquired furniture from Augsburg.

Some diplomatic gifts were also made of richly carved wood panels. One of the most impressive carved examples, designed and executed by Grinling Gibbons, master carver to King Charles II of England,

FIG. 10. Grinling Gibbons, *Panel*. England (London), 1682. Limewood. Palazzo Pitti, Florence (photo Scala/Art Resource, New York)

represents the sublime level that this art form achieved in England (fig. 10).[30] Gibbons, whose exquisite naturalistic manner of carving was unsurpassed in his day, worked at St. Paul's Cathedral, Hampton Court, Windsor Castle, and other important locations. Widely regarded as his finest carving, this limewood panel was commissioned by Charles II and presented to Grand Duke Cosimo III de' Medici in 1682. Rich in symbols of peace and love, the panel celebrates the friendship between these two princes; the carving also includes two crowns that likely signify the royal house of England and the grand duchy of Tuscany. Cosimo's connections with England had been especially close since 1669, when he visited England during his tour of Europe. Another limewood panel by Gibbons, now at the Galleria Estense in Modena, Italy, and dated to about 1686, was probably ordered by King James II of England or his wife, Mary of Modena, and sent as a gift to her father, Alfonso IV, duke of Modena.

Foreign rulers frequently received gifts of horses with noble pedigrees and elaborate horse trappings, including saddles, bridles, harnesses, caparisons, and blankets. The costly textiles with rich embroidery were considered magnificent gifts, particularly when they were accompanied with appropriate firearms, and no expense was spared in creating the most lavish horse equipment for presentation. In the early seventeenth century, King James I of England sent King Philip III of Spain six horses with saddles and other splendid trappings.[31] Horses were also presented as gifts by the king of Denmark to the Russian tsar in the early 1640s.[32]

One of the most spectacular gifts of this sort was a group of horses given by Louis XIV to King Charles XI of Sweden in 1673 (fig. 11).[33] The horses were presented during negotiations on the subject of Swedish support for an attack that Louis XIV was planning to carry out on Holland. The French ambassador in Stockholm had informed Louis XIV that riding and hunting were the Swedish king's greatest pleasures, so twelve fine Spanish horses were chosen from the royal stables and fitted out with saddles, harnesses, and blankets lavishly decorated with gold and silver em-

FIG. 11. State gift to Charles XI from Louis XIV of France, comprising saddle, harness, caparison, and blanket. France, 1673. Velvet, with embroidery of silver, gold, and colored silk; fringe and tassels of gold; harness of gold-embroidered red morocco leather, with stirrups, pommel, and buckles of gilded bronze; reins of plaited gold and silk threads; saddle girth of silk. Royal Armory, Stockholm (photo © LSH)

broidery, probably made at the Convent of St. Pierre or at the royal stables. Sophisticated techniques were used, such as appliqué embroidery in high relief, with subtle variations of shading achieved by the use of colored silks. This political gift is a rare example of the remarkable level of mastery achieved by French seventeenth-century embroiderers in creating three-dimensional patterns. Swedish court connoisseurs declared they had never seen anything to match the beauty of the horses and this equipment. King Charles was so moved that he made the unusual gesture of thanking the foreign ambassador at the presentation in French, a language he barely knew. In return for this gift, the Swedish king offered Louis XIV copper roofing for his palace at Versailles.

This gift of horses to the Swedish monarch also included numerous rifles and pistols, some chosen from the most beautiful weapons in Louis XIV's own collection.[34] Firearms were offered as gifts to rulers all over the world, but French guns made by the court gunmakers at Versailles were recognized as the best. A pair of flintlock holster pistols created about 1670, now in the Royal Armory in Stockholm, were made by D. G. de Foullois the Younger, a talented French gunsmith of the time (fig. 12).[35] The barrels of the pistols are overlaid with very finely engraved silver, the locks (signed by the maker) are silver with steel parts, and the walnut stocks are decorated with engraved silver. These pis-

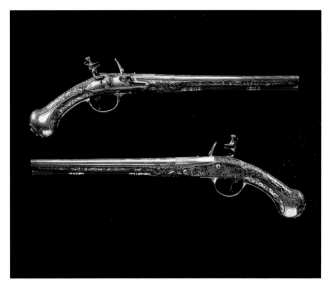

FIG. 12. D. G. de Foullois the Younger, *Pair of Flintlock Holster Pistols.* France (Paris), c. 1670. Engraved steel; inlaid and engraved silver, walnut, l. 20¹/₄ in. (51.4 cm), 12.9 mm caliber; l. 20³/₈ in. (51.7 cm), 12.8 mm caliber. Royal Armory, Stockholm (photo © LSH)

tols, embellished with symbols of triumph, are among the most sumptuous weapons ever given by Louis XIV.

Another beautiful weapon presented by Louis XIV to Charles XI is a double-barreled flintlock gun made about 1660 by Louis le Conte, a leading gunsmith in the French king's service (fig. 13).[36] Jean Berain, one of the greatest French designers and engravers of the seventeenth century, signed the gun to indicate that he had decorated it, his only surviving work of this type. This is probably the most richly ornamented French gun: the barrels are decorated with hunting scenes and figure medallions featuring Minerva, and the French king's initials appear on the upper edge of the stock.

There was a long tradition of presenting tapestries as gifts to monarchs, diplomats, and other dignitaries.

FIG. 13. Louis le Conte (gun), Jean Berain (decorator), *Double-barreled Turn-over Flintlock Gun.* France (Paris), c. 1660. Blue and engraved steel; inlaid and engraved silver; gold incrustations; walnut, l. 63 in.(160 cm). Royal Armory, Stockholm (photo © LSH)

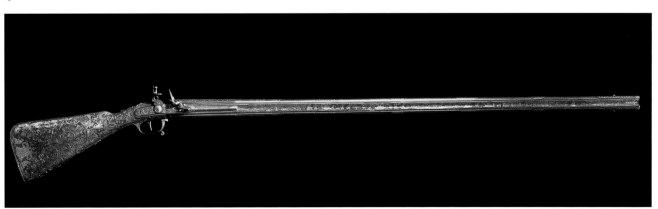

FIG. 14. After Charles Le Brun, *Tapestry (May), Château of Saint-Germain*, from the series *Les Maisons Royales*. made at Gobelins Manufactory, France (Paris), after 1668. Wool and silk, 13 ft. 3 in. x 21 ft. 7 in. (4.10 x 6.68 m). Mobilier National, Paris (photo Philippe Sébert)

In fact, luxurious tapestries richly woven with gold and silver threads were prestigious objects, especially examples made at well-known manufactories, such as those in the Netherlands, although France provided important competition. One celebrated series, probably woven at Fontainebleau between 1541 and 1550 after designs by Rosso Fiorentino and Francesco Primaticcio, reproduces the decoration of the Gallery of Francis I at the Château of Fontainebleau. These tapestries, which are in the collection of the Kunsthistorisches Museum in Vienna, were commissioned by Francis I and presented to Emperor Charles V, who was a guest of the French king at the very end of 1539, shortly after the gallery was finished.[37]

By the late seventeenth century, French tapestries made at Gobelins near Paris had acquired international status and were frequently offered as royal gifts. A group called *Les Maisons Royales* (The Royal Residences) consisted of twelve panels, one for each month of the year, each representing a French château (fig. 14). Many of these tapestries, based on designs by Charles Le Brun, include images of ornate silver owned by Louis XIV, some of which had very likely been presented as diplomatic gifts.[38] Between 1668 and 1713 the French Crown commissioned seven complete sets of *Les Maisons Royales* and a number of smaller panels, all made with gold thread. In 1682 Louis XIV offered twelve tapestries to the ministers of the king of Denmark.[39] That same year he sent six tapestries and two smaller panels to the English court (most likely for the duchess of Portsmouth, mistress of King Charles II of England), and a complete series to the Electress of Brandenburg in 1683. Later, several Gobelins tapestries, including Jean Jouvenet's series of scenes from the New Testament, now in the Hermitage in St. Petersburg, were presented by Louis XV of France to Peter the Great in 1717 at the time of the tsar's visit to Paris. Another series offered by the king to the tsar, *Les Anciennes Indes* (The Old Indies), was woven between 1692 and 1700 and included eight tapestries depicting flora and fauna, native peoples, and African slaves of the seventeenth-century Dutch-held territory of northeast Brazil. All the panels were destroyed by fire in St. Petersburg in 1837.

Extraordinary carpets made at Savonnerie outside Paris were also presented by Louis XIV as gifts to foreign rulers, ambassadors, and other high-ranking individuals. These objects, which had enormous prestige throughout the world, represented the highest level of royal patronage and artistic achievement. Moreover, symbols woven in the pattern often served as subtle propaganda that glorified the king. Nine Savonnerie carpets, delivered to Louis XIV before 1689 for the Grand Gallery at the Louvre, were presented as gifts in the late seventeenth and early eighteenth centuries to several ministers of the king of Denmark, the king of Siam, the pasha of Tripoli, and the Turkish ambassador.[40] Records for Savonnerie also show that additional carpets were given by Louis XIV to Potemkin, ambassador from Moscow in 1668; Don Jeronimo de Benavente y Quiñones, ambassador from Spain in 1669; and two ambassadors from Moscow in 1681.

Three other Savonnerie carpets were offered as gifts by Louis XIV to Grand Duke Cosimo III de' Medici while he was visiting Paris in 1669, as well as a table cover, a large bedspread, and upholstery for a couch and twenty-four chairs, all made at the celebrated French manufactory.[41] One carpet (fig. 15) can be associated with the famous series made between 1668 and 1689 for the Grand Gallery at the Louvre, while the second example (fig. 16) relates to another version designed for the Apollo Gallery at the Louvre in 1667, although the dimensions vary slightly. Eight tapestries (probably from Gobelins) were also part of this group, one of the most impressive gifts of French tapestries and carpets ever made, on a scale not to be equaled until the 1740s. Such objects were a sign of the future, when an increasing number of diplomatic gifts would be produced at workshops and manufactories owned by the donors.

FIG. 15. Savonnerie Manufactory, *Carpet*, France, 1669. Wool and linen, 26 ft. 6¹/₂ in. x 14 ft. 4 in. (8.17 x 4.37 m). Palazzo Pitti, Florence (photo courtesy Ministero per i Beni e le Attivita' Culturali)

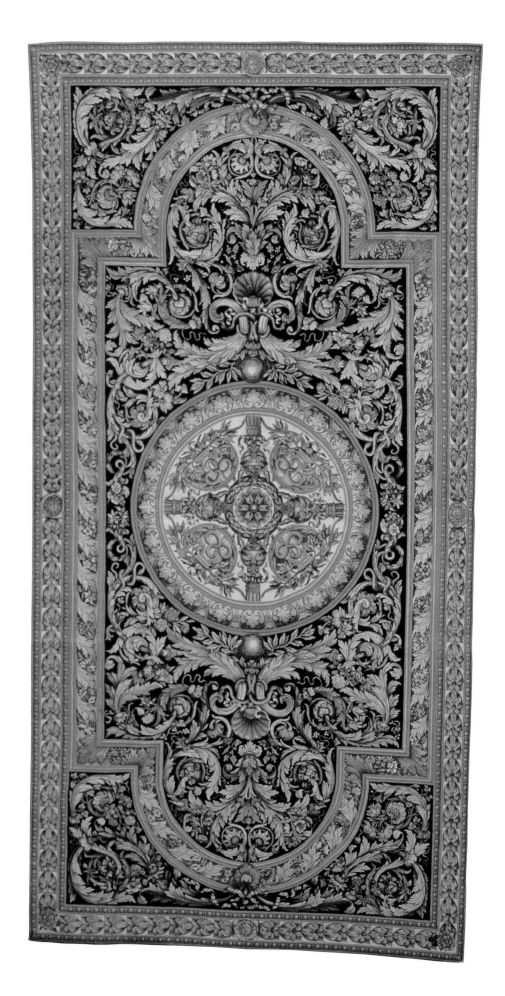

NOTES

1. Walton 1992, p. 200.
2. Cox-Rearick 1995, p. 388, no. XI-8.
3. Ibid., pp. 392–93, no. XI-11.
4. Bimbenet-Privat 1991, pp. 127–35. The Order of Saint Michael, the French equivalent of the older Burgundian Order of the Golden Fleece, was dedicated to the defense of the realm and of its church, and it had been regarded as a protector of French kings. Francis I revitalized the order, and as king he became its grand master. (See Cox-Rearick 1995, pp. 209–10.)
5. Bimbenet-Privat 1999, pp. 58–71.
6. Bimbenet-Privat and Kugel, 1998, pp. 105–9, no. 24.
7. Moncrieff 1991, p. 52.
8. *Wenzel Jamnitzer* 1985, pp. 219–21, no. 15. For a theory about this object as a gift to the emperor, see Pechstein 1974, pp. 90–121.
9. *Wenzel Jamnitzer* 1985, pp. 230–31, no. 25. I am grateful to Dr. Lorenz Seelig, curator of metalwork, Bayerisches National-museum, Munich, for his help and for suggesting this object to me.
10. Buckland 1989, p. 331. This gift also included splendid textiles and six tapestries representing Psyche. The textiles, discharged from the royal inventories, were not new when they were sent.
11. Ibid.
12. Mabille 1991, p. 79.
13. Bimbenet-Privat 1997, p. 11.
14. Syndram 1994, pp. 154–55.
15. Riccardi-Cubitt 1992, p. 98.
16. Leithe-Jasper 1970, pp. 227–42.
17. Bimbenet-Privat 1983, pp. 53–60.
18. Cox-Rearick 1995, pp. 389–91, no. XI-9. *Valerio Belli Vicentino* 2000, pp. 206–16, 308–12, cat. 6.
19. The pope also gave Francis I a tapestry woven in Flanders before 1515 reproducing Leonardo's *Last Supper* (Cox-Rearick 1995, pp. 363–64, fig. 399).
20. At some point after 1520, another Medici pope, Leo X, may have given a gilded-silver, enameled, and jeweled basin with rock-crystal insets by Belli to Duke William IV of Bavaria (Hapsburg 1997, pp. 67, 154, fig. 199).

21. Neumann 1957, p. 168.
22. Giusti 1992, p. 137. This tabletop probably influenced the emperor to order a tabletop from the Florentine manufactory, this time at his own expense and with the authorization of the grand duke (ibid., pp. 137–38, fig. 42).
23. Syndram 1999, pp. 17–18.
24. Giusti 1992, p. 84, figs. 27a–b.
25. Trusted 1985, p. 12. Fragments of the throne survive at the Kunsthistorisches Museum in Vienna.
26. Grimaldi 1996, pp. 186–91; and Rohde 1942, pp. 200–3.
27. Jackson-Stops 1985, p. 159, no. 86.
28. Ibid., and Drury 1991, pp. 54–55.
29. Saenz de Miera 1991, no. 108, pp. 29–36. I am grateful to Carmen Garcia-Frias Checa of the Patrimonio Nacional for this citation and for her help regarding these objects.
30. Esterly 1998, esp. pp. 132–45.
31. Lavin 1992, pp. 64–88. I am grateful to Donald LaRocca, Curator, Department of Arms and Armor, The Metropolitan Museum of Art, New York, for this reference and the three cited in note 34.
32. Bencard and Markova 1988, p. 46.
33. Conforti and Walton 1988, pp. 164–68, no. 51.
34. For additional gifts of arms and armor, see Thomas, Gamber, and Schedelmann 1964; Pyhrr and Godoy 1998, no. 54, pp. 278–84; and Blair 1965, pp. 1–52.
35. See Conforti and Walton 1988, p. 169, no. 52.
36. Ibid., pp. 170–71, no. 53. See also Drejholt 1996, pp. 148–50.
37. Cox-Rearick 1995, pp. 384-86, no. XI-3. Several scholars have suggested that Charles IX of France gave the Rosso tapestries, along with other famous French gold objects discussed above, to Archduke Ferdinand on the occasion of the king's marriage to Elizabeth of Austria in 1570. However, if the tapestries had remained in France as late as 1570, the series would have been listed in the royal inventory of 1551, in which it does not appear.
38. Buckland 1983, pp. 271–83.
39. Bremer-David 1997, p. 25.
40. Verlet 1982, app. B.
41. Piacenti 1986, pp. 17–20.

FIG. 16. Savonnerie Manufactory, *Carpet*. France, 1669. Wool and linen, 28 ft. 5¹/₂ in. x 15 ft. 1 in. (8.75 x 4.65 m). Palazzo Pitti, Florence (photo courtesy Ministero per i Beni e le Attivita' Culturali)

7

AMBASSADORIAL GIFTS:
MASTERPIECES OF EUROPEAN SILVER
AT THE KREMLIN ARMORY

GALINA A. MARKOVA

THERE IS NO DOUBT that the works of silversmiths in the collection of the principal Kremlin museum—the Armory—are among the most important in the world, outstanding for their unparalleled quantity and incomparable quality (figs. 1, 2). These objects have elicited great interest from scholars as well as the admiration of museum visitors. One reason the Armory collection is so impressive is the richness of diplomatic gifts brought to Muscovy by ambassadors, many of them the creations of outstanding silversmiths. These gifts included every type of standing cup and cover, vase, bowl, basin, tray, hand-washing set with ewer and basin, table fountain, candlesticks, and vessels in the shape of people, animals, ships, and globes. This bounty, bequeathed to the Armory from the ancient royal treasury, is the core of its superb collection of Western European silver (fig. 3). Nonetheless, we should note that the richness of the collection today also benefitted from the orders of the tsars, who made substantial purchases over the centuries; by the first third of the seventeenth century,

in fact, during the reign of the first tsar of the new dynasty—Mikhail Romanov—there were many hundreds of pieces in the possession of the tsars worth many thousands of rubles.[1]

The high quality of the objects that were given as gifts to the tsars was related to their historical origin. They had been painstakingly selected, because they served as instruments of diplomacy and because the high standards of the tsars were well known to donors. Therefore, foreign donors made every effort to choose gifts that represented wealth, magnificence, and rarity, novelty in form, skill in execution, and stylishness. Some objects were commissioned or purchased specifically to be given and were inscribed with the coats of arms of their donors, while others were precious heirlooms chosen from royal treasuries. The inclusion of an insignificant object in a diplomatic set of gifts was extremely rare, and only the finest works were retained from the gift offerings to be preserved in the tsar's collection.

It is not an exaggeration to call the silver objects in the Armory's collection of ambassadorial gifts masterpieces. First of all, this is accurate in the formal sense, because most of the objects represent professional ability of major artists; a silver or goldsmith became a

FIG. 1. Display of Dutch metalwork from the 17th century in the Armory Museum (formerly the Armory Palace) (photo courtesy The State Historical-Cultural Museum Preserve, Moscow Kremlin)

FIG. 4. Pangratz Storchel, *Master Goldsmith at Work*. Germany, before 1530. Watercolor on parchment. Municipal Library, Nuremberg

FIG. 5. Cuntz Rott, *Master Goldsmith at Work*. Germany, before 1542. Watercolor on parchment. Municipal Library, Nuremberg

"master" only after the guild accepted his abilities as demonstrated by his submitted masterwork, that is, his "masterpiece" (fig. 4). The process of moving to the top of the profession was a long tradition of the medieval craft organization—the guild or corporation (there were different names for this in different countries)—which was strictly regulated by laws, rules, and customs. The system was common to all European countries, although there were certain national and regional differences. The guild ensured a solid training based on mastering the skills of drawing, the tech-

FIG. 2. State Armory Museum (formerly the Armory Palace) in the Moscow Kremlin (built 1847–1851). Architect: Konstantin Andreyevich Ton (photo oourtesy The State Historical-Cultural Museum Preserve, Moscow Kremlin)

FIG. 3. Display of Western European silver in the Armory Museum (formerly the Armory Palace) (photo courtesy The State Historical-Cultural Museum Preserve, Moscow Kremlin)

niques for the artistic treatment of gold and silver, and the application of precious stones and enamel to metalwork. Artists were taught to work from a model and to use engravings and "plaques," which are bronze, tin and, more rarely, silver plates, primarily round or rectangular, with reliefs on the front side only. Plaques were used as models for ornament and figural compositions and were copied by goldsmiths coming from many sources that helped spread various motifs.[2]

At the age of ten or twelve, a goldsmith began his training as an apprentice in a workshop. Five to seven years later, he took a test and received his certificate—a document stating that he had completed his apprenticeship—and moved up to the category of journeyman for the next three to five years. (The length of this stage varied in different countries, guilds, and workshops, and it was frequently shortened for children of master goldsmiths who had inherited their father's profession.)

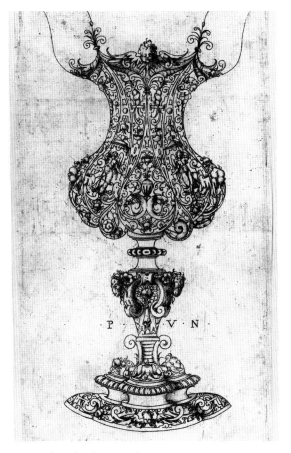

FIG. 6. Paulus Flindt, *Model for a Bell-shaped Standing Cup and Cover.* Germany, 1593. Engraving. Germanisches Nationalmuseum, Nuremberg

Apart from the guild regulations, certain social and life circumstances might also come into play in the development of a career. Someone could remain a journeyman for a long period owing to the lack of funds to start his own workshop and the money to pay his fees to the guild. (A craftsman who did not enter the guild could not obtain the title of "master" or a personal stamp to identify his works.) To complete their education, journeymen usually took, over the course of several years (from one and a half to three or more), "journeys" to other cities with major workshops, either in their country or abroad. During these journeys, they worked with famous goldsmiths if they could, often in the renowned centers of art and metalwork, such as Nuremberg, Augsburg, Paris, Rome, Florence, and Prague.[3] Contacts in the larger world outside his own town expanded a journeyman's horizons, enriched his skills with technical and artistic experience, developed his taste, gave him a sense of style, and familiarized him with what was fashionable. Returning home, a journeymen had to demonstrate the knowledge he had mastered and the skill he had accumulated by producing examination works for the title of master. Usually there were several of these works required (two or three), all of them different. For example, he might have to carve a seal or coin stamp, execute a piece of jewelry (pendant, buckle, or ring), and also make a silver vessel of fairly good size and complex decoration.[4]

The Silver of Nuremberg

In the southern German town of Nuremberg (which had an enormous influence on European art north of the Alps during the sixteenth century and the first third of the seventeenth), the most important part of the test of a potential master was the creation of a standing cup and cover (fig. 6). In a certain sense, it is even fair to say that the school of Nuremberg goldsmiths, which was dominated by the famous Wenzel Jamnitzer,[5] cultivated and refined its skill by work on standing cups with covers.[6] In fact, "Nuremberg covered cup" meant specifically a standing cup and cover with a deep and embossed bowl, and nowhere else were there more forms and decorative devices for cups than in Nuremberg workshops. The standing cups from Nuremberg at the Armory are remarkable for the diversity of their forms and profiles and for the richness of their decorative motifs. There are many types of cups: double and triple; belled and with a cylindrical band; cups shaped like beakers, conical wineglasses, pears, melons, grape clusters, pineapples, ships, figures (human and animal), flowers, and fountains, among others (fig. 7). They are decorated with embossed, cast, etched, engraved, stamped, and enameled elements and figurative depictions, as well as some sculpture in the round and some reliefs. Applied medallions and every possible type of handle, flower, and *trava,* meaning "herb" or "grass," were applied to cups. In Russian descriptions from the sixteenth and seventeenth centuries, *trava* refers to decorative details of a vegetal nature, such as bouquets on lids and applied rosettes of leaves under the bottom of the standing cup, above and below its stem. Many cups were covered with colored lacquers, much of it lost today but noted in old documents with the words "*trava* with over-colors."

In this catalogue there are two superb vessels—one an ambassadorial gift from King Christian IV of Denmark in 1644 (cat. no. 90), and one from Queen Christina of Sweden in 1647 (cat. no. 79). Both were made by famous Nuremberg artists, followers of the tradition established by Wenzel Jamnitzer. Hans Beutmüller made the sumptuous gilded-silver Late Renaissance standing cup and cover with a band around the bowl (cat. no. 79). The vertical emphasis of the tall standing cup's composition is stressed by the sculpture of the antique warrior on the lid. The horizontal articulation is especially expressive, thanks to the alternation between the lobes, or bosses, which stand out strongly on the main sections, and the low relief of the "carpet" patterns on some backgrounds.

The ornamentation of this standing cup and cover is a virtual encyclopedia of German Renaissance decorative motifs and the methods for their execution: embossed spherical, drop, and oval lobes of various sizes; large and small bundles of fruits; half-figures of putti with garlands of leaves and fruits; plant motifs, volutes; winged cherubim; busts of Venus, Mars, and Cupid with cast heads; cast lion masks; as well as a rich selection of attached handles—in the form of horns of plenty, S- or C-shaped with pearl-like ornaments and miniature heads—and grotesques (Christoph Jamnitzer proposed such to his colleagues in his *Neuw Grottessken Buch*).[7] The wide rims characteristic of this form of covered cup are decorated here with a dense engraved pattern of repeating cornucopias, birds perched on bundles of fruits, a flower, and stylized leaves. The pattern probably dates back to a sketch by Albrecht Dürer (himself the son of a Nuremberg goldsmith) from the early 1520s with cornucopias and a pelican (British Museum, London).[8] Beutmüller, however, used a greatly altered version of this drawing, and he also took liberty in drawing the bundles of fruits and garlands that derived from the designs of other Nuremberg artists. The embossed fruits on this standing cup and cover are very similar to those by the engraver Johann Sibmacher in his series of fruit

folios (four) and fruit and flower folios (six).[9] After loading the object to capacity with ornamentation, the artist demonstrated a touch of bravado by gilding and engraving the part of the standing cup that cannot be seen—the bottom of the bowl, which is hidden by a round, concave lower spindle. Attached to the inside of the cup's lid is a painstakingly cut, embossed, and stamped rosette made of long, wavy carved leaves.

Beutmüller's standing cup and cover is one of those gigantic "welcome" cups that was developed in Nuremberg in the latter half of the sixteenth century, a type that spread throughout Germany but also became famous abroad. In the northern European countries, there was a custom of presenting such covered cups to sovereigns at the time of ascension and coronation. Swearing an oath, the loyal subject would offer his ruler a vessel like this

FIG. 7. Georg Müller, *Triple Goblet.* Germany (Nuremberg), c. 1640. Silver, gilding; h. 32 cm. The State Historical-Cultural Museum Preserve, Moscow Kremlin (MZ-277)

one filled with gold coins. Polish embassies to Moscow gave coin-filled cups of this type in 1590 to Tsar Fyodor Ivanovich and in 1600 to Tsarevich Fyodor, the son of Tsar Boris Godunov.[10] In 1593, while still only a boyar during the reign of Tsar Fyodor, Boris Godunov received from Nicholas Warkoch, the ambassador of Emperor Rudolph II, "a camel made of gold and decorated with precious stones; on it sat a Moor and to either side hung baskets filled with small gold coins."[11]

In the gifts from Queen Christina of Sweden in 1647, aside from the cup and cover by Hans Beutmüller discussed above, there are two similar cups, one by him and the other by his colleague in the guild, Hans Reiff. Both standing cups are nearly five feet tall. Another large standing cup and cover by the renowned goldsmith Hans Petzolt was brought to Moscow with gifts from King Charles XI of Sweden in 1684.[12] Standing cups and covers were stored in the Kremlin and displayed with other magnificent objects on shelves and tables in the main formal hall of the Kremlin's ancient Palace of Facets.[13] In the nineteenth and twentieth centuries, these silver objects still were borrowed from the Armory for display there.[14]

The Petzolt standing cup and cover (cat. no. 90) is completely different from Beutmüller's work. It is a double cup, neo-Gothic in style, a solidly bossed gilded-silver vessel with an eight-lobed foot decorated in an engraved pattern and with applied Gothic leaves. The cup consists of two identical halves, each of which is a standing cup with bosses over the entire surface of the bowl and foot. During the Gothic period, this was a much-loved form of secular vessel, and by the late fifteenth century, the technique of embossing had become extremely popular. In a Gothic vessel the spherical lobes, or bosses, which stand out markedly from the background and cover, or "wrap," the standing cup, cease to be merely decorative: they themselves sculpt the form. As a technical device, the use of lobes makes it possible to enlarge the standing cup and its capacity by using the same amount of metal; and as an artistic device it creates an elegantly highlighted surface whose convex and concave parts reflect light differently, fragmenting and refracting it, making it play through the modu-

lations of the gilding. At the same time the qualities of silver—its malleability and its ability to hold a shape even in a thin layer and then to take polishing and gilding so that the silversmith can convincingly demonstrate his skill—can be used to great advantage. It is not surprising, therefore, that the bossed standing cup and cover enjoyed exceptional popularity in German goldsmithing as late as the eighteenth century.

In this example, Petzolt fully and accurately reproduced the technical and decorative scheme of the traditional Gothic standing cup and cover. He arranged the bosses in solid rows to which he gave characteristic long and short elements like those on the Gothic prototypes. These "tongues" unite and contain the bosses and create the impression that they flow into one another. The slanted positioning of the tongues on the bowls and of the embossed stems of the cup create a spiral movement along the vertical axis that runs through the entire form. The artist also added much-loved Gothic decorative details, such as applied curled wisps (which Heinrich Kohlhaussen, who has studied Nuremberg goldsmithing, considers a characteristic mark of German work), which emphasizes the rim of the standing cup, along with the prickly thistle leaves above it and in the garlands on the stem. The thistle is also the basis for the finely engraved pattern on the upper edge of the bowl.

Although the covered cup was unquestionably the favorite form of Nuremberg silversmiths, it did not absorb all of their creative energy. New types of centerpieces in novel forms arose in Nuremberg before they did in other centers in Germany. Supreme among them is the Merkel centerpiece[15]—a magnificent work made by Wenzel Jamnitzer, who was referred to as the "German Cellini" in nineteenth-century art-historical literature (fig. 8). A place of honor among the creations of the Jamnitzer school was the designing of table fountains, incense burners, and precious cases for writing instruments and adornments.[16] The most widespread type of centerpiece was made in the form of a round, shallow bowl on a slender baluster-stem with a low base. This form was borrowed from the Italian tazza, a bowl of silver or Venetian glass used as a vessel for

FIG. 8. Wenzel Jamnitzer, *Table Centerpiece*. Germany (Nuremberg), 1549. Silver, gilding, enamel; h. 39 in. (100 cm). Purchased in 1549 by the City Council of Nuremberg, Rijksmuseum, Amsterdam

wine during feasts. In the sixteenth and seventeenth centuries, in the paintings and engravings of mythological subjects by Italian, Dutch, Flemish, and German artists, deities were often shown holding not standing cups and covers but this kind of tazza, considered the most refined form of drinking vessel. However, in countries north of the Alps and Muscovy, the tazza was accepted as a vase for sweets, candies, as well as sugared and marinated berries and fruits. In the sixteenth

and seventeenth centuries in Russia, a marinade was known as a *raznosol*, so the dish for these delicacies was given the name *rassolnik*. Old documents mention many *rassolniks* among the silver in ambassadorial gifts, especially those from Sweden and Denmark.

The two Nuremberg *rassolniks* (cat. no. 81a,b) arrived in Moscow in 1647 along with other gifts from Queen Christina of Sweden. The bowls were originally part of a set of twelve—one for each month of the year. Like all works in the Renaissance style, they are distinguished by their balanced composition, which is emphasized by horizontal articulation and fine unity. Decoration has been applied to the major sections of the object— the bowl, stem, and base—particularly embossed ornaments, including large smooth eggs, stylized plant ornament, roll-work cartouches with bundles of fruits, and the winged heads of angels.

In the center of each bowl is a round embossed applied plaque with an allegorical figure representing a month of the year shown under the corresponding sign of the zodiac. This catalogue includes two tazzas (cat. no. 81a,b) that show two of the twelve plaques of the complete set of the zodiac cycle (see p. 266). The peasant with a scythe standing in a landscape with haystacks represents the sign of Leo the Lion and the month of July, and the peasant gathering fruits stands for the Scales of Libra and September. Allegories for the twelve months and four seasons were popular with the silversmiths of Germany and Holland, as they were with painters. Peasants, hunters, and other people depicted at their daily tasks were used to represent the months, while mythological figure served to personify the four seasons: Venus, Ceres, Bacchus, and Cronos. Other common allegorical depictions included the five senses, the four elements, the parts of the world, the virtues, the sins, the free arts, abundance, war, and peace. Very often the allegorical motif of the three ages of man was used: childhood, in the form of a head or bust of a putto (Cupid); youth as the head or bust of a young woman (Venus); and maturity as the head or bust of a soldier in a helmet (Mars). Such heads can be seen adorning the baluster in the stem of the standing cup and cover by Hans Beutmüller (cat. no. 79).

It was not necessary to include a complete sequence of these images: a single head could be repeated as a decorative motif, as we see on the Beutmüller standing cup and cover, where a woman's cast head is coupled with the embossed half-figures of sirens. The variety of heads of putti was great, as in the foreshortening of the heads or the expression on the faces. Beutmüller has six beautiful embossed cherubim viewed *en face*, in profile, at a three-quarter angle, leaning over, and looking heavenward. Their sweet little faces framed by soft short curls can be sad, smiling, serious, concentrated, or full of lively curiosity. As with the personifications of the months and the seasons, the goldsmith borrowed this imagery from the "higher" arts (painting, sculpture, drawing), and translated it into his own professional language by engravers and the designers of plaques.

Ewers and Basins

The engravings and plaques that came from abroad naturally expanded the range of the German artists. In the ornamentation of a basin with mother-of-pearl insets by Nuremberg artist Hans Brabant (cat. no. 47), the elegant rollwork with miniature volutes, bundles of fruits, and bouquets, along with putti playing with garlands, lion masks, busts of women, and complex, intersecting ribbon circles, remind us not just of the Jamnitzer workshop but also of the refined decorative art of the southern Netherlands and its principal center, Antwerp. This is not surprising, of course, since, judging from his name, the artist was likely a native of Brabant in the southern Netherlands.

Ewers and basins were used for rosewater and other fragrant waters. In Muscovy, as in sixteenth- and seventeenth-century Europe, a ewer-and-basin set was an object designated for aristocratic use.[17] More particularly, it figured as a gift in the ceremony of ambassadorial receptions (fig. 9, see also p. 269). The ambassador who visited Grand Duke Ivan IV on behalf of Emperor Maximilian II wrote this about what he had seen: "On the left side of the Grand Duke on a table stood a washbasin. On his right side sat the grand duke's oldest son, Ivan."[18] Ewer-and-basin sets, as well as large platters,

were among the most favored gifts brought by foreign ambassadors to the Russian tsars. "Between 1651 and 1672, six Polish embassies brought fifteen hand-washing sets with basins to Russia."[19] At the top of this list was Hans Brabant's elegantly sumptuous basin made with mother-of-pearl and precious stones, which had been sent with the gifts of the Polish king John II Casimir. Later on—in the seventeenth century, the Baroque era—basins became very large and represented grand artistic statements; the largest basin known is a Polish example with a plaque depicting the Freeing of Andromeda by Perseus (cat. no. 48b), also a gift from King John II Casimir of Poland. Eventually, most basins lost their functional character; the raised form in the middle of the basin, which ensured the stability of the ewer on the platter, disappeared. The ewer also acquired an identity of its own and was paired with a basin principally on the basis of subject and the ornamental motifs, as in the Augsburg and Gdańsk sets among the gifts from the Polish crown in 1647 and 1667 (cat. nos. 46a,b; 48a,b). This is also true of the basin brought from the Austrian Emperor Leopold I in 1684 (cat. no. 54).

The disciplined and relatively simple form of the basin that had originated in the Renaissance was replaced by an elaborate Baroque configuration and figurative compositions on themes taken from the Bible, mythology, and antique and modern history, as well as aristocratic daily life and even themes of everyday life (fig. 10). The predominant new form was the oval with wavy edges. Where once the interior was like a smooth mirror surrounded with an ornamented border, the interior of the platter was now stamped with a figural image and the border became a wide picture frame. We can admire the superb embossed basin "paintings" by the outstanding Augsburg artists Hans Jacob Baur I (cat. no. 46a,b), Heinrich Mannlich (cat. no. 84), and Lorenz Biller I (cat. no. 54), who created contemporary battle scenes, allegorical biblical compositions ("Triumphal Procession of Joseph the Beautiful"), and historical moments ("Captive Turks Before Emperor Leopold").

It is worth noting that the last basin presented in 1684 to the co-tsars, Ivan V and Peter I, can be viewed as a unique type of propaganda promoting the mission

FIG. 9. Johann Heinrich Mannlich the Elder, *Ewer and Basin*. Germany (Augsburg), before 1675. Silver, gilding, rock crystal, enamel, topaz, garnet, amethyst, chrysolite; h. of ewer 16 3/4 in. (43 cm); diam. of basin 25 in. (64 cm). Offered to Tsar Alexei Mikhailovich by Emperor Leopold I of the Holy Roman Empire in 1675. The State Historical-Cultural Museum Preserve, Moscow Kremlin. (MZ-1270; MZ-1271)

of the Austrian embassy, which was intended to encourage Moscow to enter an anti-Turkish military alliance. The chained captives who kneel before the throne with a group of trophies served as a vivid reminder of the most important European event of the recent past. In the fall of 1683, a combined Austrian-Polish force had obtained a victory over the Turkish army outside Vienna. The scene depicted in the center of this massive basin is the celebration of this victory in which the Holy Roman Emperor greets his marshals and commanders; at his right hand is John Sobieski (later the king of

FIG. 10. Hans Jacob Baur I, *Basin* ("Reconciliation of the Brothers Isaac and Jacob"). Germany (Augsburg), 1645–47. Silver, gilding; l. 41 3/4 in. (107 cm); w. 35 1/2 in. (91 cm); h. 3 7/8 in. (10 cm). Offered to Tsar Alexei Mikhailovich by Queen Christina of Sweden in 1647. The State Historical-Cultural Museum Preserve, Moscow Kremlin. (MZ-523)

Poland), the hero of the battle in full armor. Symbols of victory and military power surround the scene, resembling the same ornaments used by the artist, Lorenz Biller I, on the base of the silver table decoration (cat. no. 55) that was brought to Moscow with the basin. Augsburg basins are renowned not only because they are first-rate objects that reflect their own era, but also because these political commissions enabled Augsburg goldsmiths to demonstrate a high level of technical skill and artistic talent.

For these huge basins, the same amount of silver by weight as in the earlier, smaller versions was flattened and stretched into a thinner but much larger sheet. In this thin layer of metal the silversmiths embossed exquisitely intricate scenes and ornamental compositions, achieving a sense of high relief, perspective, and profound depth. The vitality of their details and the color effects created by the contrast of light and dark, of gilded and white silver, were equally impressive.

Innovation and Animals

New vessel types were also developed at this time, many of which became part of table centerpieces. The Armory has a significant group of Augsburg "horsemen": warriors on well-schooled horses like those shown here (cat. no. 55) or such figures as Diana riding a deer and a galloping centaur abducting a nymph. The models for these compositions were both Italian bronzes and German Rhenish ceramics.[20] Figures of lions were especially favored in Scandinavia. The four Augsburg beasts in the Armory—a record number among world collections—arrived as ambassadorial gifts from the Swedish crown. One of them is a ewer in the form of a lion standing on its hind legs (rampant), wearing a crown, and holding a scepter,[21] a gift to Tsar Peter I from King Charles XII in 1699 (cat. no. 85). In this ewer, Heinrich Mannlich has successfully combined naturalistic features of the beast's anatomy with a heraldic stance.

Other German silversmiths beyond Augsburg were also skilled at executing animal figures as centerpieces; compare the roaring Augsburg lion and horse (cat. nos. 55, 85), which vies with the Hamburg deer rearing on

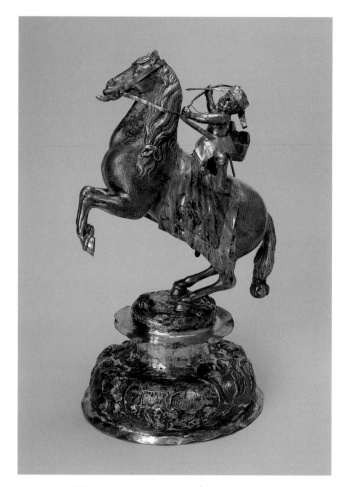

FIG. 11. *Table Decoration*. Germany (Nuremberg; maker's mark "mill"), 1675–84. Silver, gilding; h. 15^1/$_4$ in. (39 cm). Offered to Tsars Ivan V and Peter I by King Charles XI of Sweden in 1684. The State Historical-Cultural Museum Preserve, Moscow Kremlin. (MZ-586)

its hind legs (cat. no. 93). The Armory also has a table centerpiece made by a Nuremberg silversmith in the shape of a horse wearing an elegant saddlecloth and a bow in its mane carrying the figure of Cupid on its back (fig. 11).[22]

The Armory collection today reflects the observations of the learned Bishop Arseny of Elasson, who accompanied the Constantinople Patriarch Jeremiah to Moscow to attend the installation of the first Russian patriarch in 1589, and who experienced surprised admiration at the sight of the tsar's treasures on display in the formal hall of the Kremlin palace: "There were also vessels that resembled lions, bears, wolves, bulls, horses, deer, and hares, and one showed a unicorn with a long spear on its brow. Then there were roosters, peacocks with golden wings, storks, cranes, ducks, geese, and large

FIG. 12. Andreas Wickert II, *Ewer*. Germany (Augsburg), 1670–75. Silver, gilding; h. 16⅝ in. (42.5 cm). The State Historical-Cultural Museum Preserve, Moscow Kremlin.(MZ-357)

pelicans, several ostriches, large and small doves, and partridges; they all stood in beautiful order and proportion and were made of gold and silver. . . . All told, the number of bowls and vessels, as well as small and large pieces fashioned of pure gold, was tremendous."[23]

The Display of the Tsar's Silver

Since ancient times, the contents of a royal treasury has generally been considered an effective means of indicating the wealth and power of a ruler. Valuable objects were displayed in the ambassadorial ceremonies at which gifts were presented in sixteenth- and seventeenth-century Moscow, but precious vessels and utensils from the tsar's treasury were frequently used in the life of the palace, displayed in the palace's reception halls or in the private living quarters of the Kremlin. The tsar's

principal and most opulent gallery for the exhibition of such objects was in the Palace of Facets, where there were very large stands with stepped shelves, as the English ambassador Thomas Smith noted in his journal in 1604: "In the midst of this hall might seem to Stand a great Pillar, round about which, a great height stood wonderful great peeces of plate."[24] We can judge the size of the stand itself not only from the enthusiastic comments of witnesses but also from documents that describe the quantity of plate exhibited on it. In 1729, 364 and 600 objects are mentioned, and in April 1730, 500 objects were transferred to the Palace of Facets for this formal display: standing cups and covers, basins, globes, salt cellars, beakers, and tankards.[25]

The impressive nature of such a sight in the Palace of Facets is conveyed by an illustration from the *Book on the Selection to the Most High Throne of the Great Russian Realm of the Great Sovereign, Tsar and Grand Prince Mikhail Fyodorovich, Autocrat of All Russia*, which was compiled in 1672 (fig. 13).[26] This ancient custom of sumptuous displays continued for many years into the eighteenth and nineteenth centuries, as illustrated in drawings that were made to record coronations and other events. These coronation albums show four shelves with precious foreign silver rising all the way to the cornice that runs around the column in the center of the hall in the Palace of Facets, and in illustrations showing scenes of the coronation dinners of 1762 (Catherine II); 1882 (Alexander III), and 1896 (Nicholas II); numerous vessels are depicted even on a shelf above the cornice (see Chapter 4, figs. 9–12). Many of these objects can be recognized as part of the Armory Museum's current collection of ambassadorial gifts.

Augsburg Silver

The Augsburg objects in the Armory's collection are particularly outstanding (fig. 12). Without a doubt, one of the best examples of silver sculpture is the striking eagle that was made by two artists who represent the famed Augsburg dynasties of Drentwett and Mannlich (cat. no. 50). Two andirons depicting a West Indian man and woman by Johannes Kilian and Lukas Lang (cat. no. 56a b), and the figures of Mars and Minerva on the stems of the tazzas, or the fruit dishes with stands by Hans Jacob Baur I (cat. no. 83a,b) rival the eagle, although on a smaller scale. The Indian andirons represent a very rare type of object, one that seldom survives. These figures are each mounted on a base meant to hold logs in a fireplace; the materials normally used for this type of andiron were iron and bronze, and often the bronze was gilded and the objects given elegant shapes. Only in exceptional instances were andirons made of silver, and they represent a true gift on the highest royal level of prestige. Since these are works by master silversmiths, the large-scale figures are remarkable for their skilled modeling, anatomical precision, and elegance of gesture. The faces of these Indians are very expressive and reflect the Baroque era's inherent interest in the exotic. The sculpted figures of Mars and Minerva on the stems of the fruit dishes with stands are at once laconic, severe, and elegant, a classic example of the use of sculptural forms in decorative arts.

The Art of Table Decoration

In the mid-seventeenth century in Europe, the art of decorating tables for formal banquets reached exceptional heights.[27] Specialists labored over designs, creating plans and drawings for the placement of both functional and decorative vessels and for the eating utensils, creating large-scale compositions from a combination of different shapes and materials. New and more complex schemes were constantly being worked out for the decorative arrangement of the tables in the hall, as well as for the vessels and centerpieces laid out on them. The rituals for changing tablecloths and for laying out candlesticks and plates (which were changed with each new dish served) became more and more refined. Special attention was paid to the dessert table and other decorative "spectacle," or display, tables. Using colored syrup and sugar, napkins starched and folded in special ways, these designers created on the dining table a veritable garden parterre, complete with pavilions, obelisks, triumphal arches, antique rotundas, fountains, and a variety of figures. Crucial to these arrangements were the silver center-

pieces, which eventually grew to the point where they displaced the confectionary dishes. Borders or rhythmic accents could be created in a table setting by using a number of elegant fruit stands, which were grouped in turn around major centerpieces like the silver fruit stand (cat. no. 78) and the cornucopia standing cup and cover (cat. no. 80) that came to Moscow with the gifts of the Great Embassy of 1647 from Queen Christina of Sweden. Placed in several rows, one behind the other, the fruit stands themselves emphasized a vertical element of the overall decorative composition of a table. Such a display of fruit dishes with stands can be seen in an illustration depicting a royal feast in the 1672 *Book on the Selection . . .* (see fig. 13).[28]

Hamburg Silver

The group of silver at the Moscow Armory from the third renowned German metropolis, Hamburg, includes a constellation of one-of-a-kind masterpieces of goldsmithing, brilliant expressions of the high level of quality in the collection. The cornucopia cup (cat. no. 80), the melon cup (cat. no. 92), the standing cup and cover with the figure of Diana on the stem (cat. no. 91), and the multitiered fruit dish with stand (cat. no. 78) not only allow us to appreciate the art of their creators—Dietrich Thor Moye, Hans Lambrecht II, and Carsten Mundt I—but they also provide examples of the remarkable diversity of the elements that constituted German Baroque centerpieces. The opulent standing cup and cover in the form of a horn of plenty on the shoulders of Ceres, the goddess of fertility, is a composition that glorifies the divine beauty and wealth of nature (cat. no. 80). The sensuous forms of the twisting horn are modeled freely and confidently, and the sumptuous silver still life on the lid, with cast and embossed apples, pears, berries, and leaves, is faultlessly executed and skillfully arranged. The figure of the goddess kneeling on one knee is marked by a rather mannered grace, reflecting a famous bronze by the late-sixteenth-century Italian Mannerist sculptor Giambologna.[29] The German goldsmith altered the Italian composition slightly by varying the gestures of the figure: a scythe appears in

FIG. 13. Ivan Vereschchagin et al., *Banquet in the Reception Hall of the Palace of Facets, Moscow Kremlin*. Plate in *Book on the Selection to the Most High Throne of the Great Russian Realm of the Great Sovereign, Tsar and Grand Prince Mikhail Fyodorovich, Autocrat of All Russia* (Moscow, 1672–73). The State Historical-Cultural Museum Preserve, Moscow Kremlin

her right hand while the left is raised to steady the burden on her shoulder, and she wears a crown with ears of grain—the invariable attribute of Ceres. This unique covered cup, which has no parallels in other collections of German silver, has been in the Kremlin treasury for more than three centuries. It is outstanding even among the Armory's collection of ambassadorial gifts.

Other Hamburg masterpieces in this catalogue were gifts from the Danish crown to Tsar Mikhail Romanov (cat. nos. 91–93). King Christian IV of Denmark built his own collection lovingly and tastefully, and in his charming private residence, Rosenborg Castle in Copenhagen, he surrounded himself with European paintings, sculptures, jewelry, and works in silver and ivory. In

the court chapel of another residence, Frederiksborg Castle, the silver altar and pulpit, whose sculptural reliefs are among the finest creations of Hamburg silversmiths, may still be seen.[30] The Danish court retained permanent emissaries in Hamburg just to purchase artistic silver, and works by Hamburg artists predominate in the group sent to Moscow from King Christian IV and Count Valdemar in 1644. In this unique group of gifts, astonishing in every sense and including as many as two hundred silver objects, one must single out as a star of the first magnitude the standing cup and cover in the form of a melon on a plate of fruit, by Hans Lambrecht II (cat. no. 92).

Works by Hamburg goldsmiths also adorned the treasuries and castles of the Swedish monarchs (fig. 14). Among the outstanding objects received as gifts from Queen Christina of Sweden in 1647 is a table centerpiece, a fruit stand, or confectionary tree, by Dietrich Thor Moye (cat. no. 78). The natural motifs in both the still life on the melon cup (cat. no. 92) and in

FIG. 14. Peter Or, *Table Fountain*. Germany (Hamburg), 1649–52. Silver, gilding; h. 49¹/₂ in. (127 cm). Offered to Tsar Alexei Mikhailovich by King Charles XI of Sweden in 1662. The State Historical-Cultural Museum Preserve, Moscow Kremlin. (MZ-531)

the grapevines that climb up the tiers of the fruit stand (cat. no. 78) would certainly be appropriate as part of an elaborate table decoration with a landscape theme. The erotic classical mythology beloved during the Baroque period appears in the sculpture of the four tiers of the fruit tree: below is a youthful Bacchus straddling a wine barrel, holding in his right hand a ewer of wine and in his left a bunch of grapes. Above him is a seated Venus holding a burning heart; above her is Fortune (or Ceres?) with a cornucopia, her expressive right hand raised upward. The pyramid of the confectionary tree

is crowned by Cupid holding a bow and arrow. All the figures are tiny adaptations of works by the Dutch sculptor Adriaen de Vries. The skillful execution of each detail, the masterful composition of the whole, the beauty of its silhouette, and the elegant appearance allow us to place this rare object among the major achievements of German decorative art. Only one other tiered fruit stand like this is known; it too was made in Hamburg and brought to Moscow in 1644 by the Great Embassy from Denmark, among the gifts from King Christian IV and Count Valdemar. The piece is kept at the Armory.[31]

English Silver

Although German silver is particularly well represented in the Armory's collection of diplomatic gifts, the museum has a unique group of English pieces and superb examples of Dutch, Swedish, and Polish silver. The sixteenth- and seventeenth-century English silver is the finest and most extensive of any collection in the world, including England (fig. 15). We know that English silver was not in commercial circulation on the European continent, but it was, not surprisingly the dominant element in the gifts from England. These objects, from the reigns of Queen Elizabeth I (r. 1558–1603) and Kings James I (r. 1603–25), Charles I (r. 1625–49), and Charles II (r. 1660–85), were gifts from royal ambassadors and merchants to the Muscovite tsars between 1557 and 1664. All of the pieces were made by goldsmiths whose marks were registered with the Worshipful Company of Goldsmiths and bear the four mandatory London marks, which attest to the quality of the metal and the work. Two of the marks have a heraldic motif: the lion *passant*—the symbol for sterling standard—and the leopard's head—the mark of London. Next to these is the maker's mark and the "date letter," which signifies a year and allows us to date the objects within a period of two years.

This catalogue provides some fine examples that clearly demonstrate the diversity of types and styles of English silver and the features that make it unique. Although the flagons, ewers, salt cellars, livery pots,

FIG. 15. Display of English metalwork from the late 16th–17th centuries in the Armory Museum (formerly the Armory Palace). (photo courtesy The State Historical-Cultural Museum Preserve, Moscow Kremlin)

covered cups, and fruit dishes represent different stylistic groups, they share certain characteristics. The forms are based on the simple geometry of cone, cylinder, and sphere, and their contours have clear and uncomplicated profiles. The artistic language and repertoire of subjects for their decoration do not reflect the preciousness of contemporary European Mannerism of the late sixteenth and early seventeenth centuries but the influence of the Baroque floral style of the 1660s is evident.

The flagon with the coat of arms of King James I (cat. no. 57) that was most likely brought as a gift for Tsar Boris Godunov in 1604–5 vividly demonstrates the traditions of the English Renaissance. It has a conical form with decoration that successfully combines heavily embossed and engraved motifs. The horizontal elements of the design emphasize the architectural quality of the object as a whole, and the European motifs (bunches of fruit, vegetal forms, garlands, and volutes) are treated in a distinctive English manner.

FIG. 16. *Standing Cup and Cover*, England (London; maker's mark CB in monogram), 1608–09, silver, gilding, H. 45 cm.; diam of bowl: 14 cm.; diam. of base: 11.7 cm. The State Historical-Cultural Museum Preserve, Moscow Kremlin. (MZ-639/1–2)

The cylindrical standing salt probably given by ambassador Sir John Merrick to Tsar Mikhail Romanov in 1615 (cat. no. 59) is also a characteristic English work. It is one of the so-called great salts that at one time played an important role at splendid banquets, and it is impressive for its size, composition, and decoration. The tall, faceted pyramid or tower that rises above the lid is unusual, with no parallels in the work of other countries. Similar finials do appear on the lids of other English pieces in the Armory, however: a second cylindrical salt[32] and a remarkable spherical standing cup and cover whose finial is shaped like a thistle bud (fig. 16).[33]

The Armory's collection of English silver reflects the development of diplomatic and trade relations between England and Russia. The rupture that occurred during the English revolution, its civil war, and the protectorate of Oliver Cromwell explains the absence of ambassadorial silver from England in Moscow for the period 1642 to 1663, but after the restoration of King Charles II to the English throne in 1660, the first embassy arrived in Moscow in 1664. Remarkably, the gifts from this mission had come from the personal collection of the English royal family. Although the objects in this group were mostly of English manufacture, a number were from France, including a unique ewer and basin made in Paris in 1625 (cat. no. 66a,b). The English pieces from Charles II's embassy—large standing cups and covers, livery pots, flagons, and fruit dishes with stands—constitute an impressive body of work by London silversmiths of the early 1660s (cat. nos. 63–65).[34] The Baroque decoration includes floral and leaf motifs, as well as numerous animals: dogs, horses, foxes, bears, deer, and boars. The simple shapes of these objects contrast with the intricately detailed, relatively massive and picturesque ornamentation. Typical is the decoration of a flagon (cat. no. 64) that combines embossed tulips and leaves (derived from a botanical atlas) with the imposing figure of a wild boar baring its teeth at an unseen enemy as it protects its young (fig. 17). The drawing is not without fault, but the image is lively and appealing.

The decoration of the English objects from the earl of Carlisle's ambassadorial mission of 1663–64 reflects the height of the floral style that had spread from the Netherlands throughout Europe during the 1650s. Earlier in the century, the northern Netherlands had been gripped by what was called tulip mania,[35] in which the cultivation of tulips brought to Holland from Persia in the early seventeenth century merged with fashion and a popular interest in botany to create an economic boom. One of the most popular themes in Dutch paintings and engravings of the period was the floral still life, which included carnations, roses, narcissi, hyacinths, crocuses, and peonies but in which the tulip was the undisputed favorite.

FIG. 17. Robert Smithier, flagon (*flyaga*) (detail), England (London), 1663, silver, gilding, h. 14⅞ in. (38 cm). The State Historical-Cultural Museum Preserve, Moscow Kremlin. (MZ-659) (see cat. no. 64)

Dutch Silver

The Armory collection demonstrates clearly the particular inventiveness of Dutch silversmiths in the art of floral decoration. Despite obvious similarities in the patterns and motifs, the floral compositions are virtually never repeated exactly. The placement of stems and shoots with leaves and flowers is different in each of the three objects reproduced in this catalogue (cat. nos. 72, 73, 75). Artful embossing that is both elegant and realistic conveys the accurate structure of the plants, the attractive configuration of their petals, their silky texture, and even the veins on the surface of their leaves. Dutch silversmiths were capable of expressing with great delicacy the various stages of a flower's emergence from an opening bud to glorious maturity, and even its demise with a lifeless, drooping corolla and dropping petals. No other national school achieved the diversity of composition and perfection of the embossed floral pattern that can be found in Dutch silver.

The Dutch embassies of 1648, 1665, and 1676 brought groups of fine silver objects from Amsterdam, The Hague, Leiden, and Utrecht that clearly illustrate the three different artistic trends in silver from Holland's Golden Age: the "Lutma lobed style," the floral style, and a third style that tends toward simple forms and smooth surfaces (see cat. no. 77). The large wine ewer (cat. no. 70), a large candlestick (cat. no. 69), and a wall sconce (cat. no. 71) are particularly outstanding examples, with imposing dimensions and shapes. The prominence of the doubled-headed eagle from the Russian coat of arms attests to the special diplomatic purpose of these objects, which are unequaled in both scale and opulence among works of Dutch silver. The ewer and candlestick are executed in the lobed style, which is usually associated with the name of its creator, the famous Dutch goldsmith Johannes Lutma (fig. 18).[36] The smooth surfaces of objects in this style are formed of large, protruding lobes that are often free of

ornamentation, although the spaces between the lobes may be gilded. In contrast to this relative simplicity, the ewer's spout and handle are made in the shape of twisting sea monsters, executed in the full auricular style that is both decorative and expressive. The spout ends in the open mouth of one monster, while another forms the handle. The sconce (cat. no. 71), which was made in The Hague, is densely covered with a whimsically drawn embossed plant design. The ornamentation is traditional and refined, reflecting the influence of Dutch court taste.

The perfectly executed Dutch objects that represent the floral style are also decorated with auricular (or ear-shaped) motifs (see cat. nos. 72, 73, 75),[37] which were popular at the time, though relegated to a secondary role in the ornamentation. The most outstanding example of a floral work is the wonderful basin made by Hendrik tom Hulsen in 1664 (cat. no. 73). The

FIG. 18. Johannes Lutma, *Ewer and basin*, Netherlands (Amsterdam), 1647, silver, ewer: h. 19⅝ in. (50.4 cm), basin: w. 29 in. (74.5 cm), Rijksmuseum, Amsterdam, The Netherlands

flowers are executed in high relief and painstakingly worked in *poinçon*, a technique that gives the thick stems and leaves an indented outline. The stems move clockwise in an animated fashion, branching out from the compact wreath in the center of the basin and terminating in softly bending large flowers at the edge. This decorative structure is found only in Dutch and European silver.

The objects made in 1675, by contrast, are smooth and without ornament (cat. nos. 76, 77). They are distinctive for their proportions and regularity, the pure lines of their silhouette, and the simplicity of their adornment, which shows the influence of seventeenth-century classicism. Several precious gems are mounted around the basin at regular intervals, and this luxurious element, together with the gilded surface and the engraved Russian coat of arms, reflects the fact that these were intended as ambassadorial gifts to the tsar of Russia.

Polish Silver

The work of Polish goldsmiths is also represented in the Armory by fine examples that vividly express the Baroque aesthetic and demonstrate the influence on the Polish centers of the most distinguished European schools as well as their own artistic originality (fig. 19). Polish silversmiths of the seventeenth century often received their training from German and German-trained silversmiths, but they nonetheless created highly original works. There are no parallels to the astonishingly large basin and ewer brought to Tsar Alexei Mikhailovich by the Polish embassy in 1667 (cat. nos. 48a,b). All of these pieces were made in Gdańsk (Danzig), a city with a substantial German-speaking population located at the crossroads of important routes for trade and art and known as the "Golden Gates" of northern Europe.[38] The enormous oval basin with an embossed scene depicting the freeing of Andromeda by Perseus (cat. no. 48b) is the largest European silver basin known today. Its surface is embossed with large, curving forms and smaller counterspirals that diminish in width as they move toward the center from the

FIG. 19. Display of gifts from Poland in the Armory Museum (formerly the Armory Palace). (photo courtesy The State Historical-Cultural Museum Preserve, Moscow Kremlin)

edge, animating the entire surface of the basin. This free-form movement, however, is restrained by the smooth, straight edge of the basin—with its garland of large individual flowers on straight stems—and in the center, where the swirling movement ceases outside the circle that frames the plaque depicting Perseus and Andromeda. Another maker from Gdańsk, Christian Paulsen I, magnificently expressed the Baroque sense of moving mass in the body of the large ewer, which looks as though it has been twisted into a spiral (cat. no. 48a). The ewer's decoration is similar to that of the basin with the same decorative motif of embossed curving spirals.

Another unique gift from the embassy of 1667 is a large pear-shaped flask with striking gilded decoration (cat. no. 49) made by the same artist who created the Perseus basin above. The flask, however, has a completely different form and decoration, with a smooth, fluid silhouette whose shape is emphasized by the long flower stems that stream down its sides, ending in the heads of flowers and leaves. The dominant element in this original decoration belongs to the leafy auricular mask, which is alternately elongated and compressed. This flask and its mate in the Armory collection,[39] together with the remarkable basin, represent the best of seventeenth-century Polish goldsmiths' work.[40]

Swedish Silver

The largest group of ambassadorial gifts of silver at the Armory comes from Sweden and reflects the various stages of political and economic relations between that country and Russia. The groups of gifts from Queen Christina and Kings Charles X, Charles XI, and Charles XII from the period 1647–99 are dominated by silver made in Germany—masterpieces from Nuremberg, Augsburg, and Hamburg obtained by energetic emissaries of the Swedish crown and agents of aristocratic families. The market for such works was highly competitive, because agents working for the royal courts of Denmark and Poland and suppliers to the Austrian imperial court invariably sought objects from the same centers.

The works of Swedish goldsmiths are also outstanding, if less numerous, and the Armory collection includes most of the surviving examples from this period in Swedish history, as well as the most characteristic forms. The group is fairly diverse and includes bowls, tankards, flagons, basins, centerpieces with cruets for spices and candlesticks, cosmetics boxes, gift basins, candlesticks, and beakers (fig. 20). Most were made by famous masters who worked in Stockholm, and their hallmarks are those of the major goldsmiths. All the objects are made of sterling silver[41] and bear the hallmarks mandated by the Swedish guild: in addition to the maker's mark, an inspection mark in the form of a crown or the crowned head of Saint Erik and a year mark—a letter of the alphabet indicating the date the object was made. Swedish pieces were very rare among diplomatic gifts until the 1690s; not one Swedish object was among the magnificent German silver brought by the Swedish embassies in 1655 and 1684. For the most part, Swedish objects from that period are imitations of German and Dutch models.[42] The exceptions in the Armory collection are two marvelous examples from the embassy of 1647—a basin in the form of a swan and a centerpiece with a dragon.[43] The stunning originality of these pieces points to the development of a

purely Swedish style in goldsmithing, which by the late seventeenth century had become a distinctive national style, which is well represented in the objects given by Charles XII to Tsar Peter I in 1699. Two of the works in this catalogue vividly embody Swedish taste of the 1690s: candlesticks in the form of fluted columns on square bases by Anders Bengtsson Starin (cat. no. 87a,b) and a beaker with lid (cat. no. 86), pure and precise in its proportions, by Johan Nützel, who became goldsmith to Queen Hedwig Eleonora of Sweden in 1689. Beakers of this type are called "Caroline," referring to Kings Charles XI and Charles XII. The search for "magnificent, majestic simplicity"[44] was the guiding principle in the art of many Swedish silversmiths at this time, and their creations are a distinctive addition to the full range of sixteenth- and seventeenth-century European artistic silver in the collection of the Kremlin Armory.

FIG. 20. Nicolaus Breuman, *Table Centerpiece with Dragon*, Swedish (Stockholm), 1666–76. Silver, gilding; h. 15 5/8 in. (40 cm). Offered to Tsar Alexei Mikhailovich by King Charles XI of Sweden in 1674. The State Historical-Cultural Museum Preserve, Moscow Kremlin. (MZ-565/1-3)

NOTES

1. See Smirnova 1969, pp. 328–32.
2. For information, see Weber 1975, vol. 2.
3. In the late sixteenth and early seventeenth centuries, work-shops at the court of Emperor Rudolf II (1576–1612) in Prague became a meeting place for artists, including expert goldsmiths from northern Netherlands, France, and Germany. It was in Prague that the international Mannerist style was developed and solidified. For more information, see *Pragum* 1988–89; Tananaeva 1996.
4. According to the strict rules that existed in Nuremberg, a journeyman had to execute his masterpiece in the workshop under the supervision and control of a master. No one was supposed to help the applicant or even visit him, and at the end of the working day, the master would lock the work-shop for the night. A period of three months was set aside for the completion of the object, which was to be based on an example kept in the workshop, usually one made by a leading master. The journeyman was required to demonstrate a mastery of embossing, casting, and engraving (or etching) and the ability to use the technique known as *poinçon* and to apply durable gilding and, in some instances, cold enamel or colored lacquers. The result included all the sections of a standing cup and cover—the body, stem, and base, as well as the applied decorative elements, such as handles, decorative details of a vegetal nature, and figures. In the composition of an object, great importance was attached to the mastery of the techniques of mechanical reinforcement and fine soldering.
5. Wenzel Jamnitzer (1508–1585) was born in Austria at Weiner-Neustadt and received the title of master in 1534 in Nuremberg, where he became a renowned goldsmith, who, as his epitaph reads, "loyally served four German emperors, the king of France, the secular and spiritual princes of Italy, Germany, and his native city and guild." There is an extensive literature devoted to Jamnitzer; an important contribution to the study of his work is the catalogue for an exhibition held at the Germanisches Nationalmuseum, Nuremberg, in 1985 (see *Wenzel Jamnitzer* 1985).
6. See Markova 1980, pp. 91, 98, n. 17; Schürer 1985.
7. *Wenzel Jamnitzer* 1985, cat no. 460, p. 397, fig. on p. 398.
8. Kohlhaussen 1968, p. 355.
9. *Wenzel Jamnitzer* 1985, pp. 391, 392, cat. no. 431–35.
10. Zagorodnyaya 1998, p. 18.
11. Adelung 1846, pp. 262–63.
12. In 1647 Queen Christina originally presented to Tsar Alexei Mikhailovich four giant standing cups; three are now at the Kremlin Armory (MZ-515/1–2; MZ-516/1–2; MZ-517/1–2); the fourth—by Hans Reiff—was acquired, in 1931 by the Nationalmuseum, Stockholm (MZ 205/1931). See *Silverskatter* 1997, p. 206, no. 62). The Petzolt covered cup, offered in 1684, to Tsars Ivan V and Peter I, has the Kremlin Armory accession number MZ-518/1–2. It is illustrated in Böhm 1939, pl. xv, no. 8; *Schätze* 1991, pp. 116–18, no. 28.
13. The Palace of Facets was constructed in the years 1487–91 under the supervision of Italian architects on orders from Grand Duke Ivan III. Its name is derived from the white faceted stone of its facade, which faces Cathedral Square of the Moscow Kremlin.
14. These standing cups and covers, distinguished by their profiles and large size, are easily identified in the group of displayed silver recorded in the drawings and lithographs compiled in coronation albums from the nineteenth century.
15. The Merkel table centerpiece (Nuremberg, 1549), now at the Rijksmuseum in Amsterdam, is considered Wenzel Jamnitzer's earliest Renaissance work. It resembles a vase or bowl topped by a figure of Mother Earth standing among interwoven flowering grasses. From the center of the bowl rises an amphora with a tall bouquet of flowers and leaves (the overall height of the object is 39 inches). The work is published in *Wenzel Jamnitzer* 1985, cat. no. 15, pp. 219–21.
16. The sketch of the table fountain (c. 1555) by a silversmith from Jamnitzer's circle, as well as a sketch of a box of his own are published in *Wenzel Jamnitzer* 1985, p. 131, fig. 103, pp. 224–26, cat. nos. 19, 20. This type of object was not a new discovery or invention of late Renaissance Nuremberg but a continuation of the European goldsmiths' tradition. For example, scholars believe that the precious gilded and enameled table fountain was created in Burgundy in the late fourteenth century (see Link 1973, p. 73), and sketches of incense burners have been known since those of Dürer from about 1500.
17. In aristocratic homes, where forks were rarely used and food was often eaten with the fingers, it was considered in good taste to offer basins to guests during banquets and other formal meals to wash the hands when new dishes were served. It is believed that a ewer-and-basin set was the preferred gift for a princely newborn at receptions held during the week after his birth (see Seelig 1994, vol. 1, p. 35). Also found in lists of gifts in sixteenth-century Moscow are "basins" offered as "humble thanks. . . . [For] the Englishman Johnson, two gilded silver basins are indicated" (see *Sbornik* 1902, vol. 116, p. 259).
18. Quoted from Adelung 1846, p. 192. In a drawing by Erik Palmquist, a participant in the 1674 Swedish embassy, a ewer-and-basin set is shown on a small table at the right of the throne of Tsar Alexei Mikhailovich (see page 269).
19. Baklanova 1928, p. 85.
20. Examples are the basin with a centaur and nymph in the Armory and the ewer with the bust of a woman (Moscow Kremlin Armory, MZ-357, MZ-322). The former is reminiscent of a Florentine bronze of the same name by the sculptor Giambologna; the latter is related to a type of German drinking ewer that is made of solid stone and depicts bearded men.
21. The lion with a scepter in its right paw leaning on a shield introduces some heraldic symbolism, but the shield in question has not survived, so full interpretation is not possible.
22. Moscow Kremlin Armory, MZ-586.
23. Adelung 1846, p. 247.
24. Wilkins 1991, p. 166.
25. Smirnova 1984, pp. 221–25.
26. The book, which is in the Moscow Kremlin Armory (Kn-201), is referred to in short form as *On the Selection*.

27. There is extensive material on this topic in Bursche 1974.

28. Bowls for candies and sweets were used in very large numbers, and it was the custom to acquire them in large groups. For example, in preparation for the coronation of Queen Christina of Sweden in 1650, nineteen dozen dishes were purchased. At the same time we know of withdrawals from the Swedish royal treasury of many dozens of bowls for inclusion in the groups of ambassadorial gifts; about two dozen were given to Russian sovereigns by the Swedish throne in 1647, 1655, and 1674 (see Martin 1900/1, pp. 9–11, 13–15, 19–20).

29. The Armory has one other standing cup and cover on whose stem is a figure that also refers to Giambologna's sculpture (MZ-425/1–2). This is a work by another well-known Hamburg maker from the renowned Lambrecht dynasty—Hans Lambrecht III. The engravings of amorous couples on the bowl of this remarkable cup combines influences of the Nuremberg bell-shaped cup, Italian sculpture, and Dutch engravings (published in Schliemann 1985, vol. 1, p. 155, cat. no. 67; ill. in vol. 3, nos. 15–18).

30. Schliemann 1985, vol. 1, pp. 78–92; Olsen 1903, pp. 18, 20–21, 26, 29–30.

31. Moscow Kremlin Armory (MZ-533).

32. Moscow Kremlin Armory (MZ-653).

33. Moscow Kremlin Armory (MZ-638).

34. The relative scale of these pieces and the similarities in their decoration support the idea that they were intended as a unified set of formal tableware. The idea of a set in this and other instances represents a definite step in European goldsmithing toward its most striking manifestation—the full silver service, which was brilliantly realized in the eighteenth century. See also Mitchell 2000, p. 120.

35. "Rare tulips in the seventeenth century were so highly prized that their bulbs could be exchanged for a sumptuous carriage, two horses with harness, a small estate of twelve acres, or a mill" (Likhachev 1991, pp. 104–5). For more on the floral style, see Markova 1990, pp. 20–24).

36. It is not only Lutma's impressive works in museum collections that evoke our respect for this artist. Of major importance also is the fact that he was admired by the great genius Rembrandt, who painted his portrait.

37. The auricular style, based on the German word for "cartilage" or "ear," derives its name from the similarity of its component elements to the shape of the human ear. Motifs were further developed by two brother goldsmiths and draftsmen, Adam (1569–1627) and Paul (1570–1613) van Vianen of Utrecht. What is most important about these silver pieces is the unbroken integrity of their silhouette, the attractive manipulation of the metal, and the way in which

elements borrowed from both nature and abstract patterns merge and flow into one another. One encounters in these objects fantastic depictions of seashells, mollusks, crested waves and sea spray, coral branches, and anatomical parts of monsters and men. In 1620, Adam van Vianen created an album of drawings of models and ornaments for silver, *Modelli artificiosi*, in which he indicates that he executed most of these models himself. Adam's son, Christian van Vianen, engraved and published an album in London in 1650 with his own drawings.

38. See *Aurea Porta* 1997.

39. Moscow Kremlin Armory (MZ-188/1–3).

40. If one considers these objects in their role as ambassadorial gifts, one becomes aware of their reciprocal nature. Great Embassies generally brought to Moscow exceptionally rich gifts, and the silver pieces in them are distinguished by their grandeur and luxury. In the gifts from Poland, this idea is manifest in a gigantic basin, ewers, and flasks; in the gifts from Sweden it can be found in the large basins and multitiered fruit dishes with stands.

Reciprocal gifts usually surpassed the value of the gifts received but carried a different visual message. Moscow sent Russian furs and precious textiles (the latter often from the Near East), which were highly valued in the West. Thus, in 1649, "in March on the 9th d[ay] by a decree of our Sovereign Tsar and Grand Duke Alexei Mikhailovich of all Russia . . . there was sent from the ambassadorial office to . . . Queen Christina with the sovereign's great ambassadors as gifts . . . sables worth 1500 rubles" (Kologrivov 1911, p. 123). The sovereign was always presented with a detailed accounting as to the quality and value of the sables and fabrics selected for the gift: "With the great ambassadors Boris Ivanovich Pushkin and companions . . . 40 sables with tail value 250 rubles, 40 sables with tail, value 230 rubles, 40 sables with tail value 180 rubles, 40 sables with tail value 140 rubles . . . 4 forties of sables with tail, at 40 rubles apiece, and in them a sable without a tail, and all of this worth 1500 rubles" (Kologrivov 1911, p. 137).

41. The objects were not pure silver but silver with an added base metal. The content of silver in the alloy was 750, 875, or 900 parts per 1,000, or 750°, 875°, and 900°. The purity of the metal was guaranteed by an inspection mark that was placed on the finished item by an overseeing master or elder of the guild when the maker presented the item to him for inspection.

42. For more information, see Hernmarck 1951; Lightbown 1975; Lutman 1978; Seelig 1991.

43. Moscow Kremlin Armory (MZ-589, "swan" basin).

44. Silverstolpe 1996, p. 51.

THE COURT OF THE RUSSIAN TSAR

It is no accident that the title of the exhibition and this catalogue refers to the sixteenth century—even though ambassadorial gifts from that period are not represented in the Moscow Kremlin. Nor are they included in this book, in which the earliest diplomatic gifts date from the beginning of the seventeenth century. The sixteenth century, however, was a pivotal moment in Russian history because it significantly altered the country's position in the international arena. Three years before the century's midpoint, in 1547, Moscow's grand duke was crowned tsar, a title of imperial status, for the first time. This first Russian tsar was seventeen-year-old Ivan IV, subsequently dubbed "the Terrible" for the cruel and bloody acts associated with his reign. The new title of tsar he was given placed him on a par with the loftiest rulers of his day: the emperor of the Holy Roman Empire in Europe, the khans of Kazan, Astrakhan, and the Crimea, and the Ottoman sultan at Constantinople, who stood at the head of the largest and mightiest state of the day. Actually, by the 1550s, the khanates of Kazan and Astrakhan had lost their independence, having been taken over by the Russian state. In consequence, the Russian ruler claimed a higher position in the hierarchical structure of the day than the most important European kings: the English, French, Danish, Polish, and Swedish.

Detail of cat. no. 15

Such a substantial change in the Muscovite ruler's status demanded Moscow's transformation from the center of a grand duchy into the capital of a new kingdom. The development of a new, more lavish court ritual entailed the acquisition of the luxury and grandeur of European court cultures of the late Middle Ages and the Renaissance.

It is in this period that we find the first references to court workshops at the Moscow Kremlin, where the best artists of Russia as well as skilled foreign craftsmen labored and where works of the highest quality in icon painting, sculpture, gold and silver smithing, and precious embroidery were created that to this day are objects of pride and glory for Russian culture. A refined artistry of execution and elegance of shape and ornament distinguish the best works from the various workshops. These surviving fragments of the very rich material world of Russian court culture not only continue to delight us by their perfection and beauty, but they also tell us a great deal about the court of the Russian tsars, its customs and ceremonies, its traditions, and its relationships with the cultures of other countries and regions, whose influence is reflected in these objects made in Moscow.

The vivid descriptions of the Moscow court left us by many of the diplomatic emissaries and merchants who traveled to Moscow in the sixteenth and seventeenth centuries add new color to this intriguing picture. The reigning figure himself assumes the central position, and the extravagance of his regalia and ceremonial robes is frequently mentioned: "The tsar was sitting on . . . a throne. He was wearing a gold crown and surrounded by the richest porphyry. In his right hand he held a golden scepter studded with precious stones. This flash of splendor was sufficient to blind anyone."[1] The value of these testimonials is great, because portrait painting developed much later in Russia than in Western Europe, and we have only a very few depictions from which to form an image of the Russian tsars of the sixteenth and seventeenth centuries. Among their number are works by Western European artists who illustrated the written descriptions of their journeys through Muscovy. Stylized and idealized depictions of the princes and tsars appear in the frescoes of Kremlin churches and in icons (cat. no. 15). In the latter half of the seventeenth century, by a decree of Tsar Alexei Mikhailovich, a series of pictures of the Russian sovereigns illustrating the famous *Great Book of State*, or *Titulary* (see Chapter 4, fig. 1), was created in the Ambassadorial Office and Armory. This group of images played such an important role in court culture that over the following two centuries official historical portraits of Russian rulers were invariably based on the iconographic schemes of this ceremonial series or on similar pieces of Western European origin (cat. no. 21). Unfortunately, time is particularly merciless toward fabrics and allowed the survival of only a very few examples of the exquisite ceremonial raiment of the seventeenth century's Russian tsars even in the unique collection in the Moscow Kremlin. But two of these priceless objects connected with the names of the first tsar of the Romanov dynasty, Mikhail Fyodorovich, and his grandson, Tsar Peter I, are presented in this catalogue (cat. nos. 7, 16).

No less luxurious were the garments of the tsars' wives, also executed in sumptuous imported fabrics embroidered with precious stones and pearls. According to one foreigner, the tsarina's ceremonial dress left everyone quite breathless, since a tiny fraction of this magnificence would have sufficed to adorn ten sovereigns' wives. However, virtually no genuine garments and decorations of this type have survived that can be definitively ascribed to any of the Russian sovereigns apart from a few depictions from that time. This is probably owing to the status of women in Russian society and the role played by the Russian sovereign's wife in court life. That role, however, was not inflexible. Therefore, the rare depictions of sovereigns' wives in seventeenth-century Russian painting (cat. no. 15) are extremely valuable evidence and enable us to imagine not only what they looked like but also their stature at court.

We have many written descriptions of the tsar's palace, especially its arrangement and decor, to which all Russian rulers devoted so much attention. The first Russian tsar, Ivan IV, changed the appearance of the family church of his progenitors, the Muscovite grand dukes—the Cathedral of the Annunciation—by transforming it into a magnificent court cathedral, which became the ceremonial entry to the palace chambers from the ancient Cathedral Square inside the Kremlin. After one of the most terrible Moscow fires, which by sinister coincidence coincided with the year of Ivan IV's coronation and nearly destroyed Moscow, the newly crowned tsar re-created the cathedral's interior decoration. Charred frescoes were restored and new ones created, the iconostasis was restored and new icons were made for it. This may also have been the time when the precious faux-jasper stone floor and brass doors with pictures executed in gold overlay appeared. One of the tsar's final acts in redesigning his family church was to create a precious cover for the Gospel that lay on the altar of Annunciation Cathedral (cat no. 3)—one of the central objects of the cathedral's entire decor and function.

Another small icon from the Kremlin's Archangel Cathedral—"Saint Nicholas," which has a gold frame with images and ornamentation (cat. no. 4)—may also have been a gift from the tsar. This was one of the most venerated images in the cathedral. Later inventories of the cathedral note that the icon occupied a special place on one of the lecterns in front of the iconostasis. From the fourteenth to the early eighteenth century, Archangel Cathedral, which served as the burying place for Muscovite rulers, preserved quite a few donations from the tsars (cat. no. 14). Many of them were made in memory of the souls of the deceased parents of the ruling personages. Several other unique items in the exhibition are also connected with the cult of the veneration of ancestors (cat. nos. 2, 12, 13).

Foreigners' diaries mention not only the Kremlin churches, whose decor amazed visitors, but also the formal halls of the palace where the principal reception of ambassadors of various ranks took place. These descriptions of the palace frequently mention unusual objects that may have come to Moscow as ambassadorial gifts, such as royal plate and magnificent carpets. One report clearly conveys the impression produced by the tsar's wife's chamber. One of her guests wrote that the chamber was lined in pure gold and adorned with numerous birds and beasts fashioned out of precious metals. The chamber was illuminated by a chandelier in the form of a lion holding in its paw a coiled snake with gold lamps hanging from it.

Foreign guests were particularly overwhelmed by the abundance of magnificent precious vessels, many of them preserved in the Kremlin's museum, which has the richest collection of ancient Russian precious objects in the world. This catalogue includes several of the most interesting and evocative pieces in this collection (cat. nos. 1, 9–11, 17, 18). Some of them bear inscriptions executed in a special script with the sovereign's full ceremonial title (cat. nos. 1, 9–11), a rarely used method of writing his title, utilized only in acts of great international significance. Such gold vessels adorned with precious stones and pearls and bearing not only the title of the sovereign but also a depiction of the state's coat of arms—the imperial two-headed eagle—were a brilliant and precious sign of the wealth of the mighty sovereign's great power. We know that the tsar's full title enumer-

ated in detail all the lands under his authority, because an increase in the prince's holdings led to the length of his title. In the early sixteenth century, the title of Ivan IV's father—Grand Duke Vasily III—sometimes included the names of twenty-two of his holdings. But the title on the gold cup (charka) that belonged to him (cat. no. 1) mentions only six. The limited space on the vessel's lid probably forced the maker to condense some of the long list into the words "and sovereign of other [lands]." It is interesting, however, that the traditional naming of the grand duke's territories begins with the Vladimir, Moscow, and Novgorod grand duchies but is then followed by mention of Tver and finally by Smolensk. Frequently in the history of the Russian state, the ancient city of Smolensk found itself in the hands of neighboring Western rulers, and many times Moscow sovereigns won the city back again, each time noting this as a major military victory and significant political event in the nation's history. The reign of Vasily III was marked by just such a victory in 1514, which found its reflection the very next year in the grand duke's titles and in the creation of a gold vessel rare for that early period. Only two gold wine-tasting cups of Russian origin survive with the grand duke's new title that were executed before the middle of the sixteenth century. Thus a small, precious vessel may tell us not only about the refinement of the grand duke's court jewelers' work in the early sixteenth century, but also about significant events in Russia's history and about their commemoration in the objects of court culture in the Russian Middle Ages.

NOTE
1. Adams 1991, p. 39.

EAM

1. Cup (*charka*) of Grand Duke Vasily III

Russia (Moscow), Kremlin Workshops, 1515
Gold, pearl, niello, enamel
L. with handle 6¹/₂ in. (16.5 cm); h. 1¹/₄ in. (3.2 cm.)
MR-1155

In Old Russia, precious tableware was an extremely important component of the furnishings in the tsar's chambers. Magnificent gold and silver vessels were not only beautiful decorations, but they were also testimony to the wealth of the owner. Such objects were kept in cupboards or displayed on hanging shelves and on sideboards. The *charka*—a low, round cup with a horizontally soldered handle—was used in Old Russia from time immemorial for drinking alcoholic beverages.

This gold *charka* is the most venerable of all the wine-tasting cups in the Kremlin collection. On the inside of the cup is a circle on which the Russian coat of arms—the two-headed eagle—is executed in niello and adorned in the center with a pearl. Niello, an ancient technique in which a design incised in metal is filled with a black alloy, had been employed by Slavic craftsmen since at least the tenth century, but the technique flourished in Russia during the sixteenth century and can be found on many of the finest objects made in Moscow at this time. The handle is decorated with a stylized plant ornament in black enamel.

This cup originally belonged to Grand Duke Vasily III, the father of Ivan the Terrible, as indicated by the inscription around the vessel. Another inscription, which is engraved on the underside of the handle, relates how the wine-tasting cup was bought by the nun Marfa, mother of Tsar Mikhail Fyodorovich Romanov, and presented to her son at Easter in 1616. We do not know from whom she purchased the cup, nor can we even establish when or how it disappeared from the tsar's treasury, although this probably occurred in the early seventeenth century, during the so-called Time of Troubles, when Moscow was occupied by invaders and the tsar's treasury was looted. Surviving ancient documents speak eloquently of the multitude of precious items that vanished and fell into enemy hands, when they were either melted down or sold. The 1515 *charka* was one of the few objects that were returned safely to the tsar's treasury after the troubles. Later the cup was presented to a member of the church hierarchy and transferred from the tsar's treasury to the church's—the Patriarchal Sacristy—where it was carefully preserved for more than two centuries as an ancient princely relic.

SOURCES: Inventory 1923–25, fol. 14, no. 15174.
LITERATURE: Postnikova-Loseva 1954, p. 164, ill. 11; Bobrovnitskaya 1988, p. 66.

IAB

2. Pendant (*panagiia*)

Russia (Moscow), Kremlin Workshops,
first half of 16th century
Mother-of-pearl, silver, gilding
H. 7 in. (18 cm); w. 5⁷/₈ in. (15 cm)
DK-9

In sixteenth-century Russia, the word *panagiia*, used first in Byzantium to refer to a type of image of the Virgin Mary, was applied to a variety of objects, including small icons worn on the chest that were executed from various materials in a number of different techniques. Special vessels, also called *panagiias*, were used in a monastic ritual that had come to Russia from Byzantium and involved raising up the *panagiia* with the host (communion wafer) at the monks' dining table after the meal was served. This ritual was adopted in Old Russia by the courts of the metropolitans, the patriarchs, and the sovereigns. Sometimes small pieces of the host were taken on long journeys in small, round, two-chambered *panagiias*, which were for that reason called "traveling *panagiias*."

This large pendant is made of mother-of-pearl, a rare and precious material in Russian art of this period. It comes from the Annunciation Cathedral in the Moscow Kremlin—the family church of the Russian tsars. Unfortunately, the ancient inventories of the cathedral must have been destroyed during one of the many fires that occurred in medieval Moscow. Nevertheless, surviving cathedral inventories from the seventeenth century contain interesting testimonials to the *panagiia's* use in court rituals honoring ancestors of the tsar, during which it was brought into the special "requiem" chamber. This use may have determined the choice of material for the *panagiia*, since mother-of-pearl, which conveyed a number of meanings as a medieval symbol, was most often taken as a sign of the transitory nature of everything earthly.

Engraved on the outside of the *panagiia* are the Crucifixion and the church fathers St. John Chrysostom, Gregory the Theologian, and Basil the Great. Inside this *panagiia's* lids are bas-relief compositions traditional in this type of object: the Virgin Mother of the Sign (an annunciate Virgin with outstretched arms and the image of the incarnate Christ shown on her body) and the Old Testament Trinity. The latter subject combines the three angels who visited Abraham—an image regarded by the Eastern church as a prefiguration of the Holy Trinity—with the image of an incarnate Christ drawn in a chalice together with the angels, thereby relating them to the incarnation. Depicted around the Virgin Mother of the Sign are symbols of the evangelists, cherubim, and seraphim. The composition of the Trinity has an abundance of supplementary details, which is characteristic for Russian art of this period.

SOURCES: Inventory of objects for Annunciation Cathedral 1924, p. 19, no. 248; *Perepisnaio kniga Blagoveshchen skogo sobora*, 1873, p. 18.

LITERATURE: *Zoloto Kremlia* 1989, no. 15; *Das Gold* 1991, pp. 56–57, 198, no. 18; *The Gold* 1991, no. 18.

EAM

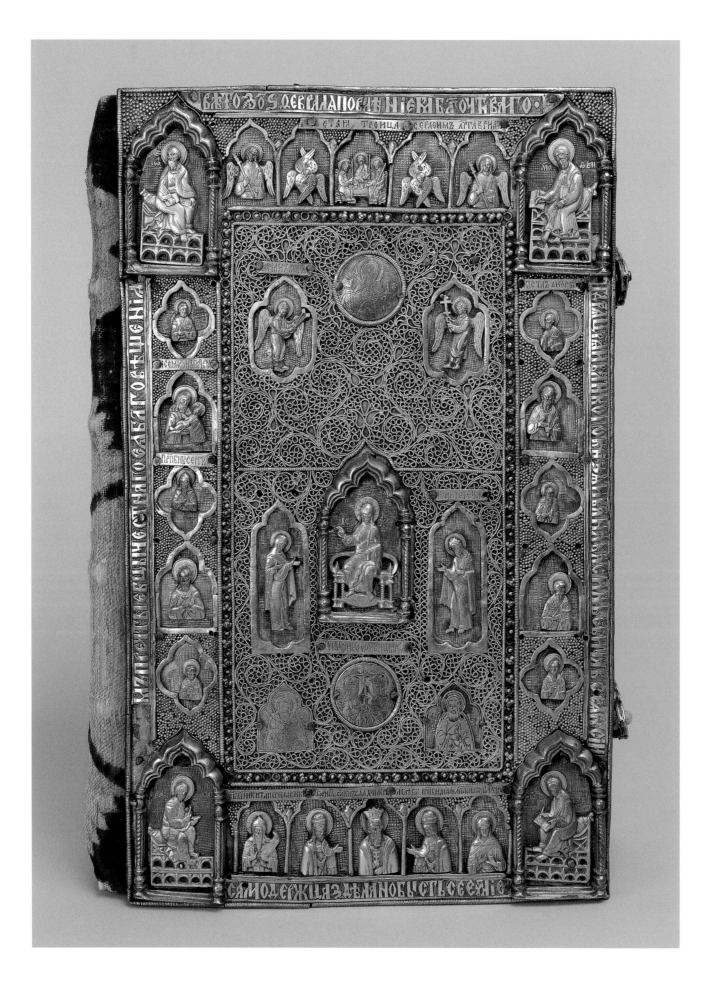

3. Gospel

Russia (Moscow), Kremlin Workshops, 1568
Silver, wood, paper, silk, gilding
H. 13 in. (33.5 cm); w. 8¹/₄ in. (21 cm)
Kn-33

In the Orthodox church, altar Gospels were typically decorated with precious covers. The Kremlin collection has several strikingly designed books of this type, one of which is presented here: an illuminated manuscript Gospel decorated with a gilded-silver filigree cover based on the Gospel cover given to the Troitsa-Sergiev Monastery outside Moscow in 1392 by the boyar Fyodor Koshka, one of the noblest figures of his day.

In accordance with Orthodox tradition, the figure of Christ is placed in the center of this 1568 cover, in this case sitting on the throne as the triumphant Savior, flanked by the Mother of God and John the Baptist. In the corners are traditional depictions of the four evangelists: Matthew, Mark, Luke, and John.

A characteristic feature of this cover's design, like that of its model, is the series of half-figures of saints placed around the perimeter of the book. The selection of saints, however, is different and may have been made, at least in part, at the initiative of the client—Tsar Ivan IV. This suggestion is supported by the presence on the cover of Anastasia Rimlianka, the patron saint of Anastasia Romanovna Zakharina-Yurieva, Ivan's first wife, who died in August 1560, nearly eight years before the cover was made. Chronicles referring to the "saintly Anastasia" claim that she "exhorted and guided Ivan to all manner of virtues." Many years after her death, Ivan is said to have remembered her with love and regret and made costly gifts to monasteries and churches in her memory, and this Gospel, which was given by the tsar to the Kremlin's Annunciation Cathedral, may have been such a memorial. It is worth noting that the father of Anastasia, Roman Yurievich, was descended from the Zakharin-Koshkin family, founded by the boyar Fyodor Koshka, whose 1392 Gospel cover served as the model for this example.

SOURCES: Inventory of objects for Annunciation Cathedral 1924, p. 24, no. 316.

LITERATURE: Postnikova-Loseva 1954, p. 196, ill. 36; Pisarskaya 1964, p. 100; Bobrovnitskaya 1988, p. 66.

IAB

4. Icon and Cover (*oklad*), "Saint Nicholas of Myra"

Icon: Russia (Moscow), c. 1600
Tempera on wood, cotton, chalk ground
Cover: Russia (Moscow), Kremlin Workshops, c. 1600
Gold, sapphires, tourmaline, pearls, niello
H. 9³/₈ in. (24 cm); w. 6 in. (15.5 cm)
Zh-563/1-2

This icon and its gold cover represent the highest level of painting and gold work in Moscow about 1600. The exquisitely made cover indicates that it must have been produced in the workshops of the Moscow Kremlin for some highly placed individual. Before entering the Armory collection, the icon was in the Cathedral of the Archangel Michael in Moscow.

The painted image combines the serious tone of the art produced during the reign of Tsar Ivan IV with the more decorative and refined artistic taste of the time of Fyodor I and Boris Godunov. The latter style is especially evident in the detailed rendering of the saint and his robe. Saint Nicholas of Myra was widely revered in Old Russia as the defender of those in trouble and a guardian of sailors and travelers.

This icon exemplifies both the precious religious objects that were an intrinsic part of life at the tsars' court and the fine craftsmanship characteristic of the best Russian metalwork of the period.

Five of the eight gold roundels on the frame depict figures generally shown on the iconostasis, or altar screen, of Orthodox churches: Christ enthroned, the Virgin Mary, John the Baptist, and the archangels Michael and Gabriel. The three roundels at the bottom are portraits of the church fathers Gregory the Theologian, John Chrysostom, and Basil the Great.

Although pearls and precious stones are used on the icon cover, the object is remarkable for its restraint, thanks to the use of niello. The figures on this icon are very much in the tradition of Byzantine art, but European influence is evident in the use of certain technical devices and in the artist's attempt to convey volume and a sense of space. The ornamentation on the gold work surrounding the icon reflects the lively arabesque forms that Russian jewelers borrowed directly from the East and from eastern-influenced designs of the European Renaissance.

SOURCES: Inventory of objects for Archangel Cathedral 1924, fol. 28v, no. 114.
LITERATURE: Bobrovnitskaya 1988, p. 64, ill. 35; *Zoloto Kremlia* 1989, no. 22.

MVM

5. Icon and Cover (*oklad*), "Virgin of Vladimir"

Icon: Russia, late 16th century
Tempera on wood
Cover: Russia (Moscow), Kremlin Workshops,
second half of 16th century
Wood, silver, turquoise, sapphires, pearls,
other precious stones, enamel, gilding
H. 14³/₄ in. (38 cm); w. 11¹/₈ in. (28.7 cm)
Zh-1764/1-2

In medieval Russia, icons were invariably found not only inside churches but in many secular buildings as well, from peasants' huts to the tsar's personal chambers. "Russians," wrote one foreign diplomat who visited the country in the early sixteenth century, "keep images in a place of honor in every home. When one of them pays a visit to another, he immediately bares his head upon entering the house and looks around, searching for the image. When he sees it, he makes the sign of the cross three times."[1]

One of the most common Russian icons was the Virgin of Vladimir, copied from the ancient Byzantine icon depicting the Virgin holding the infant Christ and pressing him close to her cheek. In Byzantium icons of this particular image with its vividly expressed emotional resonance were called "the Virgin of Tenderness." The Constantinople patriarch sent one of them as a gift to the Russian grand duke Yury Dolgoruky in the early twelfth century. In 1155, his son Andrei moved the icon to the city of Vladimir, where it acquired the name by which it is now known. In 1395 the icon, its reputation glorified by many miracles, was brought to Moscow, where it became a sacred object for all of Russia.

This Virgin of Vladimir icon is decorated with a precious cover, which, according to accepted tradition in Old Russia, refers back to the culture of Byzantium and expresses the special esteem in which this image was held. As with most other ancient Russian works in gilded silver, there are no marks or inscriptions on the cover indicating when or where it was made. A number of features in the cover decoration, however, such as the combination of filigree and enamel, the range of enamels from dark to light blue, the plant motifs in the

form of twisting stems of trefoil, enable us to say with certainty that it was made by jewelers in Moscow in the second half of the sixteenth century.

The artistic aspirations of the period are reflected in the selection and working of the semiprecious stones that adorn the cover. Predominant among them are turquoise and sapphire, which at the time were very popular in Moscow and especially among court silversmiths. More important than the beauty and rarity of these stones is the fact that they were invested with magical and symbolic power at the time; according to the Orthodox system of symbols, the shade of blue in the turquoise was considered the color of the Virgin Mary. As for the blue sapphire, Kremlin jewelers had preferred it since the time of Ivan IV, for the stone was said to have the property of "revealing treachery, dispelling fears." A mistrustful and suspicious man, Ivan IV was said to have given special significance to the sapphire, and his taste undoubtedly influenced the work of court artists during his reign and for some years afterward.

All the precious stones on the cover are cabochons ground into a convex shape. Although the first use of faceted semiprecious stones appeared in the sixteenth century, Russian jewelers continued to use unfaceted cabochons after that time, undoubtedly because they preserved the charm of natural stones and admirably suited prevailing taste.

NOTE
1. Herberstein 1988, p. 121.

SOURCES: Inventory 1927–30, fol. 16, no. 18477.

IAB

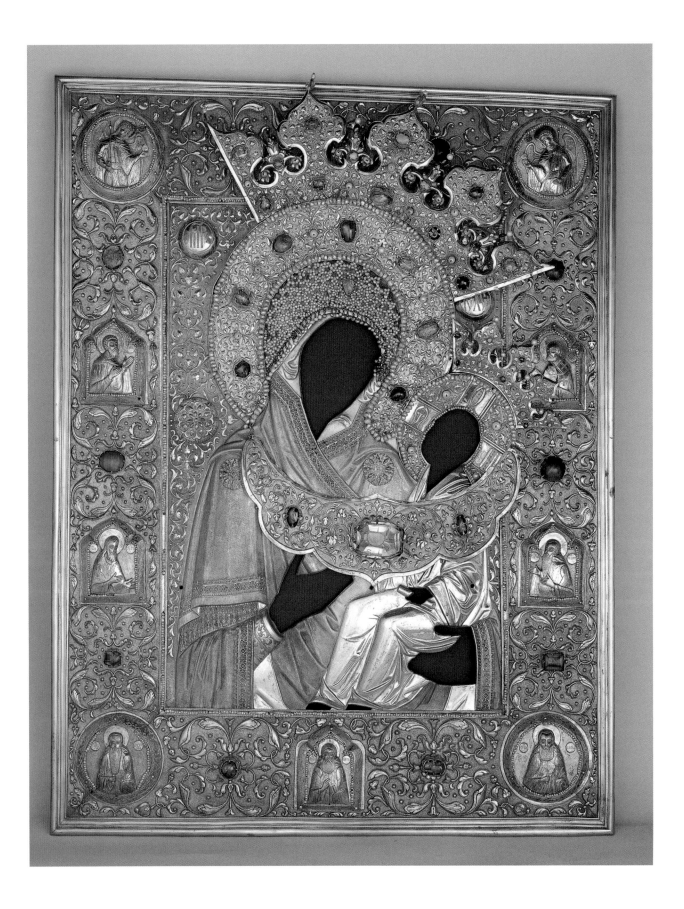

6. Icon Cover (*oklad*), "Virgin of Tikhvin"

Russia (Moscow), Kremlin Workshops,
early 17th century; robes: Russia, 19th century
Silver, pearls, sapphires, rubies, topaz,
other precious stones, gilding
H. 35¹/₂ in. (91 cm); w. 27⁵/₈ in. (71 cm)
MR-9016/1-6

This gilded-silver icon cover (*oklad*) is an outstanding example of the Russian jeweler's art of the early seventeenth century. The richness of the decoration and the variety of techniques to work precious metals are typical of the period. The beautifully rendered details—the supple drapery folds of the saints' clothing, the Virgin's pearl-embroidered head covering, the haloes, and the garlands and pendant decorated, like the frame, with an embossed plant motif—combine to create a splendid work that is aesthetically unified and distinguished by the mastery of its execution. The Virgin's halo and crown contain large sapphires and rubies weighing ninety and thirty carats respectively; two forty-carat sapphires and an enormous gilded topaz of seven hundred carats are set in the pendant.

On the frame (*riza*) of the cover are gilded-silver roundels with half-figures of saints in relief, among which the depiction of Saint Cyril (Kirill in Russian) is of special interest. Cyril lived in the latter half of the fourteenth century and the first quarter of the fifteenth. He was a literary figure and one of the best-educated men of his time. In his declining years, Cyril became a monk in the north of Russia, on White Lake (Beloye Ozero), where he founded a monastery that was eventually named after him. The Kirillo-Belozersky Monastery, the source of this precious cover, was widely known in Russia as a center of enlightenment and a guardian of Orthodox traditions.

At one time, this lavish *oklad* adorned a copy of the Virgin of Tikhvin, an icon much revered in Russia. The original icon of this image of the Virgin and Child, in which Mary's head inclines slightly toward Christ and her right hand extends toward him in a gesture of prayer, was believed in Old Russia to have been painted by Saint Luke the Evangelist. According to ancient legend, the Virgin of Tikhvin was of Byzantine origin and was brought in the late fourteenth century to the town of Tikhvin, located in Russia's northwest, hence its Russian name. There a church was dedicated to the icon, and, in the mid-sixteenth century, at the initiative of Tsar Ivan IV, the Tikhvin monastery was founded, where great miracles were said to have been performed by the icon. In 1613 it was credited with protecting the Tikhvin monastery, which helped to shelter inhabitants from the enemy during an invasion by the Swedes. Soon after this event, a holiday was established in honor of the miraculous icon, and many copies were made. It was in the presence of one of them that Russia concluded an important peace treaty with Sweden in 1617.

Icons of the Virgin of Tikhvin were very popular in Old Russia, and few churches did not have one in their collection. The revered icon was always considered a gift that bestowed merit and glory on its giver. It is quite possible that the Kirillo-Belozersky Virgin of Tikhvin icon was also a gift; if one can judge by the icon's precious cover, which was indisputably executed in Moscow, its donor may have been a member of the tsar's family.

SOURCES: Inventory 1927–30, fol. 16, no. 17667.
LITERATURE: *Russkoe serebro* 1984, p. 219, ill. 48; *Treasures of the Czars* 1995, p. 140.

IAB

7. Collar (*barma*) of Tsar Mikhail Fyodorovich

Russia (Moscow), Kremlin Workshops, 1629–45
Silk, metallic threads
Diam. around perimeter: 66⅞ in. (171.5 cm);
w. 8¾–10⅛ in. (22.5–24 cm)
TK-2858

Barmy were official attributes of the authority of the grand duke and later the tsar. This splendid example is made of a purple-gray satin, now faded, in a circular configuration with an opening where the collar closes over the left shoulder. The pattern consists of motifs of roundels and niches containing finely embroidered images of Muscovite prelates and saints, respectively.

In the central section are large medallions shaped like icon cases; in the top they are small and round. Embroidered in the icon-case medallions are full-length depictions of the saints that comprise the complete deisus—the icon composition depicting Christ in the center and the Virgin Mother, John the Baptist, and the saints turned toward him in a supplicatory stance—which is a traditional symbol of the idea of prayer and intervention. In the center Christ is on the throne, and turning toward him on either side are the Virgin and John the

Baptist along with the paired archangels Michael and Gabriel and the apostles Peter and Paul. In the eighth medallion is the most holy St. Michael Maleinos (c. 894–961), a patron saint of Tsar Mikhail Fyodorovich.

Embroidered in the small round medallions are half-length portraits of some of the Muscovite prelates, Metropolitans Peter, Alexei, and Iona, as well as the "fathers of the church"—Basil the Great, John Chrysotom, Gregory the Theologian, and Gregory Nissky. The eighth figure is Saint Alexis, man of God and protector of Tsarevich Alexei Mikhailovich, heir to the Russian throne.

Certain features, such as the saints' hands and faces, are emphasized by the use of light-colored silk floss, while the figures are outlined with a satin stitch of medium brown silk. Subtle details executed in red, blue, and green silk enliven the embroidered figures.

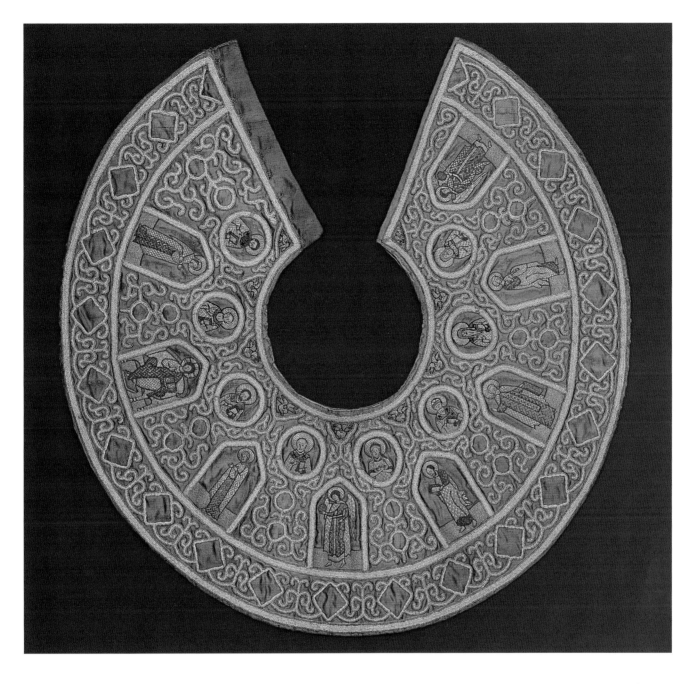

The niches and tracery surrounding the figures are embroidered with white silk, which suggests a plaited band that is then outlined with gold metallic threads. In its original form, the collar was also decorated with pearls and rhomboid metallic studs with stones that were set in an ornamental band along the lower edge. All the studs have been lost, and of the pearl design, only the backing of linen lacing to which the pearls were attached has survived.

The images on the collar indicate that it was made for Tsar Mikhail Fyodorovich. The venerable Mikhail Malein, the tsar's patron, among the saints in the deisus

series supports this conclusion. The inclusion of Saint Alexis, man of God, in whose honor the tsar's son and heir was named, narrows the collar's date to the period between the birth of Tsarevich Alexei and the death of Tsar Mikhail Fyodorovich, that is, between 1629 and 1645.

SOURCES: Inventory 1884, pt. 1, no. 77, tab. 23.
LITERATURE: *Schätze* 1991, pp. 82–84, no. 6; *Treasures of the Czars* 1995, p. 45.

IIV

8a,b. Ambassadorial Axes

Russia (Moscow), Kremlin Workshops, first half of 17th century
Damascus steel, silver, turquoise, gold, wood, gilding
a: overall l. 38¹/₄ in. (98 cm); l. of axe 15¹/₄ in. (38.5 cm);
w. of axe with head 10³/₄ in. (27.5 cm); b: overall l. 38³/₈ in.
(98.5 cm); l. of axe: 14⁷/₈ in. (38 cm);
w. of axe with head 11¹/₂ in. (29.5 cm)
OR-2238, OR-2239

The first reference to *ryndas*—bodyguards of the tsar who were armed with axes, or halberds—is in the mid-sixteenth century. These guard units consisted entirely of young men recruited from leading noble families. They escorted the tsar on his campaigns and journeys and also attended him at impressive, splendid court ceremonies. Armed with their ceremonial axes and dressed in white-and-cerise uniforms, the *ryndas* would line up on either side of the tsar's throne in what may originally have been a Byzantine tradition. (It is interesting to note that similar weapons were carried by bodyguards at the Turkish sultan's court.) In sixteenth- and early-seventeenth-century documents, these axes are called "golden" or "the tsar's."

The term "ambassadorial axe" relates to the fact that throughout the seventeenth century a guard of honor was a mandatory part of all ambassadorial ceremonies. Both Russian and Turkish ambassadorial axes are recorded in documents in the Kremlin Armory Chamber's archives. Identical in their function and construction, the axes differ somewhat in their date of manufacture and the form and nature of the heraldic depictions, although they were all styled after the traditional steel battle axe with a half-moon-shape blade, for many years one of the Russian infantry's principal weapons.

These two ceremonial axes, which were never intended for use as weapons, belong to a group of four axes made by masters of the Armory Chamber. The broad, crescent-shape blades are forged of Damascus steel and decorated with inlaid-gold foliage ornamentation. The axe heads are six-sided, the edges separated by narrow ridges that are embellished with a plant motif. The back edges of the crescent blades are cusped. A dou-

ble knob finial is located on the side of the central collar, opposite the base of the blade. This finial consists of an openwork sphere comprising eight hoops, alternately polished and damascened in gold. Joined to this is a second, smaller sphere, which is spirally fluted, with the surfaces of the fluted channels alternately polished and damascened in gold. The handle is wooden, covered in gilded silver and decorated with a stylized plant ornament in relief. The embossed lower section of the silver facing on the handle imitates the texture of leather.

The special status of these axes is underscored by the figural decoration: in a circular medallion on both sides of the center of the blade is an engraved gold Russian coat of arms—the double-headed eagle under three crowns. On one side of each blade the eagle holds a shield with a unicorn on it; on the other side is the emblem of the Grand Duke of Moscow, Saint George on horseback slaying the dragon with a spear. On both sides of the blades are lions executed in the same technique. We do not know exactly when the axes were made, but the style of the coat of arms is consistent with the first half of the seventeenth century. However, the presence of certain archaic elements—such as the combination of Moscow's coat of arms and the unicorn with the two-headed eagle—can also be found on the seal of Tsar Ivan IV (for whom the unicorn may have been a personal symbol), and the technique used to create the engraved gold foliage ornament also indicates an earlier origin. It is possible that these axes were made at the end of the sixteenth or the beginning of the seventeenth century, or that sixteenth-century axes served as the model. The presence of these axes in this catalogue is intended to evoke the ceremonial nature of the ambassadorial receptions at the Moscow Kremlin.

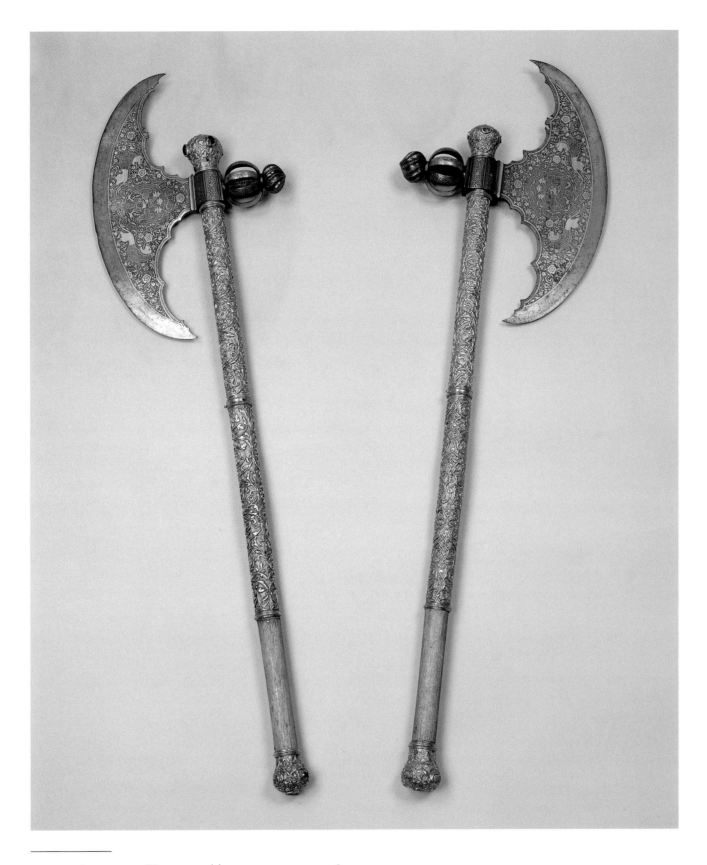

SOURCES: Inventory 1885, pt. 4, bk. 3, nos. 5275, 5276.
LITERATURE: *Schätze* 1991, pp. 194–95, no. 64; Levykin
1997, pp. 56–57; Skarby Kremla 1998, p. 104, no. 7.

AKL

The *kovsch*, notable for its beauty and the exceptional lavishness of its finish, was one of the characteristic types of early Russian vessel. Archaeological findings attest that there were such wooden dippers in Russia as early as the tenth and eleventh centuries. This is a purely Russian form, which goes back to the distant past. Drinking ladles first appeared in the north, where the many rivers and lakes were filled with wild ducks, geese, and swans and where wooden boats were built in the form of waterfowl. From the second millennium B.C. people of the region made small wooden ladles, which were later produced in gold and silver. Beginning in the sixteenth century, documents of the Moscow grand dukes frequently mention gold dippers that were bequeathed to their children. Naturally, only people of high birth had gold and silver objects adorned with precious stones and pearls.

This *kovsch* has a border with a niello-decorated inscription. Such dippers were rarely used for drinking and then only on special feast days. Most of the time they were displayed on special shelves as symbols of the owner's wealth.

At feasts Russians drank their favorite beverage, mead, from a dipper. Foreigners who visited Russia in the sixteenth and seventeenth centuries called mead "most wondrous and most delicious," comparing it with the renowned wine of Crete. Mead was traditionally prepared according to various recipes and was infused

9. Drinking Ladle (*kovsch*) of Tsar Mikhail Fyodorovich

Russia (Moscow), Kremlin Workshops, 1624
Makers: Tretyak Pestrikov and his son
(mentioned in documents of 1616–24)
Gold, rubies, sapphires, pearls, niello
H. with handle 5⅝ in. (14.5 cm); l. with handle
11½ in. (29.5 cm); w. 7⅞ in. (20.5 cm)
MR-4126

with berries and fruits, so that the results varied in color as well as taste. Red mead, an alcoholic drink similar to wine, was served in a gold *kovsch*, while white mead was served in silver. In the sixteenth century, Muscovite goldsmiths designed a special type of dipper—shallow and broad with a flat bottom.

This *kovsch*, which belonged to Tsar Mikhail Fyodorovich, is striking for the stern nobility of its form and the refinement of its decoration. The lip and handle are adorned with attached plates that bear fine niello design, and the niello inscription around the body, executed in a complicated script, contains the titles of the tsar. Such dippers, along with the regalia and other objects of court ceremony, were kept in the so-called Great Treasury. They were used during ceremonies in the reception hall of the Palace of Facets, where they also served as adornments for sideboards in order to impress visiting foreign dignitaries with the tsar's immense wealth and with the artistry and skill of Russian goldsmiths. Occasionally, mead was offered in dippers to especially important guests. Documents inform us that in 1671, during a dinner in the Moscow patriarch's Chamber of the Cross, the patriarch was served red mead in three "fancy dippers with pearls and precious stones."

SOURCES: Inventory 1884, pt. 2, bk. 1, no. 530.
LITERATURE: Uspensky 1912, no. 2, pp. 383, 384, no. 993; Postnikova-Loseva 1954, p. 161; *Tzaarien ajan aarteita* 1996, p. 8

MVM

10. Standing Cup (*kubok*) of Tsar Mikhail Fyodorovich

Russia (Moscow), Kremlin Workshops, 1628
Maker: Attributed to Jan Lent
(mentioned in documents of 1624–44)
Gold, precious stones, enamel
H. 6⅝ in. (17 cm); diam. 4½ in. (11.5 cm)
MR-1046

Standing cups were known in Old Russia from ancient times, with the earliest references appearing in chronicles of the twelfth century. During the sixteenth and seventeenth centuries, silver *kuboks* of Western European origin were quite common in the court of the Muscovite sovereign. They were frequently awarded by the rulers for services rendered; in addition, the beautiful vessels owned by the ruler served as decoration for sideboards in the formal rooms of the Kremlin.

Some examples of Russian-made standing cups date to the seventeenth century, including this elegant cup, which belonged to Tsar Mikhail Fyodorovich, as indicated by the inscription that encircles the vessel. The rim of the cup and the base of the pedestal are decorated with alternating transparent enamels; this decoration is augmented by precious stones, which intensify the brilliant colors of the object.

Archival documents suggest that this piece was made by Jan Lent, who worked in the Armory gold workshops of the Moscow Kremlin and participated in the creation of many outstanding works from the first half of the seventeenth century, including the tsar's ceremonial crown and weapon.

SOURCES: Inventory 1884, pt. 2, bk. 1, no. 535.
LITERATURE: *Drevnosti* 1849–53, vol. 5, p. 32, ill. 21; Zabelin 1853, p. 63; Postnikova-Loseva 1954, p. 177, ill. 23; *Treasures of the Czars* 1995, p. 133.

MVM

11. Loving Cup (*bratina*) of Tsar Mikhail Fyodorvich

Russia (Moscow), Kremlin Workshops,
first half of 17th century
Gold, silver, rubies, emeralds, sapphires, pearls, niello
H. 5³/4 in. (15 cm); diam. 3⁵/8 in. (9.3 cm)
MR-4188-1/2

Russians traditionally drank kvass and wine from loving cups, passing them around in a circle at the table. Among the loving cups that have survived in the Armory's uniquely large collection of Russian gold and silver objects are some very large spherical vessels, as well as some that are quite small. These were usually made in the shapes of common wooden and ceramic utensils. Vessels like this *bratina* were sometimes placed on graves filled with honey-sweetened water for the deceased. The shape of a loving cup is not as important as its decoration and the inscription around its rim,

which usually includes the name of the owner, along with some kind of exhortation.

This small, exquisite gold loving cup, decorated with multicolored precious stones, is a rare example of Old Russian secular tableware of the seventeenth century. Although such goblets existed in Russian life from early times, they were usually of Western European origin. In form, this goblet is reminiscent of a church chalice, or *potir*, although the traditional liturgical inscription has been replaced by the name of the tsar.

The loving cup was given to Tsar Mikhail Fyodorovich by the merchant brothers Sudovshchikov. The tsar later gave it to his wife, Evdokia Lukianovna, at which time the niello inscription of the cup's original donors was erased. Evidently, the tsar did not think the vessel's decoration sufficiently lavish, so he ordered a circle of pearls added to the cup, according to documentation in the tsar's archives.

The cup was made in the first half of the seventeenth century, but the somber, well-defined decoration, the combination of gold and niello, and the plant motifs are in a style related to that of the preceding century. The domed top crowns the smoothly rounded cup and is strikingly reminiscent of the gilded onion domes of Moscow's churches.

SOURCES: Inventory 1923–25, fol. 14, no. 15175.
LITERATURE: Trutovsky 1913, p. 39, ill. on p. 40; Postnikova-Loseva 1954, ill. 15; *L'URSS et la France* 1974, no. 532; Martynova 1988, p. 80, ill. 46; *Zoloto Kremlia* 1989, no. 35; *The Gold* 1991, no. 51.

MVM

12. Gospel

Printed text: Russia (Moscow), 1681
Watercolor with gold and silver
Cover: Russia (Moscow), Kremlin Workshops, 1668
Gold, silver, diamonds, rubies, emeralds, almandines,
amethysts, glass, niello, silk
H. 19¹/8 in. (49 cm); w. 11⁷/8 in. (30.5 cm)
Kn-12/1-2

The Gospel text is printed with color insets and initials, which adorn the eight miniatures depicting the apostles and their symbols, painted in watercolor with gold and silver. The striking cover, which was made by artists at the Kremlin, is remarkable for its severe elegance. Inside the roundels placed at the corners and in the central cartouche are pictures executed in niello of the Evangelists and the Crucifixion with the Virgin, Mary Magdalene, John the Theologian, and Longinus the Centurion standing in front of a scene of Jerusalem. The seventeenth-century artist has interpreted Jerusalem as a fantastic city with whimsical cupolas and towers. Russian jewelers, who achieved the highest artistry in niello engraving, used the technique widely on religious objects.

The niello roundels are framed with rows of round almandines, as are the borders, and large amethysts have been applied all over the cover. These amethysts are extraordinarily varied in shade, from deep violet to light lilac, and in combination with the dark red almandines, the velvety niello, and the gold, they contribute to the cover's astonishingly beautiful spectrum of colors.

The inscription on the Gospel cover establishes that it was executed at the behest of Tsar Alexei Mikhailovich and his wife, who donated it in 1668 to the Chudov Monastery in the Moscow Kremlin in memory of Anna Ilinichna Morozova, the tsarina's sister.

It is worth noting that this Gospel cover was created before the text was printed. Archival documents indicate that Gospel texts were often replaced when they wore out from frequent use. In this case, the replacement evidently occurred fairly quickly and for some reason unknown to us. Judging from the perfection of the facets of the amethysts that adorn the cover, they were added during the second half of the eighteenth century, when rich deposits of these stones were discovered in the Urals and amethysts became fashionable. Certainly this cover was originally adorned with colored stones, but in spite of the addition of the amethysts, the original seventeenth-century composition was preserved.

SOURCES: Inventory 1922, fol. 12, no. 13314.
LITERATURE: *Russische Schatzkunst* 1981, no. 23.

MVM

13. Censer (*kadilo*)

Russia (Moscow), Kremlin Workshops, 1676
Gold, silver, pearls
H. 12¹/8 in. (31 cm); w. 3⁵/8 in. (9.3 cm); l. of chains:
21¹/2 in. (55 cm)
MR-10547

The *kadilo*, an incense-burner suspended on chains, was traditionally used in many church services in Old Russia. In form, the censer often recalls the characteristic architecture of ancient Russian churches but in miniature, although it can also consist of two round bowls topped by a short drum with a round cupola topped off by a cross. Various techniques of the jeweler's art were used to decorate these vessels, but precious metals usually served as the basic material.

This gold and silver censer was made in the form of a single-dome church crowned with a figured cross. Its

lid is decorated with two rows of embossed wavy lines that come to a point, such as one sees along the roof-line of many Russian churches. In the middle is a drum with a smooth top, and on both the drum and the four-sided body of the censer are four openings from which smoke may escape. Attached at the midpoint of the cross are irregularly shaped pearls. On the front of the cross are carved depictions of Christ standing with a book in his hand and with cherubim and seraphim on either side. Pictured on the back of the cross are an eight-pointed cross, a cave with the skull of Adam, and symbols of Christ's passion (a flail and spears), all accompanied by appropriate inscriptions and letters. In the center of the round plate is an embossed, eight-petaled gold rosette with a ring to which five chains of round links are attached. Under the censer's four-sided body there is a smooth sphere with eight embossed protrusions. The rim of the base, echoing these forms, is slightly concave. In the circles on the base is a carved inscription indicating that the censer was made under the aegis of Stefan, Archbishop of Suzdal. Running along the censer's smooth polished sides, above and below, as well as along the lower edge of the lid, is a carved inscription on a hatched background saying that Tsar Fyodor Alexeyevich donated the censer to the Church of the Virgin in Suzdal in 1676, in memory of his father, Tsar Alexei Mikhailovich. The censer was returned from Suzdal to the Kremlin treasury in 1931.

SOURCES: Inventory 1914–30s, fol. 17, no. 19161.
LITERATURE: *Russkoe zoloto* 1987, p. 199, no. 49, ill. on p. 73.

AIR

14. Altar Cross

Russia (Moscow), Kremlin Workshops, 1677
Gold, diamonds, rubies, emeralds,
other precious stones, pearls, niello
H. 14⅝ in. (37.5 cm); w. 7¾ in. (20 cm)
MR-4228

Crosses of this type are always kept on the church altar, hence the name. In the Middle Ages, a small fragment of the cross of Golgotha, on which Christ was crucified, was inserted into altar crosses, but from the fifteenth to the seventeenth century, saints' relics were usually inserted instead. This gold cross is a typical Russian altar cross, a vertical shaft with two horizontal bars representing the concept of a triune God. The traditional image of the crucified Christ is at the center.

This altar cross combines gold, precious stones, pearls, and niello to striking effect. It was made, as the inscription attests, at the command of Tsar Fyodor Alexeyevich, the older brother of Peter I, who assumed the throne at the age of fourteen and ruled with his brother for six short years before his death, was a deeply religious youth who made frequent lavish donations to churches, monasteries, and cathedrals. These gifts were usually precious liturgical objects such as Gospel covers encrusted with gems and splendid crosses. This sumptuous example was made in his father's honor and donated to Archangel Cathedral in the Moscow Kremlin, the necropolis for Russian sovereigns for several centuries until Tsar Peter moved his court to St. Petersburg. Similar crosses were used on the altars of virtually every church in Russia.

SOURCES: Inventory 1922, fol. 13, no. 13541.
LITERATURE: Snegirev 1842–45, p. 79.

MVM

15. Icon, "Worship of the Cross"

Russia (Moscow), 1676–81
Attributed to Ivan Saltanov (Saltanyants)
Tempera, oil, colored lacquers on canvas
H. 49¹/₈ in. (126 cm); w. 35 in. (90 cm)
Zh-1714

This icon comes from the Church of the Crucifixion in the Terem Palace of the Moscow Kremlin. It was probably made by the court painter, Ivan Saltanov, an Armenian Christian who came to Russia from Turkey and soon converted to Eastern Orthodoxy, a requirement for obtaining church commissions in Russia. Like many other Armenian artists, Saltanov had studied with Italian masters and was familiar with Western European painting. Because he designed interiors as well as painting icons, the artist often painted on canvas rather than wood.

The composition centers on a cross in front of which the Emperor Constantine and his wife, Helen, stand in prayer. Both figures wear crowns and royal garments luxuriously adorned with pearls. In depicting this traditional subject, the artist has introduced images of his own contemporaries, Tsar Alexei Mikhailovich and his wife, Maria Ilinichna, who are also wearing crowns and royal garments embroidered with pearls. All four royal personages are identified by inscriptions. Below the picture of Tsar Alexei Mikhailovich is a high-ranking clergyman in full vestments, and although there is no inscription over this figure, a number of details point to its being Patriarch Nikon.

Instead of the traditional cross of Golgotha, the artist has painted a fairly accurate description of the cross acquired in Palestine at the request of Patriarch Nikon and given on August 1, 1656, to the Monastery of the Cross on Kii Island, which he had founded.[1] This cross, allegedly made in the same dimensions as Christ's cross, contained more than three hundred relics of Russian saints (Alexander Nevsky, Savva Storozhevsky, Evfimy of Suzdal, Ioann of Novgorod, and others), as well as other saints (including Anthony the Great, John of Damascus, and Theodore of the Sinai). The saints' names on the icon correspond to the genuine relics on the cross itself. The eight-pointed stars with inscriptions designate the places where stones brought from the Holy Land were placed on the actual cross—one from the mountain where Christ fasted, another from the grave of the Virgin Mary, and others.

It is believed that Saltanov was commissioned to paint this icon by the sister of Tsar Alexei Mikhailovich, Tsarevna Tatiana Mikhailovna, who was an admirer of the by-then-disgraced Patriarch Nikon. Its probable date suggests that it may also have been intended as a memorial to Tsar Alexei, who died in 1676. Maria had died in 1669.

NOTE
1. In the Soviet era, the Kii cross of Patriarch Nikon was kept at the State Historical Museum. In 1991 it was returned to the Patriarchate and is now kept in the Church of Saint Sergei in Krapivniii, Moscow.

SOURCES: Inventory of objects for Cathedral of the Dormition 1924, p. 42, no. 46.
LITERATURE: Uspensky 1907, p. 86; Posternak 1988, pp. 47–60.

NVB

16. State Robe (*platno*) of Tsar Peter I (the Great)

Russia (Moscow), Kremlin Workshops, late 17th century
Silk, metallic threads
L. 61 5/8 in. (158 cm); l. of sleeve: 20 1/8 in. (52 cm);
circ. of hem: 148 1/4 in. (380 cm)
TK-2849

The *platno* is a royal ceremonial robe worn at important events, such as coronations, major holiday appearances, and the reception of foreign ambassadors. The term *platno* first appears in the Kremlin inventories in 1628 referring to a type of robe in the tsar's wardrobe that would remain the most solemn royal ceremonial garment until the late seventeenth century. This state robe and another in the Armory's collection made of the same fabric (TK-2848) were probably the last made in this style, since Tsar Peter adopted western dress shortly afterward. The use of imported brocade whose predominant color was gold was no coincidence, since gold had from ancient times been the traditional symbol of royal power, the mark of wealth and might. The cut of the robe is directly related to that of the dalmatic, the ceremonial robe of Byzantine emperors.

The state robes of Tsar Peter I were made of seventeenth-century Venetian brocade, which was called *axamite* in Old Russia. The fabric consists of a red-silk ground with strips of gold selectively woven into the surface to create the lively and sumptuous pattern. According to documents, this state robe was once adorned with gold buttons set with emeralds and ruby chips, metallic lace, and a rich sable trim. Of the original luxurious embellishments, only the seventeenth-century European metallic lace along the hem, sleeves, and front has been preserved.

State robes did not traditionally reach the floor, which made it possible for onlookers to see a tsar's richly decorated ceremonial footwear. The length of this robe enables us to picture the young Peter, who was unusually tall at 6 feet, 7 1/2 inches.

Indirect evidence indicates that these state robes of Tsar Peter I were fashioned in 1691 from a ceremonial garment originally worn by his father, Tsar Alexei Mikhailovich.

SOURCES: Inventory 1884, pt. 1, pp. 73–74, no. 134.
LITERATURE: Schätze 1991, pp. 82–84, no. 6; *Treasures of the Czars* 1995, p. 44; *Petr Velikii i Moskva* 1998, pp. 22-23, no. 4.

IIV

17. Covered Cup (*stavka*) of Tsarevna Sofia Alexeyevna

Russia (Moscow), Kremlin Workshops, 1685
Makers: Mikhail Mikhailov (mentioned in documents
of 1664–85) and Andrei Pavlov
(mentioned in documents of 1663–85)
Silver, niello, gilding
H. 4³/₄ in. (12.2 cm); diam. 4³/₄ in. (12.2 cm)
MR-1771/1-2

One type of early Russian vessel was a small cylindrical covered cup called a *stavka*. The purpose of this piece has never been determined precisely, but we do know that wooden cups of this shape were designed to hold liquids and were widely used in monasteries, where there was a saying: "as many elders as *stavkas*." Silver *stavkas* were intended for daily use by the tsar and the boyars, who apparently used them for dessert.

Niello, important for centuries in Russian metalwork, reached new levels of brilliance during the second half of the seventeenth century. The development of the technique was owed to the presence in Moscow of two Greek jewelers who came from Constantinople in 1662. Called Constantin Manuilov and Filipp Pavlov in Russia, they obtained the permission of Tsar Alexei to open a workshop. Their exacting technique employed a sulfurous alloy of copper, silver, and lead to obtain velvety-black backgrounds.

There is no date or maker's name on this cup, but archival documents have helped us establish that it was made in 1685 by the Kremlin jewelers Mikhail Mikhailov and Andrei Pavlov. The cup is decorated with a running floral pattern interspersed with scrolled leaves. The design was created in niello, with gold engraved images set against a dark background of tarnished silver. Typical of the Moscow Kremlin Workshop designs at the end of the seventeenth century, this cup reveals the influence of Eastern art. Contemporary documents use the term *turskaia chern* (Turkish niello) to describe the work of a Moscow master. It is not clear, however, whether the term designates a style of design or the composition of the niello alloy itself.

Circling the cup in rectangular areas is a carved inscription with the title of its owner, Tsarevna Sofia Alexeyevna, the older sister of the tsareviches Ivan and Peter who served as regent during the early years of the dual reign of the two brothers.

SOURCES: Inventory 1885, pt. 2, bk. 2, no. 2089.
LITERATURE: Postnikova-Loseva 1954, p. 178, ill. 24; Martynova 1988, p. 92, ill. 58; *Treasures* 1979, no. 41; *Trésors* 1979, no. 16; *Tesoros* 1982, no. 32; *Tesori del Cremlino* 1982, no. 32; *Trezori* 1985, no. 94; *Treasures from the Museums* 1988, no. 24; *Zoloto Kremlia* 1989, no. 37; *Das Gold* 1991, no. 53.

MVM

18. Beaker (stakan)

Russia (Moscow), Kremlin Workshops,
second half of 17th century
Silver, gilding, niello
H. 9 in. (23.2 cm); diam. 6 in. (15.5 cm)
MR-1770

This tall, graduated *stakan*, or drinking vessel, represents a type widely used in Old Russia and known from manuscript illustrations dating to the fourteenth century. The niello ornamentation on this typical seventeenth-century example, one of the finest *stakans* in the world, includes leafy fruit-bearing vines that occasionally form rings shaped like cartouches. Perched among the vines are large birds that look down on a galloping unicorn, a popular image on wedding gifts.

The decoration of the beaker reveals the influence of European ornamentation, which is manifested not so much by the character of the plant motif but by the clear, disciplined arrangement of the decoration, which is atypical of Russian silversmiths.

SOURCES: Inventory 1885, pt. 2, bk. 2, no. 1594.
LITERATURE: *Schätze* 1991, pp. 150–51, no. 43; *Treasures of the Tsar* 1995, no. 33, pp. 146–47.

MVM

19. Pendant (panagiia)

Russia (Moscow), Kremlin Workshops,
second half of 17th century
Gold, silver, precious stones, pearls, enamel
L. 4⁵⁄₈ in. (12 cm); w. 3¹⁄₈ in. (8 cm)
MR-1856/1–2

Before the sixteenth century, Russian *panagiias* usually consisted of two joined round lids, but later their appearance changed somewhat (see cat. no. 2). This *panagiia* is of a ceremonial type and belonged to a member of the higher clergy. In the center of the pendant is a medallion with a relief depicting Christ Enthroned. The throne is colored with transparent and opaque enamels and includes colorfully painted herbs and flowers. Vivid precious stones create a glittering frame around the medallion, and hanging pearls add to the artistic perfection of the piece.

The art of enameling precious metals reached a high level of complexity and refinement in seventeenth-century Russia. This work suggests the brilliant technical achievements of Russian artists working in this medium at this time. The pendant opens from the back to reveal a place for holding pieces of the host (the communion wafer). There is an enamel depiction on the pendant's back cover of Virgin and Child seated on a throne.

SOURCES: Inventory 1930s, fol. 18, no. 20488.
LITERATURE: Martynova 1973, p. 22, ill. 22; Pisarskaya, Platonova, and Ulyanova 1974, p. 100, ill. on p. 101.

MVM

20. Church Vestment (*sakkos*) of Patriarch Adrian

Russia (Moscow), Kremlin Workshops, 17th century
Silk, metallic threads, pearls, silver
Embroidery: Russia (Moscow),
Kremlin Embroidery Workshop, 17th century
L. 52⅝ in. (135 cm)
TK-16

The *sakkos*, a long garment left unsewn at the sides and with a round yoke at the neck, is the most prestigious type of Russian patriarchal vestment. Its historical prototype was a ceremonial garment worn by Byzantine emperors. In seventeenth-century Russia, only the patriarch as head of the Russian church residing in the Moscow Kremlin possessed the right to perform divine service wearing a *sakkos*.

The execution of a *sakkos* was a significant undertaking. Only the most expensive fabrics were selected, and the ornamentation was distinguished by the richness of the materials used and the unusually high degree of artistry in the embroidery. Gold thread, pearls, precious stones, and appliquéd elements of gold and silver would be used to decorate the yoke, the frontlet, the cuffs and hem, and the borders along the sides, all parts of the vestment that had important symbolic meaning. After a patriarch's death, his church vestments would become the property of the Russian church and would be transferred to the Patriarchal Vestry.

The *sakkos* of Patriarch Adrian is made of imported seventeenth-century Italian cut-and-voided velvet of the highest quality. The extravagant use of gold in the form of flat strips woven into the voided ground and as looped gold threads, or *bouclé*, in raised areas of the pattern, makes this an exceptionally valuable and very beautiful garment. The fabric's large-scale pattern consists of intertwining vines, rendered in orange and green silk, that frame stylized floral motifs (reminiscent of the pomegranate motifs often seen in earlier brocaded velvets from the Italian Renaissance). The vestment's yoke, frontlet, cuffs, and hem are made of red velvet decorated with two-headed eagles (symbolic of the tsar),

unicorns, and horns of plenty embroidered in gold thread and embellished with numerous small and medium-sized pearls and embossed silver balls.

We know from documents that this *sakkos* of Patriarch Adrian was refashioned in 1691 from the state robe (*platno*) that Tsar Alexei Mikhailovich had worn during the celebration of Christmas in the Kremlin's Cathedral of the Annunciation in 1670. When the robe was made into a church vestment, the pearl embroidery with unicorns and double-headed eagles was preserved from the earlier garment.

SOURCES: Inventory 1922, doc. 13, no. 12019.
LITERATURE: *Treasures* 1979, p. 202, no. 88; Terekhova 1988, p. 313, ill. 217; 1990, pp. 313–14; *Petr Velikii i Moskva* 1998, pp. 120–21, no. 265.

IIV

21. Portrait of Tsar Alexei Mikhailovich

Unknown Russian artist
Russia, second quarter of 19th century
Oil on canvas
H. 62⅝ in. (160.5 cm); w. 46⅞ in. (120.3 cm)
Zh-2017

This nineteenth-century portrait of Tsar Alexei Mikhailovich, who wears a crown and state robe with collar and carries a scepter in his right hand, is based on a portrait by an unknown, possibly Western European, artist, painted no later than 1670.[1] This version of the portrait adds several elements to the prototype: an official document (whose text has not been preserved) in Alexei Mikhailovich's left hand and a table covered with books, alluding to the monarch's role as lawmaker, an important aspect of his reign as viewed by his successors.

The formal image of the tsar as developed by the early Romanovs, a favorite subject of court art, was used to demonstrate to the public the grandeur of Russia's crowned heads and the prestige of their realm. During Alexei's reign, the tsar's image was used as an official state representation. Political etiquette dictated that certain aspects of the portrait express the splendid ceremonial ritual with which Alexei Mikhailovich loved to surround himself and which reached its highest level during his reign. To his contemporaries, the image of the tsar in this seventeenth-century format and its carefully selected array of state regalia served as an embodiment of the sovereign (see frontispiece).

In the eighteenth and nineteenth centuries, the copying of old portraits took on a new significance. Replicas became part of the many dynastic portrait series that played an important role in furnishing the formal interiors of the tsar's palaces and of embassies, public buildings, and homes of the nobility. Along with other paintings of members of the Romanov dynasty, this portrait of Alexei was probably produced for the new Kremlin Armory during the second quarter of the nineteenth century, when extensive portrait collections were created in order to educate the public and in response to the Romanov desire to suggest the long and impressive history of Russia's rulers.

The genealogical aspect of these series of portraits reflects Romanov attitudes that date back to the time of Tsar Alexei, for it was in the early 1670s that the principal royal genealogies were written at the Moscow court. They owed their provenance largely to a general European royal and aristocratic practice. Alexei Mikhailovich had decreed that several copies of a *Great Book of State*, or *Titulary*, be compiled under the supervision of the nobleman Artamon Sergeyevich Matveyev. The very first *Titulary* to be compiled (1671–72) was the largest in format, and the tsar ordered that it be handed over to the Ambassadorial Office for safekeeping and use.[2] In addition to the text, which was the same for all these books, this copy of the *Titulary* included thirteen portraits of Russian grand dukes and tsars, from Riurik to Alexei Mikhailovich, along with many other portraits. In 1673–74, the compilers of the *Titulary*—the Romanian translator Nikolai Spafary and the scribe Peter Dolgovo in the Ambassadorial Office—composed another historical work: a *Vasiliologion*, which is an enumeration or description of the "rulers who were the most valiant from the beginning of the world until the present time."[3]

Lavrenty Khurelich, a court advisor to Emperor Leopold I and a herald of the Holy Roman Empire, was carrying out a state order in Vienna in 1673 when he compiled the *Genealogy of the Most Illustrious and Most Magnificent Grand Dukes of Moscow and the Most Invincible of Monarchs of All the Rest of Russia*. The next year, the Latin

original was sent to Moscow, where in 1675 the tsar ordered a translation of it into Russian and the production of a ceremonial copy.[4] The book concludes with a formal portrait of Tsar Alexei Mikhailovich in royal regalia that is similar in type to the portrait shown here. However, that portrait is set in a frame made up of military attributes—fittings that demonstrate the military power of the Russian tsar and underscore the victorious nature of his rule. The portrait is accompanied by a Latin device: "Munde Prudentia Rectrix" (The ruler of the world is reason).

NOTES

1. The earlier version was reproduced as an engraving by Meisens for publication in Gualdo Priorato, 1670–74.
2. The original of the first ceremonial copy of the *Titulary* is now in Moscow in the Russian State Archive of Ancient Documents (see Archive of Charters and Manuscripts, coll. 135, sec. V, cat. III, no. 7). In 1903 the St. Petersburg Archaeological Institute published all the pictures in the Moscow Archive's *Titulary* as full-size reproductions, some of them as color lithographs, as *Portrety, gerby i pechati Bol'shoi Gosudarstvennoi knigi* (Portraits, Coats of Arms, and Seals from the *Great Book of State*).
3. The title of the manuscript is based on the Greek word for "emperor." The original *Vasiliologion* is kept in Moscow in the Russian State Archive of Ancient Documents (see Archive of Charters and Manuscripts, coll. 135, sec. V, cat. II, no. 44).
4. The Latin original of Lavrenty Khurelich's *Genealogy* and the ceremonial copy of the Russian translation are kept in Moscow in the Russian State Archive of Ancient Documents (see Archive of Charters and Manuscripts, coll. 135, sec. V, cat. II, nos. 25, 26).

SOURCES: Inventory 1884, pt. 2, bk. 3, no. 3774.

VGC

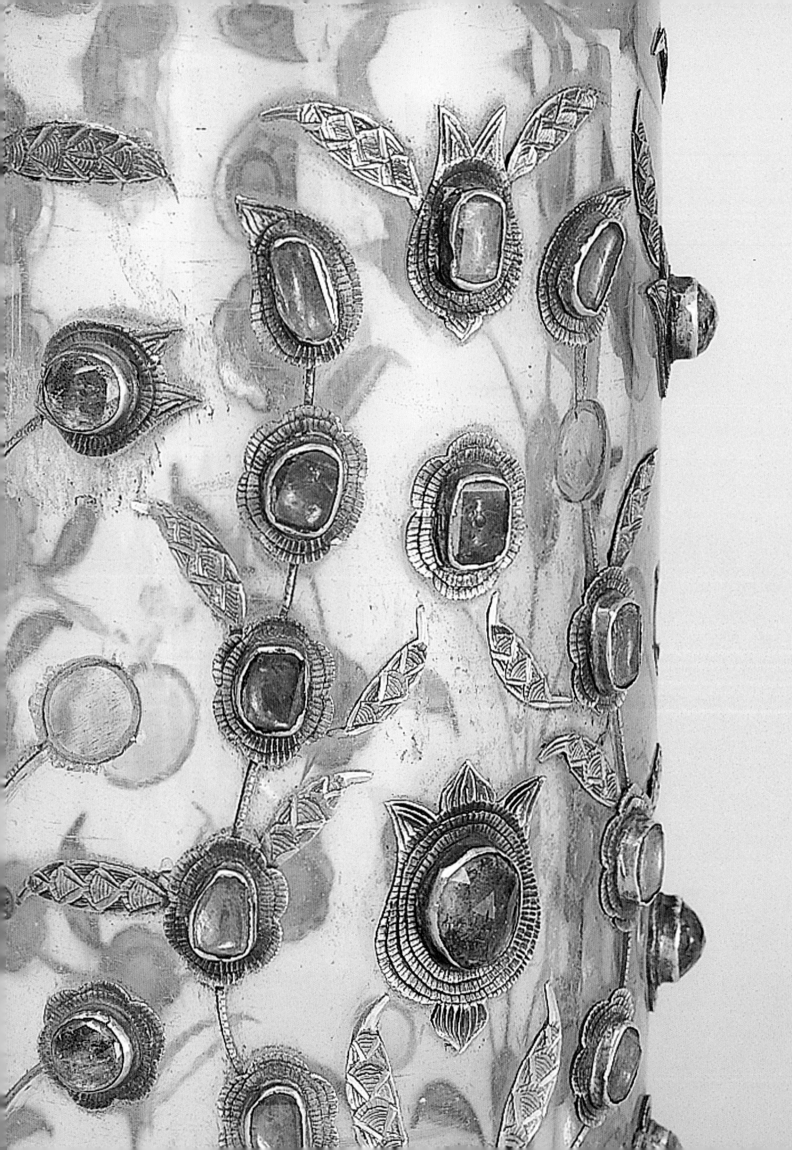

GIFTS FROM THE CHRISTIAN EAST

Ties with the many Christian centers that found themselves part of a huge Muslim state—the Ottoman Empire—after the fall of Constantinople in 1453 occupied a special place in the system of Russia's international relations in the second half of the sixteenth and seventeenth centuries. It was during this period that the Ottoman Empire reached its maximum extent, including not only what is now modern Turkey but the Holy Land and the entire Balkan peninsula, part of North Africa, Mesopotamia, and many other lands as well. The Ecumenical Patriarchs and the Orthodox monasteries and churches suffered to a greater or lesser degree and entered a difficult and protracted phase of existence under the Turkish sultans. Over this century and a half, the complex and multifaceted relations between the Christian East and Russia changed, and their history is marked by many highlights.

In 1561, only thirteen years after his coronation, the first Russian tsar, Ivan IV (the Terrible), celebrated the supreme joy of receiving a long-awaited deed from the Ecumenical Patriarchs of Constantinople, Antioch, Alexandria and elsewhere, confirming the legitimacy of his lofty new title. And by the first half of the next century, the first tsar of the Romanov dynasty, Mikhail Fyodorovich, was already looked upon by the heads of the ancient Eastern churches as their chief defender and

patron to whom they owed the miraculous preservation of Christianity in the East—a miracle that a document brought in 1644 from the Constantinople Patriarch Parpheny compared to the prophet Daniel's miraculous experience in the lion's den. In 1589, the Russian church became one of the Orthodox churches headed by its own patriarch. All the Eastern patriarchs visited Moscow during the reign of Tsar Alexei Mikhailovich.

The number of different embassies that came to Moscow from the Christian East increased steadily from the time of Ivan IV, reaching such proportions that in the seventeenth century this mighty flow had to be strictly regulated. One of the embassies' principal aims was to secure material assistance from the powerful Russian tsar. The amounts of assistance also increased during this period, thanks to which impoverished churches and cloisters were able to cope with all the calamities, natural disasters, and adversities that befell them. To this day, some of these churches still have the valuable gifts made to them by the Russian tsars.

Several of the gifts sent to Moscow from various centers of the Christian East have been preserved as well. Particularly valuable among them are the Christian relics and sacred objects that had survived in the Holy Land and Constantinople, on Mount Athos and Mount Sinai, and in the holdings of the Eastern patriarchs and metropolitans. Thus, in 1589, Constantinople Patriarch Jeremiah, who was in Moscow for the installation of the first Russian patriarch, Iov, brought Tsar Fyodor Ivanovich a silver reliquary with remains of the sainted Roman emperor, Constantine the Great. This gift undoubtedly represented a supreme blessing and was an especially suitable gift inasmuch as, since the second half of the fifteenth century, Muscovite rulers had appropriated the proud name of "the new Constantine," likening their acts to the deeds of the great emperor and their capital, Moscow, to Constantinople, which had been founded by Emperor Constantine, and then to Rome, the first capital of the great Roman Empire. The Russian tsar kept in the Kremlin's Cathedral of the Annunciation an unusually varied and rich collection of Christian relics, following in the tradition of the Byzantine emperors. Many of these objects had been gifts in the sixteenth and seventeenth centuries from embassies from the Christian East. An equally valuable collection was owned by the Russian patriarchs, some of whom were particularly renowned not only for collecting holy relics but also for their attempts to reconstruct in Russia impressive evocations of the most important Christian holy sites. The best-known and most important of such efforts was Patriarch Nikon's construction of New Jerusalem near Moscow in the mid-seventeenth century. Nikon's interest in sacred Greek objects is well known (cat. no. 15).

Along with saints' relics, miracle-working icons, and copies of them, embassies from the Christian East brought other gifts to the tsars as well as to the heads of the Russian church in Moscow, including luxury items (cat. no. 22) and ceremonial horse trappings produced in the famous workshops of Constantinople. Some of the most frequent gifts for the tsar and patriarch were carved wooden crosses (cat. nos. 23-25). *Panagiias,* or pendants worn with ecclesiastical dress, were frequently part of the offerings from the regular clergy of Mount Athos, where the art of wood carving had flourished for centuries, and from Mount Sinai. The heads of the other Orthodox churches also brought the Russian patriarchs gifts that were symbols of high pastoral authority, such as staffs (cat. no. 26), although such offerings were made only in exceptional instances. These remarkable works could not help but influence Russian court art since many were executed by the best masters from famous art centers. During some periods, Greek clerical garments and church objects for the holy service were imitated and served as models for the creation of new forms of Russian church furnishings: elements for use in the celebration of the holy mass and for the embellishment of churches.

EAM

22. Tankard

Turkey (Constantinople), first half of 17th century
Rock crystal, gold, rubies, emeralds
H. 6 in. (15.5 cm)
DK-82

This tankard was carried to Moscow by Archimandrite Amphilogios, who, along with several other secular and religious individuals, traveled with the ambassadorial caravan of Ahmed Aghā, the official representative of the Ottoman sultan Murād IV. The audience in the reception hall of the Palace of Facets of the Kremlin on February 20, 1632, included only a few of the sultan's secular Christian Orthodox subjects, so the gifts, such as this tankard, from Patriarch Cyril I Lucaris to the tsar, tsarevich, and patriarch went directly to them, bypassing any ceremonial ambassadorial presentation. Despite the donor's holy orders, which would have made a modest gift more reasonable, the objects given to the tsar were wildly expensive, and this tankard was no exception. In spite of its ecclesiastical donor, it was a secular Turkish art object, a superior piece of craftsmanship from the workshops of Constantinople.

The tankard's tall, cylindrical body is made of rock crystal and decorated with the most common ornamental motifs in Ottoman art, pomegranate flowers on long, curved stalks with leaves. These are executed in part with precious stones in characteristic rosettes and in part with fine gold wire. The gold base is decorated with leaf cartouches encompassing delicate plant forms in a technique that reached its most elegant expression in Turkish gold work of the late sixteenth and early seventeenth centuries. We can assume that, as in the case of the small rock-crystal barrel in cat. no. 29, the body of this tankard was executed at an earlier undetermined date than the handle and the missing lid. The tankard's handle is made of a crystal of different quality and could have been added to the smooth cylindrical beaker at the same time as the decoration and the lid.

Judging from documents and from the distribution of ornament on the body, the tankard must have had a crystal lid when it arrived in Moscow.

Documents cite one other gift of a crystal tankard in a gold setting, but it has not been identified. It was offered to Tsar Mikhail Fyodorovich by Ambassador Thomas Cantacuzenus in 1630 but did not go to the state. It may have remained in the tsar's personal chambers, without appraisal, from the very beginning.[1]

NOTE
1. Ambassadorial Affairs 1630, fol. 5

SOURCES: Ambassadorial Affairs 1631–32, fol. 361; Book of Receipts 1631–32, fol. 41; Inventory 1634, fol. 37 (see also Viktorov 1877–83, vol. 1, p. 12); Inventory 1884, pt. 2, bk. 1, no. 534.

LITERATURE: *Putevoditel' po vystavke iranskogo i turetskogo iskusstva* 1960, p. 10, ill. 18; Vishnevskaya 1996/2, pp. 220–21, no. 182.

IAZ

23. Altar Cross

Mount Athos, Simon Peter Monastery, 1619
Maker: Demetrios [Solunets]
Olive wood, silver, nonprecious metal, gilding
H. 17 1/8 in. (44 cm), w. 5 1/8 in. (13.2 cm), d. 1 1/8 in.(2.9 cm)
DK-1162

On this altar cross are multiple figures carved in complex compositions and other reliefs, some depicting the gospels and saints. At the midpoint on the front is the Crucifixion; above it is the Raising of Lazarus, and below it the Ascension of Christ and the Entrance of Christ into Jerusalem; flanking these scenes are the Descent into Hell and the Descent of the Holy Spirit to the Apostles, and below, on each of the volutes, are half-figures of three prelates and a series of figures that can be identified tentatively as two saints, the Apostles Peter and Paul; there are also angels with crosses and other saints. On the back in the center is the Birth of Christ; above it is the Annunciation and below it the Transfiguration of Christ and the Assumption of the Virgin; flanking these are depictions of Candlemas and the Epiphany; on each of the volutes below are half-figures of four prophets and symbols of the Virgin, and above them half-figures of four unidentified saints.

The Greek inscriptions on the mount give the titles of these scenes, and there are traditional cryptograms on the sides: one can be deciphered as "the Apostle Andrew (the first called)" and the second as "The place of execution become paradise." Of special interest is the unique inscription in Greek on the handle, which gives information about the history of the piece, who commissioned it, and its maker: "Cross, guardian of all the universe, keep and protect all those living in this Simon Peter Monastery and Simon, the father superior who adorned you, in the year of 7127 [1619], May." The second inscription reads: "My labor, Demetrios [of Thessalonica], Solunets."[1] The handle ends in a shank of ferrous metal with a screw-thread indicating that it was made for the divine service. According to Greek

tradition, these kinds of crosses were inserted vertically on the church altar on special pyramidal stands; in Russia, such altar crosses lay on the altar.

The cross's elaborate form and carving are characteristic of art from Mount Athos in the first half of the seventeenth century. Among the fairly large number of similar works, this cross stands out not only for its complex iconography but also for the high level of execution of all its details—from the carved compositions to the inscription on the handle. The piece is among the rare, precisely dated examples of Mount Athos carving. It should serve as a basis for the study of this complex and relatively under-researched artistic phenomenon.

Interestingly enough, this unique piece was made the same year Filaret came to the Russian patriarchal throne, but information has never been found about how the cross came to Russia. We do know, however, that by 1627 it had been donated by Patriarch Filaret to the Solovetsk Monastery in the distant north, where it was one of the most venerated objects at the monastery. It remained there until the 1920s.

NOTE
1. Greek inscription translated into Russian by V. L. Fonkich.

LITERATURE: Dosifei 1845, pp. 227, 291; *Trezori* 1985, pp. 38, 42, no. 45; *Grecheskie dokumenty* 1995, p. 85, no. 56, ill. on p. 84 (left).

EAM

24. Altar Cross

Mount Athos?, first third of 17th century
Mounting: Russia (Moscow), Kremlin Workshops,
1st third of 17th century
Boxwood, gold, silver, sapphires, emeralds,
rubies, turquoise, pearls
H. 14 in. (35.9 cm), w. 5⁷/8 in. (15 cm), d. 1¹/8 in. (2.9 cm)
DK-160/1

On both sides of this boxwood altar cross there are twelve compositions done in the finest relief carving; below them is a decoration of gilded foil. On the front, above the Crucifixion, is the Annunciation; on either side of the Crucifixion is the Descent into Hell and the Assumption of the Virgin; below these scenes is the Descent of the Holy Spirit and the Entrance of Christ into Jerusalem. On the back in the center is the Birth of Christ; above it, the Annunciation; to the sides, depictions of the Epiphany and Candlemas; below, the Transfiguration and Raising of Lazarus. The piece's skillful carving is echoed by its elegant and very fine gold mount, which has an enamel pattern on the filigree, a pearl border, and precious stones.

Patriarch Filaret gave the cross to the Novospassky Monastery in Moscow, where it became one of their most venerated objects, used only on especially solemn occasions: during church holidays and for receiving the most distinguished visitors. The vestry of the Novospassky cloister was one of the richest monastery treasure houses in Russia; from the moment it was founded, the monastery had been closely connected with Moscow's sovereigns. In 1613, upon the ascension of the Romanov dynasty, whose family burial vault was at the monastery, the cloister was the focus of particular attention and received numerous gifts from the tsar's family.

The history of the cross makes it possible for us to date the piece no later than 1633, when Filaret died.

SOURCES: Inventory 1925–26, fol. 15, no. 16886.

LITERATURE: Denisov 1908, p. 396; Dmitriev 1909, p. 66–67; Rechmensky 1913, p. 23, ill. 77.

EAM

25. Processional Cross

Mount Athos, first half of 17th century
Shank mounting: Russia (Moscow), Kremlin Workshops,
mid-17th century
Cypress wood, silver, gilding
H. 65 1/8 in. (167 cm)
Carved cross: 11 3/8 in. (29 cm), w. 10 1/4 in. (26.2 cm),
d. 1 in. (2.5 cm)
Sk-42

Processional crosses were carried in front of the patri-arch during formal processions and other ceremonies. This cross, which has a tall shank with a silver and gilt mounting, belonged to Patriarch Nikon. On the front and back, there are multi-figure relief compositions and depictions of the saints. On the front in the center is the Crucifixion and above it the Annunciation; flank-ing these are scenes of the Ascension of Christ and the Entrance of Christ into Jerusalem; below is a depiction of the Descent into Hell. Attached to the upper and side pieces are figured leaf-shaped elements depicting the Feast of the Presentation of the Blessed Virgin, the ox (symbol of the Evangelist Luke), and the lion (sym-bol of the Evangelist Mark). Pictured on each of the lower volutes are prophets holding unfurled scrolls, and on the almond-shape marks trailing from the volutes are half-figures of the sainted Empress Helen and her son, the sainted Emperor Constantine, shown holding crosses.

On the back, in the center, is the Birth of Christ with the Annunciation above it; flanking these scenes are Candlemas and the Epiphany and then the Trans-figuration and the Raising of Lazarus. On leaf-shape elements, the Old Testament Trinity with the figures of Sarah and Abraham (above), an eagle (symbol of the Evangelist John), and, on the sides of these images, the half-figure of an angel (symbol of the Evangelist Mat-thew); on the lower volutes are prophets with unfurled scrolls, and on the almond-shape marks trailing from the volutes are seraphim.

The Greek inscriptions give the titles of the com-positions and the names of the saints. On the butt ends of the upper piece are marks with the Greek letters τ and α in relief on a dark green ground; elsewhere the butt ends are covered with red paint.

The earliest preserved reference to the cross in written sources dates from 1658, in the inventory of Patriarch Nikon's household treasury. In the nineteenth and early twentieth centuries the cross was kept in the Synodal (Patriarchal) Vestry; it was sent to the Krem-lin Museum from the Cathedral of Christ the Savior on August 31, 1931.

SOURCES: Beliaev 1852, p. 103; Savva 1883, p. 30, table 10, no. 49.

LITERATURE: *Kratkii ukazatel' Patriarshei* 1907, p. 58, ill. 17; *Trezori* 1985, pp. 38, 42, no. 49; *Grecheskie dokumenty* 1995, pp. 85-86, no. 57, ill. on p. 84 (right).

EAM

26. Staff of Patriarch Nikon

Turkey (Constantinople), mid-17th century?
Wood, bone, mother of pearl, tortoise-shell, silver
H. 65¹/₂ in. (168 cm)
DK-1536

The tall staff was a prescribed element of an archbishop's office, symbolizing the bishop's pastoral authority over believers. This type of staff, or crozier, has been known in the Eastern church since the sixth century. In the Orthodox East, beginning in the sixteenth century, these staffs were often crowned with the heads of two snakes, a symbolic reference to the wisdom of his archbishop's pastoral leadership. In Russia, this form of staff is known from the mid-seventeenth century. One of the first examples of this type was a staff brought to Patriarch Iosif in 1650 from Parthenios II, Patriarch of Constantinople; its bone top has been preserved in the Kremlin collection.[1]

In Russia, the custom of the ruler of state presenting staffs to the patriarch, who in turn gave them to the bishops, was established in the sixteenth and seventeenth centuries, in accordance with Byzantine tradition. Especially interesting in this regard is a report from Paul of Aleppo, who visited Russia in the mid-seventeenth century along with the suite of Macharius, Patriarch of Antioch, about the preparations for this journey and the choice of gifts for the Russian tsar and the head of the Russian church. On the advice of the patriarch and metropolitans of Constantinople, a staff was commissioned for Patriarch Nikon, who at that time sat on the Russian patriarchal throne and was supposed to receive the staff from Patriarch Macharius of Antioch. This course was only possible because, although the heads of the Antioch and Russian churches were of equal status, the Antioch see was more ancient and, according to tradition, considered to have been founded by the Apostle Peter. This explains the advice given

Patriarch Macharius: "You have the authority to give the staff into the safekeeping of whosoever you desire."[2]

Unfortunately, the description of the tortoiseshell and mother-of-pearl staff that we have from the writings of Paul of Aleppo is quite laconic. However, considering that such staffs were fairly rare in Russia, we may identify this piece from the Kremlin collections as a gift probably from Patriarch Macharius of Antioch to Patriarch Nikon. True, the staff came to the Kremlin in 1919, not from the Patriarchal Vestry but from a daughter church in Moscow of the Troitsa-Sergiev Monastery. However, Nikon's connection with this church is well known, as is the practice of transferring objects from the Patriarchal Vestry to different monasteries and churches.

The mid-seventeenth-century date for the staff is at odds with some specialists' opinion on the incrustation of objects with tortoiseshell and mother-of-pearl using nails with large, rather crude heads. This, they say, is characteristic instead of eighteenth-century Constantinople artists. However, the small number of such objects with precise dates that have been preserved gives us reason to believe that such a manner of decoration could have appeared in an earlier period.

NOTES
1. See Savva 1883, p. 34; *Grecheskie dokumenty* 1995, pp. 84–86, no. 55.
2. Paul of Aleppo 1896, p. 31.

SOURCES: Inventory 1922, fol. 13, no. 13476.

EAM

GIFTS FROM
THE OTTOMAN EMPIRE AND PERSIA

O<small>NE OF THE GREATEST</small> achievements of late-sixteenth-century Russian diplomacy was the establishment of relations with the Ottoman Empire, the mighty state south of Russia's southern borders. The political and economic aspects of their relationship would always remain closely intertwined. Although grand embassies were occasionally exchanged, merchants traveled with them, and in many instances merchants served as stand-ins for the ambassadors. The Russian market, particularly in Moscow, had a strong interest in Turkish goods, especially in luxury items. The tsars themselves purchased fine objects from the workshops of Constantinople and Jerusalem, exploiting Russia's proximity to the Ottoman Empire.

The relationship between the two powers was a complicated one, with its roots in the history of the region. Access to Turkey from Moscow was across the territory of the Crimean Tatars, who were often confrontational, thanks in part to the long years during which the Russians had paid tribute to their predecessors, the Mongol khans. During the sixteenth and seventeenth centuries, the Tatars carried out devastating raids against Russia's southern lands, which had been settled by Cossacks and the Cossacks in turn raided the Crimeans and Ottomans. At times the Tatars even reached the gates of Moscow and the Cossacks the out-

skirts of Constantinople. Since the Ottoman sultans were nominal overlords of the Crimean khans, their relationship with Russia was necessarily complicated by the conflicts between the Russians and the Crimeans.

Also during this period, the European powers formed various coalitions against the Ottomans for both political and religious reasons, and efforts were frequently made to draw Russia into anti-Turkish alliances. Although Russia for many years enjoyed good relations with the Sublime Porte at Constantinople, beginning in the 1640s the alliance gradually became one of military confrontation, a situation that lasted on and off for sixty years. Nonetheless, trade with Turkey was maintained through merchants of the Christian faith, both Greek and Armenian. After 1686, and formally in 1697, Russia joined the European anti-Turkish alliance known as the Holy League. Shortly afterward, however, at the century's end, the Russians signed a peace treaty with the sultan on terms highly advantageous for Russia. (For the issue of Christians in the Ottoman Empire, see pages 167–68.)

The relations between Persia (modern Iran) and Russia generally depended on the desire of both to limit Ottoman power in the Near East. During the sixteenth and seventeenth centuries, Persia, under the Safavids, and Turkey were often at war over territorial and religious disputes, as several shahs and sultans of the time were aggressive builders of empires.

Detail of cat. no. 31b

Trade was another, equally powerful issue between Russia and Persia. Since there was a possibility that Moscow might gain a central position in trade between Europe and Persia, England, the Dutch Republic, and Schleswig-Holstein, all tried to obtain trading rights across Russia to Persia, often along the famous route through Astrakhan and across or around the Caspian Sea. The tsars were fully aware of their power in this respect and granted European trade rights (with the exception of England) only infrequently, for which they demanded significant compensation.

Monuments to the ties between Russia and countries in the Near East, including Turkey, Persia, and Crimea, can be seen in the Kremlin Armory today—masterpieces of weaving, ceremonial weaponry, jewelry, and decorative objects made of semiprecious stones, produced by artists from Constantinople, Isfahan, and elsewhere. The Kremlin collection of textiles is particularly notable because it consists not of fragments but of large pieces preserved in garments made in Russia using fabrics from Persia and Turkey, primarily church vestments for the supreme church hierarchs and the ceremonial wear of Russian sovereigns. No less outstanding is the Kremlin collection of horse trappings made by Near Eastern artists: saddles, a harness with a gold cover studded with precious stones, and elaborate caparisons (cat. nos. 32, 39). The work by Turkish and Persian arms makers and jewelers in the Kremlin museum collection originally enjoyed broad use in the official ceremonies of the Russian tsars' court.

Diplomatic missions from the Ottoman sultan included one of special importance in 1632 that brought gifts from both Sultan Murād IV and the Orthodox Patriarch of Constantinople (cat. no. 22). Another mission in 1632 brought gifts that included elaborate horse trappings. Merchants also presented splendid gifts from Turkey on several occasions, and it may be presumed that some came at the behest of the sultan. The Crimean khan sent gifts in 1616 (cat. no. 27).

The most sensational gift that accompanied a mission from Persia was the throne decorated with gold, turquoise, and rubies sent by Shah Abbas I to Tsar Boris Godunov in 1604 (see Chapter 5, fig. 2). Shah Abbas II also sent missions in the 1640s and the late 1650s, from which a number of gifts survive (cat. no. 43).

IAZ

27. Quiver

Turkey (Crimea?), 1616
Silver, leather, silk, metallic threads, gilding
L. 31 in. (79.5 cm)
OR-4479/1-2

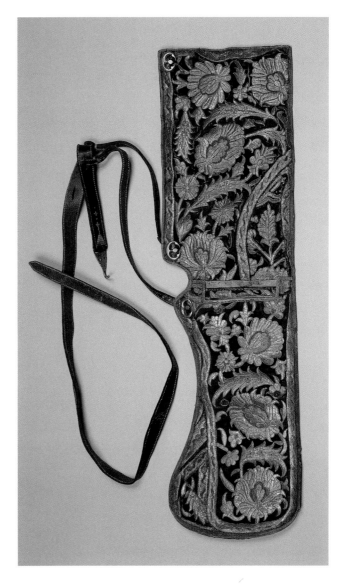

The word *saadak* is Turkic in origin. In the sixteenth and seventeenth centuries, the term meant the complete armament of the horseman, including a bow in its case with a quiver (*kolchan*) of arrows. In the sixteenth century, when the gentry cavalry was the basic element of the army, the *saadak* was mandatory and often the principal part of a Russian warrior's arms. In the seventeenth century, it is gradually replaced by firearms: saddle pistols and carbines. The *saadak* was retained as military equipment only by guard detachments and in national formations composed of representatives of the eastern region of the country. They continued to be used for hunting.

Unlike the Russian *saadaks* that have been preserved in the Armory collection, this quiver, which is part of a *saadak*, was, despite its formality and the richness of its decoration, an example not of a ceremonial item but of an expensive military or hunting outfit. (A ceremonial *saadak* was generally encrusted with gems.) Its pocket, or *kishen* (the early Russian term), could hold a large number of arrows. In the latter half of the seventeenth century, this quiver came to be called a *kalmyk*, and it is so noted in the 1687 Armory inventory. This designation was probably given to it in the Sovereign's Armory when the inventory was compiled.

The quiver is made of Moroccan leather and is covered with red velvet, which is in turn embroidered with stylized foliate ornament in metallic and blue threads. Gilded-silver decorations in the form of crescent moons have been applied at the quiver's corners. In the central area, on the outside, the quiver has three small pockets for a knife or other supplementary equipment.

This quiver was offered to Tsar Mikhail Fyodorovich on June 10, 1616, in the Golden Chamber by Ambassador Ahmed Aghā as a gift from the Crimean khan Djānbeg Girāy. The reception of the Crimean embassy of 1616 was one of the first foreign-policy actions of the young tsar from the new Romanov dynasty, related to important negotiations attempting to bring peace to the southern part of the country.

SOURCES: Inventory 1687, fol. 148, no. 25; Inventory 1885, pt. 4, bk. 3, no. 6334.
LITERATURE: *Remekmuvek a cari* 1989, no. 78; *Tesoros del Kremlin* 1990, no. 92.

AKL

28. Ceremonial Mace

Turkey (Constantinople), first half of 17th century
Jasper, gold, rubies, emeralds, turquoise, wood
L. 29¼ in. (75 cm)
OR-178

The mace was the customary weapon of the Russian cavalry until the sixteenth century. In the seventeenth century, this formidable striking weapon became instead a symbol of military power. The Armory has a large collection of weapons of this type, in which pride of place is given to a group of ceremonial maces created in the seventeenth century by Turkish and Persian artists. As a rule, these weapons went into the Russian sovereigns' Armory treasury and were gifts from Eastern rulers or merchants. They were used as part of the tsar's ceremonial military attire.

The mace, a gift to Tsar Mikhail Fyodorovich from Asan-chelibey, was presented by a member of the Turkish embassy, Ahmed Aghā, in 1631, during the reception for the embassy in the Palace of Facets in the Moscow Kremlin.

In 1654, the mace was in the treasury of campaign weapons of Tsar Alexei Mikhailovich when he took part in the siege of Smolensk, during the Russo-Polish war of 1654–66. Its high status is confirmed by the fact that the Armory treasury's inventory of 1687 and the 1654 inventory of the campaign treasury mention the mace as the first item.

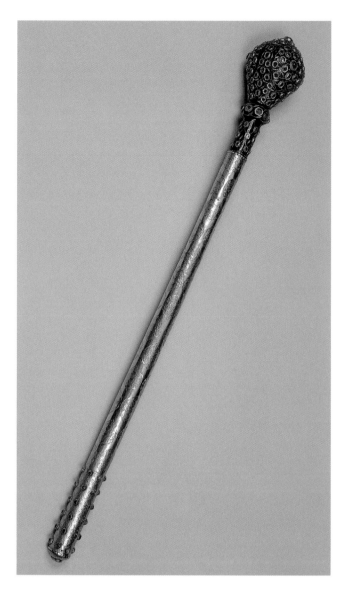

This mace is a magnificent example of seventeenth-century Turkish jewelry and was not designed for use in battle. The pear-shape head of the mace is jasper and has a relief decoration just below. The jasper's polished surface is encrusted with gold in a stylized plant motif set with rubies and emeralds in floral mounts. The wood handle is covered in a thin sheet of gold leaf and decorated with plant forms. The lower portion of the handle is mounted with rubies and emeralds. A large turquoise is set in the tip of the handle.

SOURCES: Ambassadorial Affairs 1630, fol. 288; Inventory of campaign treasury 1654, fol. 66, no. 1; Inventory 1687, fol. 102, no. 1; Inventory 1885, pt. 4, bk. 3, no. 5185.
LITERATURE: Yablonskaya 1996, pp. 102–3, no. 94.

AKL

29. Barrel (*bochonok*)

Turkey (Constantinople), first third of 17th century
Rock crystal, gold, emeralds, rubies
H. 8¹/₈ in. (21 cm); l. 4³/₈ in. (11 cm)
DK-268

This small barrel was offered to Tsar Mikhail Fyodor-ovich by Ambassador Thomas Cantacuzenus on December 27, 1632, at an audience in the Golden Chamber, as a gift from his relative Constantine Paleologue, a representative of a rich and distinguished Greek family living in the Ottoman Empire. The barrel was sent to the treasury, where it was appraised very highly for a crystal object—at 359 rubles.[1] Of all the formal plate brought by the ambassador and the three Greek merchants who participated in the audience, it alone has survived to the present day. The barrel was not listed in inventories of the treasury; evidently it was kept in the private rooms of the tsar's family.[2]

The rock-crystal body of the barrel is carved with bands, which imitate hoops, and with twisting stems, flowers, and leaves. Two round rosettes set with rubies and emeralds are attached to the barrel, and an intricate gold chain is attached to them. The spout, located between the rosettes, has a gold stopper set with an emerald. The sides of the barrel are mounted with gold bands with scattered mounted emeralds.

There is reason to think that the barrel consists of components made at different times. Originally it was probably not encrusted with precious stones but had only the carved bands and the plant ornament and was

supposed to stand vertically: one of its ends opens, and the body itself and the other end are made of a single piece of rock crystal. Most rock-crystal objects fashioned in Europe and the Ottoman Empire in the sixteenth and seventeenth centuries have an earlier, Egyptian provenance from the Fatimid period (969–1171). This barrel may well have been brought in its original form from Egypt, and the date of its carving is uncertain. The plaited handle, stopper, and precious stones could have been added in Constantinople on the instruction of the donor shortly before its journey to Moscow.

NOTES

1. The most expensive object made of semiprecious stone was a jasper scent bottle (*aromatnitsa*) set with precious gems on a stand, a gift from Ambassador Thomas Cantacuzenus appraised at 560 rubles. The diplomat's most expensive present was a (horse's) bit and breastplate worth more than 1,000 rubles (see Ambassadorial files 1640, fol. 398). It should be pointed out, however, that the appraisal of offerings from Orthodox foreigners was not always objective and was related, as was the reward given them in return, to the quality of their services to the Russian court.

2. The compiler of the 1884 inventory, G. D. Filimonov (see Inventory 1884, pt. 2, bk. 3, no. 5243), incorrectly connected a note about a rock-crystal barrel contained in the inventory of the tsar's treasury of 1640 with this small barrel. That note refers to a barrel with silver mounts and figured decoration (see Inventory 1640, fol. 200; *Drevnosti* 1849–53, vol. 5, pl. 50).

SOURCES: Ambassadorial Affairs 1632, fols. 247, 395, 398, 402; Inventory 1835, no. 2285; Inventory 1884, pt. 2, bk. 3, no. 2543.

IAZ

30. Bowl (*chasha*)

Turkey (Constantinople), first third of 17th century
Nephrite, gold, emeralds, rubies, sapphires
H. 4³/₄ in. (12.2 cm); diam. 5⁵/₈ in. (14.5 cm)
DK-267

This bowl was offered to Tsar Mikhail Fyodorovich by an Orthodox subject of the Ottoman Empire, Georgios Panagiotis, who came from a very famous family of the former Byzantine Empire and who arrived in Moscow in 1632 with Ahmed Aghā, envoy of Sultan Murād IV. Although his nephew took part in the reception held in the tsar's palace, Panagiotis himself was not among the audience. Nonetheless, his gifts to the tsar and patriarch, like those brought by Archimandrite Amphilogios from Patriarch Cyril I Lucaris (cat. no. 22), are listed in the documents of the Treasury Office as having been offered on February 20, 1632, in the Palace of Facets. In addition to this bowl, Tsar Mikhail Fyodorovich received a red velvet carpet, and the patriarch a precious liturgical set and church cloths. The gifts to Patriarch Filaret were more than twice as valuable as those brought to the tsar,[1] perhaps suggesting their Christian origin.

The bowl's round nephrite body is encrusted with floral motifs of a type well known in Turkish decorative art. The four stylized flowers on slender winding stems are made of gold threads, and precious stones are mounted in gold. The bowl's rim and base are formed of gold mounts with plant ornamentation done in carved relief that Constantinople jewelers of the time had so brilliantly mastered. This assortment of precious stones is somewhat out of the ordinary for Ottoman art; sapphires were rarely used to decorate a bowl of semiprecious stone. More often a combination of rubies and emeralds or diamonds was used.

Precious examples of this type were kept in the Kremlin's workshop or used to decorate the interiors of the tsar's palace.

NOTE
1. The bowl cost 155 rubles, the carpet 100 rubles, and the total value of the offerings for the patriarch exceeded 540 rubles. (See Book of Receipts 1632, fols. 42–42v, 47v–50.)

SOURCES: Book of Receipts 1631–32, fols. 42–42v (see also Kologrivov 1911, pp. 99–100); Inventory 1634, fol. 36 (see also Viktorov 1877, p. 12); Inventory 1835, no. 2407; Inventory 1884, pt. 2, bk. 3, no. 2506.
LITERATURE: *Drevnosti* 1849–53, vol. 5, pl. 15; *Putevoditel' po vystavke* 1960, p. 10, ill. 19; Vishnevskaya 1996/2, pp. 218–19, no. 181.

IAZ

31a,b. Ceremonial Horse Trappings

Turkey (Constantinople), first third of 17th century
Gold, silver, peridots, turquoises, nephrite,
iron, silk, metallic threads, gilding
L. of reins 41 in. (105 cm); l. breastplate 24³/₈ in. (62 cm);
25 in. (64 cm); 23³/₄ in. (60 cm)
K-420, K-225

Decorative tack was an essential part of royal horse trappings for ceremonial processions. When horses from the royal stables were put on display, they were fitted out with elaborately ornamented bridles, saddles, and other apparatus either decorated in the workshops of the Kremlin stables or imported, usually from Turkey. Turkish horse trappings were highly valued in Russia before the time of Peter the Great and were widely used by the tsars and the nobility. The type of ceremonial horse trappings that predominated in the ambassadorial gifts brought from Constantinople are unquestionably *mushtuks,* or sets of harness consisting of a bridle and breastplate.

The Armory collection has *mushtuks* brought by Ivan Velisariev (1630), Nikolai Yuriev (1631), Thomas Cantacuzenus (1632), Manuel Constantinov (1656), as they are referred to in Russian documents and others who have been identified in archival documents.

This harness set of Tsar Mikhail Fyodorovich is also one of the pieces we have been able to date on the basis of seventeenth-century documents. The 1634–35 Book of Receipts has a note dated September 28 about the reception by Tsar Mikhail Fyodorovich in the Golden Chamber of Musly Aghā, an ambassador from Ottoman Sultan Murād IV, as well as several Turkish and Greek merchants. One of these, Ivan Manuilov,

brought the sovereign a harness set with gilded-silver decorative plate made of wide and narrow straps with turquoises and peridots, which was appraised at 100 rubles and assigned to the treasury. This bridle, with its bit, is mentioned too, in the file concerning the arrival of Musly Aghā in the Ambassadorial Files of 1634–35 and in the inventory of the Stable Treasury of 1706. In this and subsequent inventories, the set is described in more detail but without any indication of the date it entered the treasury or its place of manufacture.

The bridle consists of four straps—one each for the headstall, browband, noseband, and throatlatch. The breastplate consists of three straps, two of which are attached to the saddle in front and the third to the girth underneath. The broad straps of the bridle and breastplate are studded with embossed gilded-silver plates of two types: square ones with turquoises and peridots; and narrow ones with turquoises and nephrite insets. The green peridots—semiprecious stones the color of grass—add a special charm and individuality to the set. The large, irregular peridots, which are faceted below,

are placed in the center of the bridle and breastplate straps as well as on the plates where the straps cross; small ones are on the decorative plates.

Between 1634 and 1687, the bridle was embellished in the workshops of the Stable Office with typically Russian decorations for ceremonial processions. A rounded tassel made of silk and gold threads was attached to the nose strap. The tassel itself has not survived, but in the center of the nose strap there is the silver plate with two openings where it was attached. Also added was a gilded-silver frontlet with an embossed Russian coat of arms—the double-headed eagle—looking from the forehead strap toward the nose strap. Later the steel bit and the reins made of silk with gold lace were removed from the bridle.

SOURCES: Book of Receipts 1634–35, fol. 12v; Ambassadorial Affairs 1634–36, fol. 35; Inventory 1706, fols. 70–70v; Inventory 1884, pt. 6, bk. 5, no. 8694. LITERATURE: Melnikova 1996, pp. 41–43.

OBM

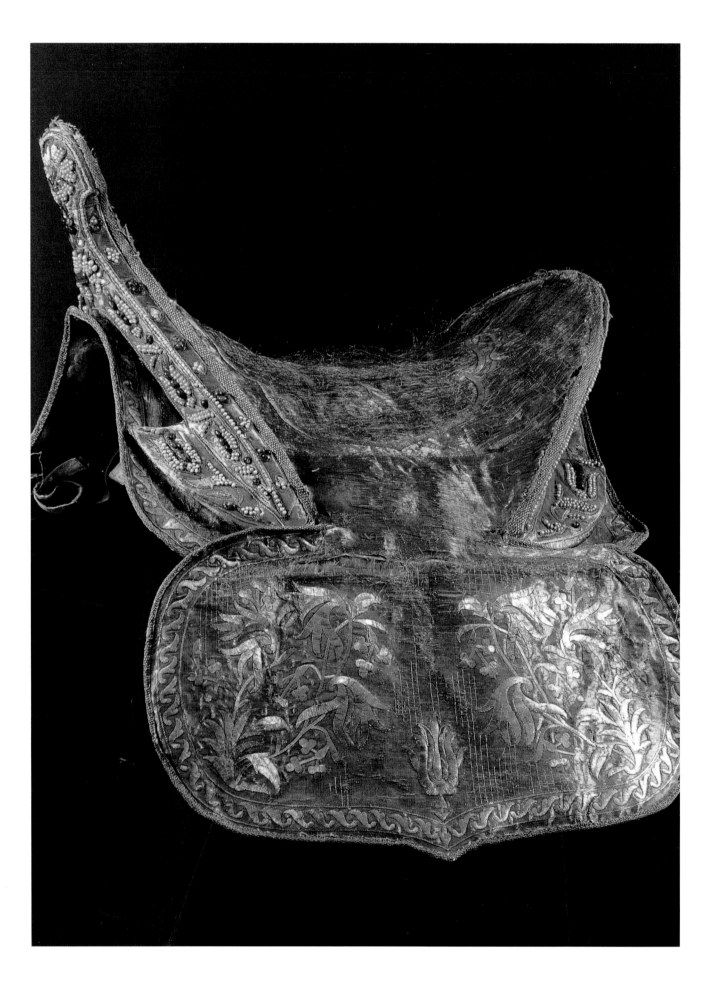

32. Saddle

Turkey (Constantinople), mid-17th century
Gold, silver, emeralds, pearls, wood, leather,
iron, silk, metallic threads
H. of pommel 1 2⁷/₈ in. (33 cm);
l. of saddle 1 7¹/₂ in. (45 cm)
K-232

In the summer of 1656, the tsar's treasury was enriched
by a large group of thirty-five precious Turkish ceremonial horse trappings: gold and silver embroidered caparisons, sumptuously decorated saddles, stirrups, and harness
sets. They had been brought by Greek merchants from
Constantinople and were offered to Tsar Alexei Mikhailovich and Tsarevich Alexei Alexeyevich on June 1 in
Moscow and August 2 in Borisoglebsk. The lists of the
gifts from Avram Rodionov and Demetrios Konstantinos
of Constantinople describe two similar Turkish saddles,
both embroidered in gold and silver, decorated with
rubies and emeralds, and ornamented with pearls. Comments in the documents indicate that the saddles were
taken by the Stable Office. The Stable Treasury inventory for 1706 lists them only as Turkish saddles with
no indication of when they entered the treasury.

Unfortunately, we cannot ascribe this saddle to the
1656 embassy with certainty, although it is very close
to the specifications for this group, as are perhaps as
many as ten other saddles kept in the Armory collection.

This saddle from Tsar Alexei Mikhailovich's treasury
has a classic form that distinguishes the pieces by Constantinople's best craftsmen from the middle of the seventeenth century. The high cantle makes a transition to the
smooth line of the seat. The saddle has a low, broad,
rounded cantle and oval flaps. It is upholstered with a
woven silver fabric made in Turkey and called "Altabas,"
which creates the illusion of a solid metallic surface. The
fabric on the seat and flaps is also heavily embroidered
with gold thread and is further embellished with small
flowers of emerald and pearl beads. It is no wonder that
such saddles are called "gold" in the 1706 inventory of
the Stable Treasury; that definition is fully justified.

sources: Inventory 1706, fols. 1 38v–1 39; Inventory
1884, pt. 6, bk. 5, no. 8527.

literature: Kologrivov 1911, pp. 148, 151; Kirillova
1996, pp. 190–91, no. 160.

OBM

33. Caparison (*chaldar*)

Turkey (Constantinople), mid-17th century
Silk, metallic threads
23³/₈ in. x 24⁵/₈ in. (60 x 63 cm);
15¹/₄ x 21³/₄ in. (39 x 56 cm)
TK-2624

Caparisons constituted a very important part of equestrian parade gear. In the seventeenth century, a significant portion of the ambassadorial and merchants' gifts brought to Muscovy from Turkey consisted of various caparisons, which in Old Russia had traditionally been the most important element of ceremonial trappings. All of them were stored in a special repository at the Stable Office in the Moscow Kremlin, where they were distributed for use at different official ceremonies. Their purpose, and consequently their shapes, varied. Some caparisons were intended to cover the entire body of the horse, while others were intended as saddle pads, and a third type was placed on top of the saddle. During ceremonial occasions, a single horse could wear several different types of caparison simultaneously.

Here we have the left side piece from one of the types of horse-cloths called a *chaldar* (caparison) in Old Russia. It was meant to cover the croup and chest of the horse. It consists of two side pieces and one front piece, which were usually cut out separately and then joined.

The side hem of the caparison consists of two pieces of different sizes embroidered all over with drawn gold threads and joined by crimson velvet that is also sewn to the edge of the horse-cloth. In the middle of each of the pieces, against a background covered with silver threads, is an area embroidered in gold thread with a stylized bouquet of pinks, tulips, hyacinths, rosettes, and rosebuds edged with a branch with burdock flowers. The edge is decorated with an embroidered spray with multi-petaled flowers and tulips. Attached to the lower edge of the horse-cloth is woven fringe.

SOURCES: Inventory 1884, pt. 6, bk. 5, no. 9107.

IIV

34. Saber and Sheath

Turkey (Constantinople), before 1656
Steel, wood, gold, emeralds, rubies, sapphires, nephrite
Overall l. 36 5/8 in (94 cm); l. of blade: 31 7/8 in. (81.5 cm);
l. of sheath: 35 in. (91 cm)
OR-199/1–2

In the seventeenth century, the Armory had more than thirty sabers categorized in the 1687 Inventory under the heading "Grand Attire." These were distinguished from other weapons of this type only by the fact that all the elements of their hilts and sheaths were fashioned of gold and silver and decorated with precious stones. In seventeenth-century Russian documents, the term "Grand Attire" was used to refer to ceremonial raiment of the tsars and to state regalia, such as the crown, scepter, and orb. Thus, sabers of the Grand Attire were either a part of the tsar's ceremonial dress or else were part of the Russian ruler's military regalia.

A magnificent example of Islamic ceremonial weaponry, this saber enjoyed the highest possible status in the tsar's armory and was numbered first among the sabers of the Grand Attire in the 1687 Inventory. Its blade is forged of high-quality Damascus steel of Persian or Turkish origin. Unfortunately, the polishing of the blade, done probably in the nineteenth century, has obscured the characteristic pattern that conveys the metal's unique texture. Incised in gold on the upper part of the blade is an Arabic inscription: "May you pass your time in bliss."

The saber's nephrite hilt is encrusted with rubies and emeralds in gold floral mounts. The sheath is covered with thin gold leaf, and its outer side is decorated in a stylized pattern of precious stones and nephrite plaques with rubies set in gold mounts. On the reverse side of the sheath a stylized plant design is incised in gold embellished with figurative niello plaques.

According to a note in the 1687 Inventory, this saber was given to the tsar by Ivan Bulgakov, a merchant in goods from Turkey, on December 10, 1656. The date of the gift coincides with the arrival in Moscow from Constantinople of a group of precious articles intended for Tsar Alexei Mikhailovich.

SOURCES: Inventory 1687, fol. 27, no. 1; Inventory 1885, pt. 4, bk. 3, no. 5909.

LITERATURE: Yablonskaya 1996, pp. 111–12, no. 102.

AKL

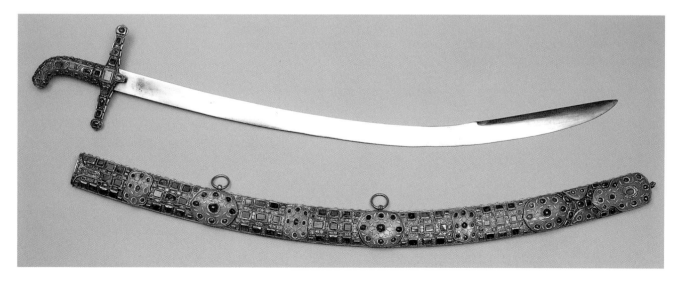

35. Scent Bottle (*aromatnik*)

Turkey (Constantinople), first half of 17th century
Rock crystal, gold, rubies, emeralds
H. 5⅝ in. (15 cm)
DK-270

The faceted crystal body of this scent bottle is decorated with gold wire and precious stones mounted in gold rosettes. Its gold decoration is ornamented with plant forms carved in a style characteristic of Constantinople goldsmiths' work of this time. The object's transparent material made it possible to see the colored perfumed oil, water, or aromatic vinegar inside the vessel, which lent additional color to the already vivid precious stones.

We know that scent bottles made of semiprecious stones on stands of the same materials were brought to Moscow several times as gifts from the sultan's diplomats and representatives of the merchant elite. For example, a crystal vessel is listed among the gifts from the ambassador Thomas Cantacuzenus to Tsar Mikhail Fyodorovich in 1630. Along with several other valuables and textiles, it was not appraised in the treasury. And although no direct evidence remains in documents, we can assume, bearing in mind well-known court practice, that these objects remained from the very beginning in the private rooms of the sovereign, bypassing the treasury altogether.[1]

This particular scent bottle may well have been a vessel mentioned in the documents. The Armory has two other vessels of this type with a similar history.[2]

NOTES
1. Ambassadorial Affairs 1630, fols. 4–5.
2. On the practice of giving objects like this to the tsar in the mid-seventeenth century, see Kologrivov 1911, p. 149; Vishnevskaya 1996/2, p. 213, nos. 177–78.

SOURCES: Inventory 1835, no. 2378; Inventory 1884, pt. 2, bk. 3, no. 2577.

IAZ

36. Writing Set

Turkey (Constantinople), 17th century
Gold, silver, lazurite, diamonds, rubies, pearls, enamel
H. 2³/₄ in. (7 cm); l. 10¹/₂ in. (27 cm)
MV-41

This writing set consists of an inkwell and a pencil case. Such sets have a long distinguished history in Islamic culture, representing symbols of knowledge and power drawn from the power of the written word. The eight-sided body of the inkwell is made of lazurite encrusted with gold and precious stones and set into a gold covering with a floral design partly executed in dark blue and green enamel. The open-work lid is formed by flowers of gold set with diamonds in the middle and joined with others of green enamel. The bottom of the vessel is decorated with a plant ornamentation done in vivid, multicolored enamel. The inkwell is attached to a large gold pencil case, which is decorated with plates in the form of large stylized flowers set with rubies and diamonds. Their winding enamel stem is of light blue enamel. The background for the ornament is translucent green enamel within the engraving, a fashionable technique at the Ottoman court from the 1630s to the 1660s. It was during these decades that the combination of rubies and diamonds became especially popular.

Precious inkwells were given by distinguished representatives of the Greek community of Constantinople engaged in trade activity in Russia, as well as by emissaries from the Orthodox church. They are listed among the gifts from the Turkish embassies of 1630 and 1631–32. For example, we know that in 1630 Tsarevich Alexei Mikhailovich was given an inkwell by Ambassador Thomas Cantacuzenus, to whom it was returned.[1] It was Cantacuzenus who in 1631–32, as part of a suite, presented a nephrite inkwell in a gold covering set with rubies and emeralds to Patriarch Filaret.[2] The current assumption that this inkwell appeared in Moscow in connection with Cantacuzenus's mission

of 1632 has not been confirmed by documents: it is not on the lists of gifts from that embassy.[3]

An alternative possibility exists to explain the origin of this gift. Judging from the inventories of the personal belongings of Tsar Fyodor Alexeyevich compiled after his death in 1682, this inkwell had belonged to his older brother, Tsarevich Alexei Alexeyevich, who died at an early age.[4] Older tsareviches in the Romanov family often received offerings from foreign visitors, including those from the East. The inkwell might have been brought to Alexei Alexeyevich as a gift by one of the Orthodox residents of the former Byzantine Empire or acquired for the young heir to the throne from a merchant. It was never listed in treasury inventories since it was kept in the tsarevich's private rooms.

NOTES
1. Ambassadorial Affairs 1630, fol. 6, 238.
2. Ambassadorial Affairs 1631–32, fols. 289, 372.
3. Vishnevskaya 1996/2, p. 225.
4. *Drevnosti* 1849–53, vol. 5, p. 69.

SOURCES: Inventory 1835, no. 277; *Drevnosti* 1849–53, vol. 5, p. 69; Inventory 1884, pt. 2, bk. 3, no. 2859.
LITERATURE: *Putevoditel' po vystavke* 1960, drawing 16; Vishnevskaya 1996/2, p. 225, no. 187.

IAZ

37. Pocket Watch with Calendar

Mechanism: Switzerland (Geneva), mid-17th century
Case: Turkey (Constantinople), mid-17th century
Metal, gold, silver, diamonds, enamel
H. 2³/₄ in. (7 cm); w. 2 in. (5 cm)
MV-4089/1, MV-4089/2

Miniature watches with complicated mechanisms in precious cases came to Russia among the offerings of diplomats from Europe and merchants from Turkey. This watch is traditionally connected with the arrival in Moscow in 1658 of a representative of the trading class of the Ottoman Empire, a Greek known in Russia by the name of Ivan Anastasov.

The Armory has two pocket watches from the tsar's treasury whose mechanism was executed in Geneva and case in Constantinople. Both have a similar decorative design, but only this watch is equipped with a calendar as well. Its case in massive gold is oval in shape and covered with translucent green enamel applied on an engraved surface, which produces the effect of the watch being lit from inside. From the 1630s to 1660s, this technique was in particular demand not only in Constantinople but also at the Muscovite court. Large diamonds with foil underneath them are mounted in settings of leaves. The inside of the lid is decorated with multicolored enamel: a handsome design of red, green, and blue flowers on spiraling stems against an opaque white surface.

The dial of the watch is decorated in Western style and equipped to indicate not only the time but also the date, day of the week, month, and phase of the moon. The drum, crown, and release wheels are engraved with floral motifs, and the open-work escutcheon with plant decoration is attached by a screw to the plate. Thomas Lentz suggests, on the basis of style, that this watch case may have been made in Mughal India at the time of Shah Jahan (r. 1628–58).[1]

NOTE
1. Correspondence with Barry Shifman, February 2001.

SOURCES: Inventory 1884, pt. 1, no. 509.

LITERATURE: *Putevoditel' po vystavke* 1960, p. 16; *Sokrovishcha Irana i Turtsii* 1979, no. 163, ill. on p. 60; Vishnevskaya 1996/2, p. 224, nos. 185, 86; *Sokrovishcha Kremlin* 1997, no. 13.

IAZ

38. Dagger and Sheath

Persia, first half of 17th century
Steel, gold, rubies, turquoise, pearls, glass
Overall l. 12 in. (30.8 cm); l. of blade 6¹/₂ in. (16.8 cm); l. of
sheath: 7¹/₄ in. (18.5 cm)
OR-208/1-2

In the sixteenth and seventeenth centuries, a mandatory part of the Russian tsar's campaign or military uniform was a dagger that hung from his belt or from the sash girdling the long narrow tunic (*chuga*) he wore under a chain-mail shirt or armor breastplate. This Safavid Persian example, one of the few richly decorated examples of this type of weapon to be preserved in the Armory, was presented to Tsar Mikhail Romanov in 1617 by the Persian merchant Mohammed Qasim. The documents recording its receipt make no mention of the fact that the merchant was executing the will of Shah Abbas I, so it may have been a personal gift. The dagger was transferred to the Armory a year later, on September 22, 1618; however, throughout the seventeenth century, it was not kept in the Armory but in the Master's Chamber, together with objects of the Grand Attire, the ceremonial garments of the Russian rulers.

The double-edged blade, forged of Damascus steel, is lozenge-shape in cross section with a long groove in the middle. The hilt and the sheath are covered in gold with an embossed plant design and lavishly decorated with turquoise, rubies, and pearls, many of which are arranged in a floral configuration. Pieces of turquoise decorate the edge of both the grip and the sheath.

SOURCES: Inventory 1884–93, pt. 4, bk. 3, no. 6169.
LITERATURE: Yablonskaya 1988/1, ill. 135; Yablonskaya 1996, pp. 95–96, no. 90.

AKL

39. Caparison (*chaldar*)

Persia, late 16th to early 17th century
Silk, metallic threads, cotton
62⅞ x 56½ in. (161 x 145 cm)
TK-606

The Armory has a group of beautiful Safavid Persian horse-cloths. Some of them are made of magnificent, harmoniously colored fabrics distinguished by their exceptional beauty and diversity of patterns; others by their gold and silk embroidery. At one time, they were widely used in Old Russia as ceremonial horse trappings for outings of the tsar's court, adding a special celebratory feeling as well as a sense of refined luxury. These horse-cloths were made especially in Persian court workshops as presents for the Russian rulers and distinguished persons close to the court; consequently they were made by the best craftsmen of the day. The process of selecting objects for the gifts for Moscow took into consideration not only the material value of the objects but also the perfection of the work, its rarity, and even how well it corresponded to current fashion.

This caparison (*chaldar*) is unique. It is an extremely interesting example of Persian decorative embroidery of the sixteenth and early seventeenth centuries. Executed on canvas, it gives the impression of brocade, since its entire surface is solidly embroidered with gold thread. The relief informs the pattern with an almost palpable vitality. Even at that time embroideries by Persian artists were considered works of art, and people remarked on the quality of all sorts of embroidery but especially gold and silver embroidery on heavy cloth, silk, and leather.

A two-headed eagle under a crown and the lion of Saint Mark, the coat of arms of the Venetian Republic, are embroidered on the caparison. The lion is holding a small shield with the inscription Pax Tibi Marce Evangelista Meus. The caparison was apparently commissioned by the Doge of Venice as a gift for the Muscovite court. Testifying to this is the depiction on it of the coat of arms of the Russian state. Therefore, there is reason to think that the caparison must have come to Russia as a diplomatic gift.

One frequently encounters in seventeenth-century archival documents indications that textiles and embroidered goods were made in the shah's court workshops—even those whose ornamentation included elements of European heraldry—and that they were made especially for export, often specially commissioned by ruling courts abroad. However, the date and the specific embassy that brought this caparison cannot be traced in currently known archival sources. Information contained in a 1706 document indicates that in the second half of the seventeenth century the caparison was already in the tsar's Stable Treasury in the Moscow Kremlin.

SOURCES: Inventory 1706, article "Caparisons," no. 3.
LITERATURE: *Pamiatniki diplomaticheskikh i torgovykh* 1890, pp. 135–40; Denisova 1954, p. 278, ill. on p. 285; Kirillova 1988, p. 386, ill. 261; *Tesoros del Kremlin* 1990, no. 40.

LPK

40. Saddle Cloth (*cheprak*)

Persia, early 17th century
Refashioning: Moscow, Kremlin Workshops, 17th century
Wool, silk, metallic threads
25³/₈ x 57 in. (65 x 146 cm)
TK-2205

Among the ambassadorial gifts brought from Safavid Persia in the seventeenth century, ceremonial horse trappings occupied an important place. We know that in 1644 Asān Aghā, the ambassador from Shah Abbas II of Persia, brought several heavy embroidered horse-cloths to Russia, of which this splendid example is one.

This saddle cloth consists of a woven green wool broadcloth embroidered with metallic threads in various shades of gold, with a few details executed with brightly colored silk floss. The center of the ornamental composition is a large, stylized lotus blossom, and on both sides, symmetrically placed, are slender branches with flowers and two lions *passant*. Along three sides of the horse-cloth the edging is embroidered with a pattern of large curving leaves and multipetaled flowers. The marking of the place for the saddle with embroidery and the placement of the edging indicate that this is a specific type of horse-cloth called a *cheprak*. While it was in Russia, this *cherpak* was refashioned and widened somewhat with insets of cloth in another color.

SOURCES: Inventory 1884, pt. 6, bk. 5, no. 9123.
LITERATURE: Denisova 1954, p. 278, ill. on p. 282; Kirillova 1964; *Sokrovishcha Irana i Turtsii* 1979, no. 26; Mironova 1996, p. 183, no. 153.

IIV

41. Helmet

Persia, late 16th-early 17th century
Gold, steel, silk, precious stones, pearl, enamel
Diam. 8³/₄ in. (22.2 cm)
OR-164

In the sixteenth century, helmets worn in the eastern Islamic world underwent changes to strengthen their protective qualities. Instead of a mantle of mail reaching the shoulder to cover the warrior's neck, there appeared a solid metal neck guard and ear flaps. In Russia, this kind of helmet began to be used in the second half of the sixteenth century and was known as an *erikhonskaia*, or "Jericho cap." As a rule, these helmets were a part of the protective arms of distinguished commanders, as well as part of the ceremonial and battle armor of the Russian tsars.

This particular Jericho cap was kept in the Great Sovereign's arms treasury and listed in a 1687 inventory as a "Kuchum Jericho cap." Earlier, in 1654–55, under this designation, it had been chosen for the "campaign treasury" of Tsar Alexei Mikhailovich during the war with Poland.

It is very hard to explain how the helmet acquired the name "Kuchum." Kuchum was a khan of the Siberian horde who suffered a defeat at the hands of Cossacks led by Ermak, the subjugator of Siberia, in the latter half of the sixteenth century. However, according to the above-mentioned inventory, the helmet ended up in the Armory as a gift to Tsar Alexei Mikhailovich from the boyar Boris Petrovich Sheremetev—the great-uncle of Tsar Peter I's renowned comrade-in-arms Field Marshal Boris Petrovich Sheremetev. An alternative possibility is that the helmet was confiscated from an earlier Sheremetev in the first decade of the seventeenth century.

The helmet is forged of steel and decorated with a stylized plant ornament whose character and technique attest to the fairly early origin of this battle headgear and allow us to date it at the end of the sixteenth or beginning of the seventeenth century. Decorated with gold inlay, gold plaques, and colored stones, the neck guard, ear flaps, and nose guard, as well as the plume tube, which is mounted in gold with enamel, may have been made later.

SOURCES: Inventory 1687; Inventory 1884, pt. 3, bk. 2, no. 4414.

LITERATURE: Yablonskaya 1988/1, p. 207, ill. 138.

AKL

42. Ceremonial Shield

Persia, first half of 17th century
Leather, gold, emeralds, rubies, pearls, turquoise, silk
Diam. 21 5/8 in. (55.5 cm)
OR-169

Shields were virtually never used in the seventeenth century by Russian rulers in military ceremony. However, they were frequently objects of gift-giving to the Russian tsars from Muslim rulers of Safavid Persia and Ottoman Turkey. Made of various materials—leather, cane, brocade, Damascus steel—and decorated with precious stones and turquoise, they were not intended for battle but were primarily works of the jeweler's art combined with that of the armorer.

The decorative design of this shield is elegant and refined. Its black leather surface is a magnificent background for the gold decorations, precious stones, and pearls. Attached in the center is a large convex gold plate scattered with rubies, turquoise, and pearls. The gems are surrounded by a carved open-work stylized gold ornamentation. An exquisitely executed turquoise mosaic, set in gold and surrounded by a band of pearls, frames the central cluster of gems.

The shield was offered to Tsar Mikhail Fyodorovich and his heir, Tsarevich Alexei Mikhailovich, by Assan-bek, ambassador of Shah Abbas II of Persia, evidently between 1641 and 1643, the time when the Persian embassy was in Moscow. The shield's accession to the Armory Treasury is dated December 29, 1644. The Treasury Office's Book of Receipts of 1644–45 calls the shield "single-horned," that is, made of rhinoceros hide. More than likely, however, this reflected the usual exaggeration of the merits ascribed to a gift.

SOURCES: Book of Receipts 1644–45, fol. 126v; Inventory 1884, pt. 3, bk. 2, no. 5056.
LITERATURE: Yablonskaya 1996, pp. 94–95, nos. 88, 89.

AKL

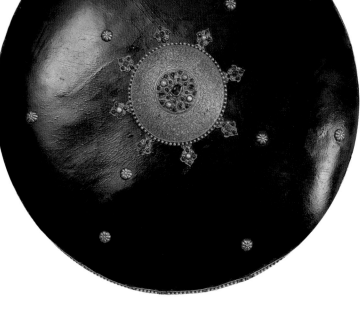

43. Ceremonial Mace

Persia, mid-17th century
Gold, wood, turquoise
Overall l. 20¹/₄ in. (52 cm)
OR-187

In Russia in the sixteenth and seventeenth centuries, *pernaty* was the term used for a mace, the head of which consisted of more than six solid flanges. Maces served in the Russian landed gentry's cavalry both as menacing battle weapons and as symbols of military authority. The Armory collection includes maces made by Safavid and Ottoman craftsmen. These often came to Russia as ambassadorial gifts from Eastern rulers. Made of precious metals—gold and silver—and decorated with precious stones, they are true masterpieces of the jeweler's art.

The head of this mace consists of seven gold flanges radiating from a tubular socket. Its wooden handle is covered in gold and has open-work ornament. The main element of the mace's design is a turquoise mosaic set into the gold cap of the head and handle.

This mace was offered as a gift to Tsar Alexei Mikhailovich from Shah Abbas II of Persia, presented on February 3, 1658, by the Shah's ambassador, Khan Dakun-saltan, during the formal reception for the embassy in the Palace of Facets at the Moscow Kremlin. In the inventory of 1687, this mace was ranked first among others of this type of weapon, confirming its high status in the arms treasury of the Russian rulers.

SOURCES: Inventory 1687, sh. 116, no. 1; Inventory 1885, pt. 4, bk. 3, no. 5241.
LITERATURE: Yablonskaya 1996, p. 106, no. 97

AKL

GIFTS FROM POLAND AND LITHUANIA

DURING MOST OF THE SIXTEENTH and seventeenth centuries, the Polish state was a confederation consisting of Poland, Lithuania, and several territories whose ownership was disputed by Russia, the Ottoman Empire, and the Holy Roman emperors. The positions of king of Poland and grand duke were elective, although members of the Vasa family (originally from Sweden) ruled Poland and Lithuania from 1587—1668. (In 1660, however, King John II Casimir was forced to renounce his rule over Lithuania.) Sovereignty was shared by the king and by the Rzeczpospolita (Polish-Lithuanian Commonwealth), which consisted of various assemblies of the nobility and the upper middle class of Poland-Lithuania. Most embassies sent abroad to deal with other nations were sent both by the kings and by the Rzeczpospolita.

Since the Polish and Russian states were in direct competition for territories along their eastern and western borders, the history of their relationship is a complex one. Diplomatic relations between Kievan Rus and Poland were already established in the 960s, during the territorial formation of the two states. For the following seven centuries, attempts to resolve the issue of the border between them were made both on the battlefield and through peace negotiations.

Impressive gifts from Poland to the tsars and the documentation of them began in the year 1493. Six-

teenth-century ambassadorial documents refer to only one important group of gifts, the 1584 gift from King Stefan Batory of Poland to Tsar Ivan IV.[1] Gold coins, brought in standing cups, were standard items in the groups of Polish gifts and were included in an ambassador's gift of 1543 to Tsar Ivan, and similar gifts of coins occurred in 1590 and 1600. The purpose of the 1590 ambassadorial visit was to conclude a truce, and that of 1600 was to receive a reconfirmation of the treaty from the new Tsar Boris Godunov. Horse trappings and saddles were included with other gifts in 1600; these items were often sent as gifts from Poland, later accompanied by carriages. Statues in precious metal are occasionally noted; for example, one document indicates that Boris Godunov received an eagle of gilded silver and a statue of a fawn.

Relations with Poland were one of the major aspects of Russian foreign policy during the seventeenth century, because at the beginning of the century, during the years of intervention and disturbance, Russia had incurred substantial territorial losses to the west. Several times during the years that followed, Russia would be at war with her Polish-Lithuanian neighbor. During the 1620s and the early 1630s, Russia carried on negotiations with Sweden and Turkey regarding an alliance against the Rzeczpospolita, but the controversies existing between Russia and these neighbors excluded the possibility for any lasting alliance.

Russia's attempts in 1632–34 to resolve the issue of the western lands by means of military action without the support of any allies ended in failure. The Russians did, however, achieve one goal, the recognition of Tsar Mikhail Romanov as Russia's sovereign ruler. At that point, military confrontation was replaced by a period of rapprochement between Russia and the Polish-Lithuanian state on the grounds of their common anti-Ottoman political interests. This might have lasted if it were not for events in Ukraine, where a war for independence from Poland broke out in 1648, followed by Ukraine's unification with Russia six years later. The 1654 decision of the Muscovy government to launch a new war for Smolensk ended all prospects for peace. The Andrusovo armistice of 1667 marked the end of that war, which was a victory for Russia, and the tsar's rule was restored over many formerly Polish territories. However, the most significant result of the diplomatic activities of the Polish and Russian governments was the later signing of the Eternal Peace agreement in 1686, as a result of which Russia joined the Holy League, which was able to some degree to push back the borders of the Ottoman Empire.

Traces of almost all the visits of great ambassadors from Warsaw can be seen in various collections of the Moscow Kremlin Armory. Among the silver objects—valuable evidence of the ambassadorial missions of 1647, 1667, and 1686—are splendid works by German craftsmen of Hamburg and Augsburg, as well as masterpieces from the city of Gdańsk, the main center of goldsmith art in Poland. The greatest of the German objects is a splendid eagle made by Abraham Drentwett I, a magnificent work of sculpture executed in silver presented to Tsar Alexei in 1671 (cat. no. 50). Quantitatively, the later gift of 1686, which restored peace between the countries for more than a decade, was more important than the embassy that carried the eagle, as seems reasonable given the issues discussed.

NOTE

1. The best and most substantial modern discussion of the Polish gifts to the tsars is by Zagorodniaia 1998, pp. 15–37. The notes contain the references to the basic documents.

IAZ

44. Hussar Saddle

Poland, late 16th century
Wood, silver, silk, metallic thread, turquoise, glass
H. of pommel 14 in. (36 cm); l. of saddle 14³/₄ in. (38 cm)
K-52

On October 6, 1600, an important embassy from Poland made its ceremonial entry into Moscow to conclude a peace treaty that would establish friendly relations between the new tsar, Boris Godunov, and King Sigismund III and to congratulate the tsar on his elevation to the throne. The Dutch merchant Isaac Massa, who was living in Moscow at the time, witnessed the sumptuous reception given the embassy, which consisted of more than 900 people, 2,000 finely bred horses, and numerous carriages. The four Hungarian or Turkish horses given to the tsar were reportedly difficult to handle, despite the fact that their legs were hobbled. Their trappings were extremely valuable. Included in a list of the gifts presented to the tsar and his son, Fyodor Borisovich, were fifteen riding horses. The trappings for these horses were described only briefly, but at least three sets included Hussar saddles. Two other Hussar saddles of Polish origin in the Armory collection have traditionally been included with the saddles in the group brought by the 1600 embassy (K-55, K-78).

The saddle shown here is covered in raspberry-colored velvet decorated on the seat and flaps with appliqués of navy, cream, and light-blue velvet and embellished with gold embroidery. On the pommel and cantle are mounted silver plaques ornamented with turquoise and pieces of dark-blue glass; seven plaques are visible on the pommel, but of the seven on the cantle only one has been preserved.

The saddle is mentioned for the first time in the state Book of Receipts for the years 1613–14. On December 28, 1613, it was "taken from upstairs, from the tsar and grand prince Mikhail Fyodorovich and brought to the treasury." After a detailed description of the saddle appears a note, "taken," which attests that the saddle brought from the palace had passed into state hands. Indeed, on the inside of the saddle flap, a barely visible inscription in ink on leather indicates the year 1613/14, according to the old Russian dating system, which coincides with the notation in the book of receipts.

———————

SOURCES: Book of Receipts 1613–14, fol. 46; Inventory 1706, fol. 179; Shpilevsky 1850; Massa 1874, pp. 73–74; Inventory 1884, pt. 6, vol. 5, no. 8516.
LITERATURE: Denisova 1954, p. 290; Kirillova 1996, pp. 144–45, no. 127 (K-55). *Skarby Kremla* 1998, p. 153, no. 39.

OBM

45. Tankard

Königsberg, first half of 17th century
Amber, wood, silver, gilding
H. 9 in. (23 cm)
DK-222

During his audience at the Palace of Facets held on January 26, 1645, Ambassador Gabriel Stempkowski presented Tsar Mikhail Fyodorovich with this tankard, or wine mug, as a gift from King Wladislaw IV of Poland. Along with the other objects to the tsar, it was submitted to the treasury, where it was appraised at 12 rubles. The tankard was the second most costly amber object given to the Russian court at this time. The most expensive amber piece was a large casket whose value,

including the value of the numerous standing cups, tazzas, and amber rosary beads in boxes it contained, was estimated at 100 rubles.

The proportion and decoration of the tankard's body, as well as the artistry of the silver frame, are typical of objects created by craftsmen in Königsberg, the leading European center of amber carving in the late sixteenth and seventeenth centuries. The cylindrical body is composed of three registers of amber; the middle register is decorated with fruit and flowers and birds intertwined with grapevines.

The history of amber carving dates back to prehistoric times. Amber amulets have been found from as early as 3500–1800 B.C. European works of amber are almost invariably made of Baltic amber, and as amber working flourished, guilds sprang up along the Baltic coast. In Gdańsk, Poland, about one hundred miles west of Königsberg, secular objects in amber were made for the Polish court, along with devotional items, and contemporary sources indicate that in the seventeenth century carved ambers were a highly regarded aspect of Polish art and craftsmanship.

SOURCES: Book of Receipts 1644–45, fol. 162; Ambassadorial Book 1644–46, fol. 142v; Inventory 1676, fol. 29; Inventory 1679, fol. 43; Inventory 1721, fol. 36v; Inventory 1884, pt. 2, vol. 3, no. 2456 (misstates the date when the object was brought over and the name of the ambassador).

LITERATURE: Pelka 1920, pp. 98–99, 100, ill. 76; Markova 1966, p. 50, color ill.; *Skarby Kremla* 1998, pp. 116–17, no. 16.

IAZ

46a,b. Ewer and Basin

Germany (Augsburg), 1635–40
Maker's mark for Hans Jacob Baur I (Seling 1980, vol. 3,
no. 1369), Augsburg (Seling 1980, vol. 3, no. 62)
Silver, gilding
Ewer: H. 21 1/2 in. (55 cm); weight 5,694.7 gr
Basin: H. 34 3/4 in. (89 cm); w. 42 1/4 in. (108.3 cm);
weight 10,200 gr
MZ-172/1–2, MZ-168

This basin (which weighs 22 pounds) and ewer (which weighs 13 pounds) were offered, among many other royal gifts, to Tsar Alexei Mikhailovich by Jan Kazimierz Pac and Hieronim Ciechanowicz, two ambassadors of the king of Poland, Wladislaw IV, during an audience in the reception hall of the Palace of Facets on October 24, 1647. Along with the rest of the gifts, this set was submitted to the treasury, where it was kept permanently. The ewer and basin, although designed for washing the hands, were never actually used except for display purposes. The inventory listed two sets of ewers with basins, which, after the standing cups, were the gifts of greatest prominence during the first half of the seventeenth century.[1] This set, however, is the most valuable silver gift brought by the 1647 embassy.

The decoration of the set is based on the combination of traditional Baroque elements—auricular forms, seashells, and a lavish floral ornament—and military motifs typical of the first ruler from the influential Lithuanian Radziwill family. Several generations of this family, including Krzysztof Radziwill, successfully carried out military activities on behalf of the Polish crown. Embossed images of an armed soldier and a drummer are situated on the ewer's body; the lid is decorated with military accessories and a floral ornament. Seventeenth-century records of the treasury indicate that a figure of Cupid with a wreath and a branch was initially situated on the top of the ewer. The current ornamentation of the lid appeared in the nineteenth century. The spout of the ewer looks like the half-figure of a woman holding a dolphin in her hands. The handle, consisting of volutes, is decorated with a female herm, and the lid is embellished with auricular motifs.

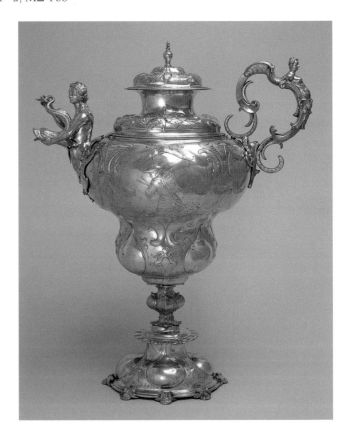

The center of the basin is embossed with a battle scene that is taking place against the background of engraved city walls with towers, which gives the impression that this is a depiction of an actual historical event. One of the mounted soldiers fighting with swords holds a flag with the emblem of the Grand Duchy of Lithuania. According to one scholar, the basin depicts an episode of the recent war between Poland-Lithuania and Sweden. In this manner, the gift perfectly exemplified the purposes of this ambassadorial mission—to win Russia as an ally against Turkey.

The Thirty Years' War did not disrupt the crafts of gold and silver work in Augsburg, and artists continued

to perfect the forms and decorations of precious metal. Military scenes and figures of soldiers borrowed from contemporary engravings were popular, and the figures that appear on the body of this ewer undoubtedly refer to an engraved source.

The Polish eagle with the coat of arms of the Radziwill family is engraved on the reverse of the basin and under the ewer's handle; the first letters of all words comprising the following inscription and indicating the titles of the ruling family are engraved on the sides: CHRISTOPHORUS RADZIWIL DEI GRATIA DUX BIRZENSIS ET DUBINKENSIS SANCTI ROMANI IMPERII PRINCEPTS PALATINUS WILNENSIS ET MAGNI DUCATUS LITHUANIAE DUX GENERALIS MOSCOWITICUS AC SUETICUS CAMPIDUX BELLATOR. This inscription enables us to specify the date of the set, which belonged to Krzysztof Radziwill, governor of the city of Vilnius, capital city of the Grand Duchy of Lithuania during the period 1635–40.

An inscription with the number and the weight of the piece is also engraved on the underside of the basin; a similar inscription, including information regarding the circumstances under which the ewer was received into the treasury, is engraved on the bottom of its base.

NOTE

1. The gift of 1647 also included six standing cups with weights ranging from 7 to 13 pounds. Five standing cups are preserved in the Kremlin Armory.

SOURCES: Ambassadorial Book 1647–48/2, fol. 129v; Book of Receipts 1647–48, fols. 87v–88; Inventory 1676, fols. 183v–184; Inventory 1679, fol. 155v; Inventory 1835, no. 980 (basin); Inventory 1884, pt. 2, vol. 2, nos. 1196, 1463.

LITERATURE: Seling 1980, vol. 2, ill. 469; vol. 3, no. 1369b; Markova 1996, pp. 53–54, nos. 48–49; *Skarby Kremla* 1998, pp. 122–25, nos. 21, 22.

IAZ

47. Basin

Germany (Nuremberg), mid-16th century
Maker's mark for Hans Brabant (Rosenberg 1922–28, vol. 3,
no. 3842), Nuremberg (Rosenberg 1922–28, vol. 3, no. 3687)
Silver, mother-of-pearl, diamonds, rubies, garnets
enamel, glass, paper, gilding
Diam. 18¾ in. (48 cm); weight 4,147 gr
MZ-1235

This sumptuous basin was offered by King John II Casimir of Poland through his envoys Stanislaw Witowski and Filip Kazimierz Obuchowicz and the secretary of the Polish legation, Krzysztof Antony Obrynski, to Tsar Alexei Mikhailovich at a reception in the Palace of Facets held on April 11, 1651. The basin was evaluated at a very high price because of the superb quality of its execution. The only piece among the royal gifts more expensive than this basin was a painted glass tankard mounted in a gold frame.

The basin is typical in structure to seventeenth-century examples, with a foot and a pronounced central raised medallion, on which could be placed a ewer with a base corresponding in shape and size. In this case, the medallion is decorated with gold painting on paper under glass surrounded by a band in high relief.

The basin is set with six cartouches of mother-of-pearl and decorated with *verre églomisé*, enameled ornament, and garnets against a rich background of arabesques and cast Renaissance relief work. The relief decoration is unique in its variety of form and originality; it con-

sists of scrollwork cartouches with female herms and medallions with precious stones set in mounts trimmed with enamel.

Hans Brabant (master 1535; d. 1569), who made this magnificent basin, is one of the finest early Renaissance goldsmiths in Nuremberg. Unfortunately, very little is known about him, and there are only three pieces by his hand, two of them in Russia. One is this object; the other is in St. Petersburg. The third work, a gilded-silver double standing cup, is part of the Waddesdon Bequest in the British Museum.

SOURCES: Ambassadorial Book 1651, fol. 105; Book of Receipts 1650–51, fol. 107; Inventory 1884, pt. 2, vol. 2, no. 1225.

LITERATURE: Rosenberg 1922–28, vol. 3, p. 69, no. 3842c; Markova 1975, no. 6; Markova 1980, p. 102, no. 7; Rashkovan 1988/2, pp. 280–81, fig. 195; *Skarby Kremla* 1998, pp. 25–26, 126, no. 24.

IAZ

48a. Ewer

Poland (Gdańsk), 1630–50
Maker's mark for Christian Paulsen I (Czihak 1908, p. 57,
no. 312), Gdańsk (Czihak 1908, p. 44, no. 1)
Silver, gilding
H. 28⁷/8 in. (74 cm); weight 8,594.4 gr
MZ-162

48b. Basin

Poland (Gdańsk), c. 1667
Maker's mark: "HPL" (Rosenberg 1922–28, vol. 2, no. 1558),
Gdańsk (Gradowski 1993, no. 4)
Silver, gilding
H. 39³/4 (102 cm); w. 49⁷/8 in. (128 cm); weight 18,050 gr
MZ-170

This ewer (which weighs 20 pounds) and basin (which weighs 40 pounds) were royal gifts delivered during an audience with Tsar Alexei Mikhailovich on October 20, 1667, by the ambassadors Stanislaw Bieniewski and Cyprian Pawel Brzostovski, and the secretary of the legation, Wladislaw Szmeling as a gift from King John II Casimir of Poland. The group of gifts contained only one silver set, in addition to which the king had sent a horse-drawn carriage. During the reign of Regent Sofia, in the 1680s, this ewer was documented among the belongings of her favorite, Prince Vasily Vasilievich Golitsyn, and in 1690, after she lost her position, it was returned to the tsar's treasury.

In the opinion of N. V. Rashkovan, the basin was commissioned from the goldsmith to go with the ewer especially for the ambassadorial mission. Certainly, the ewer was used as a model for the form and decoration of the basin, but beyond that, the diameter of the raised medallion in the center of the basin exactly matches that of the ewer's base. The medallion has a scene of Perseus rescuing Andromeda, an image based on a print by Hendrik Goltzius. The basin is decorated with swirls, and the body of the ewer is embossed with reliefs. The curvilinear rim of the basin is highlighted with alternating daffodils and tulips. The ewer's spout is finished with an embossed male mask, while the corresponding decoration on the lid is the mask of a dolphin. The enormous size of this ewer and basin, the use of gilding in specific areas, and the abundant floral decoration characterize the set as a Baroque masterpiece. In addition to typical Baroque details, the ewer has features characteristic of the work produced by Gdańsk craftsmen of the period: the handle is decorated with a pearl-like border and the lid with a double hinge. This ewer and its matching basin are the largest gifts of silver preserved in the Kremlin Armory.

Two similar ewers made by Christian Paulsen I and brought to Moscow by the same embassy as the set discussed here, according to Dr. A. Fischinger, are in the Moscow Kremlin Armory (MZ-163, MZ-164). The Russian documents do not confirm this theory but suggest that they may have come with the 1686 mission. According to the records of the Ambassadorial Book, the royal gifts of 1686 included two ewers of a similar weight, but they were not recorded in the inventory of the tsar's treasury until 1690.

At the foot of this ewer's base and on the reverse of the basin are inscriptions with information about weight, value, and date of acceptance into the treasury, as well as sources. The gift inscription on the ewer indicating that it was a gift from the ambassador is erroneous. All archival documents list it among the king's gifts.

Along with other valued objects, two ewers with spirals stood on the grand sideboard set up in the reception hall of the Palace of Facets for a ceremonial banquet given after the coronation of Empress Catherine II in 1762 (see Chapter 4, fig. 10).

SOURCES: Ambassadorial Book 1667, fols. 296, 317v; Book of Receipts 1667–68, fol. 31; Inventory 1676, fols. 191, 196; Inventory 1679, fol. 162; Ambassadorial Book 1686, fol. 477v; Books of Receipts 1689–90, fol. 121; Inventory 1690, fol. 163; Inventory 1721, fols. 72, 97v; Inventory 1884, pt. 2, vol. 2, nos. 1171–1173, 1220.

LITERATURE: *Oruzheinaia palata* 1902, p. 237, fig. on p. 256; *Oruzheinaia palata* 1914, p. 914; *Treasures* 1979, cat. no. 96, pp. 128, 210; *Trésors* 1979, cat. no. 96, pp. 189, 191; *Illustrated Bartsch* 1980–81, vol. 3, pt. 1, p. 149; Fischinger 1983, pp. 318, 322; Rashkovan 1988/3, p. 243, figs. 167, 168; Markova 1996, pp. 86–87, no. 78; *Aurea Porta* 1997, p. 325, no. VIII.57; *Skarby Kremla* 1998, pp. 128–31, nos. 26, 27.

IAZ

49. Flask

Poland (Gdańsk), c. 1667
Maker's mark: "HPL" (Rosenberg 1922–28, vol. 2, no. 1558),
Gdańsk (Czihak 1908, p. 44, no. 3)
Silver, gilding
H. 22⅝ in. (58 cm); weight 5,721 gr
MZ-189/1-3

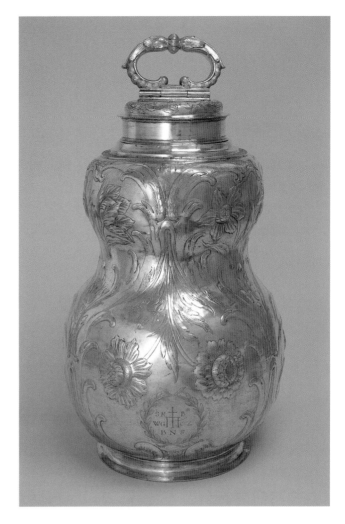

This vessel, which weighs 13 pounds, was one of the gifts offered to Tsar Alexei Mikhailovich by the ambassador Stanislaw Kazimierz Bieniewski during an audience in the reception hall of the Palace of Facets on October 20, 1667, after he had presented gifts from the Polish king John II Casimir. Among the ambassador's gifts is a mate to this flask, which is in the Moscow Kremlin Armory (MZ-188). The ambassador also brought a ewer-and-basin set—by now a mandatory element of ambassadorial audiences during the second half of the seventeenth century—as well as an enormously costly automatic calendar table clock, an object very rarely included in Polish gifts.

This bottle-gourd-shape vessel is decorated with long-stemmed daffodils, tulips, and peonies. The images are ornamented with auricular motifs. Engraved on the body of the vessel is the coat of arms of the Bieniewski-Radwan family. There is also the Wieniawa family coat of arms, which belonged to Bieniewski's wife. Under the screw cap, which is embossed with a wreath of flowers, is a smooth, gilded cork with a hinged handle, an indispensable detail of this type of plate.

In the second half of the seventeenth century, such flasks were common among the gifts of the Polish and Swedish rulers as well as diplomats, but objects with dimensions like this example were extremely rare. Flasks equal in size to the Polish examples were presented in Moscow only once, in 1647, as a gift from Queen Christina of Sweden. Judging by the 1721 inventory of treasury plate, a pair of silver flasks—along with several confectionary and candy trees, fruit dishes on stands, and trays—were used during the formal dinner on the occasion of the coronation of Peter I's wife, for the purpose of keeping and serving wine.

On the bottom of this flask is an engraved note stating the object's weight, value, and source, and the date it was admitted to the tsar's treasury.

SOURCES: Ambassadorial Book 1667, fols. 300, 318v; Book of Receipts 1667–68, fol. 31v; Inventory 1676, fol. 53; Inventory 1679, fols. 62v–63; Inventory 1721, fols. 78v–79, 80, 178–178v; Inventory 1835, no. 1727; Inventory 1884, pt. 2, vol. 2, no. 1896.
LITERATURE: Fischinger 1983, p. 321, fig. 6; *Aurea Porta* 1997, p. 325, no. VIII.57.3; Silverskatter 1997, p. 83, nos. 10–11; *Skarby Kremla* 1998, pp. 131–32, no. 28.

IAZ

50. Heraldic Eagle

Germany (Augsburg), figure 1665–70, base c. 1670
Maker's mark for Abraham Drentwett I (eagle) (Seling 1980,
vol. 3, no. 1507k) and for Heinrich Mannlich (base)
(Seling 1980, vol. 3, no. 1613b); Augsburg (on eagle)
(Seling 1980, vol. 3, no. 98) and on base (unclearly stamped)
Silver, gilding
H. 34³/₈ in. (88 cm); w. 25³/₄ in. (66 cm); diam. of base:
22⁷/₈ in. (59 cm); weight 15,810 gr
MZ-191

On December 8, 1671, ten members of a Polish embassy to Moscow witnessed a ceremony in the Palace of Facets during which Ambassadors Jan Gmniński and Cyprian Pawel Brzostovski and the secretary of the legation, Jan Kotowicz, presented to Tsar Alexei Mikhailovich a gift from King Michael Wisniowiecki—the silver figure of an eagle.

Abraham Drentwett I, *Silver Throne.* Germany (Augsburg), 1650. Made for the coronation of Queen Christina of Sweden in 1650. Hall of State, Royal Palace, Stockholm (photo by Lennart of Petersen's courtesy Swedish Royal Collection, Stockholm)

The Armory museum possesses the world's largest collection of Augsburg silver with more than four hundred impressive objects dating from the sixteenth to the early eighteenth century. Situated on trade routes running from the south to the north, Augsburg flourished because of its favorable geographical position, and between 1525 and 1575 there were about a hundred goldsmiths working there. Like Nuremberg, Augsburg was famous for its families of goldsmiths, in which jewelry-making skills were passed down from one generation to the next. The Drentwett family of goldsmiths worked in Augsburg over a very long period, and they were well known throughout Europe.

This splendid object, symbolic of the Polish monarchy, is a truly royal gift and a very rare example of German silver. The eagle itself, with its outspread wings, is depicted in a heraldic stance holding in its talons emblems of royal power, the orb and scepter, which suggests its function as a heraldic beast. A flat plate at the top of the eagle's head serves as a base for the royal crown. Although this object has been housed in the Moscow Kremlin for centuries, it does not represent the eagle of the Russian Empire, which was adapted from the Byzantine eagle after 1472 (when Ivan III married a Byzantine princess, Sofia Paleologue), but can be identified with the kingdom of Poland. This eagle is similar to one that served as a stand for the crown during the reign of King John II Casimir of Poland.

Abraham Drentwett I was born in 1614, the son of goldsmith Philipp Jakob Drentwett; he attained the rank of master goldsmith in 1641 and died in 1666. One of his most significant works—the silver throne of

Queen Christina of Sweden (Stockholm, Royal Palace)—testifies to the international reputation of this superb craftsman, who is counted among the most distinguished representatives of the German Baroque style.

The decoration of the round, massively worked base, made by Heinrich Mannlich, consists of bundles of fruit that flank small images of eagles. The base was apparently added at a later time so Mannlich (active 1658–98) was obliged to adopt a motif appropriate to the eagle. The object must have been chosen as a gift because of its impressive character, but as a symbol of Polish royalty it could hardly have been used in Russia as a pedestal for a crown. In the tsar's collection it could serve only as an extraordinary example of royal plate. Engraved on the disk is an inscription indicating the number, weight, and date, as well as information about how the object passed into state hands.

SOURCES: Ambassadorial Book 1671–72, fol. 203v, 218v, 319v; Book of Receipts 1671–72, fol. 35; Inventory 1676, fol. 52v; Inventory 1690, fol. 39v; Inventory 1721, fol. 46; Inventory 1835, no. 1077; Inventory 1884, pt. 2, bk. 2, no. 1931.

LITERATURE: Filimonov 1893, pt. 7, vol. 10, p. 34; Smirnova 1964, p. 244; Augburg 1968, pp. 300–301, no. 441, ill. 272; Fischinger 1990, pp. 85–90; Rashkovan 1988/3, vol. 3, p. 247 (where the wrong accession date is indicated); Grzybkowska 1994, p. 260; *Silber und Gold* 1994, pp. 204–5, ill. 36 (where the wrong accession date is indicated); Nowacki 1995, p. 146; Szmytki 1995, p. 66; *Narodziny Stolici* 1996, p. 383, no. XII 32, ill. 75; *Skarby Kremla* 1998, pp. 135–36, no. 31.

IAZ

51a,b. Pair of Vases (*tsvetniki*)[1]

Germany (Augsburg), 1685
Maker's mark for Abraham Drentwett II (Seling 1980, vol. 3,
no. 1728), Augsburg (Seling 1980, vol. 3, no. 136)
Silver, gilding
H. (a) 19 1/8 in. (49 cm); (b) 18 3/4 in. (48 cm); weight (a)
2,821.2 gr; (b) 2,880.8 gr
MZ-359; MZ-360

During their audience in the Palace of Facets held on November 11, 1686, Ambassadors Krzysztof Grzymutowski, governor of Poznań, and Marcjan Oginski, chancellor of the Grand Duchy of Lithuania, presented the co-tsars Ivan V and Peter I with this pair of silver vases, the first weighing 7 pounds (10 ounces), the second 7 pounds (9 ounces), as a gift from King John III Sobieski.[2]

The handles are composed of two eagles perched on the shoulders of each vase, standing on applied turbans and trophies of war. The surface of each vase is embossed with bundles of fruit and acanthus leaves.

Shaped like amphoras with a tall profile, the vases are Baroque in style, with gilded decoration (see Chapter 4, fig. 15). The curved gilded acanthus leaves at the neck of each vase, supported by eagles with spread wings, serve as handles. The center portion of each vase's body is decorated with two cast busts of the helmeted goddess Bellona,[3] the patron of cruel, swift, and bloody war.

The victorious 1683 battle at Vienna between the Polish army, under the leadership of John Sobieski, and the Turks is reflected in the decoration of silver objects made by the famous goldsmiths of Augsburg—the Drentwetts, the Billers, Lukas Lang, and Johannes Kilian—during the period of 1670–85.[4] For this reason, the decoration on the vases discussed here is dominated by anti-Turkish motifs. The busts of ancient warriors emerging from the side of the vases, and especially the eagles, can certainly be understood as symbols of the Holy Roman Empire and the Hapsburgs. The turbans in the claws of the eagles clearly represent the conquered Ottoman foe.[5]

Depictions relating to the war in Europe against the Turks appeared often on basins and vessels of the time; a pair of silver vases made by Lorenz Biller II about 1695–1700 has a similar iconographic motif and is also engraved with views of the taking of Turkish fortresses in Hungary.[6] Another silver example, by Lorenz Biller I (cat. no. 54), also alludes to the defeat of Turkey at the Siege of Vienna.

An inscription indicating with a letter the weight of the piece and its treasury number is engraved along the edge of the reverse of the base.

NOTES

1. The term *tsvetnik* was used in old Russian inventories published by Filimonov.

2. In the past, the city mark was read incorrectly (1680–84, Seling 1980, vol. 3, no. 128), which led to the incorrect assumption that these objects were gifts from Emperor Leopold I in 1684.

3. The busts of Bellona on the vases from the Kremlin collection are probably the work of Abraham Drentwett II (1647–1729) on the basis of the same model used for the bust of Bellona made by him in 1680–85. See *Silber und Gold* 1994, pp. 229–32, no. 45, ill. 45.

4. For more detail, see Augsburg 1968, p. 295, nos. 428, 429, ill. 288; p. 298, no. 437, ill. 286.

5. According to Dr. Lorenz Seelig, the most similar contemporary parallel to this pair of vases are the ciboria found in Protestant churches. The vessels created by Abraham Drentwett II in 1677 for St. Ulrich's Church in Augsburg are similar in construction, whereas the altar vases at the same church are more slender and delicate. See *Silber und Gold* 1994, pp. 218–19, no. 42.

6. Florence, Palazzo Pitti, inv. nos. 67, 68/A.s.e.; see Seling 1980, vol. 2, figs. 1057, 1059; vol. 3, no. 1753e.

SOURCES: Ambassadorial Book 1686, fols. 447, 457v, 477; Inventory 1835, nos. 1647, 1648; Inventory 1885, pt. 2, vol. 2, nos. 1980, 1981, table 296.

LITERATURE: *Pamiatniki diplomaticheskikh snoshenii* 1862, p. 579; Rosenberg 1922–28, vol. 3, no. 651r; Markova 1969, pp. 338–42; Seling 1980, vol. 3, no. 1728c; *Silber und Gold* 1994, pp. 218–19, no. 42; *Skarby Kremla* 1998, pp. 29–31, 144–45, no. 37.

IAZ

52. Saddle

Poland, second half of 17th century
Silver, silk, leather, metallic threads, wood, gilding
H. of cantle 13¹/₄ in. (34 cm); l. of saddle 16 in. (41 cm)
K-53

This saddle is covered with raspberry-colored velvet attached to gilded silver, with hammered plant patterns, including flowers, tulips, and leaves on slender stems. The seat and flaps are embroidered with silver and gold threads in the forms of stylized flowers and leaves.

Seven saddles of a similar type have been preserved in the collections of the Kremlin Armory. In imitation of Turkish saddles, they have a high, wide cantle. In the inventories of the Stable Treasury, they are recorded either without an indication of the place where they had been made or as Turkish. They may have been received into the tsar's treasury as part of the ambassadorial gift from Poland-Lithuania; however, owing to the lack of detailed description of the saddles in the Books of Receipts and the Ambassadorial Books, this cannot be proved. For example, in 1686, the great ambassadors and members of the ambassadorial mission presented co-tsars Ivan V and Peter I with a gift consisting of eight horses in full ceremonial trappings; they also presented Princess Sofia Alexeyevna with a carriage and six horses. However, only a brief description of the horse trappings is included in the records.

This saddle is an exception. In the inventory of the Stable Treasury for 1706, it is called a Polish saddle, which suggests that it was part of the gifts brought by the ambassadorial mission of 1686.

SOURCES: Inventory 1706, fol. 185; Inventory 1884, pt. 6, vol. 5, no. 8531.
LITERATURE: *Skarby Kremla* 1998, p. 165, no. 52.

OBM

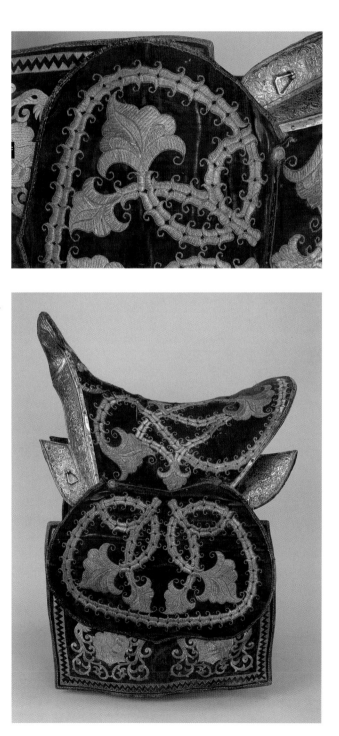

53a,b,c. Ceremonial Horse Trappings

Poland (?), second half of 17th century
Gold, silver, rubies, copper, rock crystal, brass, leather, silk,
metallic threads, iron, enamel, niello, gilding
L. of bridle 34³/₄ in. (89 cm); l. of breastplate straps 22¹/₄ in.
(57 cm), 22⁵/₈ in. (58 cm), 26¹/₈ in. (67 cm);
l. of frontlet 5 in. (13 cm)
K-1013 (bridle); K-637 (breastplate); K-1063 (frontlet)

This set of ceremonial horse trappings consisting of a bridle, a breastplate (to keep the saddle from slipping back), and a frontlet (a head ornament), was intended for use on one of the eight saddle horses presented as a gift to co-tsars Ivan V and Peter I by the members of the Polish ambassadorial mission of 1686. Evidence of this can be found in the inventory of the Stable Treasury for 1706, where the set is described, among others, as Polish "mushtuks," in which the bridle includes an iron curb bit.

There are two types of silver plates on the bridle in this set. Rectangular gold plaques, each with a pattern covered with blue enamel and three rubies, are soldered on some of the plates; silver plaques with a niello pattern are soldered on other plates of gilded silver. The bridle was originally equipped with an "Arab" curb bit, and gold and silk reins.

The frontlet, a curved figured plate, was designed to be suspended on a silver chain attached to the bridle

over the horse's face; a silk noseband was also attached to the bridle. The gilded and carved silver-plate decoration of the frontlet is like those on the bridle and breastplate. A gold plaque with blue enamels and five mounts for precious stones, of which one ruby and two rock crystals are preserved, is soldered in the center. Two silver plates with a carved pattern, originally covered with niello, are soldered to the sides. Unique to this particular frontlet is the fact that not only its silver chain but also the woven band of silk with metallic threads has been preserved.

SOURCES: Inventory 1706, fols. 92, 93, 118; Inventory 1884, pt. 6, vol. 5, nos. 8703, 9020.
LITERATURE: *Skarby Kremla* 1998, pp. 166–68, nos. 53–55.

OBM

GIFTS FROM AUSTRIA

Diplomatic relations between Russia and the Holy Roman Empire[1] and the exchange of ambassadorial missions between them began in 1486, when Emperor Frederick III expressed his desire to enter into a dynastic alliance with Grand Duke Ivan III Vasilievich. Such a connection would mean that the emperor would gain an Eastern ally whose land holdings were larger than he could possibly imagine. For Russia, the alliance would open a trade route into Europe and the expansion of its international contacts without the need to pass through the territories of a frequently hostile Poland. The prospects of this dynastic alliance failed, but in 1489, the first agreement regarding strong and friendly relations "between the two Courts, based on mutual defense from common enemies" was signed,[2] and the long, complicated history of their relationship began.

In Moscow, the emperor's ambassadors were always greeted with splendor and great honor.[3] The grandeur of the Russian ambassadorial mission of 1493 to the court of Emperor Maximilian I, son of Frederick III, was impressive enough to deserve mention in the notes of European diplomats a hundred years after the fact. Tsar Boris Godunov was particularly happy when the emperor presented him with regalia, which was seen as imperial recognition of his own status as a ruler.

Detail of cat. no. 54

But the alliance between Russia and Austria was not just beneficial to Moscow, and their economic relations were constantly under discussion. However, when Vienna was besieged in 1683 by the Turkish army under the leadership of Mustafa Pasha and then saved by John Sobieski, head of the Polish army,[4] Austria recognized just how important the military alliance with Russia was. The power of the Turkish military was so great and its commanders' desire for revenge was so obvious that Austria felt an urgent need of alliance with her neighbors, Poland and Russia.

For this purpose, a Grand and Plenipotentiary Ambassadorial Mission headed by Christof Baron von Zyrova Zyrovsky and Sebastian Reichs-Freiherr von Blumberg was dispatched to Moscow in 1684. The Holy Roman Emperor Leopold I assigned the ambassadors the task of persuading the Russian government of the young co-tsars Ivan V and Peter I to enter into an alliance with Poland, Austria, and the Venetian Republic. All these countries were at risk from Ottoman power—Poland and Austria in the southeast, and the Venetians in their several holdings that abutted the Ottoman Empire. The ambassador was also given the task of persuading Russia to sign a peace agreement with Poland, not a simple matter given the recent history of Russian–Polish relations. In light of the fact that Leopold I had already entered into a similar agreement with the Polish king, John III Sobieski, the

Anonymous, *The Arrival of the Austrian Embassy in Moscow on April 19, 1698*, plate from Johann-Georg Korb's *Diarium Itineris in Moscoviam . . .* (Vienna, 1700). Cleveland Public Library

ambassadors were instructed to promise Moscow the emperor's assistance in negotiations with Warsaw. The potential success of such a coalition had already been demonstrated during the battle at Vienna. As a result of long and complicated, yet successful negotiations, Russia joined the Holy League of Poland, Austria, and Venice, which is viewed by some experts as the beginning of active participation by Russia in European affairs.

The magnificent gifts that the 1684 ambassadorial mission brought to Tsars Ivan and Peter stand out by virtue of their high artistic value. The silver objects were made in the best workshops of Augsburg, which was considered the center of European goldsmith's art in the second half of the seventeenth century. Emperor Leopold I was one of Augsburg's greatest patrons, and so Russia received the most exquisite silver objects that the Augsburg craftsmen could produce. The decoration of virtually every object is inspired by the triumph of the allied armies near Vienna. For example, the flag of Mustafa Pasha with two crescent moons thrown down at the feet of the victors is depicted on a basin (cat. no. 54), along with Turkish captives and captured trophies.

Anti-Ottoman sentiment in the foreign policy of Austria and Russia continued to connect the two countries for some time. One of the most important issues for Russia was access to the shores of the Black Sea. When Tsar Peter I needed support in his war against Turkey in 1695 as he prepared to march on Azov in Tatar and Ottoman territory, he approached former allies, including the emperor of Austria. However, by the end of the 1690s, the political situation had changed. Austria had become involved in the struggle over the Spanish succession and had moved the Eastern question further down on its foreign policy agenda. Peter was unable to make progress in this regard when he visited Vienna in 1698. Then Tsar Peter's new goal—the Baltic sea coast—shifted his interest somewhat from the Austrian alliance, and the Holy League fell into decline and ambassadorial exchanges were less frequent.

NOTES
1. From the twelfth century, as one of the strongest principalities in the Holy Roman Empire, Austria held a leading position in it and generally from 1438 on, members of the Austrian Hapsburg dynasty were its emperors.
2. For more detail, see Adelung 1846, p. 100.
3. See Chapter 3.
4. Danilevsky 1991, pp. 334, 550.

AGK

54. Basin ("Captive Turks Before Emperor Leopold I")

Germany (Augsburg), c. 1683–84
Maker's mark for Lorenz Biller I (Seling 1980, vol. 3,
no. 1524), Augsburg (Seling 1980, vol. 3, no. 130)
Silver, gilding
H. 30³/₈ in. (78 cm); w. 36¹/₄ in. (93 cm); weight 5,333.5 gr
MZ-345

This spectacular basin was presented to co-tsars Ivan V and Peter I at an audience in the Palace of Facets on May 16, 1684, by ambassadors Christof Baron von Zyrova Zyrovsky and Sebastian Reichs-Freiherr von Blumberg on behalf of Emperor Leopold I of the Holy Roman Empire. The purpose of the embassy was to announce Austria's recent victory over the Ottoman Turks, who

had attacked Vienna in 1683, and to persuade the Russian government to consider an alliance to continue the war against Islam and the Ottoman Empire.

The basin is part of a set with the ewer in cat. no. 55. Both pieces were executed in the Baroque style by Lorenz Biller I (active 1644–85), one of the most distinguished masters of the celebrated Augsburg dynasty. It

was traditional for silversmiths of the Biller family to address significant events and historical figures in their work.[1] The central relief on this basin celebrates the victory of the combined forces of Austria and her allies, specifically John Sobieski, later king of Poland, over the Turks at the Siege of Vienna on September 12, 1683.

The goldsmith has chosen to depict the culminating moment of the victors' triumph, when the captive Turks were presented to the emperor in one of the formal halls of the Viennese court, probably in the Hofburg. In the center foreground, we see the defeated Turks bound in chains, bowing on their knees with heads hung low. The emperor is seated on his throne under an elaborate canopy crowned by a two-headed eagle, and at the base of the throne are strewn the trophies of battle— banners and weapons, kettledrums and standards. At the right, apart from the crowd, one of the captives holds a standard bearing an Arabic inscription, and on both sides are lines of armor-clad guards carrying swords and halberds.

The fact that depictions referring to the ongoing war in Europe against the Turks often appeared on basins and vessels is attested to by a pair of silver vases, created by Lorenz Biller II about 1695–1700, which have a similar iconographic motif and are engraved with views of the taking of Turkish fortresses in Hungary.[2]

The basin is embellished with unusually complex imagery. The emperor's left hand rests on a staff, and his left foot is trampling Turkish standards and a turban. Before him stand a page and two captains, one of whom holds an unrolled map of the siege. Above the throne soars the figure of victory holding a laurel wreath in one hand and a palm branch in the other. To the left of the emperor stand three Austrian marshals carrying the imperial staff, sword, and orb, and the future king of Poland dressed in knight's armor.[3] Above each of these four figures is a shield with a coat of arms topped by a crown. Below them are representatives of the victorious army wearing armor and sumptuous wigs. Sobieski's soldiers are shown to the right of the emperor, and above them hang laurel wreaths denoting victory.

The relatively low relief of the central scene is surrounded by an embossed ring of acanthus leaves surrounded by a wide rim, lushly decorated in highly embossed images of the attributes of war and peace. Bundles of fruits are interspersed with gilded trophies, two of Roman and medieval armor and two displaying modern arms. At the top, the gilded figure of an eagle under an imperial crown rests its feet on the orb.

On the reverse of the basin is engraved an inscription indicating its weight, ownership by the state, and official number in Cyrillic.

NOTES
1. The Armory has one other hand-washing set, which was part of the 1686 gift of King John III Sobieski of Poland. It depicts the same theme by Albrecht Biller (basin MZ-524; ewer MZ-585). For more detail, see *Skarby Kremla* 1998, pp. 141–43, nos. 35–36.
2. Florence, Palazzo Pitti, inv. nos. 67, 68/A.s.e.; see Seling 1980, vol. 2, figs. 1057, 1059; vol. 3, no. 1753e.
3. Lorenz Seelig tentatively deciphered the figures on Lorenz Biller I's basin in his article for the catalogue *Silber und Gold* 1994, pp. 32–56.

SOURCES: Ambassadorial Book 1683–84/2, fols. 468, 596v; Inventory 1835, no. 987; Inventory 1885, pt. 2, bk. 2, no. 1193, table 252.

LITERATURE: Markova 1969, pp. 338–42; Markova 1975, ill. 66; *Treasures* 1979, p. 211, no. 98; *Trésors* 1979, p. 192, no. 98; *Schätze* 1991, pp. 138-41, no. 39; *Silber und Gold* 1994, pp. 196–200, no. 32, *Treasures of the Tsar* 1995, pp. 272–73, no. 94; Markova 1996, pp. 59–62, nos. 53, 54.

AGK

55. Ewer

Germany (Augsburg), c. 1680–84
Maker's mark for Lorenz Biller I (Seling 1980, vol. 3, no.
1524), Augsburg (Seling 1980, vol. 3, no. 130)
Silver, gilding
H. 17³/₄ in. (45.5 cm); weight 3,232.3 gr
MZ-355

During their audience in the Palace of Facets held on May 16, 1684, Ambassadors Christof Baron von Zyrova Zyrovsky and Sebastian Reichs-Freiherr von Blumberg presented co-tsars Ivan V and Peter I with this ewer, in the form of a warrior on horseback, as a gift from the emperor of the Holy Roman Empire, Leopold I. This ewer is part of a hand-washing set and is the mate to the basin in cat. no. 54 ("Captive Turks Before Emperor Leopold"). The opening for the spout is in the horse's head, hidden by the forelock.

The figure represents a horseman dressed in the armor of a Roman warrior sitting on a horse raised on its hind legs. A sense of dignity and state power emanates from the horseman's appearance. The ideals of the Holy Roman Empire appealed to the monarchs of the seventeenth century who strived toward the establishment of absolute power. It is for this reason that similar table decorations, often made in Augsburg, are so frequently listed as ambassadorial gifts.

Biller's work, with its characteristic diagonal composition, possesses the dynamic quality that is so typical of Baroque art. Aside from Biller, David Schwestermüller also created table ornaments and other objects in the form of equestrian figures, often modeled on European monarchs, including Gustavus Adolphus of Sweden, Christian IV of Denmark, and Charles I of England. An equestrian statue of Charles I, created in Augsburg between 1640 and 1645 by Schwestermüller, is in the Armory collection (MZ-356).

In the Baroque period, objects of this type were much in demand for banqueting tables, alongside tradi-tional tableware. The idea was to overwhelm one's guests with the sumptuous, dramatic, and exuberant character of such pieces, which were often made in materials other than silver.

A Cyrillic inscription indicating the weight of the object is engraved on the reverse of the base.

SOURCES: Inventory 1835, no. 573; Inventory 1885, pt. 2, vol. 2, no. 1913, table 252.

LITERATURE: Rosenberg 1925–28, vol. 1, no. 568; Markova 1969, p. 339; Seling 1980, vol. 3, no. 1524b.

AGK

56a,b. Pair of Andirons

Germany (Augsburg), 1680
Maker's marks for Johannes Kilian (figures),[1] (Seling 1980, vol.
3, no. 1673), Lukas Lang (bases),[2] (Seling 1980, vol. 3, no.
1655), Augsburg (figures and bases) (Seling 1980, vol. 3, no. 131)
Silver
H. 37 in. (95 cm); weight (a) 10,304.5 gr; (b) 10,111.4 gr
MZ-361; MZ-362

During their audience in the Palace of Facets held on May 16, 1684, Ambassadors Christof Baron von Zyrova Zyrovsky and Sebastian Reichs-Freiherr von Blumberg presented co-tsars Ivan V and Peter I with fireplace sculptures of an "Indian Man" and an "Indian Woman," as a gift from Emperor Leopold I of the Holy Roman Empire.

The seventeenth century was the heyday of Augsburg silver and brought fame to many craftsmen in that city. The best of the Augsburg goldsmiths created large objects and entire sets of silver plate for European monarchs, such as the throne of Queen Christina of Sweden (see cat. no. 50),[3] but to a large extent they owed their success to the objects they fashioned for ornate interiors. Augsburg workshops produced sets of matching objects that permitted customers, including several European courts, to furnish rooms according to their own taste. In Russia, as in Europe, palaces were filled with silver furniture, mirrors, chandeliers, wall sconces, and decorative fireplace accessories. Monumental scale and extravagant decoration invested these utilitarian objects with brilliance and grandeur.

Andirons, like fireplaces, were relatively rare in Russian interiors at the end of the seventeenth century (palaces and houses alike still used tile-decorated stoves), but they were quickly becoming fashionable. Unlike the basin discussed above (cat. no. 54), there is no obvious connection between the content and decoration of these andirons and the purpose of the diplomatic mission, that of bringing Russia into the Anti-Turkish coalition. However, the massing of war trophies—armor, helmets, and bundles of flags—that serves as a pedestal for the figures could be a general allusion to this effort.

Moreover, the figure of a cherub at the top of the base blows a trumpet, perhaps a symbol of victory.

This set of andirons came with a set of fire irons to which "two tongs and a shovel made of iron, with silver-tipped handles" also belonged, according to the inventory. They still exist at the Armory. This is one of the few surviving sets in Russia of Augsburg andirons made of silver. The clothing and features identify both figures as West Indians: a loincloth made of feathers, which covers a loosely hanging dress on the woman and is worn by the man without additional materials other than a kind of sash; the feathered crown of the female figure and the feather-decorated turban of the male; the arrow in the woman's hand, and the bow in the man's.

The motif of exotic lands, be it the Far East or, as here, the West Indies, was a favorite element of interior decoration at this time. This particular motif is encountered in numerous sketches by Jean Lepautre, although designed for a candle stand rather than andirons. The purpose of these fireplace ornaments is apparent in the open, projecting iron-frame construction at the back, which is not covered in silver.

A Cyrillic inscription indicating the treasury's inventory number appears on the base under the figure of the female Indian figure. An engraved Cyrillic inscription indicating the number of the object according to the inventory of the treasury as well as the total weight of the object (i.e., the weight of the silver and the currently missing iron stand) is preserved on the base of the male figure to the left under the armor. The metal supports now on the andirons were made in 1882.

NOTES

1. About 1685 Johannes Kilian (1623–1697) created a figure of the Virgin in silver nearly three feet high intended for Mary's chapel in Würzburg; see Seling 1980, vol. 3, p. 223.

2. A skillfully crafted gilded-silver chandelier nearly 62¹/₂ inches high, made in 1676 on the occasion of the marriage in Passau of Emperor Leopold I and Eleonora Magdalena of Neuerburg, is the only preserved piece made by this craftsman, who died in 1680; see Seling 1980, vol. 3, p. 218, no. 1655a.

3. See Tydén-Jordan 1997, pp. 13–22.

SOURCES: Ambassadorial Book 1683–84/2, fols. 468, 597; Inventory 1835, nos. 1385–1389; Inventory 1885, pt. 2, vol. 2, nos. 1985–89, table 294, p. 210.

LITERATURE: Hernmarck 1978, pl. 516; *Silber und Gold* 1994, pp. 325–36, no. 75, *Treasures of the Tsars* 1995, pp. 278–79, nos. 97, 98.

AGK

GIFTS FROM ENGLAND

IN 1553, A FIRM WITH the unwieldy name of Trading Company for the Discovery of Countries, Islands, States and Possessions Not Yet Known and Not Yet Connected via Sea was established in London. Equipped with funds provided by London merchants, the company sent an expedition under the leadership of Richard Chancellor in search of Eastern countries with fantastic riches. Two of the expedition's ships were destroyed, but the third managed to reach the mouth of the North Dvina on the Barents Sea, the very place where the city of Archangel would be founded some thirty years later. It was from this point that Chancellor was brought to the court of Tsar Ivan IV, where he was received with ceremony at the palace. These events marked the beginning of the active use of a sea route between England and Muscovy.

Two years later, in 1555, the Muscovy Company of English merchants was founded. It had close ties with the English court and the nobility and was the main rival to Dutch merchants in the Russian market over the next century. From this time on, Russia and England would play an exceptionally important role in each other's foreign affairs. The commercial aspect of this relationship was a central factor, but under Ivan IV and Boris Godunov, a number of other, more traditional, diplomatic exchanges occurred as well.

Detail of cat. no. 62

Ivan IV and his successors kept careful control over foreign trade, using the eagerness of countries such as England to trade with (and across) Russia as a means of furthering his political goals. The tsar's desire for a military alliance with England's Queen Elizabeth I, which she consistently refused, remained an unresolved issue for some thirty years. In the meantime, she struggled to obtain concessions for English merchants.

England's first formal embassy to Russia was led by Sir Thomas Randolph in 1568, and this ushered in a long period of cordial trade relations. Russia's "Time of Troubles" brought several embassies from King James I, both to congratulate the successive tsars on their ascension to the throne and to preserve English trading rights. The embassy of Sir Thomas Smith in 1604–5 was particularly important, as evidenced by the major gift of a splendid state coach now in the collection of the Kremlin Armory (see Chapter 5, fig. 10). An important description of the journey was published as a book, anonymously, in 1605: *Sir Thomas Smithes Voiage and Entertainment in Rushia, with the Tragical Ends of Two Emperors and one Emperesse*. The list of Smith's English gifts is preserved in the Central Public Record Office in Moscow: "A charyott [the state coach], Two greate flaggons, A christall cuppe, A bason and ewre, Two haunche pottes, One standinge cuppe. One peece of scarlett and fowre peeces of other fine cloathe."[1]

Simon van de Passe, *Sir Thomas Smith*, 1616. Engraving, sheet: 6⁵/₈ x 4 in. (17.1 x 10.25 cm). National Gallery of Art, Rosenwald Collection, Washington D.C. (photo Ricardo Blanc, © 1999 Board of Trustees)

An embassy in 1614–15, headed by Sir John Merrick, was noteworthy for the ambassador's role in negotiating a peace treaty between Russia and Sweden (the Peace of Stolbovo, 1617). A list of the gifts presented to the tsar also survives: "A large cup with a gilt cover . . . weight 14 *grivenka*, 35 *zolotniki*; and likewise ten goblets parcel-gilt, with a lid, a bowl of chalcedony on a foot, with a cover, the foot and cover silver-gilt; three tureens and for them a cover 15 *grivenka*, 42 *zolotniki*; two large pots silver-gilt, with spouts; a cup of silver-gilt and in it four beakers of silver, the lips gilt and for them one cover, a salt gilt with a cover, a basin also silver-gilt. A chafer silver, the handle wooden; three pieces of cloth of gold and silk, two pieces of satin, a piece of damask."[2]

Another important embassy followed in 1620, and still another in 1634. By the middle of the seventeenth century, however, relations between Moscow and London became somewhat complicated. English merchants were banished from Moscow and permitted to trade only in Archangel. This restriction was related to the upsurge in activity of Russian merchants and to the economic policy of the Moscow government aimed at winning their support, although the official pretext was the execution of King Charles I, an act that had shocked Tsar Alexei Mikhailovich. After the restoration of the monarchy in England in 1660, relations improved somewhat, but the English merchants never managed to reestablish their privileged position in Russia.

The Armory's unique and enormous collection of more than 300 pieces of English silver contains about 150 objects that were brought to Russia between 1557 and 1663, most of them by diplomats. Of the surviving gifts, the largest number is from the 1663–64 embassy

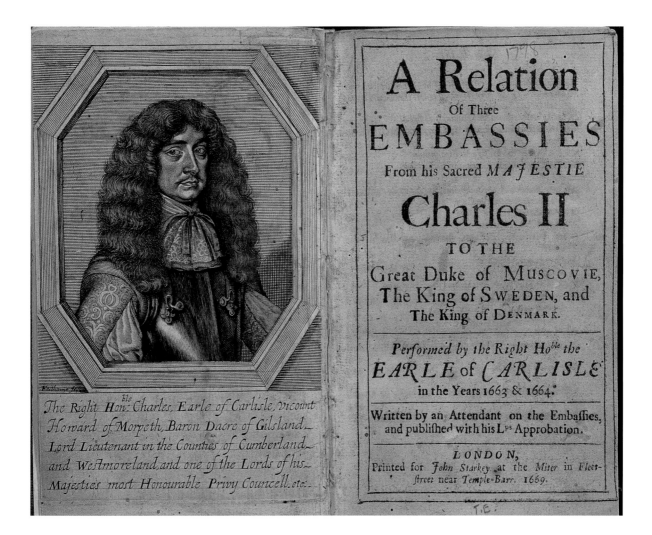

Frontispiece and title page from [Guy de Miège], *A Relation of Three Embassies From his Sacred Majestie Charles II To The Great Duke of Muscovie, The King of Sweden, and The King of Denmark Performed by the Right Noble the Earle of Carlisle in the Years 1663 & 1664* (London, 1669). Rare Books Division, The New York Public Library, Astor, Lenox and Tilden Foundations

led by the earl of Carlisle, which was a failure diplomatically but a grand event of the Russian court. Guy de Miège described the journey and reception by the tsar in a book published in London in 1669: *A Relation of Three Embassies from his Sacred Majestie Charles II to the Great Duke of Muscovie, The King of Sweden and The King of Denmark Performed by the Right Hon*ble *the Earle of Carlisle in the years 1663 & 1664.*

When Carlisle and his companions met Tsar Alexei, de Miège wrote: "[The tsar] . . . being most magnificently placed upon his Throne with his Scepter in his hand, and having his Crown on his Head. His Throne was of massy Silver gilt, wrought curiously on the top with several works and Pyramids; and being seven or eight steps higher than the floor, it rendered the person of this Prince transcendently Majestick."[3]

De Miège also described the presentation of the gifts, which must have been a spectacular sight: "The whole consisted in Vessels of gold and silver, in cloth, velvets, satins, and damaske of diverse colours; there was also great quantities of stufs, and table linnen, two gold-watches, and two carabins, besides six pieces of cast Canon, a great quantity of *Cornish* tynne, and a hundred piggs of lead."[4]

NOTES
1. Oman 1961, p. 29.
2. Ibid., p. 31.
3. *English Silver Treasures* 1991, pp. 117–18.
4. Ibid., p. 118.

IAZ

57. Flagon (*flyaga*)

England (London), 1580–81
Maker's mark: "FT" (Jackson 1989, p. 97), London,
sterling standard, 1580–81 (Jackson 1989, p. 50)
Silver, gilding
H. 17 1/8 in. (44 cm); diam. of base 4 3/8 in. (11.4 cm);
weight 2,979.2 gr
MZ-657

Flagons of this type are known today as pilgrim flasks. (The word *flagon* refers to a container with chains.) Special miniature flagons for holding scented water were also made by English silversmiths at this time. Many silver flagons were made in England and France during the sixteenth and early seventeenth centuries.

This flagon is one of a pair in the collection of the Kremlin Armory (MZ-656), which has a total of six similar flagons dating from 1580 to 1663. These objects constitute the only known group of this rare type, a conical shape with an elongated neck on a tall base and a richly ornamented surface. The body of the flagon illustrated here is decorated with sea creatures in oval strapwork cartouches and clusters of fruit and acanthus leaves. Lion's-head masks with rings are attached to each side, linked by a chain that garlands the flagon and is fastened to the lid by two grotesque scrolls. The engraved birds, draperies, and military trophies on the neck of the vessel were popular decorations at the end of the sixteenth century in the Netherlands; the stylized gilly-flowers, marguerites, and rosettes are typical of English floral engraving found later at the beginning of the seventeenth century.

The other flagons in the Armory are well documented: one pair hallmarked for 1619–20 was presented by Sir John Merrick on behalf of James I in 1620 to Tsar Mikhail Fyodorovich; a similarly decorated example of 1606–7 was presented by Simon Digby for King Charles I in 1636 to Tsar Mikhail; the sixth flagon is dated for 1663–64 and was presented by the earl of Carlisle to Tsar Alexei Mikhailovich.

This flagon and its mate may have been brought as a gift to Tsar Boris Godunov by the English ambassador Sir Thomas Smith in 1604–5. The presence of the coat of arms of King James I engraved in a medallion on the flagons indicates that the pair came from the Royal Jewel House, which was authorized to provide objects for diplomatic purposes. However, according to documents relating to Smith's embassy, the two "great flagons" he presented weighed more than 28 pounds each, more than four times the weight of the present example. Nevertheless, there is no other documentation of any flagons of such great size and value among gifts presented to the Moscow court at any time, nor are there any similar objects in the collection of the Kremlin Armory.

A letter representing the weight of the flagon and an inscription indicating that it belonged to the tsar's treasury are engraved on the bottom.

SOURCES: Inventory 1634, fol. 83v; Inventory 1663, fol. 149v; Inventory 1835, no. 1365; Inventory 1885, pt. 2, vol. 2, no. 1538.

LITERATURE: Cripps 1903, p. 482 (VI); Jones 1909, p. 25, pl. 2, g. 1; Jackson 1921, p. 81; Goldberg 1954, p. 500, fig. 53; Oman 1961, p. 72, pl. 11; *English Silver Treasures* 1991, pp. 140–43, no. 94; *Anglichane v Moskve* 1997, pp. 451–54.

IAZ

58. Livery Pot (*krushka*)

England (London), 1606–7
Maker's mark: "TS" (Jackson 1989, p. 105), London,
sterling standard, 1606–7 (Jackson 1989, p. 51)
Silver, gilding
H. 15 in. (38.5 cm); weight 1,979.1 gr
MZ-701

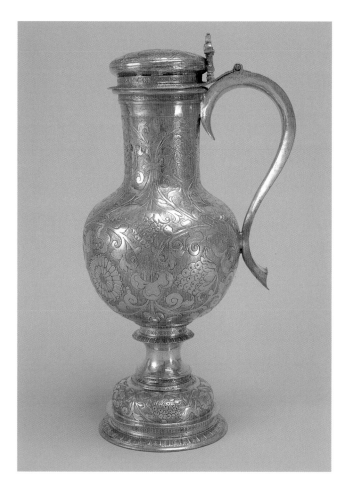

Livery pots are among the most substantial pieces of Elizabethan silver.[1] Unlike tankards used for drinking, vessels like this, inspired by Rhenish stoneware jugs, were used to distribute the daily allotment of beer (or livery, from the French *livrée*, meaning allocation) to servants in addition to wages. Silver livery pots were likely made for the purpose of displaying wealth or position rather than holding beer for servants; they were especially fashionable between about 1575 and 1610 and usually bore similar decorative elements, such as Tudor roses enclosed in strapwork.

This handsome livery pot is typical of the form, with a high-profile base, a pear-shaped body with a lid, and an S-shaped handle. The surfaces are embossed with designs in shallow relief; foliage shoots form circles and end in bunches of grapes, daisies, and roses. The ornament includes an engraved monogram of King James I. The pitcher is characteristic of English Renaissance metalwork, with its harmonious blend of form and decoration. Five similar examples are in the Armory collection, four of them presented to the tsar by the Muscovy Company (in 1615, 1617, and 1620) in order to gain trading concessions.

T. Goldberg has suggested that this livery pot is one of the gifts brought to Russia with the embassy of Sir John Merrick in 1614–15. As with the flagon in cat. no. 57, the coat of arms of James I is engraved on the body of the vessel, which may indicate that it was also a diplomatic gift to Tsar Mikhail. Supporting this conclusion is the fact that the inventory submitted by the treasury to the Ambassadorial Office specifically lists two of the objects donated in 1615 as *krushkas*, along with a number of other different types of vessels.

However, the inventory contains neither a description of these objects nor an indication of their weight, so these conclusions must be considered speculative.

An inscription indicating the weight of the piece is engraved on the bottom, along with the information that at some point after 1640, the pitcher was given by the tsar to one of the patriarchs, who placed it in the Patriarchal Treasury; it was returned to the Armory in 1920.

NOTE
1. For more on the nomenclature of the livery pot or flagon, see Oman 1961, p. 43, n. 22. See also Glanville 1990, pp. 266–69.

SOURCES: Ambassadorial Book 1614–17, fols. 57–58v (see also Kologrivov 1911, p. 20).
LITERATURE: Cripps 1903, p. 483 (VII); Hayden 1915, p. 351; Jackson 1921, p. 82; Goldberg 1954, p. 471, fig. 10 (stamp deciphered incorrectly); *English Silver Treasures* 1991, pp. 130, 160–61, no. 100; *Treasures of the Moscow Kremlin* 1998, p. 83, no. 53.

IAZ

59. Standing Salt

England (London), 1611–12
Maker's mark: "RB" (Jackson 1989, p. 108), London,
sterling standard, 1611–12 (Jackson 1989, p. 51)
Silver, gilding
H. 17$^1/_2$ in. (45 cm); weight 1,280.5 gr
MZ-652

Great significance was always attached to salt containers, or salts, in Renaissance Europe, because of the relative scarcity and high cost of salt. A symbol of wealth and status, the salt was usually given a prominent position at the table, where a guest's relative importance was indicated by how close to it he was seated (the closer, the better). Lavish amounts were spent on the fashioning of silver salts; some were made in the shape of human figures carrying bowls on their heads, while others were given architectural shapes.

This beautiful gilded-silver piece, with its tall cylindrical body, has a particularly interesting feature: its lid is topped by a turret, a typical English motif found on palaces and cathedrals as well as on decorative objects. Its smooth sides, ball-shaped feet, and the round lid rising above the bowl that holds the salt are characteristic of English silver salts of the early seventeenth century.

The object was likely included in the same group of gifts as the livery pot (cat. no. 58) presented by Sir

John Merrick for King James I during his audience with Tsar Mikhail in the Golden Chamber on January 1, 1615. Documentation survives indicating that a salt was submitted to the treasury along with the rest of the objects in the Merrick embassy, but there is no description nor any indication of weight, making the attribution only a conditional one.

An inscription consisting of a letter indicating the weight of the vessel (2 pounds, 14 ounces) is engraved on the bottom.

It should be noted that there is no mention of salts among the gifts that Sir John Merrick took to Russia during his other journeys to Moscow, although an example similar in weight to this one (2 pounds or 64 *zolotniki*) is listed in the 1630 inventory of the possessions of Patriarch Filaret as having come from Merrick. Since other discrepancies exist in the weights indicated in documents and on the objects, Goldberg and Oman have argued that the salt in the treasury is probably the same as the one brought by the mission of 1614–15.

SOURCES: Ambassadorial Book 1614–17, fols. 57–58v (see also Kologrivov 1911, p. 20); *Opis' keleinoi kazny* 1630, vol. 3, p. 932; Inventory 1640, fol. 25 (see also Viktorov 1877–83, p. 20); Inventory 1663, fol. 151v; Inventory 1676, fols. 214v–215; Inventory 1835, no. 1317; Inventory 1885, pt. 2, vol. 2, no. 1493.
LITERATURE: Cripps 1903, p. 415; Jones 1909, pl. VII, 2; Goldberg 1954, p. 493, fig. 46; *Oruzheinaia palata* 1954, pls. 285–288; Oman 1961, p. 32, pl. 16; *Great Britain–USSR* 1967, no. 17, Markova 1996, p. 37, no. 33.

IAZ

60. Livery Pot (*krushka*)

England (London), 1604–5
Maker's mark: "IH" (not published), London, sterling standard,
1604–5 (Jackson 1989, p. 51)
Silver, gilding
H. 19 in. (48.7 cm); weight 3,758.5 gr
MZ-644

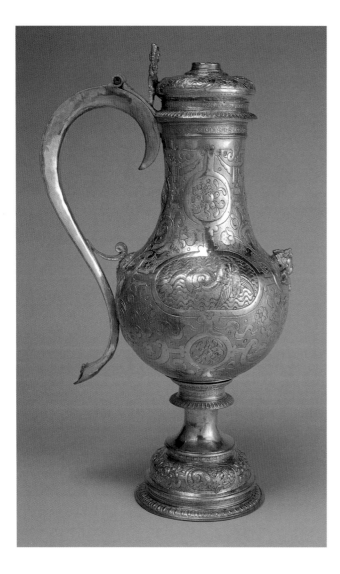

This livery pot, one of a pair, is the same type of vessel as that in cat. no. 58 and formed part of a personal gift presented by Sir John Merrick, who split the pair between Tsar Mikhail and his father, Patriarch Filaret. The gift of King James I to Filaret included a crystal vase mounted in gilded silver, four covered cups, and a gilded-silver ewer-and-basin set. Merrick presented the tsar and patriarch with the gifts from King James I during his audience in the Golden Chamber on December 15, 1620.

This object is decorated with strapwork enclosing shells and sea monsters, typical decorations for this kind of vessel. An inscription consisting of a letter indicating the weight of the vessel is engraved on the bottom.

An identical pot with a similar weight has also been preserved in the Kremlin Armory (MZ-645) and is thought to be the one that Merrick gave to Patriarch Filaret.

SOURCES: Ambassadorial Book 1620–21, fols. 172v, 570; Ambassadorial Book 1620–21, fols. 38, 77; Inventory 1640, fol. 120 (see also Viktorov 1877–83, p. 20); Inventory 1663, fol. 147; Inventory 1676, fols. 182v–183; Inventory 1679, fol. 154v; Inventory 1721, fols. 72v–73; Inventory 1835, no. 844; Inventory 1885, pt. 2, vol. 2, no. 1182.

LITERATURE: *Drevnosti* 1849–53, vol. 5, pl. 29; Cripps 1903, p. 482 (VII); Jones 1909, p. 39, pl. x; Hayden 1915, p. 351; Jackson 1921, p. 82; Goldberg 1954, pp. 469–70, fig. 9; *Oruzheinaia palata* 1954, pls. 290–291; Oman 1961, p. 35, pl. 22.

IAZ

61. Letter of King James I of England (James VI of Scotland) to Patriarch Filaret dated June 24, 1620

Parchment, ink, decorative heading and a large initial letter
decorated with the state emblems
H: 22⅝ in. (58 cm); w: 24⅝ in. (63 cm)
Russian State Archive of Ancient Documents, Moscow

Ambassador John Merrick arrived in Moscow to negotiate with Tsar Mikhail Fyodorovich on December 4, 1620, with the usual credential letter for the tsar and this communication for the tsar's father, Patriarch Filaret. The letter includes congratulations from the king of England and Scotland to Filaret on his return from a long period of captivity in Poland. Filaret had been arrested on an embassy to Smolensk in 1610 and taken to Poland, where he was detained for eight years, returning finally to Moscow in July 1619. In this letter, King James also thanks Filaret for protection that he had given English merchants trading in Russia.

SOURCE: Russian State Archive of Ancient Documents, Moscow, fol. 35 "Anglo-Russian Relations," work 2, doc. 28.

62. Flagon (*krushka*)

England (London), 1613–14; lid: 1611–12
Maker's mark: "WR" (Jackson 1989, p. 107), London,
sterling standard, 1613–14 (Jackson 1989, p. 51)
Silver, gilding
H. 16 in. (41 cm); diam. of base 6⅞ in. (17.4 cm); weight
2,449.2 gr
MZ-699

The flared base of this vessel is embossed, chased, and stamped with strapwork and formal motifs, while the cylindrical body, which tapers slightly, is decorated with grotesques, winged masks, shells, canopies, and three oval cartouches enclosing vignettes of two mermen that flank Neptune, riding sea monsters and blowing conches.

The group of handsome drinking vessels of this type in the Armory collection includes nine examples dating from 1585 to 1663, two pairs of them having been presented to Tsar Mikhail in 1615 by Sir John Merrick. Sixteenth-century nomenclature was not entirely consistent, but most inventories apply the term *flagon* to a tall, pear-shaped vessel with a narrow neck and equipped with a chain; vessels such as this example are generally referred to in contemporary records as a "livery pot" and only became known as a "flagon" around the middle of the following century. This livery pot is of the so-called Hanseatic type, being of tall cylindrical form and similar in outline to vessels that were made up to the eighteenth century in Baltic coastal towns.

Details of the decoration—the faces of dragonfly-winged sirens and the horn-blowing tritons—reflect the influence of Dutch ornament, which was very popular in England, particularly sea-related motifs such as dolphins, sea monsters, and fish, which were often found on marine maps.

This flagon, one of a pair,[1] was presented by Ambassador Simon Digby to Tsar Mikhail on January 3, 1636, in the Golden Chamber. In addition to this pair of flagons, the gifts of English silverplate—the last such group that the Muscovy Company sent to Russia—included standing cups, another pair of flagons, and small candelabra.

Although the list of gifts for this embassy mentions one pair of flagons, another similarly decorated pair (dated for 1617–18 but lacking a maker's mark) is recorded as having come through Simon Digby, possibly as his personal gift to the tsar. This latter pair bears the Stuart coat of arms, indicating that the flagons must once have been provided by the Royal Jewel House.

On the underside of the base, engraved letters denote the weight of this flagon and indicated that it belonged to the Tsars' Treasury. Also inscribed is the name of Patriarch Josaphat and the information that this flagon was presented to him and became part of the Patriarchal Treasury. In 1920 the vessel was acquired by the Moscow Armory from the Patriarch's Wardrobe.

NOTE
1. Moscow Kremlin Armory, MZ-667. This object is dated for 1611–12.

SOURCES: Ambassadorial Book 1635–36, fol. 56; Book of Receipts 1636–37, fols. 33v–34 (see also Kologrivov 1911, p. 105).
LITERATURE: *Drevnosti* 1849–53, vol. 5, pl. 34; Jones 1909, pp. 36–37, fig. 15; Goldberg 1954, pp. 496–97, fig. 49; Oman 1961, p. 37, fig. 26a; *English Silver Treasures* 1991, pp. 166–69, no. 103; *Tesori del Cremlino* 1993, p. 182, no. 63.

IAZ

63. Standing Cup and Cover (*kubok*)

England (London), c. 1663
Maker's mark for Francis Leake (Jackson 1989, p. 123)
Silver, gilding
Height: 27⅞ in. (71.5 cm); diam. of base: 8⅛ in. (20.7 cm);
weight 4,075.5 gr
MZ-621/1-2

This covered cup, one of a pair at the Kremlin Armory (MZ-620/1–2), is a superb example of the elaborate style in English silver that accompanied the Restoration, characterized by naturalistic representations of birds and animals against grounds of overblown flowering plants.

The circular foot of the cup is boldly embossed with a dog, a wild boar, and an abundance of vegetation, with a partially matted baluster stem rising to the cup's beaker-shaped bowl. The bowl is richly decorated on one side with an eagle and on the other with a hare and a stag against a background of tulips and leaves. The detachable cover is also embossed with foliage, and its finial is cast in the form of an equestrian warrior wielding a spear.

Although this piece is marked for Francis Leake, it was embossed by a skillful chaser, probably a foreigner, such as Wolfgang Howzer or Jacob Bodendick.[1]

The cup was presented to Tsar Alexei on February 18, 1664, during an audience in the Palace of Facets by Ambassador Charles Howard, earl of Carlisle, on behalf of King Charles II.

NOTE
1. Mitchell 2000, p. 120.

SOURCES: Ambassadorial Book 1663–64, fols. 201v, 284; Inventory 1690, fol. 55v; Inventory 1721, fol. 59v; Inventory 1884, pt. 2, vol. 1, no. 1124.
LITERATURE: Cripps 1903, p. 460; Jones 1909, pl. XX, no. 2; Goldberg 1954, p. 486, fig. 24; Oman 1961, p. 39, pl. 29; Oman 1970, vol. 2, pl. 2b; *English Silver Treasures* 1991, pp. 180–83, no. 1207; *Tesori del Cremlino* 1993, p. 190, no. 67. Mitchell 2000, pp. 120–21, fig. 12.

IAZ

64. Flagon (flyaga)

England (London), 1663
Maker's mark for Robert Smithier (Jackson 1989, p. 126)
Silver, gilding
H. 14⅞ in. (38 cm); weight 4,310 gr
MZ-659

At an audience in the reception hall of the Palace of Facets on February 18, 1664, Ambassador Charles Howard, earl of Carlisle, presented this flagon to Tsar Alexei on behalf of the English king. After Charles II's accession to the English throne in 1660, the government dispatched Howard to Russia at the head of a large embassy to try to recover its privileges lost after the execution of Charles I. The gifts that the embassy brought to the Russian tsar were exceptionally valuable and included fine gilded-silver candlesticks, goblets, and dishes made in London. Unlike earlier objects made by English silversmiths, these were decorated with bold-relief chasing (see Chapter 7, fig. 17). Although this piece is marked for Robert

Smithier, it was embossed by a skillful chaser, probably a foreigner, such as Wolfgang Howzer or Jacob Bodendick.[1]

This flagon, originally one of a pair, is decorated with chains that connect the screw-on lid and the masks soldered to the sides. The body of the vessel is embossed with a leaping unicorn and a wild boar with its young amid flowers and leaves. This object is an example of a form common primarily in England, where there was a great demand for luxury objects of all types after the restoration of Charles II.

The lavish treatment of flowers on this flagon reflects the influence of the Dutch floral style (see cat. no. 73), which became highly fashionable in England during the mid-seventeenth century, when many Dutch silversmiths were among the numerous foreigners working in London. (Oddly, the Dutch influence on English silver ended when the Dutch-born King William III ascended the English throne in 1689.) By 1665 nearly everything English, from the grandest royal display plate to the most ordinary cup or beaker, was decorated in the same style.

On the bottom of the flagon, an engraved inscription gives the number, weight, date, and value, as well as information about how the object came into state hands. An accurate and detailed color lithograph of the flagon, including the inscriptions, appears in the multivolume work by Fyodor Grigorievich Solntsev printed between 1849 and 1853.

NOTE
1. Mitchell 2000, p.120.

___

SOURCES: Ambassadorial Book 1663–64, fols. 201, 284v; Inventory 1676, fol. 53v; Inventory 1885, pt. 2, bk. 2, no. 1540.

LITERATURE: *Drevnosti* 1849–53, vol. 5, pl. 37; *Khudozhestvennye sokrovishcha* 1902, p. 256, table 110, nos. 9, 10; Cripps 1903, p. 482; Jones 1909, pl. 20, no. 2; Hayden 1915, p. 351; Goldberg 1954, p. 501, ill. 52; Oman 1961, p. 39, pl. 28; Oman 1970, pl. 2b; Markova 1996, pp. 41, 43, no. 38.

IAZ

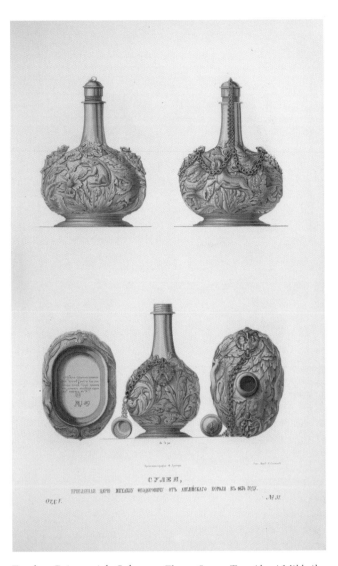

Fyodor Grigorevich Solntsev, *Flagon, Sent to Tsar Alexei Mikhailovich by King Charles II of England in 1664.* Plate 37 in Solntsev, *Drevnosti Rossiiskogo gosudarstva,* vol. 5 (Moscow, 1849–53). Slavic and Baltic Division, The New York Public Library, Astor, Lenox and Tilden Foundations

65. Footed Fruit Dish

England (London), 1663
Maker's mark: "TH" (Jackson 1989, p. 118), London,
sterling standard, 1663 (Jackson 1989, p. 52)
Silver, gilding
H. $3^1/_2$ in. (9 cm); diam. $16^1/_2$ in. (42.5 cm);
weight 1,931.1 gr
MZ-646

During his audience in the Palace of Facets on February 18, 1664, Ambassador Charles Howard, earl of Carlisle, presented Tsar Alexei with this footed fruit dish as a gift from King Charles II.

The fruit dish stands on a short, squat base that is framed by a band of high-relief decoration. Figures of a dog, wild boar, lion, and deer are depicted among poppy and tulip flowers. The originality of the English silversmiths' treatment of the floral ornament can be seen in the images of animals worked into the decorative foliage.

The royal gift carried by the earl of Carlisle originally comprised six footed fruit dishes of about the same weight and similar decoration, the only difference between them being the choice of embossed animals along the border. Three other dishes are also preserved in the Armory (MZ-647, MZ-648, MZ-649).

Such dishes or bowls were used in Old Russia for serving various delicacies, such as macerated berries and fruits. In England they were used as trays to carry fruit. Often the dishes were made in pairs with two-handled cups, or porringers. In Russia these held pickled items such as berries and fruits and were called *rassolnik* vases (*rassolnik* being a soup containing pickled cucumber).

This dish formed part of a presentation including gilded-silver goblets, dishes, and other impressive objects to Tsar Alexei brought by the first embassy after the English Civil War. Information about this gift is preserved not only in the inscription engraved on the dish itself but also in the 1676 inventory of the tsar's collection in the Treasury Palace and in the 1663–64 Ambassadorial Book.

Although hallmarked for "TH," this piece was likely embossed by a skillful foreign chaser.

SOURCES: Ambassadorial Book 1663–64, fols. 202, 284; Inventory 1676, fol. 210v; Inventory 1690, fol. 137v; Inventory 1885, pt. 2, vol. 2, no. 1284.

LITERATURE: Jones 1909, pl. xx, no. 2; Hayden 1915, p. 351; Jackson 1921, pp. 83, 141; Goldberg 1954, p. 491, fig. 43 (the mark has been deciphered incorrectly); *English Silver Treasures* 1991, pp. 176–79, no. 106; *Treasures of the Moscow Kremlin* 1998, p. 81, no. 51; Mitchell 2000, p. 117, fig. 8.

IAZ

66a. Basin

France (Paris), 1625
Maker's mark for Antoinette Marqueron, Paris, 1625
(Bimbenet-Privat and de Fontaine 1995, no. 119)
Silver, gilding
Diam. 27³/₈ in. (75 cm); weight 10,156.7 gr
MZ-1780

66b. Ewer

France (Paris), 1625
Maker's mark for Claude Couturier, Paris, 1625
(Bimbenet-Privat and de Fontaine 1995, no. 119)
Silver, gilding
H. 17¹/₂ in. (45 cm); weight 4,408 gr
MZ-1781

These unique objects are among the most important and splendid pieces of French silver made during the early seventeenth century; few examples of this quality have survived. The marks on both the ewer and the basin are not those of a goldsmith from the king's household (Garde Robe or the Galerie du Louvre), but of recognized Paris goldsmiths. Each object is marked with a crowned D, which confirms that they were made in Paris between December 1624 and December 1625. The ewer is marked with the stamp of Claude Couturier, a goldsmith whose workshop was located on the Pont au Change from 1613. The basin bears the stamp of Antoinette Marqueron, widow of the French goldsmith Nicolas de Villars. The beautiful chasing on the basin is in the fluid style of de Villars, like that on examples in the Museo Sacro of the Vatican Library and in the Los Angeles County Museum of Art.[1]

The ovoid body of the ewer is faceted and decorated with nine figures of dancing women, each holding a musical instrument (lute, viola, flute, triangle, rattle, tambourine, trumpet, and others). The vessel's tall handle is adorned with a female figure and below the spout is a male mask.

The circular basin is formed by eighteen concentric lobes, and along the rim are eighteen leafy masks. In the center of the basin, a scene in very high relief shows soldiers on horseback and foot soldiers. This scene may have been inspired by an episode in Greek or Roman history, or it may be from the Bible; one scholar has speculated that this is a scene from *Jerusalem Delivered* by the sixteenth-century Italian poet Tasso. In composition it resembles a painting by the Flemish painter Ambroise Dubois, *View of the Crusaders' Camp under the Walls of Jerusalem*. One of the episodes on the vessel is definitely the story of Scylla from Ovid's *Metamorphoses* (Book VIII).

Stylistically, the two objects are very restrained for French Renaissance and Baroque royal plate. Ewers and basins—originally utilitarian objects intended for washing the hands before and after a meal—were increasingly used during this period to decorate sumptuous buffets on ceremonial occasions and holidays, which explains the large proportions and the lavishness of the ornamentation.

Ewers and basins were used in Russia for both practical and ceremonial purposes. They might have adorned either a sideboard in the personal chambers of the tsar and his family or one in the formal halls of the palace. Frequently, as in this case, the ewer and basin were created by different silversmiths but were kept as a set, like those in which both items were produced by the same maker. Instances have been recorded in which separate ewers and basins brought to Moscow by ambassadors were later paired to form sets. Some sets in the tsar's treasury are the work of silversmiths from different countries or were from ambassadorial gifts of different periods.

As is often the case with royal plate, the reference to antiquity is clear in these objects, not only in their deco-

ration, but also in their general form: this ewer was inspired by images of amphoras and antique vases disseminated beginning in the sixteenth century by the engravings of Enea Vico, Agostino Veneziano, and Polidoro da Caravaggio, among others. The ornamental details—the grotesque masks, terms, acanthus vines, and garlands—are characteristic of the late Mannerist style, while other aspects of the decoration are inspired by the auricular style, initiated by the important goldsmiths of the Van Vianen family of Utrecht and spread throughout Europe in the first decades of the seventeenth century.

In 1663 King Charles II of England sent to Moscow a large embassy directed by Charles Howard, earl of Carlisle. This French ewer and basin, among other impressive English gilded-silver objects, was offered to Tsar Alexei, and the precise circumstances of its transfer to Russia are known, thanks to the testimony of the writer Guy de Miège.

On June 20, 1663, the earl of Manchester authorized the transfer from the inventory of the Royal Jewel House: *"one Bason & Ewer* (the French ewer and basin), *a pr.* [pair] *of flagons, a pr. of bottles, a pr. of standing bowles, & covers, a pr. of candlesticks, & one p*[er]*fuming pot, six fruite dishes, all large & curiously enchased & gilt, the whole to amount in weight to two thousand ounces or thereabouts, with cases of leather gilt."*[2] The English gifts brought by the earl of Carlisle to Moscow were offered to Tsar Alexei on February 18, 1664. Two pistols were offered as a personal gift to the tsar from King Charles II.

The French basin discussed here was carried by two men and led the procession of gifts. It and the ewer are the only French objects to be found among the numerous early diplomatic gifts in the Kremlin collection. Compared with the fashionable floral style of the English Restoration silver presented by the earl of Carlisle's embassy, the ewer and basin seem slightly archaic in style, but they may have been chosen for their royal provenance rather than their stylishness.

In 1625 Henrietta Maria, the last child of the French king Henri IV and Marie de' Medici, was married at the age of twenty to King Charles I of England. This royal marriage was a carefully calculated move. Long negotiations were undertaken in England by the comte de

Anthony van Dyck, *King Charles I and Queen Henrietta Maria of England,* 1632. Oil on canvas. Archepiscopal Castle and Gardens, Czech Republic

Tillières, *ambassadeur extraordinaire* of King Louis XIII, and in France by the duke of Buckingham and the earl of Carlisle. The marriage ceremony took place at the Cathedral of Notre Dame in Paris on May 11, 1625, and on June 12, Henrietta Maria and her suite left French soil for England.

There is no complete description of the silver and gold objects made for this royal wedding, and this ewer and basin are not recorded in the personal inventory of the French-born English queen. It was probably ordered by the French crown to decorate the splendid buffet at the wedding banquet and was most likely offered to the royal couple by King Louis XIII, Henrietta Maria's brother. Later, the ewer and basin are listed in the English royal treasury in 1664 as property of the crown, having escaped the fate of much of the treasury that was sold at the time of the English Civil War.

On the bottom of both the ewer and basin are engraved inscriptions giving weight, date, and value, as well as information regarding the circumstances under which they were received into the tsar's treasury.

NOTES
1. Much of this entry is taken from Bimbenet-Privat 2000. The information regarding year stamps on the ewer and basin provided by Michèle Bimbenet-Privat, chief curator, Archives Nationales, Paris, enabled us to decipher the names and makers and to clarify a number of points. She also provided the early history of these objects, as did Philippa Glanville, director of the James A. de Rothschild Bequest at Waddesdon Manor, the National Trust, Great Britain.
2. Oman 1961, p. 39 n. 47.

SOURCES: Ambassadorial Book 1664–65, fols. 201v, 283v; Inventory 1885, pt. 2, vol. 2, nos. 1217, 1467, pl. 255. LITERATURE: Veltman 1844, fig. 255; Jones 1909, fig. 355; Arsenev and Trutovsky 1914, p. 204, ill. p. 203; *Oruzheinaia palata* 1954, fig. 355; Smirnova 1964, p. 249; *Le XVI siècle en Europe* 1965–66, pp. 90–91, fig. 117; *L'URSS et la France* 1974, no. 524; Hernmarck 1977, vol. 1, p. 244, vol. 2, pl. 661; Rashkovan 1988/4, pp. 290–92, figs. 203–4; *Versailles et les tables royales en Europe* 1993, p. 37; *Prikladnoie iskusstvo Frantsii* 1995, pp. 34–35, nos. 21, 22, figs. 21, 22; Markova 1996, pp. 44–45, nos. 39, 40; Bimbenet-Privat 2000.

IAZ, AGK, and BS

GIFTS FROM THE DUTCH REPUBLIC

Although the Dutch followed the pioneering English into the Russian market, Dutch traders played a major role in the developing economy of the tsars' state, beginning as early as the sixteenth century. During the seventeenth century, the Dutch Republic gradually gained the upper hand over their English competitors.

The States General was the old bicameral legislative body of the northern Netherlands. With the revolt against Hapsburg (Spanish) domination in 1579, the name was adopted by the federal assembly of the United Provinces (Holland, Utrecht, Zeeland, Friesland, Gelderland, Groningen, and Overijssel). The States General claimed sovereign power, a claim first supported by the formation of a triple alliance with the rulers of France and England in 1597. Since the economic and naval power of this new country made it a force to contend with, a rationale was needed for the Russian tsars to deal with a form of government that they did not wish to recognize. The Dutch proffered the concept of the States General as a sovereign entity. The difference of approach was at first officially unremarked by the Russians.

By the 1580s, Dutch traders had made a significant appearance in the Russian north. The city of Archangel, founded in 1584, was a major point of contact between Dutch and Russian tradesmen. In Russia the Dutch

bought potash, resin and mast timber, and many other products, which were resold in Spain and Portugal at great profit. Persian raw silk, a basic need of European weavers, was also bought from Russian intermediaries. The Russian government was careful to control access to this profitable trade, and the issue of trade with Persia via Moscow was on the agenda of nearly every Dutch embassy to Russia.

During the early seventeenth century, the Russians sought to enlarge the scope of the relationship between the two states, as the political power of the newly created Dutch Republic burgeoned. Holland came to be considered a world economic and military power, not only in Europe, but in Asia as well. The Dutch obtained trade rights with Japan and Indonesia, the latter producing lucrative trade in spices. Furthermore, the Dutch navy became an important, even victorious, rival to the British at this time.

During the Thirty Years' War (1618–48), the Dutch Republic frequently turned to Tsar Mikhail's government for various kinds of support in its conflict with the Catholic League (Austria, Spain, among others), and they became in turn, mediators in certain Russian controversies. Russian-Dutch trade also extended over time into an area of critical importance to the tsars, modern weaponry and the recruitment of arms experts.

Insofar as trade with Russia was concerned, the Dutch Republic turned out to be a major beneficiary of

Dish (cat. no. 73)

the English Civil War, benefiting in particular from Tsar Alexei's decision to limit the almost limitless trade rights of the English. English merchants were confined to traveling to Archangel, as punishment for the execution by Parliament of King Charles I. But since this action was something of an excuse to allow the tsar to respond to Russian criticism of foreign trade rights, the Dutch also suffered. A few Dutch-owned factories were confiscated by the tsar. But after 1649 the English were never again able to obtain their original powerful situation.

An embassy of 1648, headed by Koenraad Burgh, was typical of the period. The tsar was asked for help with a number of commercial problems, and certain specific issues were resolved, although the tsar refused to grant the broad privileges requested by the Dutch, who wished to obtain the full rights of the English traders. This embassy gained some prestige, since it was officially related to dynastic matters of the princes of the House of Orange, the stadtholders or military leaders of the Dutch armies, and its announced purpose was to report the death of Frederick Henry and the

succession of his son William III. The Dutch gifts were exactly like those that would have been given by other monarchs.

The recognition of the Dutch Republic by the tsar was an ongoing problem for Dutch diplomats, since the tsar found it difficult, no matter how important the need, to recognize the government of anyone other than a prince. The Russians seized on the idea of addressing the government as regents, stand-ins for a prince, a title actually used by the governing committee of the country. When they served as diplomats in Russia, however, these regents were annoyed not to be recognized as holders of sovereignty.

The issue of sovereignty was brought out by the embassy of 1665, and the issue of the regents' status actually reached the agenda, probably because at that moment there was no stadtholder to serve as stand-in for a prince. In spite of the awkward problem of sovereignty, the Dutch ambassador, Jacob Boreel, was successful in reaching agreement on most items on his agenda. First, earlier agreements were reaffirmed, and then equality in the treatment of Dutch merchants with

those of England was achieved, and other more minor commercial issues on the table were resolved. Perhaps, most important, an agreement was reached about the building of special housing for foreign residents in Moscow, since there were several limitations on foreign residents. The gifts presented by the embassy were princely in character in spite of the absence of a royal donor.

Jacob Boreel's mission had to its credit another achievement: explaining Russia to the world. Traveling with the ambassadors was a young man from Amsterdam, Nicolaas Witsen, who wrote an account of his travels in Russia. He included the following remarks about the audience with Tsar Alexei: "His majesty's person is exceedingly corpulent, so that he filled his entire seat, into which he seemed to have been crammed. . . . He remained motionless, no matter how we bowed and scraped. Even his clear eyes hardly moved at all."[1] More important, Witsen must be counted to be among the first writers from the West to correctly assess Russia's vast potential. The immense size of Russia, which was commonly ignored by Western Europeans, was realistically represented on his map *Noord en Oost Tartarye . . .* [North and East Tartary] of 1687 (see also Chapter 1, fig. 2).

A less successful embassy headed by Koenraad van Klenck arrived in Moscow in 1676.[2] He asked for the aid of some troops to fight Sweden, a state that was currently the ally of Holland's enemy, the French. The request was refused because of previous treaty commitments to Sweden. Issues of trade also fared poorly. In fact, in order just to continue trading in Archangel for some months the embassy had to agree to buy a large quantity of grain from the Russians. Van Klenck was able to leave a permanent Dutch representative in Moscow, which was symptomatic of an increased curiosity about foreigners and a willingness to receive them, said to have been characteristic of the late seventeenth century.

The most famous Moscow embassy of the seventeenth century was certainly the Great Embassy of Tsar Peter I (the Great) in 1697–98, but this was travel abroad rather than the reverse. Peter's travels became legendary, including the story "The Tsar Carpenter," which refers to Peter's study of shipbuilding in the shipyard of Zaandam. Peter traveled incognito in the entourage of other official ambassadors, Admiral-General François Lefort, Admiral-General Fyodor Golovin, and Chancellor Prokopy Voznitsyn. This allowed Peter plenty of time to follow his non-diplomatic interests, these mostly related to military matters. Nonetheless, he expected to be treated as a ruler, and there were splendid receptions at the Dutch seat of government at The Hague, and gifts that were presented in an informal manner in the hope of retaining the tsar's favor.

NOTES
1. Witsen 1966–67.
2. van Klenck 1677. See also Chapter 3, fig. 10.

IAZ and GW

Romeyn de Hooghe, *Arrival of the Dutch Embassy of Koenraad van Klenck in Moscow in 1675.* Plate in K. van Klenck, *Historisch Verhael . . .* (Amsterdam, 1677). Cleveland Public Library

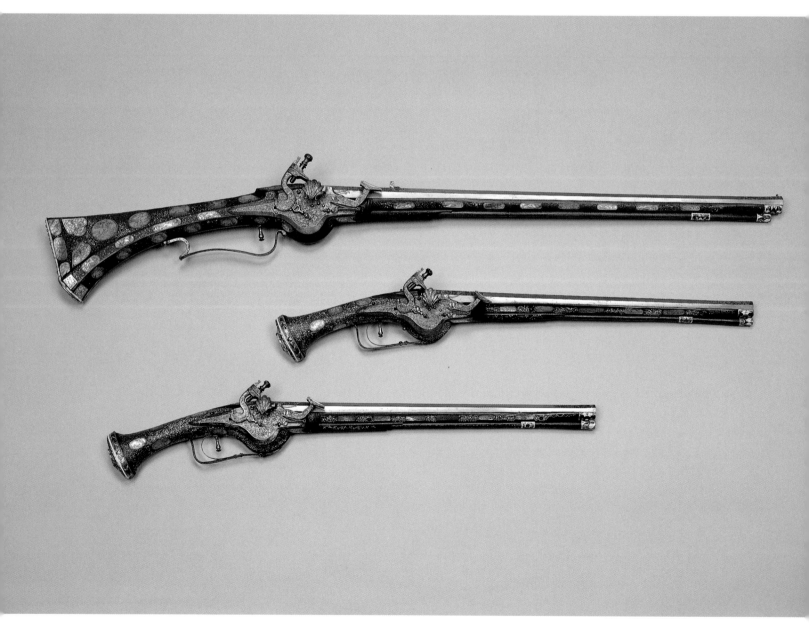

67, 68a,b. Set of Firearms
(Carbine and Pair of Pistols)

Holland (Amsterdam), c. 1630
Steel, wood, gold, rubies, emeralds,
mother-of-pearl, enamel, gilding
Overall l. of carbine: 40 in. (102.5 cm);
l. of barrel: 25⅞ in. (66.3 cm); caliber: 15 mm
Overall l. of pistols: 25⅛ in. (64.5 cm);
l. of barrels: 17½ in. (45 cm); caliber: 14 mm
OR-283/1–2, OR-284/1–2, OR-285/1–2

This unique set of ceremonial firearms is one of the finest examples of its type. The set was presented to Tsar Mikhail Romanov by a trading agent from Amsterdam, Carl Desmoulins, on January 3, 1630. The earliest description of these guns appears in a 1630 book of receipts and expenditures for goods and objects. The carbine and pistols were appraised in an Armory document by Conrad Frik, a foreign jeweler working in the Kremlin.

The name of Carl Desmoulins appears in Russian archival documents beginning in 1613, when he obtained commercial privileges. He executed orders from the tsar's court on several occasions and purchased precious goods in Europe for the Russian state. In addition, he had a rope manufactory in Kholmogory and held a monopoly on the production and export of potash. An enterprising merchant, industrialist, and diplomat, Carl Desmoulins knew Russia well and was welcomed at the tsar's court, whose customs he understood.

The Russian coat of arms (the two-headed eagle beneath three imperial crowns) appears on the barrels of the carbine and the pistols shown against a background of gilded embossed plant forms. The stock of the carbine and the handles of each pistol are decorated with silver plant forms to create the impression of filigree. On this ground are numerous mother-of-pearl plaques of horsemen, hunters with long spears, Roman profile portraits with laurel wreaths and helmets, and images of Saint George on horseback attacking a winged dragon. Enameled depictions of the saint also appear on the butts of each firearm, framed in precious stones set in gold. Clearly the client knew that Saint George, the protector of knights in European countries, was especially revered in Russia.

The firearms are equipped with snaphaunce locks of Anglo-Dutch design.[1] The surface of each lock is engraved with a plant design on a background worked in tiny hatching. The fittings of each piece, including the tips of the barrels, the butts, and the ramrod pipes, are made of gold and decorated with enamel. The pistol triggers are equipped with springs to prevent accidental firing.

NOTES

1. The details characteristic of the Dutch version of this type of lock are an S-shaped cock, a steel on a curved stem, an upright guard (fence) in the form of a shell on the side of the priming pan, and a lock plate, as in wheellocks of this period.

SOURCES: Notes 1630, fols. 1–2; Book of Receipts and Expenses 1630, fols. 33–34v; Inventory 1639, fols. 11–12; Inventory 1647, fol. 19; Inventory of campaign treasury of Tsar Alexei Mikhailovich 1654, fols. 23–24; Inventory 1687, fols. 332, 359v–360; Inventory 1886, pt. 5, bk. 4, nos. 7809, 8313.

LITERATURE: Sobolev and Ermolaev 1954, p. 424; Yablonskaya 1988, p. 198; Hoff 1978, p. 71; *Dutch Guns in Russia* 1996, pp. 78–81; Yablonskaya 1996, pp. 134–37, nos. 118–121.

EAY

69. Candlestick

Netherlands (Amsterdam), 1646
Maker's mark for Jan van den Velde (Voet 1912, no. 83;
Citroen 1975, no. 1000), Amsterdam (Voet 1912, 7 alf, p. 115)
Silver, gilding
H. 20¹/₄ in. (52 cm); weight 1,878.1 gr
MZ-143

During his audience at the Golden Chamber on June 20, 1648, Ambassador Koenraad Burgh presented Tsar Alexei Mikhailovich with a candlestick weighing 2 pounds, 8 ounces, as a gift from the States General of the Dutch Republic. Among the gifts brought over by the ambassadorial mission was the mate to this candlestick (Moscow Kremlin Armory, MZ-144).

This gilded-silver candlestick is unusually light, in spite of its seeming massiveness and its large dimensions. The surfaces are formed by six silver lobes with gilding in the grooves between them. The base is decorated with three medallions showing the symbol of Russia (a two-headed eagle under three crowns), in the middle of which is a shield representing the emblem of Moscow — Saint George on horseback piercing a dragon with his spear. The base is elevated on ball-shaped feet grasped by talons — an element that had become fashionable in European decorative art in the middle of the seventeenth century. The craftsman emphasized certain individual details with gilding.

An engraved Cyrillic inscription under the base indicates the weight of the piece and the date and circumstances under which it was received into the treasury.

SOURCES: Ambassadorial Book 1647–48/1, fols. 165, 180; Book of Receipts 1647–48, fol. 120–120v; Inventory 1835, no. 1104; Inventory 1884, pt. 2, vol. 2, no. 2010, table 293.

LITERATURE: Filimonov 1893, nos. 968, 969; Markova 1990, pp. 80–81, nos. 54, 55.

AGK

70. Jug

Netherlands (Amsterdam), 1646 or 1647
Maker: Jan van den Velde?
Marks: Amsterdam, 1646 or 1647 (Voet 1912, 7 alf, p. 115)
Silver, gilding
H. 31¼ in. (80 cm); weight 7,320 gr
MZ-112

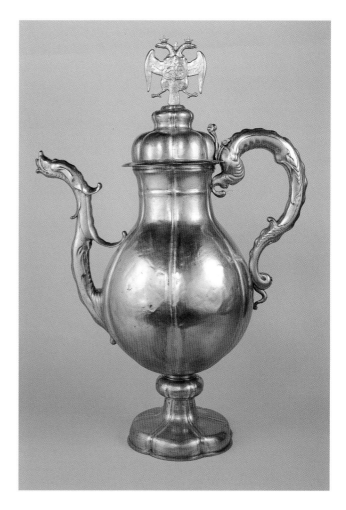

During his audience at the Golden Chamber on June 20, 1648, Ambassador Koenraad Burgh presented Tsar Alexei Mikhailovich with a jug weighing 16 pounds, 5 ounces, as a gift from the government of the Dutch Republic. Among the gifts brought over by the ambassadorial mission was the mate to this jug (Moscow Kremlin Armory, MZ-111). The majority of the objects are executed in the style created by the Dutchman Johannes Lutma. According to Galina Markova, these jugs were specifically ordered for this embassy; all of them were made between 1646 and 1647.

The pear-shape body of this gilded-silver jug is divided into six large vertical sections. The base, foot, and lid are also divided into six sections. The jug's spout is executed in the form of the head of a sea monster; the maker has emphasized the softness of the monster's skin by means of folds at the point where the monster's neck is connected to the body of the vessel. The handle is shaped like a dolphin. The top of the lid is decorated with a double-headed eagle, the symbol of Russia, with the emblem of the capital city of Moscow in the middle.

An engraved Cyrillic inscription on the bottom of the base indicates the weight of the piece and the date and circumstances under which it was received into the treasury.

Two large gilded-silver candlesticks also made by Jan van den Velde (act. 1630–86) were brought to Moscow with the same embassy (Moscow Kremlin Armory, MZ-143, MZ-144). One of them is discussed in cat. no. 69. The similarities between the large size of the jugs and candlesticks, their shape, and type of decoration have led Markova to conclude that the jugs were the work of the same craftsman.

SOURCES: Ambassadorial Book 1647–48/1, fols. 165, 180; Book of Receipts 1647–48, fol. 120–120 v; Inventory 1676, fol. 189v.; Inventory 1679, fol. 160v; Inventory 1721, fol. 72–72v; Inventory 1835, no. 887; Inventory 1884, pt. 2, vol. 2, no. 1169, table 274.
LITERATURE: Filimonov 1893, no. 972; *Oruzheinaia palata* 1954, pl. 350; Smirnova 1964, p. 229; Markova 1988, pp. 234–35, fig. 180; *Russen en nederlanders* 1989, p. 62, no. 83; *Gollandtsy i russkie* 1989, p. 62, no. 83; Markova 1990, pp. 18, 70, 84–85, nos. 57–58; Markova 1996, pp. 72–73, no. 65.

AGK

71. Wall Sconce

Netherlands (The Hague), 1647
Maker: Hans Koenraad Breghtel
Marks: The Hague (Rosenberg 1922–28, vol. 4, no. 7620;
Voet 1963, p. 11, no. 3), 1647 (Voet 1963, p. 32)
Silver, gilding
35¹/₂ x 15⁵/₈ in. (91 x 40 cm); weight: 3,842.5 gr
MZ-140

During his audience at the Golden Chamber on June 20, 1648, Ambassador Koenraad Burgh presented Tsar Alexei Mikhailovich with this wall sconce weighing 8 pounds, 8 ounces, as a gift from the Dutch Republic. Sconces go back to the Middle Ages and were still being made of base metals at the end of the fifteenth century. The Moscow Kremlin Armory has three other identical sconces by Breghtel that were also from the same 1648 embassy (MZ-139, MZ-141, MZ-142). Born in Nuremberg in 1608/9, Breghtel received the title of master in 1634 and was one of the most celebrated Dutch silversmiths of the time.

This sconce, made to accommodate a single candle, consists of two intersecting shields decorated with a chased pattern of intertwined, stylized acanthus leaves. It also emphatically displays elements of the auricular style, popular in the seventeenth century and characterized by smooth, rippling forms resembling the human ear. The smooth boss on the larger shield has a gilded, round medallion with a chased depiction of the Russ-

ian two-headed eagle under two crowns with an eight-point star between them. On the smaller shield on the eagle's breast is Saint George slaying a dragon.

An engraved Cyrillic inscription on the bottom of the candlestand indicates the weight of the piece, the date and circumstances under which it was received into the treasury, and its number in the inventory of the treasury.

SOURCES: Ambassadorial Book 1647–48/1, fols. 165v, 180v; Book of Receipts 1647–48, fol. 121v; Inventory 1663, fol. 161v; Inventory 1884, pt. 2, vol. 2, no. 1991.
LITERATURE: Filimonov 1893, nos. 1077–1080; Schätze 1987, no. 105; Markova 1988, pp. 236–37, fig. 161; *Russen en nederlanders* 1989, p. 62, no. 85; *Gollandtsy i russkie* 1989, p. 62, no. 85; Markova 1990, pp. 156–57, nos. 149–52; *Tesori del Cremlino* 1993, no. 70; Markova 1996, pp. 74–75, no. 67.

AGK

72. Dish

Netherlands (Amsterdam), 1664
Maker's mark for Koenraad Breghvelt (Voet 1912, no. 100;
Citroen 1975, no. 122), Amsterdam, Dutch control (Rosenberg
1922–28, vol. 4, no. 7622), 1664 (Voet 1912, 9 alf, p. 116)
Silver
H. 2³/₈ in. (6 cm); diam. 19¹/₂ in. (50 cm); weight 1,163 gr
MZ-114

During his audience at the Palace of Facets held on January 23, 1665, Ambassador Jacob Boreel presented Tsar Alexei Mikhailovich with this dish weighing about 2¹/₂ pounds, as a gift from the Dutch government.

This dish has a low base, a smooth and gently convex interior decorated with a wide border of eight palmettes. Each of these is ornamented with tulips and daffodils on short, undulating stems, a popular motif in Dutch silver work of the 1650s and 1660s. The palmettes are further embellished with auricular ornament, widely used in Dutch decoration up to the end of the seventeenth century. Dishes like this were often treated as decorative objects in Russia and hung on walls; they were also placed on dressers in the royal apartments.

In 1665 Dutch goldsmiths used two styles in the decoration of their metalwork. At the beginning of the century, Utrecht masters—the brothers Paul and Adam van Vianen—asserted the so-called auricular style. Starting in the 1650s, largely thanks to the works of Amsterdam silversmiths, plant ornament became especially popular, led by the tulip. The shape of this deep dish and the name *lokhan*, given it in the nineteenth century, suggests that it was used as part of a hand-washing set. However, Dutch still lifes of the period show similar dishes filled with fruit.

The sign of the treasury and a Cyrillic inscription indicating the weight of the piece are engraved on the bottom of the base.

SOURCES: Ambassadorial Book 1664–65, fols. 91, 98v, 142; Inventory 1884, pt. 2, vol. 2, no. 1223, table 236.

LITERATURE: Filimonov 1893, no. 1007; Schätze 1987, sec. 125, no. 106; *Tesoros* 1988, no. 83; *Russen en nederlanders* 1989, p. 63, no. 88; *Gollandtsy i russkie* 1989, p. 63, no. 88; Markova 1990, pp. 118–19, no. 86; *Treasures of the Czars* 1995, p. 120; Markova 1996, pp. 76–77, nos. 68, 69.

AGK

73. Dish

Netherlands (Amsterdam), 1664
Maker's mark for Hendrik tom Hulsen (Voet 1912, p. 99,
Citroen 1975, no. 372), Amsterdam, Dutch control (Rosenberg
1922–28, vol. 4, no. 7522; Voet 1912, p. 116),
1664 (Voet 1912, 9 alf, p. 116)
Silver, gilding
Diam. 30³/8 in. (78 cm); weight: 3,005 gr
MZ-113

On January 23, 1665, Ambassador Koenraad van Klenck gave Tsar Alexei Mikhailovich this dish, which was appraised at fifty-six rubles, as a gift from the Dutch Republic. One of the most important examples in the Moscow Armory representing the Dutch floral style, the dish was made by Hendrik tom Hulsen and is the only major work by this master still in existence.

In 1630 Hulsen was born in Munster (Westphalia) to a family of goldsmiths, and he studied with his father from 1641 to 1647. He became a master in 1657 and died only six years later.[1] Hulsen's sons were also goldsmiths. Most of the surviving works by Hulsen are spoons.

This dish is rare also for its size and magnificence. It is decorated with various long-stemmed spring flowers, including tulips, carnations, and anemones, embossed realistically across the entire surface in relatively high relief. The floral style emerged about 1640, influenced by Dutch enthusiasm for the science of botany and the tradition of horticulture. The cultivation of tulips, which were first imported from Persia at the beginning of the seventeenth century, became an important factor in the national economy of the Dutch Republic. Accurately rendered images of tulips occupied a revered place in illustrated scientific works and in still-life paintings and engravings. Floral decoration, much of it influenced by ceramics imported at the time from the Near East, became virtually ubiquitous in embroidery, woodwork, and tooled leather wall hangings, as well as in metalwork, for which Amsterdam was an important center. The Kremlin Armory's collection includes about 150 objects by Amsterdam silversmiths.

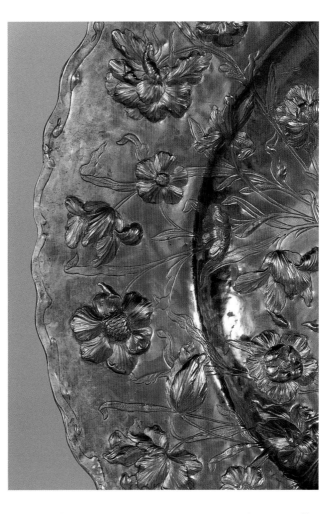

On the rim an inscription is engraved in Cyrillic indicating the dish's weight, its inventory number, and how it came into state hands.

NOTE
1. Hulsen died in 1663, yet this dish bears a mark corresponding to the year 1664. It is possible that the finished work was not marked until after his death by the heir to his workshop, perhaps his widow or one of his sons. Another explanation is that a new type of year marks was introduced in Amsterdam on December 1, 1663, possibly before Hulsen's death (the exact date of which is unknown).

SOURCES: Ambassadorial Book 1664–65, fols. 91, 98v, 141; Inventory 1676, fol. 231v; Inventory 1835, no. 1759; Inventory 1884, pt. 2, vol. 2, no. 2039, table 293.
LITERATURE: *Drevnosti* 1849–53, vol. 5, pl. 64; Filimonov 1893, no. 970; Markova 1988, pp. 238–39, fig. 163; Markova 1990, pp. 134–35, no. 113.

AGK

74. Letter of the Prince Stadholder William Henry to Tsar Alexei Mikhailovich dated May 12, 1675

Parchment, ink, decorative ornament
H. 27¹/₂ in. (70.5 cm) x 19⁷/₈ in. (51 cm)
Russian State Archive of Ancient Documents, Moscow

Captain Richard-Henrich Reiser brought this message to Tsar Alexei in 1675 announcing the future arrival of a Dutch embassy. Ambassador Koenraad van Klenck arrived in Moscow in January 1676 with a large suite and bringing many gifts, some of which survive. The mission, however, was not a success. Van Klenck's request for military help in the war of the Dutch provinces against France and Sweden was refused by the tsar on the basis of previous Russian commitments to Sweden. Furthermore, the tsar was unwilling to grant Dutch merchants the trading privileges requested by the ambassador.

SOURCE: Russian State Archive of Ancient Documents, Moscow, fol. 50 "Dutch-Russian relations," work 2, doc. 36.

LITERATURE: *Russen en nederlanders* 1989, p. 60, no. 80.

75. Ewer

Netherlands (Leiden), 1659
Maker's mark for Gillyaem Belle or Barend Gast,[1] Leiden
(Rosenberg 1925–28, vol. 4, no. 7644), 1659
Silver
H. 10¹/8 in. (26 cm); weight: 1,052.6 gr
MZ-28

During his audience at the Golden Chamber on January 17, 1676, Ambassador Koenraad van Klenck presented Tsar Alexei Mikhailovich with this ewer weighing nearly three pounds, as a gift from the Dutch States General.

The ewer on a small base is executed in the Baroque style. Its surface is vertically divided into three fields by acanthus leaves; each of the fields is adorned with two flowers. The decoration of the lower portion of the vessel is an elegant combination of acanthus and auricular motifs. The handle, executed in the auricular style, consists of three "fish" devouring one another. Its surface is embossed so as to simulate fish scales, and the ending is a gracefully arched fish tail. By dividing the massive cup and base, the smooth, wavy shelf in the middle of the foot gives the vessel a certain lightness of silhouette. The concave base is embossed with acanthus leaves, which repeat the acanthus of the lower portion of the body. The floral style is a characteristic feature of Netherlandish metalwork from the mid-seventeenth century. The silversmiths achieved amazing realism not only in individual flowers but also in the creation of floral compositions.

A Cyrillic inscription indicating the weight of the piece and its number in the treasury inventory is engraved on the bottom of the base.

NOTE
1. Regarding the interpretation of the master's mark, see Markova 1990, p. 161.

LITERATURE: Filimonov 1893, no. 1081; *Oruzheinaia palata* 1958, pl. 318; *Leids Zilver* 1977, p. 26; Markova 1990, pp. 160–61, no. 153.

AGK

SOURCES: Inventory 1676, fol. 186; Inventory 1679, no. 157; Inventory 1884, pt. 2, vol. 2, no. 1482.

76. Ewer

Netherlands (Amsterdam), 1675
Marks: Amsterdam, Dutch control (Voet 1912, p. 116), 1675
(Voet 1912, 9 alf, p. 116; Rosenberg 1925–28, vol. 4, no.
7566), maker's symbol of two boots
Silver, gilding
H. 9³/₄ in. (25 cm); weight: 982.1 gr
MZ-30

During his audience at the Golden Chamber on January 17, 1676, Ambassador Koenraad van Klenck presented Tsar Alexei Mikhailovich with a pitcher weighing 2 pounds, 2 ounces, as a gift from the Dutch government.

The soft, streamlined forms of the pitcher are in contrast with the sharp, slightly raised spout and the large, geometrically rigid handle finished with a cast curl. The smooth polished silver of the body is shaded with a thin gilded band in only three places: along the crown, along the edge of the shelf, and along the base.

A Cyrillic inscription indicating the weight of the piece and its number in the treasury inventory is engraved on the bottom of the base.

SOURCES: Inventory 1676, fol. 231v; Inventory 1835, no. 1759; Inventory 1884, pt. 2, vol. 2, no. 2039, table 293.

LITERATURE: Filimonov 1893, no. 970; Drevnosti 1849–53, vol. 5, pl. 64; Markova 1990, pp. 140–41, no. 121; Treasures of the Tsar 1995, pp. 258–59, no. 87.

AGK

77. Dish

Netherlands (Amsterdam), 1675
Maker's mark for Evert van Heerden (Citroen 1975, no. 878),
Amsterdam (Rosenberg 1922–28, vol. 4, no. 7563), Dutch
control (Rosenberg 1922–28, vol. 4, no. 7575; Voet 1912, p.
116), 1675 (Voet 1912, 9 alf, p. 116)
Silver, emeralds, sapphires, gilding
Diam. 26³/8 in. (67.5 cm); weight: 3,803.3 gr
MZ-98

During his audience at the Golden Chamber held on January 17, 1676, Ambassador Koenraad van Klenck presented Tsar Alexei Mikhailovich with a dish weighing 8 pounds, 6 ounces, as a gift from the Dutch government.

The round, smooth plate is gilded, and the Russian two-headed eagle is engraved in the center. The dish is set with emeralds and sapphires, although it is very rare to find Dutch silver with precious stones. The extravagance of this type of decoration is most likely related to Russian taste. The presence of the coat of arms suggests that the dish was created as an ambassadorial gift especially for the tsar.

A Cyrillic inscription indicating the weight of the piece and the date and circumstances under which it was received into the treasury is engraved on the reverse of the border. On the underside of the dish there are traces of an inscription: "Treasury Property, sent to the great ruler by the Dutch States in the year 1676."

Another, similar plate with the maker's mark of two boots, set with tourmalines and rock crystal, is at the Armory.[1] Both pieces stand out from the usual Dutch silver by virtue of the complete gilding and the use of precious and semiprecious stones in the decoration.

NOTE

1. Moscow Kremlin Armory, MZ-99; published in Inventory 1884, pt. 2, vol. 1, no. 583, table 235; Filimonov 1893, no. 1061; *Russen en nederlanders* 1989, p. 64, no. 91; *Gollandtsy i russkie* 1989, p. 64, no. 91; Markova 1990, pp. 142–43, no. 122.

SOURCES: Ambassadorial Book 1675–76, fols. 225v, 237v, 509v; Inventory 1835, no. 429; Inventory 1884, pt. 2, vol. 1, no. 582.

LITERATURE: Filimonov 1893, no. 1062; Markova 1990, pp. 34, 138–39, no. 120.

AGK

GIFTS FROM SWEDEN

SWEDEN WAS RUSSIA'S GREAT (and frequently victorious) rival in northeastern Europe from 1579 to 1709. During the previous half century, better relations had prevailed, because the Swedish king Gustavus Vasa (c. 1494–1560) was grateful to the tsar for recognizing his right to the Swedish crown, especially at a time when the king of Denmark continued to claim the right to govern Sweden.

Soon after Gustavus Vasa's death, the city of Revel (today Tallin) asked his son Erik XIV for incorporation into the kingdom of Sweden. This request provoked a major confrontation with Tsar Ivan IV, whose victories had acquired for Russia a substantial part of the nearby Baltic Sea coast; the ultimate result was the Livonian War (1579–82), which Russia lost. That loss was a major setback to Ivan's ambitions, since it cut off Russia from the Baltic, leaving Sweden with a small Baltic empire since the peace treaty concluding the war awarded her Livonia as well as Revel. Later conflicts added Ingria and Karelia to Sweden's holdings.

Sweden's expansion into Russia followed during the Time of Troubles (1605–13), when Novgorod the Great was captured, a great triumph for Sweden and a humiliation for a Russia in turmoil. At the time, Sweden's ambitions seemed limitless. A young King Gustavus Adolphus (Gustaf II Adolf, 1594–1632), who ascended the Swedish throne in 1611, even dreamed of putting himself (or one of his generals) on the throne in Moscow, but this was not to be, as the situation in Russia improved and both Poland and England were strongly opposed to the expansion of Swedish power. The English ambassador, John Merrick, at the request of King James I of England, brokered the Treaty of Stolbovo (1617), affirming Sweden's gains in the Baltic area, although Gustavus Adolphus returned Novgorod to Russia and recognized the succession of Tsar Mikhail Romanov.

Gustavus Adolphus then turned his attention to the cause of European Protestantism, gaining fame as one of the great generals of the Protestant cause in the Thirty Years' War (1618–48) in Germany. He found the Romanov rulers sympathetic with his anti-Catholic politics and that, plus his interests in preserving the Russo-Swedish borders in the Baltic area, led him to establish permanent diplomatic representation in Moscow in 1631. After Gustavus's death at Luzen in 1632, the Swedish government continued the policies he had put in place, and by the combination of his German victories and those of the regency that followed, Sweden gained a reputation as a great European military power, a reputation that would endure for another half century.

When Gustavus's daughter, Queen Christina, began her personal rule in 1644, she decided to play the role of peacemaker. Her ambassadors moved Europe toward peace, and as a result of her efforts, Russia was brought into the negotiations and was one of the signatories of the Peace of Westphalia (1648). Christina's efforts included a Great Embassy to Moscow (1647), which was intended to clarify the position of the two nations on European issues and, more secretly, to determine what benefits Sweden might gain from the increasingly strained relations between Russia and Poland. The pretext for the embassy, however, was to congratulate Tsar Alexei Mikhailovich on his succession to the throne. It may be noted that the issue of Swedish espionage was on the Russian agenda. Christina sent numerous gifts of gilded silver, about seventy impressively grand pieces, including four gigantic standing cups (cat. no. 79).

The second half of the seventeenth century brought many Russo-Swedish diplomatic exchanges and Great Embassies. The first of these was in 1655, the year after Christina abdicated her throne. King Charles X, looking to the military resolution of problems with Denmark and Poland, sought Russian support. The many gifts he sent were very much of the type sent by his predecessor, and as his ambassador noted, they were more of value for their goldsmiths' art than for their enormous weight in precious metal. As with Christina's gifts, many were from the great German silvermaking centers of Augsburg and Hamburg.

Another important Swedish embassy arrived in Moscow in 1674. King Charles XI, on the brink of war with Denmark and allied with France's King Louis XIV in his war against the Dutch, sought Russian support at a time when the Dutch were seeking the same. This notoriously frugal monarch sent only thirty-four pieces of gilded silver, but the objects that can still be identified in the Moscow Armory appear to have been large and showy. A most interesting insight into the real feeling of the Swedes about Russia at the time may be had from a fine manuscript book, a Russian atlas with drawings (see page 269), maps, and short commentaries made by a Swedish officer who accompanied the embassy as a spy. Erik Palmquist asserted that his book was written in the hope that the result would contribute to a victorious outcome of future Swedish military campaigns in Russia, but he also noted: "I have not

been able to learn more from this suspicious and difficult nation than this trival work contains."[1]

When Charles XI sent another embassy in 1684, ostensibly to congratulate the new co-tsars Ivan V and Peter I, his aims had substantially changed. Stung by losses after his army's support of Louis XIV, King Charles was of a decidedly more conciliatory frame of mind and concentrated on the reorganization of his government. He had established a new royal absolutism in his kingdom and his major interest in Russia during the 1680s was in the protection of his holdings in the southeast Baltic area. The seriousness with which he regarded this diplomatic initiative is suggested by the size of his gift of silver, about twice that of 1674.

A 1699 embassy was motivated by very different concerns. Charles XI had died in May 1697 leaving his underage son Charles XII to rule. The following year,

F. Jollain, *Tsars Ivan V and Peter I in 1685*. Plate in *Materialy dlia russkoi ikonografii* (St. Petersburg, 1884–90). Slavic and Baltic Division, The New York Public Library, Astor, Lenox and Tilden Foundations

Erik Palmquist, *Reception of the Swedish Envoy Count Oxenstierna March 30, 1674, in the Reception Hall of the Palace of Facets.* Drawing from Palmquist's *Some Observations of Russia . . .* (Stockholm, 1674). Pen-and-ink wash. The Swedish National Archives, Stockholm

Sweden's traditional enemies, Denmark and Poland, along with German Saxony, decided to form a grand alliance to conquer Swedish lands, particularly in the Baltic area and in parts of northern Germany. The Swedish ambassador, Baron Johan Bergenhielm, sought to improve Sweden's position by neutralizing Russia, asking for a reaffirmation of previous treaties and agreements, particularly those related to the Russo-Swedish borders in the Baltic area. Tsar Peter I, then ruling alone, agreed. The gifts, not surprisingly given Sweden's position, were very numerous and splendid. However, before the treaties negotiated in Moscow could be returned, signed, Tsar Peter decided to join the anti-Swedish alliance and prepared to begin a war.

The resulting Great Northern War (1699–1721) became the heroic confrontation of two important military rulers whose victories were the talk of Europe for decades. Ultimately Peter prevailed, although the war was a very long one. After Russia's victory at Poltava (1709), Sweden lost much of her empire and Russia gained a Baltic coast. Sweden was ultimately reduced to the status of a second-class power, never to recover her great power status. Two credential letters from the Swedish kings have survived in the Moscow State Archives (cat. nos. 82, 88).

GW

NOTE

1. See *Silverskatter* 1997, pp. 163–66. For Palmquist, see Poe 1995, p. 178.

78. Fruit Dish with Stand

Germany (Hamburg), 1633–44
Maker's mark for Dietrich Thor Moye
(Scheffler 1965, no. 172), Hamburg (Hüseler 1950, no. 21)
Silver, gilding
H. 33 1/8 in. (85 cm); weight 8,589.3 gr
MZ-233

The Swedish ambassador Erik Gyllenstierna presented this stunning fruit dish with stand, or confectionary tree, as a gift from Queen Christina to Tsar Alexei Mikhailovich on September 2, 1647.

The maker of this splendid object, the German master Dietrich Thor Moye, selected for the different tiers four classical deities representing plenty and success: Bacchus holding a bunch of grapes and a pitcher as he sits on a cask; Venus holding a flaming heart; Ceres with a horn of plenty; and Cupid with a bow and arrow. Master goldsmiths frequently united Venus, Bacchus, and Ceres in their works, evidently in accordance with the saying "Love grows cold without food and wine." The base of the centerpiece is decorated with six bunches of fruit; the inclusion of silver still lifes in objects like this is characteristic of Dietrich Thor Moye's work. The grapevines that connect the tiers emphasize the upward movement of the composition and unite the small shell-shaped dishes that are attached to the central portion of the tree. The grape leaves were originally colored with green lacquer, or, as the inventory of 1663 reads: "the tree's grass [leaves] are green."

The Armory has several other objects by Dietrich Thor Moye, who was one of Hamburg's most accomplished silversmiths: a covered cup, which is included in this catalogue (cat. no. 80), a nautilus cup (see Chapter 2, fig. 8),[1] and numerous sets of fruit dishes with stands.[2] Many objects made by Hamburg silversmiths were acquired in the seventeenth century for the royal treasuries of Denmark and Sweden, some for use as diplomatic gifts. It is interesting to note that this fruit dish is almost identical to another example at the Armory (RK-76), marked by Hans Lambrecht II and dated for 1631–33, that was presented by an ambassador of King Christian IV of Denmark to Tsar Mikhail Romanov on January 28, 1644.[3]

An inscription engraved in Cyrillic on the base of the fruit stand indicates the weight of the object.

NOTES
1. Inv. no. DK-179/1–2. Offered to Tsar Mikhail Romanov by King Christian IV of Denmark and Norway in 1644.
2. Inv. nos. MZ-234, MZ-235, MZ-236, MZ-237, MZ-239, MZ-240, and MZ-243.
3. See Bencard and Markova, 1988, pp. 70–71, n. 92.

AGK

sources: Inventory 1663, fols. 154, 156; Inventory 1676, fol. 166v; Inventory 1885, pt. 2, bk. 2, no. 1301, table 220.

literature: *Drevnosti* 1849–53, vol. 5, pl 52; Martin 1900/1, pp. 29–30, pl. 5; Kologrivov 1911, p. 39; Scheffler 1965, vol. 1, 869 ill.; Bursche 1974, p. 35, ill. 221; Markova 1975, p. 47; Schliemann 1985, p. 161, no. 85, ills. 104, 105; Smirnowa and Heitmann 1986, pp. 122–23, no. 25; Bencard and Markova 1988, fig. 51; Markova 1988, p. 242, ill. 166; Markova 1996, pp. 70–72, nos. 63, 64.

79. Covered Cup

Germany (Nuremberg), 1588–1622
Maker's mark for Hans Beutmüller
(Rosenberg 1922–28, vol. 3, nos. 4054, 4055),
Nuremberg (Rosenberg 1922–28, vol. 3, no. 3757)
Silver gilding
H. 52^1/$_4$ in. (134 cm), diam. 10^1/$_4$ in. (26.3 cm),
weight 10,231 gr
MZ-516/1-2

During his audience in the Palace of Facets held on September 2, 1647, Ambassador Erik Gyllenstierna presented Tsar Alexei Mikhailovich with a silver standing covered cup, weighing 23 pounds, as a gift from Queen Christina of Sweden.

This lidded goblet is of late Renaissance design. It tapers at the waist and is decorated with spherical bosses, garlands, and fruit clusters; the decoration also includes half-length female figures, small cast heads, horns of plenty, and arabesques. At the very top is a plant motif with birds and horns of plenty, and on the baluster of the foot are the figures of Mars, Venus, and Cupid.

This cup is one of the four "giant" standing covered cups (*riesenpokal*) that were sent by Queen Christina to Russia, three of which are in the Kremlin Armory.[1] The lids of all of the cups are crowned with figures of knights in ancient armor, each one of which is unique. Outstanding "giant" cups of this type were created in Nuremberg during the second half of the sixteenth century; the style quickly spread throughout Germany and became known in other countries as well. In northern Germany, it was customary for cups like this one to be presented on specific events, such as accessions and coronations. Faithful subjects swearing allegiance would present them to their ruler filled with valuable coins.

Nuremberg was one of the leading cities for goldsmiths' work from the beginning of the sixteenth century until about 1625. Strict guild regulations and high quality gave Nuremberg silver an outstanding reputation and attracted buyers from outside Germany. The goldsmiths themselves were employed in court workshops and on commission for the rulers of Florence, Paris, Prague, and elsewhere. Hans Beutmüller, who

became a master in 1588 and died in 1622, was a prolific goldsmith working in Nuremberg. Beutmüller was a gifted rival to Hans Petzolt, who was at that time preeminent among the Nuremberg goldsmiths (see cat. no. 90). Beutmüller left a significant body of work, which suggests that he had a large workshop. At the time of his death, he was described not only as a goldsmith, but also as a silver merchant.

The standing covered cups offered to Tsar Alexei Mikhailovich by Queen Christina in 1647 were made by the best silversmiths of Nuremberg and had been a significant part of the Stockholm treasury since the times of the conquests of the Queen's father, King Gustavus Adolphus. It was probably these cups that impressed the French diplomat Charles d'Ogier in 1634, when he and the French ambassador d'Avaux, on their travels in Sweden, saw in the Swedish treasury "four large gilded silver cups, four or five feet high, big enough to hold a small child: these are called loving cups and can be drained ten or twelve times in the course of a drinking party."[2] They may have been acquired by Christina's grandfather King Charles IX, or taken as booty in Germany. Their unusual size and lavish decoration suggest that they were designed to be displayed, probably on a sideboard in a public room. In Russia, the cups may have graced a table in the large reception hall at the Palace of Facets on ceremonial occasions; they were removed from the Armory for this purpose during the nineteenth and twentieth centuries.

A Cyrillic inscription indicating the weight of the piece, the year it was presented, and the name of the donor is engraved on the reverse of the base.

NOTES

1. Besides the cup by Beutmüller discussed in this entry, the two other cups at the Armory include an example by Hans Reiff (MZ-515/1–2) and another by Beutmüller (MZ-517/1–2). A fourth cup, also presented in 1647 by Queen Christina to Tsar Alexei, was later acquired in 1931 by the National-museum in Stockholm (MN 205/1931; see *Silverskatter* 1997, p. 206, no. 62).

2. See *Silverskatter* 1997, p. 160.

SOURCES: Inventory 1663, fol. 76v, 77; Inventory 1676, fols. 55, 56; Inventory 1835, no. 623; Inventory 1884, pt. 2, vol. 1, no. 853.

LITERATURE: Martin 1900/1, p. 29, pl. 3; *Khudozhestven-nye sokrovishcha* 1902, nos. 9–10, p. 257, pl. 112; Markova 1980, no. 74; Rashkovan 1988/3, pp. 250–51, fig. 172; *Silverskatter* 1997, p. 70, no. 1; Kudriavtseva 1997, p. 52.

AGK and BS

80. Covered Cup

Germany (Hamburg), 1633–35
Maker's mark for Dietrich Thor Moye (Scheffler 1965, no.
869),Hamburg (Hüseler 1950, no. 18)
Silver, gilding
H. 26¹/8 in. (67 cm), weight 5,102 gr
MZ-521/1–2

During his audience in the Palace of Facets held on September 2, 1647, Ambassador Erik Gyllenstierna presented Tsar Alexei Mikhailovich with a standing covered cup, with a weight of 11 pounds, 4 ounces, as a gift from Queen Christina of Sweden.

The ambassadorial mission of Queen Christina included precious gifts totaling 10,699 *riksdalers*. Most of the gifts are still kept in the Kremlin Armory. The standing covered cup, made in the form of a cornucopia, is one of the most unusual and rare objects.

This covered cup is supported by a cast figure of Ceres, the goddess of plenty. The kneeling goddess is derived from the well-known bronze statue *Bather Crouching* by the Italian Renaissance sculptor Giambologna. More of a table decoration than a drinking vessel, everything about the cup is on a grand scale: the ample shapes of the twisted horn are freely and confidently modeled. A remarkably opulent still life adorns the lid. The cast and chased apples, pears, berries, grapes, and leaves are superbly executed and artistically arranged. Some of the fruits and leaves were originally painted with enamel, which is mentioned in the description of the cup in a seventeenth-century inventory.

An inscription indicating the weight of the piece, the date it was sent, and the name of the donor is engraved on the reverse of the base; there is also a barely legible inscription indicating the weight of the piece, and below it a later inscription also indicating the weight of the piece and its number according to a nineteenth-century inventory.

SOURCES: Inventory 1663, fol. 94; Inventory 1676, fol. 114, 114v; Inventory 1835, no. 638; Inventory 1884, pt. 2, vol. 2, no. 1158, table 215.

LITERATURE: *Drevnosti* 1849–53, vol. 5, pl. 23; *Khudozhestvennye sokrovishcha* 1902, nos. 9, 10, pp. 222, 263; Martin 1900/1, p. 31, pl. 12; Hüseler 1950, vol. 1, no. 172; Scheffler 1965, vol. 1, no. 869 A; Markova 1975, no. 44; Schliemann 1985, p. 160, ills. 34, 35; Smirnova and Heitmann 1986, pp. 118–19, ill. 23; Rashkovan 1988/3, p. 253, fig. 173; Markova 1996, p. 70, no. 62; *Silverskatter* 1997, p. 73, no. 5.

AGK

81a,b. Tazzas (*rassolniki*)

Germany (Nuremberg), first quarter of 17th century
Maker's mark for "HB" (Rosenberg, 1922–28, vol. 3, no. 4095), Nuremberg (Rosenberg 1922–28, vol. 3, no. 3760)
Silver, gilding
H. (a): 7⁷/₈ in. (20 cm), (b) 7³/₈ in. (19 cm), diam. of cups: (a) 10⁷/₈ in. (28 cm), (b) 11¹/₈ in. (28.5 cm), weight (a) 996.3 gr, (b) 1,012.2 gr
MZ-538; MZ-1018

During his audience in the Palace of Facets held on September 2, 1647, Ambassador Erik Gyllenstierna presented Tsar Alexei Mikhailovich with two tazzas, as a gift from Queen Christina of Sweden.

The design of this pair of small round bowls on baluster feet was borrowed by German goldsmiths from Italy, where it was used for cups. Too flat to be used as drinking vessels, these bowls were used in Russia as table decorations or as dishes for cakes and sweetmeats, such as candied fruit. The Russian name for these bowls is *rassolniki*, a reference to the fact that fruits were candied with salt as well as sugar; the name occurs in documents from the seventeenth century. In many other countries, the Italian name *tazza* became current, as well as the Renaissance way of decorating the interior of the bowl with a boss. This might cover the entire interior or be a medallion in the center, as with these examples.

In the middle of the bowls the goldsmith has embossed a sinuous allegorical depiction of one of the months of the year under the corresponding sign of the zodiac. These two tazzas represent July and September. This pair and six others now in the Kremlin Armory formed part of an original collection of twelve, one for each month and zodiac signs, as indicated by the inscriptions underneath the foot of each bowl and a note in the 1676 inventory. It is known that in 1640 all the bowls were in the Swedish Royal Treasury. Since the beginning of the twentieth century, one pair has been in the State Hermitage Museum in St. Petersburg.

Subjects from the daily life of peasants and the holidays of city dwellers constitute the basis of each composition. The sign for Libra (September) is depicted in the top left portion of the first tazza discussed here and a peasant gathering crops is in its center. The second tazza shows a peasant with a scythe on a background of a landscape with haystacks, a barn, and a hay wagon; the sign of Leo (July) is presented in the top left portion. A sign, possibly of the author, is engraved on the reverse of each plaque. There are different signs on each plaque, some of them with the Roman letters "N" and "S" and others with more complicated configurations.

A Cyrillic inscription indicating the weight of the piece, the year it was received, and the name of the donor, as well as a later inscription indicating the number and weight, are engraved on the reverse of the base of one of the tazzas (a); a Cyrillic inscription indicating the weight of the piece, the year when it was received, and the name of the donor is engraved on the reverse of the base of the second tazza (b).

SOURCES: Inventory 1663, fols. 155–156; Inventory 1676, fols. 173–174; Inventory 1884, pt. 2, vol. 2, nos. 1334–1341, table 220.

LITERATURE: Veltman 1844, pp. 132–33; Martin 1900/1, p. 31, pl. 11; Rosenberg 1922–28, vol. 3, no. 4095 g–o; Markova 1980, p. 120, nos. 100–107.

AGK

82. Charter of Ratification of the Peace Treaty of Kardis and the Pliusa Agreement, sent by King Charles XI of Sweden to co-tsars Ivan V and Peter I, dated January 7, 1684

Parchment, ink, gold, silk cover, decorative ornament with
the king's portrait and the emblems of the towns
H. 18³/₄ in. (48 cm); w. 12¹/₂ in. (32 cm)
Russian State Archive of Ancient Documents, Moscow

Although both Sweden and Russia were from the first in agreement about the renewal of the Kardis treaty that had ended the Swedish-Polish War of 1656–58, and the Treaty of Perpetual Peace (1661), as well as the reconfirmation of much older agreements such as the Treaty of Stolbovo (1617), some few disagreements remained. A meeting of Russian and Swedish envoys took place in 1668 on the banks of the Pliusa River, where another agreement was signed. After Tsar Alexei's death it was necessary for the new tsars to confirm all the agreements between the two countries. Ambassador Conrad Gyllenstierna, assisted by Jonas Klingstedt and Otto Stackelberg, presented the two tsars this charter of renewal at an audience at the Kremlin on May 2, 1684. On May 28, 1684 the tsars took an oath to observe the various treaties and agreements mentioned in the documents, thus agreeing to the border between Russia and Sweden's land holdings along the southeast shore of the Baltic Sea. The ambassadors also agreed to six additional agreements, known as the Moscow Resolution. These decisions presumably reflected the policies of the Regent Sofia.

SOURCES: Russian State Archive of Ancient Documents, Moscow, fol. 96 "Swedish-Russian Relations," work 3, doc. 59.

83a,b. Tazzas (*rassolniki*)

Germany (Augsburg), before 1653
Maker's mark for Hans Jacob Baur I (Seling 1980, vol. 3,
no. 1369), Augsburg (Seling 1980, vol. 3, no. 92)
Silver, gilding
H. 11 3/4 in. (30 cm); diam. of cups: (a) 12 in. (30.7 cm),
(b) 11 7/8 in. (30.5 cm); weight (a) 1,754.6 gr, (b) 1,662.7 gr
MZ-546; MZ-549

During his audience in the Golden Chamber held in 1684, Ambassador Conrad Gyllenstierna presented co-tsars Ivan V and Peter I with tazzas, each weighing about 4 pounds, as a gift from Charles XI, King of Sweden.

The tazzas, or marinade bowls, used for a traditional Russian practice of serving fruit in a salty sauce (*rassol*), are shallow bowls chased into six leaves. The foot of the first bowl is cast in the form of Mars wearing antique armor and a helmet. The other bowl is identical to the first in form and decoration, but the foot takes the form of Minerva in antique half-armor and helmet. The tazzas were made by the Augsburg goldsmith Hans Jacob Baur I (active 1622–53), a skilled and highly gifted master craftsman. Surprisingly, the majority of his known work exists in the Armory's collection, which includes fourteen of the original eighteen tazzas. These tazzas form pairs, with either Mars or Minerva depicted at the base. Baur was the first goldsmith in Augsburg to employ auricular motifs. These, along with thirty-five other objects, form the greater part of the surviving work attributed to Hans Jacob Baur I.

Although these tazzas were referred to as "confectionary dishes with Roman figures" in the Swedish inventory, they are designated in the Russian inventory of the seventeenth century as "*rassolniki*."

A Cyrillic inscription indicating the weight of the piece is carved on the reverse of one of the tazzas (a); an inscription indicating the weight of the piece is engraved on the other (b).

SOURCES: Inventory 1885, pt. 2, vol. 2, p. 57, nos. 1343–1360, table 220.

LITERATURE: Martin 1900/1, p. 37, fig. 32; Seling 1980, vol. 3, p. 163, no. 1369k; *Silber und Gold* 1994, pp. 206–10, fig. 38.1, 2; Schätze 1991, pp. 119–21, nos. 29, 30; *Silverskatter* 1997, pp. 106–7, nos. 30, 31; Kudriavtseva 1997, pp. 50–54.

AGK

84. Basin (The Legend of Joseph the Beautiful)

Germany (Augsburg), 1698
Maker's mark for Heinrich Mannlich (Seling 1980,
vol. 3, no. 1613), Augsburg (Seling, vol. 3, no. 156)
Silver
H. 36¹/₄ in. (93 cm).; w. 42¹/₈ in. (108 cm); weight 8,000 gr
MZ-1635

During his audience in the Palace of Facets held on November 11, 1699, Ambassador Baron Johan Bergenhielm presented Tsar Peter I with a basin weighing 18 pounds, as a gift from King Charles XII of Sweden. The 1699 ambassadorial mission headed by Bergenhielm came to Russia with the purpose of proposing an alliance with King Charles in the event of a war between the Northern Crown and its long-time enemies, Denmark, Poland, and Saxony, who had entered into a military alliance as early as 1698. The gifts from the Swedish king were substantial in quantity and splendid in execution—they included 124 magnificent gold and silver objects, the work of the most renowned goldsmiths from Sweden and Germany, among which was this silver basin by Heinrich Mannlich (act. 1659–98), part of a hand-washing set that included a ewer (cat. no. 85). In Russia, such basins were often called *lokhans* (washbasins).

"The Triumphal Procession of Joseph" is represented on the basin, and on its rim are six oval cartouches depicting episodes from the Old Testament legend of Joseph the Beautiful. The cartouches on the upper row illustrate scenes of his suffering and false accusation, while those on the lower half show his rewards for patience and steadfastness. The episodes are arranged clockwise, starting with the top left image: the sale of the young Joseph by his brothers into slavery to a traveling merchant; the false accusation of Joseph by the wife of Potiphar; Joseph's appointment by the pharaoh as a joint ruler, who gives him a signet ring from his own hand as a confirmation of the appointment.

In the lower row the images include Joseph selling bread to his brothers for silver, the meeting between

Joseph and Benjamin, and the meeting between Joseph and his father. Inscriptions in old German revealing the contents of the depicted events are engraved within each cartouche—on the columns, on parts of the interiors, such as the throne and the table, or on rocks in the landscape.

The cartouches are arranged vertically in two sections, which allowed the silversmith to represent the stages in the development of the story, to outline its main characters, or to demonstrate the conflict between good and evil, truth and falsehood, ingratitude and justice. The triumph of the righteous man is represented in the center of the basin. Each scene of the fable is depicted in extraordinary detail: in order to convey the texture of clothing and objects and the depth of the spatial dimensions of the interiors and landscape, the goldsmith combined the techniques of chasing, pouncing, and engraving. The genre characteristics of the scenes, the attempt to disclose the image of each character, and the attention to the smallest naturalistic details are artistic traits that link this work and Baroque silver as a whole to paintings of the period.

The Old Testament parables and legends that were widely used in paintings and decorative arts were familiar and understandable to Russians of the seventeenth century. There could not have been a better choice as a gift for the Russian tsar than a basin depicting the parable of the virtuous master of Egypt, for Russian works of art contain many references to Joseph the Beautiful. A sixteenth-century icon depicting him is in the iconostasis of the Kremlin's Annunciation Cathedral, and the northern wall and part of the eastern walls of the Palace of Facets are decorated by a fresco devoted to his legend. The image of a wise statesman, a zealous master, and a far-sighted politician striving for the greater good of the state was the ideal model for the Russian rulers.

Mannlich's interest in biblical subjects is not coincidental considering his voluminous work for the church. The sculptural qualities of the embossed figures, typical of the silver objects by this artist, are also characteristic of this basin, which was made in the prime of the silversmith's life, evidently not long before his death in 1698.

A Cyrillic inscription indicating the weight of the object is engraved on the reverse.

SOURCES: Inventory 1885, pt. 2, vol. 2, nos. 2032–2038.
LITERATURE: *Drevnosti* 1849–53, vol. 5, pl. 64; Martin 1900/1, p. 40, pl. 40; Kudriavtseva 1998, pp. 4–13; *Petr Velikii i Moskva* 1998, p. 143, no. 313.

AGK

85. Ewer

Germany (Augsburg), 1674–80
Maker's mark for Heinrich Mannlich (Seling 1980, vol. 3,
no. 1613), Augsburg (Rosenberg 1922–28, vol. 1, no. 170)
Silver, gilding
H. 18 in. (46 cm); weight 2,334.9 gr
MZ-588/1–2

In the Palace of Facets on November 11, 1699, Ambassador Baron Johann Bergenhielm of Sweden gave to Tsar Peter I for King Charles XII this unusual ewer made in the shape of a lion. Since the reign of King Gustavus Adolphus, who was called the "Lion of the North," lions were often depicted in Sweden's gifts as an embodiment of the king's brilliant victories and a commemoration of Sweden's influence in Europe. Queen Christina, his daughter, even added a live lion to the Swedish royal collections, part of the booty taken after the Swedish capture of Prague (1647). Housed in a special building she had constructed for him, the lion was one of the most popular sights in Stockholm.

The lion on this fine ewer stands rampant and bears the attributes of power: a crown on its head and a scepter in its right paw. The other paw was evidently intended to hold a shield, judging from the engraved lion in a similar pose on the sheath of a hunting set that once belonged to King Charles XII of Sweden.[1]

It is impossible to determine the original use of this ewer. It was not made for the king who presented it to Peter I, but for his father, Charles XI. In fact, the date of the work suggests a connection with the celebration of Charles XI's victories over Denmark in the Scanian War (1675–79), a subsidiary conflict in the Dutch Wars of Louis XIV of France. It is not surprising that an object of this quality from the Swedish royal collections should have been included among the 124 gifts presented to Peter I. Not only is it a superb piece of German silver, but it was also clearly an attempt to remind the tsar of Swedish power at a time when Charles XII's government was trying, without success, to maintain peace with Russia. Less than a year after the gift was presented,

following the lead of Saxony, Poland, and Denmark, Peter declared war on Sweden and thus entered the Great Northern War in which Sweden was defeated.

The animal's body is chased to look like fur, and the sculptured mane, tail, and fur on the paws are carefully delineated. The tall, oval base, which is shaped for ease in handling, is embossed on the top to suggest a grassy ground. On the lower part of the base, a plowman relaxing at his plow and a shepherdess with her crook are depicted against the background of a rural landscape in two oval silver plaques. Crossed horns of plenty are embossed between the plaques. The removable crown of this lion serves as a lid for the ewer, while the animal's mouth, with its slightly protruding tongue, serves as a spout.

The image of a rearing lion with crown and scepter was a popular one with Augsburg's goldsmiths and was often used in decorative tableware and clocks. Many lion-shaped vessels are known to have been made in Augsburg in the 1630s and 1640s. Another Augsburg ewer in the form of a lion was given to Tsar Alexei Mikhailovich by King Charles X of Sweden in 1655 (Moscow Kremlin Armory, MZ-587/1–2).

Foreign envoys who attended banquets in the reception hall of the Palace of Facets in the Kremlin reported that the tables bore a variety of silver and gold vessels in the form of lions, horses, cockerels, ostriches, and other animals.[2]

On the reverse side of the ewer's base an inscription is etched in Cyrillic indicating the weight and number according to an inventory made in the nineteenth century, and on the plug of the crown its number from another nineteenth-century inventory is engraved.

NOTES

1. In the 1830s, by order of Emperor Nicholas I, the hunting set (sheath, knife) of King Charles XII, as well as the marshal's staff of King Gustavus II, were moved from the study of Peter I and preserved in the Kunstkammer to the Armory. A lion is embossed on the staff as well.

2. *Treasures of the Tsar* 1995, p. 270, no. 93.

LITERATURE: Filimonov 1893, pt. 7, vol. 10, p. 35, no. 322; Martin 1900/1, p. 41, table 43; Rosenberg 1922–28, vol. 1, no. 611f; Seling 1980, vol. 1, p. 114, vol. 2, ill. 462, vol. 3, no. 1613p; *Treasures from the Museums* 1988, p. 6, ill. 66; *Schätze* 1991, p. 136, no. 38; *Treasures of the Tsar* 1995, pp. 270–71, no. 93; *Petr Velikii i Moskva* 1998, p. 143, no. 314.

AGK

SOURCES: Inventory 1835, no. 1075; Inventory 1885, pt. 2, bk. 2, no. 1927, table 308.

86. Beaker

Sweden (Stockholm), 1698
Maker's mark for Johan Nützel (*Svenskt Silversmide* 1963, no.
261), Stockholm (*Svenskt Silversmide* 1963, no. 260),
1698 (*Svenskt Silversmide* 1963, no. 35).
Silver, gilding
H. 12⁷⁄₈ in. (33 cm); weight 1,440 gr
MZ-571/1-2

During his audience in the Palace of Facets held on November 11, 1699, Ambassador Baron Johan Bergenhielm presented to Tsar Peter I a covered beaker, part of a set consisting of twelve such beakers, as a gift from King Charles XII of Sweden. As early as 1885, only ten beakers out of the original group remained in the Kremlin Armory. Even then, two of them were missing their lids. In 1931–32, these beakers were offered at international auctions. Currently, eight from the 1699 gift are in the Armory. Two examples are in the Nordiska Museet in Stockholm.

Tall goblets, candlesticks, containers for tea and spices, and filigree boxes made in Stockholm were among the objects presented in 1699 by Bergenhielm's embassy. In spite of the influence of German goldsmiths, Swedish silverware has unique forms, and a variety of techniques were used in the creation.

Johan Nützel (act. 1674–1716) was one of the founders of the new national style established in Sweden at the end of the seventeenth century: the so-called Caroline style, named for King Charles XI and King Charles XII, who were in favor of classical simplicity in art. The silversmith made a dozen tall, cone-shape, gilded beakers of equal size, each having a lid decorated with a pine cone with five cast, carved, and engraved leaves. This beaker is distinguished by its austere elegance, and everything about it is simple and expressive, including the harmony of the pure lines and proportions and the smooth surface. It is also a good example of Swedish originality and taste, and Charles XII in particular preferred this style, which may have been influenced by contemporary trends in England, Holland, and France.

A Cyrillic inscription indicating the weight of the beaker and its number according to the inventory of the treasury is engraved on the reverse of the base.

SOURCES: Inventory 1835, nos. 1440–1449; Inventory 1885, pt. 2, vol. 2, nos. 1566–1575.

LITERATURE: Martin 1900/1, p. 43, fig. 49; *Svenskt Silversmide* 1941–63, pp. 75–76; *Treasures* 1979, p. 212, no. 99; *Schätze* 1987, p. 127, no. 108; *The Triumph of Simplicity* 1988, no. 9; Rashkovan 1988/3, vol. 3, p. 256, fig. 177; *Svenskt Silver* 1990, pp. 50–51; *Schätze* 1991, pp. 144–45, no. 41; *Vier Jahrunderte Schwedisches Silber* 1991, pp. 9–10, ill., inv. no. 205, 468; Markova 1996, pp. 88–89, no. 80; *Silverskatter* 1997, p. 118, nos. 45, 46; Markova 1998, pp. 14–21, flyleaf; Kudriavtseva 1998, pp. 4–13, flyleaf.

A G K

87a,b. Pair of Candlesticks

Sweden (Stockholm), 1698
Maker's mark for Anders Bengtsson Starin (*Svenskt Silversmide*
1941–63, no. 422), Stockholm (*Svenskt Silversmide* 1941–63,
no. 416), 1698 (*Svenskt Silversmide* 1941–63, p. 35)
Silver, gilding
H. (a) 9¹/8 in. (23.5 cm), (b) 9³/8 in. (24 cm);
weight (a) 580.4 gr, (b) 584.1 gr
MZ-768; MZ-1258

On November 11, 1699, during his audience in the Palace of Facets, Ambassador Baron Johan Bergenhielm presented Tsar Peter I with candlesticks from King Charles XII of Sweden. The shape and decoration of this pair, made to resemble a stylized cluster of pillars on a square base, are extremely simple, but the partial gilding, which emphasizes the distinctive proportions of the objects, makes the decoration appear less severe. Candlesticks with square bases and square stem feet most probably originated in France in the second half of the seventeenth century. Their appearance in other European countries, including Sweden, demonstrates the increasing influence of French craftsmen upon the art of the European goldsmith.

The last thirty years of the seventeenth century were a very dynamic period in Swedish silversmithing. Anders

Bengtsson Starin (act. 1694–1715/17) was prominent among the seventeenth-century silversmiths in Stockholm. His plain candlesticks brilliantly epitomize the classical emphasis of Swedish metalwork.

Twelve candlesticks originally constituted the set, which were made by one of the famous representatives of the Caroline style in Swedish silver. This style evidently suited the tastes of the Russian court, and no later than a week after the departure of the Swedish embassy, Grand Duke Alexander Danilovich Menshikov selected thirty objects from the Ambassadorial Office, where all gifts were initially kept, for his trip to Preobrazhenskoe, the monarch's residence at that time.

The inventory of 1885 mentioned only seven candlesticks, and two of them have since been acquired by the Nationalmuseum in Stockholm at an auction held in 1931–32. Only five candlesticks have been preserved in the Kremlin Armory.

A Cyrillic inscription with the number of the piece according to the nineteenth-century inventory and its weight is engraved on the reverse of the base of one candlestick (a); the number and weight of the object appears on the other candlestick (b).

SOURCES: Inventory 1885, pt. 2, vol. 2, nos. 2032–2038. LITERATURE: *Drevnosti* 1849–53, vol. 5, pl. 64; Martin 1900/1, p. 43; Rosenberg 1922–28, vol. 4, no. 8638; *Svenskt Silversmide* 1941–63, pp. 75–76; *Treasures* 1979, p. 146, no. 42; *Svenskt Silver* 1990, p. 56; *Vier Jahrhunderte Schwedisches Silber* 1991, pp. 12, 13, ill.; *Schätze* 1991, pp. 146–47, no. 42; Markova 1996, p. 88, no. 79; *The Triumph of Simplicity* 1988, no. 12; *Silverskatter* 1997, p. 117, nos. 43, 44; Markova 1998, pp. 14–21; Kudriavtseva 1998, pp. 4–13.

AGK

88. Charter of Ratification of the Peace Treaty of
Kardis, the Pliusa Agreement, and the Moscow
Resolution, sent by King Charles XII of Sweden to
Tsar Peter I, dated February 1, 1699

Parchment, ink, gold, silk cover, decorative ornament with
the king's portrait and the emblems of the towns
H. 18 in. (46 cm); w. 13 in. (33.2 cm)
Russian State Archive of Ancient Documents, Moscow

The necessity of renewing the older treaties was probably motivated by two factors: Tsar Peter Alexeyevich
had become sole ruler after his brother Ivan's death in
1696, which might have called for reconfirmation, but
more important still was the realization by the Swedish
government that the new alliance of Denmark, Poland,
and Saxony was a threat to Swedish security. It would
have been much to Sweden's advantage to guarantee
peace along her border with Russia. After preliminary
negotiations, Tsar Peter agreed to accept an embassy from
Sweden. Ambassador Baron Johann Bergenhielm, accompanied by Anders Lindenhielm and Samuel Eosander,
handed the present document to Tsar Peter at the Kremlin on November 16, 1699. Tsar Peter promptly took an
oath to implement the agreements and treaties mentioned in the charter and sent the ambassadors home.
Before final versions of the agreement could be returned
to the tsar, Peter had already begun preparations for
war against the young Swedish king. Therefore, Russian confirmation of the agreements remained in Stockholm and none was returned to Moscow as was usual.

SOURCE: Russian State Archive of Ancient Documents,
Moscow, fol. 96 "Swedish-Russian Relations," work
3, doc. 64.

LITERATURE: *Petr Velikii i Moskva* 1998, pp. 142–48, no.
312. See also *Silverskatter* 1997, pp. 208–9, nos. 71, 72.

GIFTS FROM DENMARK

Twice—at the beginning of the seventeenth century and again at mid-century—Denmark failed at attempts to enter into a dynastic alliance with Russia. In the first attempt, in 1602, Duke Hans the Younger of Schleswig-Holstein, a member of the royal family of Denmark, sought in marriage Princess Kserisia, the daughter of Tsar Boris Godunov. It was important that the newly elected Russian monarch strengthen his ties to the royal families of Europe, but, upon his arrival in Moscow, the duke fell severely ill and died. Unfortunately, none of the valuable gifts brought to Moscow in 1602 is preserved, because the Kremlin treasuries were pillaged during the Polish-Lithuanian occupation of Moscow in 1611–12.

In 1640 King Christian IV of Denmark had good reason to consider the possibility of a Russian alliance once again. During the chaotic Thirty Years' War (1618–48), Denmark gradually lost prestige and risked domination by Sweden, its traditional enemy. Negotiations between Russian diplomats and the Danes concerning a marriage between Princess Irina, the eldest daughter of Tsar Mikhail Fyodorovich, and Count Valdemar Christian, son of King Christian IV, began as early as 1641.[1] The numerous visits of Danish ambassadors and messengers to Moscow at the beginning of the 1640s, especially the secret meetings of the Danish resident in Moscow, Peter Marselis, with the tsar and

his courtiers, convinced the Russian court of the advantage of a dynastic alliance with Denmark. These talks prepared the ground for the arrival of a first ambassadorial mission headed by Count Valdemar.

Sweden tried to discourage the developing relations between Denmark and Russia in every way, not simply because of the tsar's wish to make a matrimonial connection with a European royal family, but because a close tie between the two countries threatened the safety of Swedish borders. The threat to Swedish territories along the Baltic Sea south of Finland could potentially lead to the loss of the market that supplied the Swedish army in Livonia with important supplies, so the upcoming marriage and the possible severance of relations with Sweden were regarded cautiously.

In order to clarify the circumstances of the future match and to find out more about the bridegroom, Tsar Mikhail sent Hans Becker von Delden (also known as Ivan Fomin), a Russified Dane who served in the Ambassadorial Office in Moscow, to Copenhagen to investigate. In any case, the first visit of the Danish ambassadorial mission headed by Count Valdemar in 1641 was such a failure that the diplomats and the bridegroom were forced to go home empty-handed. However, in the spring of the following year (1642), Russian ambassadors arrived in Copenhagen and negotiations were resumed. The Danish court assigned the task of making the match to the skilled diplomat Peter Marselis, and at the end

Detail of cat. no. 89

of October 1643, the Great Ambassadorial Mission with Count Valdemar once again headed for Russia via Poland.

The Polish king Wladislaw IV, who wished to see the marriage agreement completed, since he viewed Sweden as an enemy, gave the ambassadors a cordial welcome, and the mission reached Moscow without obstruction. In January 1644, the count and the diplomats in his escort were given a particularly splendid formal reception in the Kremlin, but Sweden immediately responded by sending her army into Danish territory. Christian IV's ambassador was taken by surprise, and Polish diplomats who arrived in Moscow tried to force Russia to launch a war immediately against Sweden in Livonia, in order to stop the advance of the Swedish army before it reached Poland.

However, the successful actions of the Swedish diplomats at the Russian court managed to alert the tsar and his advisors to the intrigues of Poland and Denmark, and as a consequence the marriage of Count Valdemar came to be seen unfavorably by Tsar Mikhail. It did not take long to find a formal pretext for the refusal of the count's marriage proposal; the Russians demanded that Valdemar convert to Orthodoxy (although this issue had not been previously presented in such firm terms). The Danish diplomats demanded warranties that Russia would become involved in the war, but the tsar did not want to damage relations with Sweden, a close neighbor and an old and reliable partner in trade. Count Valdemar therefore refused to consider the possibility of a religious conversion and was finally placed under house arrest. It was only after Tsar Mikhail's sudden death in 1645 that the new monarch, Alexei Mikhailovich, allowed Valdemar to return home, thus ending the negotiations.

An alliance between Denmark and Russia was established much later, at the end of the seventeenth century, when Tsar Peter I sought allies in the upcoming Northern War (1700–1721) with Charles XII, the king of Sweden.

Of the ambassadorial gifts of Denmark to the Russian monarchs, the gifts of 1644 are outstanding for the great variety of splendid, beautifully crafted silver objects. The way in which the gifts were accumulated by the Danes is a complicated story, involving the loss

Fyodor Grigorevich Solntsev, *Cup in the Form of a Melon, Sent to Tsar Alexei Mikhailovich by King Christian IV in 1644*. Plate 22 in Solntsev, *Drevnosti Rossiiskogo gosudarstva*, vol. 5 (Moscow, 1849–53). Slavic and Baltic Division, The New York Public Library, Astor, Lenox and Tilden Foundations

of a first group and the rapid purchase of replacements.[2] Most of the silver was created by the best craftsmen of Hamburg, and it was of a type that suggests it was intended for use during the so-called Sweet Feasts. These feasts were organized in the tsar's wife's residence to celebrate the birthdays, name days, christenings, and wedding ceremonies of members of the tsar's family. A table was covered with colossal cakes baked in the shape of cities; fruit preserved in honey, candied fruit, candies, and sweet wines were served in vessels of unusual shapes: lions, cranes, deer, clusters of grapes.

NOTES
1. For more details, see Vainshtein 1947, pp. 202–10; Bencard and Markova 1988, pp. 43–72.
2. Bencard and Markova 1988, pp. 52–60.

AGK

89. Tablecloth

Denmark (Copenhagen), 1621
Maker: Karel Thijssen (initials "KT" woven into fabric)
Silk
87 x 169¹/₄ in. (223 x 434 cm)
TK-527

This red tablecloth with a gold pattern (the colors of the Danish crown), now rather faded, is a rare example of European weaving and includes images depicting various themes. Along with a similar blue-and-white tablecloth (Moscow Kremlin Armory, TK-2184), it was brought to Russia from Copenhagen in 1622 by the Moscow ambassadors Grand Duke Alexei Mikhailovich L'vov and Deacon Ždan Šipov. Recent research has shown that the embassy had as its secret objective a possible marriage between the tsar and a young princess

of Gottorp, a niece of King Christian IV of Denmark. She refused the offer but since the negotiations were secret, the gifts were not returned as they normally would have been after such a refusal.[1]

The center section of the tablecloth emulates a tabletop covered with a cloth of small-pattern fabric on which are placed many round dishes with food and sixteen plates with four half-dishes and forks and knives. Fruits and vegetables are depicted on the cloth as well. This central area is bordered by two narrow strips, one of which contains a garland comprising bunches of small flowers, leaves, and fruits, and the other depicts putti flying in pairs and holding shields with the inscription "GLORIA."

Along one of the long sides of the tablecloth is the scene of a battle between ships sailing under the flags of various European countries, and along the other long side are scenes of a royal hunt with dogs and hunting birds. Views of a medieval city with a town hall, a cathedral, tall houses, and a mill serve as the background of the two hunt scenes. The two short sides of the tablecloth each depict two large heraldic shields with the monogram of King Christian IV and the emblem of Denmark, surrounded by sixteen small shields with the coats of arms of various lands and provinces belonging to the state or connected to it through dynastic ties, as well as one blank shield. The words "ANNO 1621" are woven under the emblem of Christian, and between the small shields appear the initials "KT" (Karel Thijssen). Each of the sides is marked with a single-line inscription: CHRISTIANUS IV VAN GHODES SHENANDEN FRIS IN ALLEN SINNE DADEN ISI ANNO 1622. The corners of the tablecloth depict figures symbolizing the four seasons.

The tablecloth is executed using a double-face weaving technique, which produces a negative image of the pattern on the reverse side. The manufacture of similar fabrics became quite common in sixteenth- and seventeenth-century European silk weaving, although most of the fabrics made were of a single color with a floral pattern. This richly ornamented tablecloth with finely designed images is unique among European textiles of this type. Objects like this were intended for use during court ceremonies and could not be produced in large quantities. The composition of the tablecloth's

pattern, in which the central area and the border are emphasized, is clearly related to the Danish crown and to the formal purpose of this object, which in its size and skillful manufacture was entirely worthy of being a diplomatic gift. Another cloth with the same pattern but woven white on white exists in a Danish collection.[2]

This large cloth is a great rarity in its size, its technical refinement, and its monetary value. Works of this quality are generally thought to have been the unique achievement of the weavers of Courtrai in Flanders. Karel Thijssen was brought to Copenhagen from Flanders about 1621 by King Christian IV when he sought to upgrade a textile manufactory that he had established in 1605, turning it into a training center for weavers. A silk-weaving workshop was founded within the manufactory in 1621, and this piece was an early and exceptionally ambitious example of its work. Mogens Bencard has suggested that the king probably wished to encourage orders from the tsar for such objects, but such were not forthcoming and the manufactory failed in 1626.

NOTE
1. Bencard and Markova 1988, pp. 27–32.
2. The center of a white linen tablecloth (in the Rijksmuseum) made by Passchier Lammertijn in Haarlem about 1604 shows a table set with dishes and knives. Lammertijn (c. 1562–1621) was the foremost Dutch linen weaver at the time; see Rijksmuseum 1995, p. 419, fig. V.

SOURCES: Inventory 1884, pt. 2, vol. 3, no. 3699.
LITERATURE: Martin 1900/2, p. 13, pls. 2, 3; Bencard and Markova 1988, pp. 27–32, 90–91; Kondrikova 1996, pp. 262–65, nos. 218–222.

IIV and GW

90. Double Cup

Germany (Nuremberg), early 17th century
Maker's mark for Hans Petzolt (Rosenberg 1922–28, vol. 3,
nos. 4002, 4003),
Nuremberg (Rosenberg 1922–28, vol. 3, no. 3758)
Silver, gilding
H. 18³/₈ in. (47 cm); weight 1860.8 gr
MZ-227/1–2

On January 28, 1644, the ambassadors Oluf Parsberg and Sten Bille, representing Christian IV, King of Denmark and Norway, and his son Count Valdemar Christian, gave to Tsar Mikhail Romanov and his son, the tsarevich Alexei Mikhailovich, a double cup weighing 56 *zolotniks* (four pounds). Foreign embassies often brought double cups as gifts to the Russian tsars, and the Armory's unusually rich collection offers a unique opportunity to trace the development of this type of silver vessel.

Christian IV's embassy had been sent to Russia to negotiate the final terms of the projected marriage of Valdemar Christian, the king's natural son, to the tsar's daughter. By virtue of its distinguished maker, Hans Petzolt (master 1578–1633), this double cup would have been considered outstanding among the many valuable gilded-silver objects presented to the tsar by that embassy.

Petzolt was one of the most important silversmiths working in Nuremberg during the late sixteenth and early seventeenth century, overshadowed only by the great artist Wenzel Jamnitzer. Petzolt worked for emperors and princes and carried out many commissions for his native city. He was an outstanding representative of the neo-Gothic (*Neugotik*) style, of which this double cup is an exemplary work.

The shape of the double cup seems to have developed out of the custom of using a lidded vessel for wine. The tall, slender shape was, of course, particularly well suited to Petzolt's revival of the Gothic style, but the master has also retained the vertical axis and strong horizontal divisions of traditional Renaissance forms. He has skillfully combined a curvilinear quality with protruding lobes, or bosses, a feature of the late German Gothic style popularized about 1507 in Nuremberg by Albrecht Dürer. The applied ornament and the engraved band around the lip are typical of the late sixteenth century.

Petzolt's workshop must have been extensive because as many as forty of his marked pieces still exist, despite the heavy losses of Renaissance silver. The influence of his Nuremberg workshop spread rapidly to other centers, especially in northern Europe. We know that Petzolt received regular orders from the Nuremberg City Council for spectacular, tall presentation cups, which were given to visiting dignitaries and honored citizens. Between 1595 and 1615 he sold at least eighty-four of these cups to the council, the majority of which are described as decorated with bosses in the Gothic style.

On the bottom of one of the cups (MZ-227/1) is an engraved Cyrillic inscription that gives the weight of the object and the date and manner in which the double cup came into state hands.

SOURCES: Inventory 1663, fol. 58v; Inventory 1676, fol. 122; Inventory 1835, no. 604; Inventory 1884, pt. 2, bk. 1, nos. 1056, 1057, table 206.

LITERATURE: Lessing 1883, p. 379; Martin 1900/2, p. 18, pl. 17; Bartenev 1916, vol. 2, p. 208, ill. 222; Falke 1919, vol. 40, p. 83, ill. 7; Rosenberg 1922–28, vol. 3, nos. 3758, 4002–3c; Markova 1975, p. 24; Markova 1980, p. 117, no. 58; Markova 1996, pp. 48–49, no. 45.

A G K and B S

91. Covered Cup

Germany (Hamburg), 1628–43/44
Maker's mark for Carsten Mundt I (Hüseler 1950, no. 139),
Hamburg (Hüseler 1950, no. 19)
Silver, gilding
H. 20⅝ in. (53 cm); weight 1,140 gr
MZ-228/1–2

During their audience in the Palace of Facets, held on January 28, 1644, ambassadors Oluf Parsberg and Sten Bille presented to Tsar Mikhail Fyodorovich and Tsarevich Alexei Mikhailovich a standing cup with a weight of 2 pounds, 8 ounces, as a gift from the King of Denmark, Christian IV, and Count Valdemar Christian.

The gilded-silver cup with a closely fitted lid resembles a cluster of grapes. The figure on the stem represents the goddess Diana holding a bow in her hand and carrying a hunting horn on her back. The figure of Diana is reminiscent in its pose of the late Gothic portrayals of Saint Sebastian.

A Cyrillic inscription indicating the weight of the piece and the date and circumstances under which it was received into the treasury is engraved on the underside of the base.

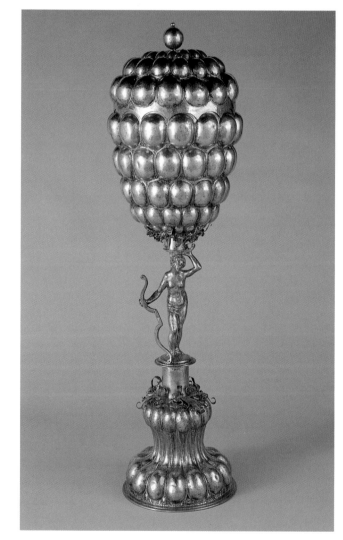

SOURCES: Inventory 1835, no. 601; Inventory 1884, pt. 2, vol. 1, no. 1072.

LITERATURE: Martin 1900/2, p. 19, pl. 19; Scheffler 1965, vol. 1, p. 845; Schliemann 1985, p. 146, no. 31; Smirnowa and Heitmann 1986, pp. 108–109, no. 17; Bencard and Markova 1988, pp. 87–88, no. 19, fig. 42.

AGK

92. Cup

Germany (Hamburg), 1631–33
Maker's mark for Hans Lambrecht II (Hüseler 1950, no. 19),
Hamburg (Hüseler 1950, no. 19)
Silver, gilding
H. 14⅞ in. (38 cm); weight 1,909 gr
MZ-230

On January 28, 1644, the ambassadors Oluf Parsberg and Sten Bille presented this cup to Tsar Mikhail Fyo-dorovich and Tsarevich Alexei Mikhailovich as a gift from the king of Denmark, Christian IV, and Count Valdemar Christian (see also page 290).

Hans Lambrecht II, who made the cup in the form of a melon, may have been inspired by the numerous tazza forms intended for the serving of fruit. The strik-ing gilded-silver still-life on the object, consisting of apples, cherries, and grapes, was originally more elabo-rate. The fruit and leaves were once painted with col-ored lacquers, and the melon had a top that served as a lid and completed the arrangement. The figure of Ceres, goddess of fertility, perches on the stem of the cup holding a cornucopia. During the Baroque period, when the dining table was elaborately decorated, candy

bowls and vessels like this were grouped around large centerpieces or placed on special stands.

Hans Lambrecht III, the silversmith's son, evidently received the principal order for the production of silver gifts to be sent in 1644 to the Russian tsar. He gath-ered together about seventy objects and sent them to Copenhagen. Most of them were lost at sea en route to Moscow, but a few surviving objects by Hans Lam-brecht II arrived safely in the Russian capital. The ambassadorial gifts of 1644 also included objects rap-idly assembled by unknown means en route to Moscow and may have included other objects from Christian's treasury. The cup discussed here may have come with the first order, part of which was lost at sea, or it may have been added later to the gift on its way to Moscow.

A Cyrillic inscription indicating the weight of the piece and the date and circumstances under which it was received into the treasury is engraved on the reverse of the base; the number in the nineteenth-cen-tury inventory and the weight are engraved on one of the reliefs on the base.

SOURCES: Inventory 1663, fol. 154v; Inventory 1676, fols. 79v–80; Inventory 1835, no. 600; Inventory 1884, pt. 2, vol. 1, no. 1154, table 215.

LITERATURE: *Drevnosti* 1849–53, vol. 5, pl. 22; Martin 1900/2, pl. 17, pl. 14; Rosenberg 1922–28, vol. 2, no. 2417b; Hüseler 1965, no. 167; Scheffler 1965, 862 ill.; Markova 1975, p. 50; Schliemann 1985, p. 158, no. 77, ill. 41; Smirnova and Heitmann 1986, pp. 116, 117, no. 22; Bencard and Markova 1988, p. 89, no. 25, fig. 47; Markova 1996, pp. 68–69, no. 61.

A G K

93. Table Decoration

Germany (Hamburg), 1635–44
Maker's mark for Johan Jans (Hüseler 1950, no. 148), Hamburg
(Hüseler 1950, no. 22)
Silver, gilding
H. 15⅝ in. (40 cm); weight 2,201.5 gr
MZ-248

During their audience in the Palace of Facets on January 28, 1644, ambassadors Oluf Parsberg and Sten Bille presented to the tsar and his son a table decoration in the form of a stag weighing 4 pounds, 14 ounces, as a gift from the king of Denmark, Christian IV, and his son, Count Valdemar Christian.

Evidently, the sculpture was made as a water or wine vessel: the opening in the mouth of the deer may have served as a spout, while the round detail on its head, now soldered, on which the long branchy antlers are mounted, may have served as a lid. The body of the animal is chased to give the appearance of hair. The top of the base is embossed to resemble earth, and the lower section of the base is decorated with auricular motifs.

The object may have been a component in a set of table decorations with a hunting theme, but it may also have served as a splendid single work of art to be displayed on a sideboard.

A Cyrillic inscription, "in white deer," and the weight of the piece are engraved on the bottom of the base.

Johan Jans (act. 1617–53/58) is well known as a maker of standing cups; two cups made by him are in the Moscow Kremlin Armory (MZ-223/1–2, MZ-434).

852 d.; Schliemann 1985, p. 151, no. 52, fig. 38; Smirnowa and Heitmann 1986, p. 112, no. 19, illus. p. 11 and p. 113; Bencard and Markova 1988, p. 89, no. 26, fig. 55; Markova 1988, p. 241, fig. 165.

AGK

SOURCES: Inventory 1676, fol. 189v; Inventory 1679, fol. 160v; Inventory 1721, fol. 72–72v; Inventory 1835, no. 887; Inventory 1884, pt. 2, vol. 2, no. 1928.

LITERATURE: Kologrivov 1911, p. 39; Martin 1900/2, p. 16, pl. 14; Hüseler 1950, p. 148; Scheffler 1965, 1,

94. Wheellock Hunting Rifle

Germany, c. 1640
Steel, iron, copper, silver, wood, gilding
Overall l. 49⅞ in. (128 cm); l. of barrel 38⅜ in. (98.5 cm);
caliber: 88 mm; grooves: 6
OP-473

The hunting rifle presented here is one of a pair of identical weapons in the Armory collection (the mate is OP-474). The tradition of making twin hunting rifles dates from the seventeenth century. Such arms were intended to enable hunters to shoot on a similar gun without wasting time on reloading. During hunting, while the hunter was shooting at game, his huntsman quickly loaded the second gun, preparing it for the next shot.

In the inventory of 1687, the two guns are entered under the category of first class, i.e., best quality, firearms. The inventory contains information regarding the fact that, in the words of the boyar Boris Ivanovich Morozov, these guns had been presented as gifts of the prince of Denmark, Valdemar Christian. Firearms of this type were included in the "field arm reserves" of Tsar Alexei Mikhailovich of the Russian-Polish war of 1654–55. After a brief description, the Inventory of Field Reserves notes the following: "Humbly presented to His Majesty by the Danish Prince."

The German rifle is a magnificent example of gunsmith craftsmanship. Its decoration is typical of the German school of the 1640s, when the inlaying of the gunstock with bone and mother-of-pearl was gradually replaced by cut and engraved silver plate as well as by miniature cast silver figures.

The stock of the rifle is inlaid with silver wire, and openwork silver plaques are placed on gilded-silver plates. The plaques depict hunting scenes and the ancient goddess of agriculture and fertility, Ceres, holding a cornucopia in her hands; on the other side of the stock, opposite the lock plate, is the representation of a griffin.

The rifle is equipped with a wheellock firing mechanism. The cover plate of the wheel is embellished with two cast putti and two engraved dragons. A cast figure of Saint George on horseback fighting a winged dragon is located on the lock plate. Saint George was among those saints associated with the Russian tsars (see cat. nos. 67, 68). The breech, middle, and muzzle portions of the polygonal barrel are engraved with a floral ornament, which was originally gilded. The trigger is executed in the form of a partial, nude female figure.

SOURCES: Inventory of campaign treasury of Tsar Alexei Mikhailovich 1654, fol 28; Inventory 1687, fol. 218; Inventory 1886, pt. 5, vol. 4, no. 6450.
LITERATURE: Yablonskaya 1996, pp. 138–39, no. 122.

EAY

GIFTS FROM SCHLESWIG-HOLSTEIN

DURING THE PERIOD 1630–40 Duke Frederick III of Schleswig-Holstein developed a grand project to lift his small duchy into the ranks of major European economic powers, which included four missions to Moscow, in 1632, 1634, 1636, and 1639. A Hamburg merchant, Otto Brügmann, proposed opening a new trading route to Persia through the Swedish territory of Livonia (on the Baltic Sea) to Moscow, and south to Isfahan, capital of the great Persian empire built by Shah Abbas I. The Swedes readily acquiesced to the scheme, and Brügmann left for Moscow in 1632 to negotiate transit rights with Tsar Mikhail Fyodorovich. Holstein's gift of twelve cannons, ammunition, permission for Russia to purchase Western European military equipment and to send recruiting agents to Holstein was received warmly, since Tsar Mikhail was about to launch a military campaign against Poland. Later the duke sent cannoneers and even one of his physicians.[1]

When Brügmann left for Russia in 1633, he took with him Adam Olearius, a German scholar from Anhalt. Olearius's account of his mission and of later travels through Muscovy to Persia became a standard work about Russia and Persia. Published in German in 1647, *Neue Orientalische Reise Beschreibung* [New Travel Descriptions in the Orient], was promptly translated into Dutch, English, and Italian; a Russian edition did

Detail of cat. no. 95a

August John, title page from Adam Olearius's *Neue Orientalische Reise Beschreibung* (Schleswig, 1647). Schleswig-Holsteinische Landesbibliothek, Kiel

not appear until the nineteenth century. Olearius provided a carefully written account that was liberally illustrated with engravings. The following is an excerpt from his list describing the diplomatic gifts presented by the duke to the tsar on August 19, 1634:

> a black stallion covered with a beautiful cloth; a dapple-gray gelding; another gray horse; a horse's harness, finely worked in silver and embedded with turquoises, rubies, and other stones; a cross, almost a quarter of an ell in length, made of chrysolite and encased in gold, carried on a basin[2]; a costly chemical-apothecary apparatus; a cabinet was made of ebony and stamped in gold; boxes were also made of gold and decorated with precious stones; a crystal receptacle stamped with gold and set with rubies; a large mirror, five quartiers long and an ell wide, framed in ebony, adorned with pictures and thick layers of silver leaf; a chiming clock, shaped like a mountain, on which was portrayed the story of the prodigal son; a gilded silver walking stick which housed a magnifying glass; a large ebony clock decorated with silver.[3]

The archival documents confirm Olearius's story and preserve the names of the ambassadors, Philip Crusius and Brügmann. Among the documents of the Book of Receipts for August 19, 1634, the gifts are listed and noted as having been "taken to the treasury." This evidence leads us to conclude that the set of ceremonial horse trappings preserved in the Armory are the same as those described by Olearius (cat. no. 95a,b).

Tsar Mikhail proved to be a tough negotiator, insisting on the enormous sum of 800,000 *Reichsthalers* for each of the ten years of the transit agreement. Nonetheless, Brügmann and Olearius set out from Holstein across Russia to Isfahan in 1635, returning to the duke's court only in 1639. The results of this trip were disastrous for most of those concerned. The new Shah Sefi I refused to accept Holstein's trade proposals, and the entire scheme collapsed. The duke later disengaged himself from his agreement with the tsar, after bidding farewell to a Persian ambassador who returned to Holstein with the duke's embassy.[4] Brügmann was beheaded. Only Olearius made something of the matter with his successful book, which he revised and expanded over the years; at the Holstein court Olearius was given a comfortable sinecure, which enabled him to continue his studies of Russia and Persia and to found a museum. Indeed, he became something of a cultural figure of the duke's court.

NOTES
1. Baron 1967, pp. 3–30.
2. The length of an ell varied from place to place. Olearius may have used the Flemish ell, which equals 27 English inches, or a smaller one.
3. Baron 1967, pp. 60–61.
4. See Bier 1995, pp. 9–19, 70–75.

OBM and GW

95a,b. Set of Ceremonial Horse Trappings

Bohemia (Prague), early 17th century
Maker: Johann Michael (worked in Prague at
the beginning of the 17th century)
Silver, silk, garnets, emeralds, pearls,
filigree, enamel, gilding, fabric, leather
L. of bridle 41 3/8 in. (106 cm); l. of breastplate 30 in. (77 cm)
K-429, K-64

On August 19, 1634, Philip Crusius and Otto Brüg-mann, ambassadors of Frederick III, duke of Schleswig-Holstein, presented the duke's gifts to Tsar Mikhail Fyodorovich. Among them was the set of ceremonial horse trappings mentioned in the Book of Receipts for August 19, 1634.[1]

The comparison of the texts of the Book of Receipts, the inventories of the tsar's treasury for 1640,[2] and the inventory of the stables treasury for 1706,[3] led to the discovery of the set of horse trappings discussed here.[4] Initially, the set included four objects: a bridle with reins, a frontlet, a breastplate, and a crupper. Two of the objects, the bridle with reins and the breastplate, survive. The bridle consists of three straps—a head-stall, a browband, and a throatlatch—and the breast-plate consists of two long straps that fastened to the saddle and a short strap that dangled on the horse's chest. All of the straps are of leather fitted with blue silk, trimmed with gold cord, and decorated with large gilded-silver plates with filigree floral motifs enhanced with blue, turquoise, and green enamel. Larger plates in the form of flowers with abundant petals are located

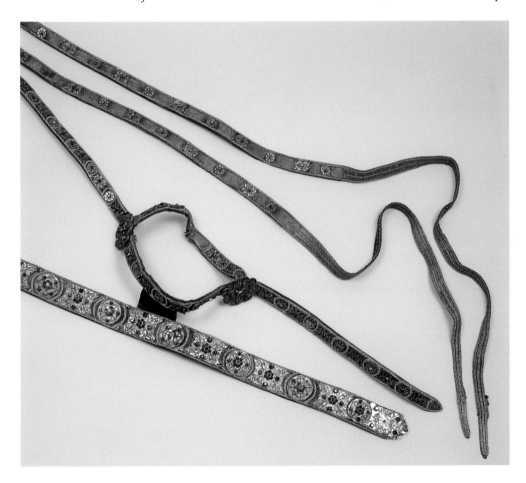

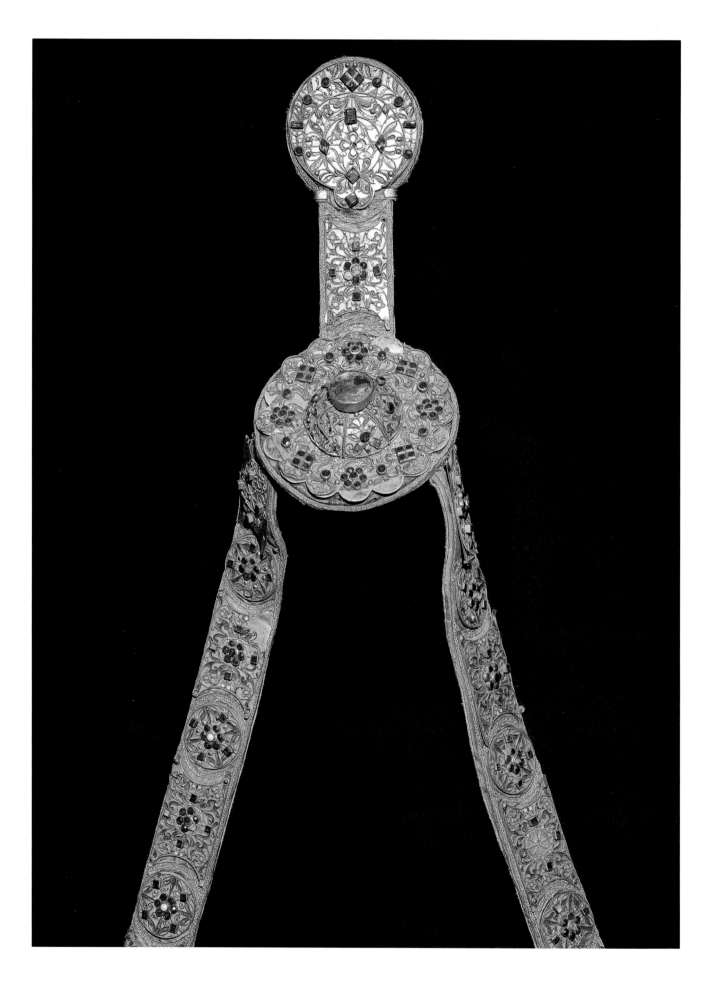

at the fastening points of the straps. Cut garnets, mounted on the surface of the silver plates, and a flower with a garnet or pearl cup are in the center of each plate. The reins are also decorated with similar rosettes of enamel, filigree, and semiprecious stones.

Similar examples of horse trappings and arms—with blue and green enamel with filigree on a smooth gilded-silver ground with inset gems—are found in museum collections in Dresden, Munich, Vienna, and Prague. These luxurious so-called Turkish-style sets were manufactured in the court workshops of Prague, and experts attribute them to the Prague craftsman Johann Michael.

SOURCES: Book of Receipts 1633–34, fols. 139v–141; Inventory 1640, fol. 376–376v; Inventory 1706, fol. 71; Inventory 1835, no. 3273; Inventory 1884, pt. 6, vol. 5, no. 8802; Olearius 1906, pp. 29–34.

LITERATURE: Kirillova 1996, p. 144, no. 126; Melnikova 1996, pp. 41–43.

NOTES

1. The Book of Receipts describes the set in the following manner: "with silver filigree on gold trimming, plants coated with blue and green enamel."
2. The 1640 Inventory gives the following description of the set: "Bit, cruppers, breastplates, frontlet, and reins without bit, made of silver, stones, and pearls; gilded plants coated with enamel; sky-blue silk braid sewn on the straps; beautiful edges and sockets trimmed with a gold thread weave; one stone fallen out of the socket on the breastplate, price one hundred rubles. Sent to His Majesty as a gift by the Grand Duke of Holstein in the year 1634, on the 19th day of August."
3. In the 1706 inventory, the set is called a "Holstein bit."
4. Owing to the stylistic similarity between the breastplate and the work of Prague jewelers from the early seventeenth century, L. P. Kirillova suggests that the breastplate was brought to Moscow from Prague in 1604 by the ambassadorial mission of Heinrich von Logau as a gift to Tsar Boris Godunov from Emperor Rudolf II. However, convincing evidence exists for the connection between this set and the Schleswig-Holstein ambassadorial mission of 1634.

OBM

BIOGRAPHIES OF TSARS, PATRIARCHS, AND DONORS

THE TSARS

Ivan IV, the Terrible (1530–1584), Grand Prince of Russia (r. 1533–47), Tsar of Russia (r. 1547–84)

> There was a majesty in his countenance proportionable with the excellency of his estate.
>
> RICHARD CHANCELLOR, 1553

Ivan Vasilievich was tall and well made with high shoulders and a broad chest. His eyes were small and restless, his nose hooked, he had a beard and moustaches of imposing length. He was Russia's first ruler to bear the title of tsar, a title previously used by Russians for Byzantine, Bulgarian, and Middle Eastern emperors, including the khans of the Golden Horde and their successors. Although his father, Grand Prince Vasily III (r. 1505–33), and grandfather, Ivan III, known as Ivan the Great (r. 1462–1505), had used the title hesitantly and on only a few documents, Ivan IV proclaimed himself tsar at his coronation in the Moscow Kremlin in 1547. He was the penultimate prince of the Riurikid dynasty.

Tsar Ivan inherited his grand-dukedom at the age of three in 1533. His difficult childhood included the four-year regency of his mother, Elena Glinskaia (d. 1538) and various governments run by viciously competitive boyar (noble) factions. At the beginning of his personal reign, Ivan IV embarked upon radical reforms within the government and a reduction of the boyars' power, which he achieved in part during the 1550s. These were his glory days, which saw not only significant reforms but also great military victories, such as the taking of the cities of Kazan (1552) and Astrakhan (1554), and the conquest of Russia's former oppressors. Ivan commemorated the capture of Kazan by building the Church of St. Basil the Blessed, a masterpiece of Russian architecture near the walls of the Moscow Kremlin. Ivan then turned his attention to Livonia and the Baltic Sea area, where in 1558 he captured forts along the Baltic, including Narva, which briefly brought Russia into closer contact with Western Europe.

The period after 1560 is seen as the second, "terrible," phase of Ivan's reign. Having lost a wife and a son and repudiated his ministers and friends, the tsar began to live in an atmosphere of such fear and apprehension that by 1565 he decided to abdicate. He consented to remain only after major demonstrations of popular support were mounted, but then he insisted on dictating his own terms, including the establishment of the *oprichnina*, a separate court under his direct control. Ivan moved on to the second wealthiest city in his tsardom, Novgorod, which he punished by murdering thousands of residents and destroying the roofs of all houses and secular buildings there. In 1581, in an uncontrollable rage, he killed his son and heir, Ivan. Repentant, Ivan IV again sought to resign his throne, but no one in authority was willing to accept his gesture.

Ivan's fortunes at war declined markedly when his troops faced the able Polish king, Stephan Batory, and the tsar surrendered most of his conquests in the Baltic area under the treaty known as the Peace of Zapoli in 1582.

On his deathbed, Ivan joined an order of hermits and died (wearing a cowl) as the monk Jonah. His son Fyodor I (1557–1598), the last of the Riurikid dynasty, who was said to be "slow-witted, but very gentle," then ascended the throne.

Ivan's relationship with England is an interesting story. He graciously exchanged favorable trading rights with Richard Chancellor, an English captain who sailed to the White Sea and proceeded to Moscow. When Chancellor returned to Russia in 1555, Ivan permitted the establishment of an English-

Ivan IV (the Terrible). Color lithograph, no. 26 in *Portrety, gerby i pechati Bol'shoi gosudarstvennoi knigi* (Moscow, 1672; St. Petersburg repr., 1903). 13¼ x 10½ in. (34 x 27 cm). Slavic and Baltic Division, The New York Public Library, Astor, Lenox and Tilden Foundations

Boris Godunov. Color lithograph, no. 30 in *Portrety, gerby i pechati Bol'shoi gosudarstvennoi knigi 1672 g.* (St. Petersburg, 1903). 9³⁄₈ x 12½ in. (24 x 32 cm) (photo courtesy The State Historical-Cultural Museum Preserve, Moscow Kremlin)

Russian trading company, for which he built a structure that still stands today. The tsar corresponded with Queen Elizabeth I, in hopes of establishing a place of exile for himself in England in the event of troubles at home, and he eventually proposed marriage to Lady Mary Hastings, the queen's cousin. (His proposal was refused.) In 1558 Ambassador Thomas Randolph presented to Ivan "a great Cuppe of silver curiously wrought with verses graven on it expressing the histories workmanly set out on the same." Queen Elizabeth said, "We doo send him that same rather for the newnes of the devise than for the value." In 1571 Anthony Jenkinson brought further tokens of Her Majesty's esteem: "a paire of Candlesticks... (and) two standinge Pottes gilte." In 1586 the queen sent another emissary to Tsar Fyodor I, Jerome Horsey, who carried impressive presents, including dogs, lions, bulls, pistols, armor, drugs, and wine.

Although the busy exchanges of embassies during a reign that often looked to expand foreign relations must have produced a prodigious quantity of gifts, few if any of these appear to have survived, in part because of a fire in the tsar's treasury and in part because of the Time of Troubles (1605–13) between the Riurik and Romanov dynasties. Ivan's treasures are represented in this catalogue by a splendid Russian gospel cover

commissioned by the tsar and donated by him to a monastery (cat. no. 3).

Boris Godunov (c. 1551–1605), Tsar of Russia (r. 1598–1605)

> He is a comely person, well favored, affable...
> of good capacity, affected much to necromancy,
> not learned but of sudden apprehension...a natural
> good orator...subtle...revengeful...sent rich
> presents to foreign princes.
>
> SIR JEROME HORSEY, 1586

Boris Fyodorovich was a member of an ancient Tatar family that had migrated to Moscow during the fourteenth century. He had no blood connection to the Riurikid Moscow tsars but rose in power through political astuteness at the court of Ivan IV. His sister, Irene, was married to Ivan's son Tsar Fyodor, who named Boris to the regency council on his deathbed. Although Boris was loaded with honors in this position, he accepted second place to Nikitich Romanov (father of Patriarch Filaret, q.v.), whose early death left Boris with only Filaret as a rival for power. But Filaret lost out and Boris remained the power behind the throne during Fyodor I's reign (1584–98), dealing like a prince with other princes. In foreign policy Boris agreed to aid the Austrian emperor with subsidies in his wars against the Ottoman sultan, and he encouraged English merchants by exempting them from tolls. He strengthened Russia's position along the northeastern and southeastern borders of the realm by building numerous towns and forts. During Boris's era, the office of metropolitan of the Moscow church was raised to that of a patriarchate. However, his governance was tainted by suspicion that he was responsible for the sudden death of Tsar Fyodor's half-brother Dmitry in 1591, seen widely as a move to take the throne, although it is doubtful that Boris was involved.

The death of Fyodor, who left no Riurikid heir, produced an unprecedented and critical situation. Boris's election to the throne was proposed by the Moscow patriarch Job. The national assembly unanimously elected Boris tsar in 1598.

Boris negotiated with Elizabeth I of England in the hope of marrying his son and daughter to members of the English aristocracy. In 1603–4 he sent four young Russians to England to study, and fourteen others were later sent to Western Europe. Few of them returned to Moscow.

Whatever his abilities, Boris's reign as tsar was marked by a series of disasters more or less beyond his control. Famine and drought were widespread in the years 1601–3, resulting in serious social unrest and even open revolt, in spite of heroic efforts by the tsar to organize famine relief. In response to the landowners, who had difficulty retaining their peasants during these difficult times, Boris introduced laws binding the peasants to the land, thus establishing the basis for the development of serfdom.

In 1604 an army marched to the gates of Moscow, led by a man who pretended to be the dead Prince Dmitry, Ivan IV's son. Although he was defeated, the "False" Dmitry escaped and returned to take Moscow after Boris's sudden death in 1605, inaugurating the instability that would become known as the Time of Troubles (1605–13). Boris and the False Dmitry were the subject of a poem by Pushkin, which served as the basis for the famous opera *Boris Godunov* by Moussorgsky.

Boris seems to have been viewed favorably from abroad, and he received many embassies, such as those from King James I of England (q.v.), which produced many gifts—even a massive state coach (Chapter 5, fig. 10). The Austrian emperor Rudolf II sent Boris regalia (crown, orb, scepter, and so on), and Shah Abbas I (q.v.) of Persia sent him a golden throne (Chapter 5, fig. 2), probably to encourage his anti-Ottoman policies, since the Ottomans were a rival power to Persia.

Mikhail Fyodorovich Romanov. Color lithograph, no. 31 in *Portrety, gerby i pechati Bol'shoi gosudarstvennoi knigi 1672 g.* (St. Petersburg, 1903). 9 x 11½ in. (23 x 29.5 cm). Slavic and Baltic Division, the New York Public Library, Astor, Lenox and Tilden Foundations

Mikhail Romanov (1596–1645), Tsar of Russia (r. 1613–45)

> A gentle and pious prince, Michael was afflicted even when young with weak legs and a tic in the left eye. . . . He himself can not write and I am not sure whether he can read.
>
> ISAAC MASSA, 1614

Mikhail Fyorodovich was the first tsar of the Romanov dynasty (1615–1918). His parents were Maria Ivanovna Shestova and Fyodor Nikitich, a cousin of Tsar Fyodor I (r. 1584–98), and his great-aunt Anastasiia had been the first wife of Tsar Ivan IV. Mikhail's parents were accused of treason, sorcery, and witchcraft by Boris Godunov and were forced to take religious vows and undergo imprisonment in monasteries. Mikhail's father became the monk Filaret (q.v.) and his mother the nun Marfa. After Boris's death, Mikhail often lived with his mother, and the family was occasionally reunited, although the church forbade Fyodor and Maria to resume married life.

After a chaotic interregnum (1610–13), when several men sought the crown, the national assembly rejected all of these and settled on Mikhail, whose youth and inexperience proved

Alexei Mikhailovich Romanov. Color lithograph, no. 32 in *Portrety, gerby i pechati Bol'shoi gosudarstvennoi knigi 1672 g* (St. Petersburg, 1903). 10⁷/₈ x 13¹/₄ in. (28 x 34 cm). Slavic and Baltic Division, the New York Public Library, Astor, Lenox and Tilden Foundations

positive attributes in contrast to someone tainted by the complicated political situation of the previous years. It took some months before the tumult and the rebellion died down and law and order were restored. Although progress was gradually made, Mikhail's kingdom was impoverished and his army was too weak to take on Poland and Sweden, which occupied some of his territories (including Novgorod), and to secure the release of his father, who was imprisoned in Poland. The most serious problems were eventually solved with the Treaties of Stolbovo (Sweden, 1617) and Deulino (Poland, 1619), and Filaret finally returned home.

Enthroned as the Moscow patriarch, he became co-ruler with Mikhail, who was apparently content to be a submissive son. Mikhail's second wife, Evdokiia, bore him ten children, securing the Romanov succession. While he occupied himself with the rituals of tsarship, his father took over the ship of state in the ecclesiastical, military, domestic, and international areas. A census was begun to find monies to replenish the empty treasury. A modest financial success and the fact that Poland was at war on two fronts enabled Filaret and Mikhail to undertake their own war with Poland (1632–33) in order to win back lost territories (particularly Smolensk). This venture was unsuccessful at first, and when Filaret died during a second siege of Smolensk, Mikhail rapidly negotiated for peace,

obtaining little except the withdrawal of King Wladislaw's (q.v.) claim to the Russian throne (1634).

The international outlook improved in some respects as the Thirty Years' War (1616–48) wound down. The pacific Queen Christina (q.v.) began to rule in Sweden, and King Christian IV of Denmark (q.v.) appeared willing to marry his son Valdemar to one of Mikhail's daughters. The marriage arrangement was of potentially great importance since by that time (1644–45) only a single male heir of Mikhail's, Prince Alexei, had survived.

The present catalogue discusses many objects from Mikhail's reign. There are diplomatic gifts from Turkish officials (cat. nos. 29, 30) and the Crimean Tatar khan (cat. no. 27). Silver gifts from James I of England and Christian IV of Denmark (cat. no. 60) and horse trappings from the celebrated Schleswig-Holstein embassy (cat. no. 95a,b), along with Dutch and Danish guns, are also included (cat. nos. 67, 68). An indication of Mikhail's political situation is the gift of a golden wine-tasting cup (*charka*) from his mother (cat. no. 1), which originally belonged to Vasily III (the Great), Ivan IV's father. The gift was certainly intended to suggest the continuity of the Romanov and Riurikid dynasties.

Alexei Mikhailovich (1629–1676), Tsar of Russia (r. 1645–76)

The kind of sovereign all Christian peoples desire, but few ever obtain.

JACOB REUTENFELS

His Imperial Majesty is a goodly person . . . of a sanguine complexion, light brown hair, his beard uncut, he is full and fat, of a majesterial Deportment, severe in his anger, bountiful, chairitable, chastly uxorious, very kind to his sisters and Children, of a strong memory, strict in his Devotions, and a favorer of his Religion.

SAMUEL COLLINS

Alexei Mikhailovich Romanov ascended the Russian throne at the age of sixteen in 1645 on the death of his father, Tsar Mikhail Romanov (q.v.). Alexei's background had been the sheltered world of the Kremlin Terem Palace, where his mother lived a traditional life, supplemented by the political tutorials of the boyar Boris Morozov. The young Alexei mastered the fine points of church music and liturgy.

During the first few years of Alexei's reign, Boris Morozov was the dominant figure. His foreign policy was pacific, and his domestic policy was aimed at relieving governmental burdens on the people. He arranged for the tsar to marry Mariia Miloslavskaia, who was a member of an important but unpopular boyar family. Ten days later Morozov married Mariia's sister Anna and became the tsar's brother-in-law. Five months after that, both Morozov and members of the tsarina's family, the Miloslavskis, were driven from the court by riots in Moscow. The success of the riots culminated in dangerous rebellions at Novgorod and Pskov, which were settled by a near surrender of the government, but the riots also resulted in Alexei's promulgating an improved legal code favorable to the merchant class. The peasants did less well, however, since their status as serfs was further institutionalized.

The metropolitan of Novgorod, Nikon (later patriarch, q.v.), caught the tsar's attention by his tactful and courageous conduct and was brought to Moscow. Nikon was installed as patriarch of Moscow in 1652 and later granted the title Supreme Sovereign. For a period he served as a virtual co-ruler with Alexei. Their extraordinary relationship is largely demonstrated by the tsar's intense interest in religious issues. Alexei was scrupulous in observing religious rituals, deeply interested in theology, and concerned about the state of the Russian church. Nikon converted Alexei to his controversial theology, and these doctrines continued to be supported by the tsar even after Nikon fell from his favor.

In 1654 Russia went to war with Poland, using that country's weakness as an excuse to regain territory linguistically Belorussian and Ukrainian. At first, Alexei was successful with his objectives, such as the expulsion of Polish forces from Ukraine, the conquest of Belorussia, and the capture of Smolensk. His efforts were aided by the invasion of Poland by Sweden, and he returned in triumph to Moscow in December 1655, but eventually things went less well for Russia. Alexei was forced to give up his ambition to conquer territory near the Baltic Sea, and the war with Poland continued for thirteen long years. The Treaty of Andrusovo (1667) nonetheless resulted in an important settlement of the Russian-Polish border, one favorable to Russia. Smolensk was gained and, even more important, Kiev and the parts of Ukraine east of the Dnieper River were added to Alexei's realm.

Although Alexei's court in most respects held fast to its traditional character, he was willing to accept some Western European influence in limited areas, particularly in the military and for the economic development of Russia. His attitude is perhaps best reflected in his decision to establish in 1657 a German quarter outside Moscow to house merchants and others working in Russia. They had their place but one well outside that of the mainstream.

The memorial icon *Worship of the Cross* (1676–81) (cat. no. 15) shows the tsar, his wife, and Patriarch Nikon with Saints Constantine and Helen. The subject matter and the costumes emphasize the traditional character of the Russian rulers. Alexei decreed: "Courtiers are forbidden to adopt foreign, German and other customs, to cut their hair on their heads, and to wear robes and hats of foreign design" (1675). Yet Alexei also built his palace and gardens at Izmailovo, a westernized ensemble that paralleled the earlier residence of Matveev, his minister.

Artamon Matveev, Alexei's closest adviser toward the end of his reign, has been called the "first Russian to live in the Western manner." He dressed like a European and entertained foreigners in his home, even with his wife present, an unprecedented occurrence.

In military matters the tsar was a reformer, creating new regiments of Russian soldiers commanded by foreign officers. He sponsored the publication of books on modern warfare and energetically recruited engineers and other technical experts. Alexei also attempted to bring modern manufacturing to Russia, even establishing factories on some of his own estates, where he also developed experimental farms. A poet and historian, Alexei appears to have been open to the influence of Western writers. The birth of his son Peter in 1672 was actually celebrated by the performance of a play, *Esther*, in spite of the strong disapproval of theater by the Orthodox church hierarchy.

The peace with Poland held until the end of Alexei's reign and with the exception of the serious Razin rebellion and a minor war with Turkey in Ukraine, the later years of his life were reasonably tranquil.

Alexei received a large number of embassies, many relating to various wars and treaties and to the steady growth of foreign trade with Russia. Gifts from Polish embassies (1647, 1667, and 1671), Dutch embassies (1648, 1665, and 1676), and English gifts from 1663, are included in this catalogue. A Gospel cover given by Alexei and his wife, Mariia, to the Chudov Monastery at Moscow (cat. no. 12) may illustrate this tsar in his role as "favorer of his religion."

Sofia Alexeyevna (1657–1704), Regent (r. 1682–89), Autocrat (1686–89)

Said to possess great wit and judgment.
JOHANN HÖVEL, 1682

A shapeless body, monstrously fat, a head as big as a bushel measure [with] hair growing on her face.
F. NEUVELLE, 1699

When Alexei died in 1676, he was succeeded by his surviving eldest son, who was fourteen at the time and who ruled as Fyodor III (r. 1676–82). Fyodor was well educated and devout and had literary talent; his ill health has always been mentioned, though mostly exaggerated. There were no radical departures from the policies of the previous reign, although a brief period of Polish cultural influence may be mentioned in connection with his first marriage to the daughter of an orthodox Polish nobleman. This wife died within a year, and Alexei's second marriage was also brief. Fyodor died shortly afterward without naming an heir and was survived by his brother Ivan and a half-brother, Peter, under the regency of his half-sister, Sofia.

Sofia Alexeyevna, daughter of Tsar Alexei and his first wife, Mariia, shattered precedent by appearing in the quarters of her brother, the tsar, to nurse him while male ministers were in his presence. When he died in 1682, she attended his obsequies, although it was traditional for only tsars' wives and mothers to attend.

After Fyodor's death, Sofia found herself and members of her mother's family at a disadvantage, since her younger brother, Ivan (1666–1696), was passed over for the throne because of his physical and mental limitations and her half-brother, Peter (q.v.), was proclaimed tsar. Peter's mother, who was Alexei's second wife, Natalya, of the Naryshkin family, was declared regent.

Sofia emerged as a major public figure after playing a role in the 1682 revolt of the Streltsy Guards of the Kremlin, which resulted in the murder of several members of the Naryshkin family. Sofia then used her relationship with the Streltsy to force Natalya to resign as regent and to have Ivan proclaimed co-tsar with his half-brother, Peter. With Ivan's ascension, Sofia emerged as the dominant figure at court and eventually assumed the title of regent herself. She befriended the highly westernized member of Fyodor's government, Vasily Vasilievich Golitsyn (1643–1714), and used him as an adviser in many areas.

As an able and determined woman, Sofia proceeded with a program of reforms, but she was also scrupulous, even fanatical, about her religious obligations, which are reflected in the extraordinary Baroque architecture erected in Moscow at this time. Much of Sofia's attention had to be devoted to maintaining her position, however, an increasingly difficult task in the face of Ivan's weakness and Peter's robust physical and intellectual development. Peter recognized the difficulties of his situation and chose to lead a life apart from Sofia's court, but he represented a continual threat to her.

Sofia's ambition to remain in power probably transcended the position of regent. She married Ivan off with the idea of producing a rival heir to Peter, but Ivan fathered only daughters, and Peter remained a threat. Motivated to maintain the positions of the Miloslavskiis and their clients versus the Naryshkins and theirs, Sofia certainly considered simply seizing the crown for herself—her portrait as tsarina appeared on coins and medals in 1684 and two years later she assumed the title of autocrat—but she never actually did so.

In foreign affairs, Sofia and Golitsyn sought to stabilize the situation in Russia. With the Treaty of Eternal Peace (1686) Poland officially recognized Russia's permanent acquisition of Kiev, and Russia agreed to join an alliance with Austria against the Turks. However, this peace did not achieve stability on Russia's southern frontier, which was constantly threatened by the Crimean Tatars and the Ottoman Turks.

In spite of her cunning, Sofia was gradually undone by her relationship with Golitsyn, who proved unsuccessful as a

A. Afonas'ev after L. Tarasevich, *Sofia Alexeyevna*. Engraving, no. 1 in *Rovinsky's Materialy dlia russkoi ikografii* (St. Petersburg, 1884–90). 13⅝ x 9 in. (35 x 23 cm). Slavic and Baltic Division, the New York Public Library, Astor, Lenox and Tilden Foundations

general in spite of his great ministerial talents. He fought two campaigns against the Crimean Tatars (1687, 1689) at great expense and loss of life and withdrew short of his goals. Sofia refused to admit these shortcomings and treated his campaigns as great victories.

In 1689 both she and Peter realized that a political showdown was at hand. Over a period of time many officials came to Peter to show their support, and Sofia finally handed over her advisers to him and retired to the Novodevichy Monastery. Golitsyn was exiled, and Sofia remained confined at Novodevichy for some years, where she was, however, treated as a princess. The Streltsy Guards rose up again during Peter's absence abroad (1698), and Sofia was suspected to have had a role in the attempted coup, so after Peter succeeded in putting down the revolt, he forced Sofia to take the veil, and she remained at Novodevichy as Sister Susanna.

Although Sofia had not been present at receptions held for diplomats by the young co-tsars, she received some ambassadors while crowned and enthroned in a nearby room. Most of the ambassadorial gifts were formally presented to the tsars, but she certainly understood these to be official, not personal. For example, the gifts from the mission of Charles XI of Sweden to the tsars on the occasion of their coronation in 1684 consisted of the usual gilded-silver objects, hardly personal gifts suitable for young men. Another Great Embassy, held on the occasion of the ratification of the Treaty of Eternal Peace with Poland in 1686, is represented in the catalogue by

Peter I (the Great), 1697?. Drawing on paper, 8⁵/8 x 7³/8 in. (22 x 19 cm). Rijksmuseum, Amsterdam, Rijksprentenkabinet

various valuable horse trappings among other objects, including a splendid pair of silver vases (see cat. no. 51a,b).

Peter (1672–1725), Tsar of Russia (r. 1682–1721), Emperor of Russia as Peter I (r. 1721–25)

> The Tsar was a very tall man [six feet, seven inches], exceedingly well made, rather thin, his face somewhat round, a high forehead, good eyebrows, a rather short nose, but not too short, and large at the end, rather thick lips, complexion reddish brown, good black eyes . . . his look majestic and gracious when he liked, but when otherwise severe and stern . . . a twitching of the face . . . was frightful to see; it lasted for a moment, gave him a wild and terrible air.
>
> DUC DE SAINT-SIMON, 1719

Peter Alexeyevich's earliest education was relatively traditional. Essentially Peter was a self-taught man, his education having come mostly through his contact with foreigners resident in Moscow, and eventually he was to gain some command of Dutch and German.

Peter was primarily attracted to the study of the military. He struck up friendships with foreign military figures who lived in Moscow's German quarter, which he often visited. These friendships were long-lasting, particularly those with the Swiss François Lefort and the Scot Patrick Gordon. Two

principal interests dominated Peter's early life: the army and the navy. He developed an independent military unit (which by 1689 numbered more than a thousand men), drilled it, and staged mock battles. He was also interested in boats, and his navy—a departure for a ruler of landlocked Russia—is legendary. These interests, though ostensibly related to his education, later gave Peter the power to stand up to the politically influential Kremlin Streltsy Guards.

After Sofia's downfall in 1689, Peter continued to remain on the periphery of the court. At first, the traditionalists appeared to gain the upper hand, as the Patriarch Joachim attempted to suppress Western influence both at court and in the church. However, what emerged was a dual monarchy in which the new and the old coexisted—Ivan in the jeweled robes of earlier tsars attending an endless series of church functions, while Peter generally donned Western dress. After Joachim died in 1690, the anti-Western influence fell off rapidly, although Ivan continued to play the ritual role of tsar, which freed Peter to pursue his military and scientific interests. After Ivan's death in 1696, Peter would rule alone until 1725.

Peter's first great undertaking was intended in part to set right the Russian military failures in the Crimea in 1687 and 1689. Drawing on advice from his foreign military friends, he launched a surprise siege, not on the Tatars but on the Ottoman-held town of Azov (1695), which although audacious, was unsuccessful. Later, in 1696, with the use of a newly built navy to block the arrival of supplies to the besieged, he captured Azov, and his prestige in the world rose markedly. Even the *London Gazette* noticed. "The loss of this place [Azov] is like to be of very ill Consequence both to the Turks [Ottomans] and to the Tatars." Peter was able to negotiate an alliance with Venice and Austria against the Ottomans on the basis of this achievement (1697).

In 1697 Peter decided to send a prestigious embassy to Europe to visit the courts of allies and potential friends. Although Lefort and the others were the official ambassadors, Peter insisted on going along, and the trip was decisive for his reign in many ways. He was able to compare Russia to other countries, determining that Old Russia might not be able to hold its own against Europe's powers. More specifically, he learned about European technology; indeed, the months he spent working in a Dutch shipyard became part of his legend.

The fact that Peter chose to travel incognito only increased international interest in both the tsar and his country. While in Vienna, Peter was forced to rush home to put down a revolt of the Streltsy Guards, which he did unmercifully, using torture and executing hundreds, but as a result he was able to stabilize his political position and secure firm control.

The European experience had a powerful influence on Peter and caused him to accelerate certain aspects of Russia's westernization. One symbolic and highly visible gesture was Peter's trimming of the boyars' beards in 1698 and his insistence that they wear Western clothes at court. Peter's trip had convinced him that he should contemplate military moves against Sweden along the Istrian Baltic coast. When he had visited the Swedish city of Riga in 1697, he must have noted that the fortifications, though state-of-the-art, were incomplete. King Charles XI of Sweden (q.v.) must also have been aware of Peter's appraisal of the Swedish military situation. It was probably to buy him off that Charles offered the tsar a gift of three hundred iron cannons (which did not actually arrive until 1698), an exceptionally impressive gift but one ineffective in maintaining peace.

King Charles XII of Sweden (q.v.), who succeeded his father in May of 1697, was also concerned about the Russian threat to Sweden's Baltic territories. In August 1698, Charles wrote that he would like to send an embassy to Moscow to renew peace treaties, a proposal that Peter found "highly pleasing." A year later he swore to observe the treaties, but before the documents could be signed and returned by both sides, Peter declared war on Sweden because of the alleged illegal occupation of Russian territory; what ensued was called the Great Northern War, which lasted from 1700 to 1721.

The most famous period of Peter's reign was to follow. His early losses and later victory over the Swedish king (Poltava, 1709) mark a turning-point in Russian history. His successes on the Baltic front allowed for the founding of the Russian capital of St. Petersburg. Peter added the title of emperor to that of tsar in 1721 and henceforth became known officially as Peter I and popularly as Peter the Great.

THE PATRIARCHS

Filaret (c. 1554/5–1633), Metropolitan of Rostov (1605–9), Patriarch of All Russia (r. 1608–10, 1619–22), Supreme Sovereign (r. 1619–33)

> Of medium height and bulk, [he] had some knowledge of theology, was irritable and mistrustful, and so overbearing that even the Tsar was afraid of him. . . . To clerics he was kind and not avaricious.
> BISHOP PACOMIUS OF ASTRAKHAN

Born Fyodor Nikitich Romanov, Filaret was the father of the first Romanov tsar, Mikhail Fyodorovich (q.v.). He was the grand-nephew of Tsar Ivan IV's first wife, Anastasia, and the cousin of Tsar Fyodor (r. 1584–98), whom he served as a soldier (fighting against the Swedes) and as a diplomat (negotiating in 1593–94 with the ambassadors of Austrian Emperor Rudolf II). When Tsar Fyodor died childless, Fyodor Nikitich was a strong candidate for the throne, but he did not prevent Boris Godunov's (q.v.) succession in 1598.

In 1602 Fyodor Nikitich Romanov and his wife were forced by Godunov to divorce and to enter separate monaster-

Patriarch Filaret. Color lithograph, no. 54 in *Portrety, gerby i pechati Bol'shoi gosudarstvennoi knigi 1672 g.* (St. Petersburg, 1903). 10 1/2 x 12 7/8 in. (27 x 33 cm). Slavic and Baltic Division, the New York Public Library, Astor, Lenox and Tilden Foundations

ies, where as the monk Filaret he suffered imprisonment and humiliation. After Godunov's death, Filaret reappeared in public and was named metropolitan of Rostov (1605). Later in 1608, during the Time of Troubles (1605–13) he was named Patriarch of All Russia by the Tsar False Dmitry II, although his authority was extremely limited by that tsar's small territory. Filaret later became something of a hero as the leader of Rostov's resistance against the Poles (1609). He was imprisoned in Poland when, at the head of an embassy, he had refused to accept King Sigismund III's (q.v.) claim that his son Wladislaw (q.v.) should become tsar of Russia.

When Mikhail Romanov ascended the Moscow throne, he tried at once to secure his father's release, but Russian military strength was insufficient to secure his goal for some years. Mikhail eventually conceded much to Poland in the Peace of Deulino in 1619, and his father returned home. Within eight days Filaret was confirmed as patriarch and installed as co-ruler with the unprecedented title of Supreme Sovereign. Afterward, Filaret frequently transacted affairs of state without consulting the tsar.

In spite of his lack of a church vocation, Filaret was a zealous supporter of orthodoxy, insisting that all Catholics in the realm be rebaptized in the Orthodox religion. He sought a faith more directly aligned with the Greco-Byzantine tradition and was close to Patriarch Cyril of Constantinople (q.v.), an ardent anti-Catholic who persuaded Filaret to follow a strongly anti-Catholic and anti-Austrian policy. Filaret encouraged the publication of theological works and formed the nucleus of the famous Moscow Patriarchal Library. Every Russian archbishop was commanded by him to establish a seminary for the clergy.

In spite of his religious traditionalism, Filaret attempted to reorganize the Russian army along more modern lines by recruiting foreign officers, and although his military strength was not enough to challenge Polish power, he twice sought to take back the city of Smolensk. He died during the second try in 1633, and his death put an end to the Russian-Polish War when Tsar Mikhail recognized its futility.

As co-ruler and father of the tsar, Filaret was present when ambassadors were received at the Kremlin. However, an image of such an audience shows him near the tsar, but to one side, suggesting that in the diplomatic context he was willing to play the role of a more traditional patriarch. Nonetheless, Filaret received presents as co-ruler, in addition to those of the sort more generally given to patriarchs (such as relics and altar crosses [cat. no. 23], jeweled pendants, and ecclesiastical garments sewn from precious fabrics), most of them from the hierarchy of the Greek Orthodox Church. He received a jeweled staff from Shah Abbas I of Persia, now in the collection of the Kremlin Armory.

Nikon (1605–1681), Patriarch of All Russia (r. 1652–66), Supreme Sovereign (r. 1652–58)

> Patriarch Nikon is bestial in appearance, of towering
> height [six feet, six inches] with an enormous head;
> his hair is still black at age 60, his brow low and fur-
> rowed, his eyebrows thick and wild, his ears long
> and satyr-like, his speaking voice grandly resonant.
> PAISIUS LIGARDES, 1663

Patriarch Nikon was born Nikitich Minin, the son of a poor peasant. His talent and self-education earned him the support of some Moscow merchants, who encouraged him to move to Moscow. After the death of his three children, he decided to become a monk, took the name of Nikon, and retreated to a desolate hermitage in the far north on the White Sea. After moving to the Kozhurersky Monastery near Novgorod, Nikon rose to the rank of abbot in 1643. In 1646, on business in Moscow, he met Tsar Alexei (q.v.), who came under his influence. Other offices were heaped upon Nikon, but it was only after hesitation and the acceptance by the church of a number of conditions that he assumed the Moscow patriarchate in 1652.

The patriarch took office at a time of ecclesiastical reform. After considerable consultation and study, he embraced a radical reform of the Orthodox prayer book and other elements of church practice. During a synod his church declared that "the Greeks [Constantinople] should be followed rather than our

Portrait of Patriarch Nikon, no. 57 in Portrety, gerby i pechati Bol'shoi gosu- darstvennoi knigi 1672 g. *(St. Petersburg, 1903). Slavic and Baltic Division, The New York Public Library, Astor, Lenox and Tilden Foundations*

own ancients." Dissidents from this position, known as "Old Believers," embraced an unappeasable hatred of Nikon's views, which resulted in a schism within the Russian Orthodox church.

Nikon erected buildings on a royal scale that were related either to his powerful position at court or to his "reformed" Orthodox faith. At the Kremlin in 1652–56, he rebuilt the patriarch's palace, which had been first erected in 1643. His audience hall, Krestovaya Palata, rivaled in size that of the tsar's in the Palace of Facets, although it was decorated in a rather restrained manner. The patriarch's own Cathedral of the Twelve Apostles (see Chapter 1, fig. 7), built along with the palace, was a major addition to the cathedrals of the Kremlin. More ambitious were Nikon's plans for the New Jerusalem (Resurrection) Monastery in the country to the west of Moscow. A truly monumental ensemble of a great church and surrounding buildings was intended to serve as the cult center for his reformed faith. Other priorities prevented completion of this work while he was in power, and it was not continued until the regency of Sofia (q.v.).

While Tsar Alexei generally favored and propagated Nikon's church reforms, the patriarch's vast power in this and other areas eventually brought about his downfall. From 1652 to 1658, his position approached that of co-tsar, and he was given the title Supreme Sovereign. When Alexei's affection toward his "own familiar friend" cooled, Nikon publicly divested himself of office and retired to a monastery. After 1658 the Moscow church remained without a patriarch until 1666, when an ecumenical council deposed Nikon and enthroned a new patriarch. Surprisingly, Nikon resumed something approaching his former intimacy with the tsar from 1671 until his death five years later, although he did not return to the Kremlin.

A number of splendid ecclesiastical garments that belonged to Patriarch Nikon are among the highlights of the textile collection of the Kremlin Armory (see Chapter 2, fig. 5). The precious textiles from both Europe and the Near East, woven of silk, gold, and silver thread, were either given directly to the patriarch as diplomatic gifts or were given to the tsar and passed along to the patriarch; some were purchases made by the patriarch himself. It must have been widely understood that Nikon considered his personal appearance at church and court functions of the utmost importance. A staff (cat. no. 26) was given to Nikon by a member of the hierarchy of the Greek Orthodox church; it may represent Nikon's theology, which called for rapprochement with the Greek church.

DONORS OF GIFTS

CHRISTIAN EAST

Cyril I Lucaris (1572–1638), Greek Orthodox Patriarch of Alexandria, Egypt (r. 1602–20), and Patriarch of Constantinople (r. 1620–37)

Born in Crete (then a Venetian territory), Lucaris studied in Venice and Padua. During the 1590s he served as a parish priest and teacher in Polish-held Vilnius and L'viv, and he became strongly anti-Catholic. In 1596 he refused to agree to the union of Orthodox and Catholic churches supported by the Polish King Sigismund III (q.v.). A friend of Anglicans and other Protestants, Lucaris became a virtual Calvinist; the Austrian ambassador to the Ottoman sultan called him "the arch-fiend of the Catholic Church." He was enthroned as patriarch in Alexandria in 1602 and in Constantinople in 1620.

The Constantinople patriarch's close links with the Moscow patriarch Filaret (q.v.), father of Tsar Mikhail Romanov (q.v.), were important in the areas of both politics and religion. Lucaris was instrumental in bringing Russia into the anti-Hapsburg coalition in the second half of the Thirty Years' War (1632–48). He wished to reinforce the connection between the Russian and Greek churches, but his patriarchate in Constantinople was troubled with church disputes, and he was temporarily deposed several times. Finally Sultan Murād

IV (q.v.) accused him of plotting with the Ukrainian Cossacks against the Ottomans and had him killed.

Lucaris sent gifts to Tsar Mikhail with the Ottoman embassy of 1632, including textiles and a rock crystal tankard (cat. no. 22). A carved wood altar cross from Mount Athos given to the Moscow patriarch Filaret in 1629 may have come indirectly from Lucaris. In 1655, long after his murder (which some in the church considered a martyrdom), a splendid *sakkos*, or church vestment, that had belonged to Lucaris was brought to Moscow by a Greek merchant traveling with an embassy. The *sakkos* has been regarded as a saint's relic and is called the *sakkos* of Iosif II.

CRIMEA

Djānbeg Girāy (?–1635), Khan of the Crimean Khanate (r. 1610–35)

The Crimean Khanate comprised the Crimean peninsula in the Black Sea, areas to the north of it, and considerable territories around the Sea of Azov. The khanate, one of several successor states of the Golden Horde, was ruled by members of the Turkic Girayid dynasty, which traced its descent from Genghis Khan (1162–1227). By the sixteenth century, however, the Crimean khans were simply local rulers and had become vassals of the Ottoman sultans, who had the right to choose a member of the Girāy family to rule over the khanate.

Djānbeg Girāy's life was an amazing story of ups and downs. He and his parents spent years in exile, and after his father was killed, his mother returned to the Crimea and married Khan Selymet. When Selymet died in 1610, Djānbeg Girāy obtained the sultan's permission to rule, but his stepfather's brothers fomented plots against his succession for years. The tables turned on Djānbeg Girāy when his stepuncle Shahīn Girāy won a major victory against the Ottomans at the head of a Persian army, and a new sultan began to reign and made peace with the Persians. Shahīn's brother obtained the khanate (as Mehmet III Girāy) in 1623, although he lost the sultan's support in 1627 and Djānbeg again became khan. For some time Djānbeg's reign was as often as not in name only, since his step-uncles retained military power, but his tribulations ended when, owing to a miscalculation, the step-uncles were defeated by other enemies.

The Crimean Tatars, although deeply divided, were perceived as troublesome throughout the seventeenth century. A Tatar invasion of Russia in 1633 was an alarming reminder of the vulnerability of Russia's southern frontier. From 1613 to 1651 the Russians paid 363,970 rubles in tribute to the Tatars.

One gift believed to have been given by Djānbeg Girāy to Tsar Mikhail Romanov in 1616 is a velvet quiver embroidered in gold (cat. no. 27), an appropriately military object, though ceremonial in character.

Konstantin Kapidağli, *Murād IV, Ottoman Sultan of the Sublime Porte,* 1815. Colored engraving printed in London, 15 x 10 3/8 in.(38.5 x 26.5 cm). Library, Topkapi Saray Museum, Istanbul

Attributed to Muhammad Zaman, *Abbas II, Shah of Persia,* c. 1663?. Gouache and gold on paper, pasted on blue cardboard, 8 x 12 1/2 in. (20.5 x 32 cm). Prince and Princess Sadruddin Aga Khan

OTTOMAN EMPIRE

Murād IV (1612–1640), Ottoman Sultan of the Sublime Porte (r. 1623–40)

Sultan Murād inherited the throne at the age of eleven, when his immediate predecessor, Mustafa I, was deposed a few months after succeeding Osman II, who had been murdered. During the first nine years of his reign, Murād ruled over an anarchic state alternately controlled by the army, Janissary corps, and the Sufis. Displaying a savage ruthlessness, he eventually asserted his authority. Some historians have estimated that as many as 100,000 people were condemned to death during his reign, sometimes for such minor offenses as drinking or smoking.

Murād was an ardent adherent of Sunni Islam, and his campaigns against Persia were largely motivated by a desire to destroy the Shia heresy. The sultan was known to amuse his entourage by demonstrating feats of strength, and he also published books of poetry under the name Murādi.

Several military initiatives proved quite successful during Murād's reign, and he was able to retake some territories lost to the Persians before his time. In 1638 he instituted a number of important reforms, including the establishment of a new military system and the reduction of the Janissary corps, and he reorganized the Ottoman system of military fiefs. He also abolished the tradition by which Christian children were paid in tribute to the Ottomans.

Murād's diplomatic contacts with Russia stemmed mostly from a common desire to restrain and reduce Polish and Aus-

trian power in lands bordering on the two countries, to restrain Persia, and to deal with problems related to the not-always-loyal Cossacks and Crimean Tatars, who held semiautonomous lands between Russia and Ottoman Turkey. The tsar in turn wished to protect the interests of the Orthodox Christians who lived under Ottoman rule

Murād's gifts to the tsar are said to have included small treasures made in the famous workshops of Constantinople, ceremonial arms, and horses with trappings. These gifts were highly regarded by the tsars, who made regular purchases of similar items and imported Ottoman craftsmen to work in the Kremlin workshops.

PERSIA (IRAN)

Abbas II (1631?–1677), Shah of Persia (r. 1642–77)

Named for his great-grandfather Abbas I (the Great), this son of Shah Safi (r. 1629–42) inherited the throne of Persia before he was ten years old. Abbas I had mounted the throne after a period of near-anarchy in Persia, and through long and severe struggles, he was able to acquire a vast empire, which at his death stretched from the Tigris to the Indus Rivers. His capital, Isfahan, was an important center of Islamic art and culture. Although the reign of Shah Abbas II lacked the brilliant achievements of his namesake's, he did manage to hold together much of the Persian Empire with a minimum of military force. His reign was one of peace and prosperity, marred by only occasional periods of conflict with the Turkish Ottomans. A notable feature of his reign was the first Russian mission to Isfahan (1664), the same year in which Persia was opened to trade with the French.

Several splendid gifts from this reign are in the Kremlin Armory, including shields, maces, and horse trappings, although it is not always clear what objects came through diplomacy and which were obtained through trade.

POLAND

Sigismund III (1566–1632), King of Poland (r. 1587–1632) and Sweden (r. 1592–99), Grand Duke of Lithuania (r. 1587–1632)

Heir to King John III Vasa of Sweden (1537–1592) and the son of Katarina Jagiellonika, a Polish princess. Sigismund shared his father's goal of creating a united kingdom of Sweden and Poland. His mother raised him a Catholic in Lutheran Sweden, and the first part of the dual-kingdom project was fulfilled when Sigismund was elected king of Catholic Poland (1587) while his father continued to rule in Sweden. Sigismund succeeded to the Swedish throne in 1592 and was crowned at Uppsala in 1594, but he was eventually outmaneuvered by his uncle Charles, duke of Södermanland (later King Charles IX of Sweden), and Sigis-

Studio of Peter Paul Rubens, *Sigismund III, King of Sweden, King of Poland*, c. 1630. Oil on canvas, 103 3/8 x 71 3/4 in. (265 x 184 cm). Nationalmuseum, Stockholm

mund was unable to retain the Swedish throne because of his Catholic faith and the shrewd politics of his uncle.

A long series of skirmishes and wars occupied Sigismund's reign, mostly in the Baltic states and, most important, in Russia, which Sigismund saw as a crusade for his faith. But these wars failed to resolve the issue of his Swedish succession and eventually aided the Swedish expansion in the Baltic area and in Russia. The Poles occupied Moscow in 1610 but were subsequently forced to withdraw, and Sweden took Novgorod and most of Ingria (along the southeast Baltic coast) from Russia in 1617.

King Sigismund III played a major role in Russian history, especially during the Time of Troubles, when Polish armies occupied and sacked the Moscow Kremlin. The purpose of the 1610 Polish invasion of Moscow was to enthrone Sigismund's son Wladislaw (q.v.) as tsar of Russia. In less turbulent times, Sigismund often sought peace with Russia in order to pursue his military adventures against Sweden and her Baltic territories and against the Ottomans in Ukraine. Thus there were numerous embassies and many gifts, including armor and ostrich eggs

Daniel Schultz the Younger, *John II Casimir, King of Poland, Grand Duke of Lithuania*, 1651. Oil on canvas, $81\frac{7}{8}$ x 60 in. (210 x 154 cm). Nationalmuseum, Stockholm. Photo: Rikard Karlsson

Wladislaw IV, King of Poland, Grand Duke of Lithuania, after 1632. Oil on canvas, $80\frac{3}{8}$ x $49\frac{3}{4}$ in. (206 x 127.5 cm). Palace Museum, Wilanow, Warsaw. Photo: M. Kwiatkowska

and rock crystal mounted in silver. Most cannot now be identified, with the notable exception of a saddle (cat. no. 44).

Wladislaw IV (1595–1648), King of Poland and Grand Duke of Lithuania (r. 1632–48)

Wladislaw ascended the Polish throne in 1632, after the death of his father, King Sigismund (q.v.). A Russian invasion of Poland ensued, which Wladislaw was finally able to repel with a vigorous offensive. He took a more pragmatic approach to political and religious issues than had characterized his father's reign, and in 1634 an armistice was concluded with a virtual surrender by the Russians. The only gain for Russia was the Polish king's renunciation of his claim to the Russian throne, for Wladislaw IV recognized Mikhail Romanov as tsar. Since Wladislaw had a legitimate claim to the Swedish throne, he pursued the dream of his return in a relatively mod-

est way with various military efforts throughout his reign, but he was never successful. He sent important embassies to Russia in an attempt to pursue his Swedish goal through alliances with Russia. Russian support was also needed to neutralize the Ottoman threat to Polish territories in Ukraine and other southern territories.

Wladislaw's gifts to the tsars appear to have been particularly sumptuous. The embassy of 1645 has been called the Amber Embassy, and a table, chess set, wine cups of various sizes, a large mug (cat. no. 45), a carved scene of the Crucifixion, carved boxes, and more, all made of amber, were sent to Russia, along with fashionable table clocks (one in the shape of an elephant), ebony furniture, and armor.

John II Casimir (1609–1672), King of Poland (r. 1648–68), Grand Duke of Lithuania (r. 1648–67)

The youngest son of Sigismund III, John Casimir was a Jesuit novice when he traveled abroad before his election to the Polish throne in 1648 at the death of his brother Wladislaw IV. John Casimir's reign was a turbulent one, disturbed by the Khmelnitsky revolt of the Ukrainian Cossacks, who changed their allegiance from the Polish crown to Tsar Alexei, a revolt that resulted in the Thirteen Years' War with Russia (1654–67). The year 1655 was particularly disastrous, because Russian forces took Minsk, Vilnius, L'viv, Kovno, and Moghilaú, and the Swedes invaded Poland and captured Warsaw. Through the treaty of Oliva with Sweden (1660), John Casimir renounced the Vasa claim to the Swedish throne and ended those long hostilities. Since he had no heir, the Russians aspired to put a Romanov on the Polish throne, and civil war broke out in Poland. Because of difficulties he had with the Polish nobility, King John was obliged by the Swedes to give up the Grand Duchy of Lithuania. The Treaty of Andrusovo with Russia, signed in 1667, brought an end to the war and gave Russia Smolensk, the parts of Ukraine east of the Dnieper River, and the right to hold Kiev until 1669 (though Tsar Alexei refused to give it back then). Embittered by his continued failures, John Casimir abdicated in 1668 and went to France. Several of his gifts to Tsar Alexei Mikhailovich survive; of special interest are those presented in 1667 at the mission confirming the Andrusovo Treaty, which included coaches and important silver objects.

Michael Wisniowiecki (1640–1673), King of Poland (r. 1669–73)

Michael emerged as the king of Poland from a highly contested election in which the oligarchic nobles were bettered by the lesser nobility, who demanded a native-born king after eighty-one years of rule by the Swedish house of Vasa, who had little affection for the country they ruled. The election was something of a surprise, since it was assumed that an opposing party strongly backed and financed by Louis XIV of France would carry the day. However, the vote in the lower house was unanimous and there was public rejoicing at the return of Polish rule. Michael's principal talents were said by his enemies to be multilingualism and overeating. Within a few weeks he encountered a series of conspiracies whose purpose was to dethrone the sovereign. Throughout the brief reign a figure of greater stature was in the picture, namely his successor John Sobieski (q.v.), who occupied himself with opposing a serious threat to Poland by the Crimean Tatars and the Ottoman sultan. It is said that Michael's exclusive goal was to retain the throne.

In 1671 he sent important gifts to Tsar Alexei, including a fabulous silver eagle by Abraham Drentwett I (cat. no. 50).

John III Sobieski (1629–1696), King of Poland (r. 1674–96)

A Polish general and national hero, John Sobieski served in wars against Sweden and Russia, and his fame increased with his victory over the Ottomans at Khotin. He was elected king of

Daniel Schultz the Younger, *Michael Wisniowiecki, King of Poland*, 1669. Oil on canvas, 76¼ x 47 in. (195.4 x 120.5 cm). Wawel Royal Castle, Cracow

Poland in 1674. He continued fighting the Ottomans and was able to regain for Poland much of Ukraine, which had been lost during the two previous reigns. He also played a decisive role in defeating the Ottomans at their Siege of Vienna (1683), a feat regarded as a brilliant victory for Christendom.

From the Polish point of view, his reign of twenty-two years was a failure. His belated attempts to reform the constitution to assure a more stable government led to conspiracies against his crown and life. Even the French faction, of which he had been a part, deserted him, while Lithuania remained in a state of chronic revolt and the country went bankrupt. He is said to have died brokenhearted.

Sobieski convinced Russia during the regency of Princess Sofia (q.v.) to join in a league against the Ottomans with the Vatican and Austria, and in 1686 the Treaty of Eternal Peace

John III Sobieski, King of Poland, after 1676. Oil on canvas, 40¹/₂ x 24¹/₈ in. (104 x 62 cm). National Museum, Warsaw

(with Russia) was signed. The price for Poland was high, including the permanent concession of Kiev to Russia and the other territories conquered by Russia from Poland in previous decades. Splendid gifts were presented by the confirmation embassy of the Treaty of Eternal Peace, including a unique silver centerpiece with trays, candle holders, a pair of vases (cat. no. 51), and a silver ewer in the form of a horse. Large numbers of amber pieces figured among the gifts, including a box, a huge mirror, and candle holders brought by ambassadors in 1686.

AUSTRIA

Leopold I (1640–1705), Holy Roman Emperor
(r. 1658–1705), King of Hungary (r. 1655–1705),
King of Bohemia (r. 1656–1705)

The second son of the Hapsburg Emperor Ferdinand III, Leopold was at first destined for the church, but the death of his older brother changed his prospects. In 1655 he was chosen king of Hungary and in 1656 king of Bohemia, and in 1658 he was elected emperor at Frankfurt. Leopold regarded himself as an absolute sovereign. He was a man of industry and education and showed political ability in his later years.

Though not a warrior himself, Leopold's long reign encompassed numerous wars, including those on a European level (Europe's "First World War") and a number of difficult struggles near home, especially those with the Hungarians and the Ottomans. Leopold was able to organize alliances that challenged the enormous military potential of Louis XIV's France, although the most memorable Austrian victory of his reign was the lifting of the Ottoman Siege of Vienna in 1683. This was accomplished by his allies, most notably John Sobieski, since the emperor had withdrawn from Vienna.

During the War of the Grand Alliance (1689–96), Leopold managed victories on two fronts, one in Western Europe and the other against the Ottomans. The Vienna victory was followed with a series in Hungary and in Serbia. In 1697 the Ottoman Sultan Mustapha II signed the Treaty of Karlowitz, which acknowledged the rights of the House of Hapsburg over most of greater Hungary, bringing an end to these long wars, and in the same year Louis XIV signed the Treaty of Ryswick, ending the wars in the West.

Leopold's Russian policy was most often aimed at obtaining aid from the tsars for his wars with Ottoman Turkey. His embassy to Russia in 1684 during the regency of Sofia, after the lifting of the Vienna siege, brought brilliant works to Russia, some of which rank among the greatest examples of Augsburg craftsmanship (cat. no. 54).

Leopold I, Holy Roman Emperor, King of Hungary, King of Bohemia, c. 1700. Oil on canvas, 90⁷/₈ x 67⁷/₈ in. (233 x 174 cm). Heeresgeschichtliches Museum, Vienna, on loan from the Kunsthistorisches Museum, Vienna

Always a strong supporter of business enterprises in his kingdoms, James I was pleased to add his royal prestige to four major embassies to Russia in 1604, 1607, 1614, and 1620. Ostensibly concerned with royal–imperial relations, such as reporting James's ascent to the English throne (1604) or extending congratulations on the coronations of Russian rulers (Vasily Shuisky in 1607; Mikhail Romanov in 1614), the embassies were primarily intended to lend support to the English Muscovy Company, founded in 1555 to promote trade with Russia and across Russia to Persia and even China. Treaties establishing English trade rights required renegotiation with each new monarch.

The expensive presents given to the tsars were largely paid for by the Muscovy Company and recorded in lists that still survive. In 1604: a coach ("charyott"; see Chapter 5, fig. 10), two great flagons, a rock-crystal cup, a ewer and basin, two pots with handles, a standing cup, and five bolts of precious textiles. In 1615: a large cup (with a gilded cover), two gilded goblets with lids, a chalcedony-footed bowl with a gilded cover, three tureens, two large pots, four beakers, a large salt cellar, a basin, a chafing dish, and three cloth bolts of silk and gold, two of satin and one of damask. (The tableware was made of gilded silver.) The gifts of 1620 were similar to those of 1615 but somewhat more modest.

Charles II (1630–1685), King of Great Britain and Ireland (r. 1660–85)

Charles's public career began when he accompanied his father, King Charles I, during the later campaigns of the English Civil War (1639–49). The execution of his father in 1649 caused Charles II to inherit the British crown, but much of the first part of his reign was spent in exile in France, Holland, and Germany. After Oliver Cromwell became Lord Protector of England in 1653, and for the rest of Cromwell's life, the prospect of Charles's ascending the throne was indeed bleak. Even those friendly to him saw little hope for his restoration, and many deserted his cause. However, Tsar Alexei (q.v.) offered occasional financial support. Charles's fortunes changed radically after Cromwell's death (1658), and a triumphant restoration of the British monarchy ensued (1660).

Charles II's reign is often seen as something of a scandal, a time of lax morality in both social and political areas. Cronyism determined many of the king's major appointments. The embassy to Russia of 1664 appears to have been a case in point, inspired by the idea that trade with Russia, which had been abruptly terminated by Tsar Alexei when he learned of Charles I's execution, might be restored to the benefit of the crown. The embassy was sent ostensibly to thank the tsar for his earlier support of the English king when he was in exile, but the possibility of restoring English trading rights was the important item of the agenda. It failed, in part because of the choice by Charles of his ambassador, Charles Howard, earl of Carlisle.

Daniel Mytens, *James I, King of England*, 1621. Oil on canvas, 58 x 39¼ in. (148.6 x 100.7 cm). National Portrait Gallery, London

ENGLAND

James (1566–1625), King of Scotland as James VI (r. 1567–1625), King of Great Britain and Ireland as James I (r. 1603–25)

The son of Mary Stuart, Queen of Scots, became King James VI of Scotland at the age of one in 1567 after the forced abdication of his mother. As a child he was used as a figurehead king during a tumultuous period and began to rule himself only in 1583. Although the young king was sometimes intimidated by the violence around him in Scotland, he gradually was successful in cultivating those who could support his claim to the English throne both at home and in England. Although some have found his behavior dishonorable with regard to his reaction to the execution of his mother by Elizabeth I of England in 1587, this act helped pave the way for his assumption of the English throne (as King James I) in 1603 after Elizabeth's death. Well educated and a published writer, James's greatest fame resulted from his patronage of a brilliant translation of the Holy Bible into English.

John Michael Wright, *Charles II, King of England*, after 1661. Oil on canvas, 110 x 93¹/₄ in. (281.9 x 239.2 cm). The Royal Collection, Her Majesty Queen Elizabeth II

David Beck, *Christina, Queen of Sweden*, 1650. Oil on canvas, 42⁷/₈ x 35⁷/₈ in. (110 x 92 cm.). Nationalmuseum, Stockholm

The Russian resident in London reported in dismay to Samuel Pepys that at court "nobody attends to business, but every man himself or his pleasures." Carlisle seems to have accepted an assignment that would give him a hunting and shooting holiday on a grand scale. "Ignorant and arrogant, he spent a lot of time showing resentment at unintended insults," Pepys recorded, and Carlisle insulted the tsar by returning his presents.

The selection of presents for the tsar was, however, carefully arranged. Eighteen impressive silver objects and twelve knives with agate handles were given, most of the silver stamped with the London hallmark for 1663–64. A splendid ewer and basin presented before the Civil War to the king's mother was also included (see cat. no. 66a,b).

SWEDEN

Christina (1626–1689), Queen of Sweden (r. 1632–54)

Christina was the daughter and heir of Gustavus Adolphus Vasa, "Lion of the North," champion of the Protestant cause in Germany during the Thirty Years' War (1619–48) until he died a hero's death in battle in 1632. His earlier conquests in Eastern Europe had succeeded in cutting off Russia's access to the Baltic Sea (Treaty of Stolbovo, 1617).

An outstandingly gifted, intelligent, educated, and willful woman, as well as an Italophile and Francophile, Christina

began to rule in 1644. Her interest in art, theater, and literature transformed the Swedish court; René Descartes once traveled to Stockholm to discuss philosophy with her and died there. She abdicated her throne in 1654, traveled through Europe, and converted to Catholicism. She then settled in Rome, where her court at the Palazzo Riario was considered a great center of European culture (1656–89).

The queen perceived herself as a peacemaker, possibly because she believed the high cost of foreign wars infringed on her royal lifestyle. Certainly this was a factor in her desire to conclude a Russian alliance. Her 1647 embassy was intended to congratulate Alexei on his ascent to the Moscow throne. She sent him about fifty gifts of fine German and Swedish silver from Nuremberg, Augsburg, Hamburg, and Stockholm (cat. no. 79). An earlier exchange of gifts is documented by the presence at the Stockholm Armory of a Persian caftan sent to Christina by Alexei Mikhailovich, when he was still tsarevich (see Chapter 5, fig. 3).

Charles XI (1655–1697), King of Sweden (r. 1660–97)

Christina's heir was Charles X of Pfalz (1622–1660), who accomplished astonishing military feats before his death, when his son, Charles XI, inherited the throne at the age of four. After he began to rule in 1672, Charles undoubtedly harbored ambitions similar to those of his father. Following the

David Klöcker Ehrenstrahl, *Charles XI, King of Sweden*, 1685. Oil on canvas, 41 3/8 x 32 in. (106 x 82 cm). Nationalmuseum, Stockholm

Scanian War (1675–79), which consolidated some of his father's conquests, Charles XI then settled down to a peaceful reign, considered the prosperous peak of the history of Sweden's time as a Baltic power. However, early dreams of Russian military campaigns of the sort suggested by Palmquist's Russian atlas of 1674, commissioned for Charles, never materialized. Charles maintained a well-trained army at home where in order to balance the budget, support a substantial defense establishment, and control the power of the nobility, he promulgated an absolutist form of government in 1680.

Apart from an embassy sent during his minority, Charles dispatched two important embassies with gifts to Russia, one to Tsar Alexei Mikhailovich (q.v.) in 1674 and another in 1684 on the occasion of the coronation of the co-tsars, Ivan V and Peter I (q.v.). About thirty pieces of gilded silver were presented to Alexei, while Ivan and Peter together received sixty-seven gifts, according to the inventories. A later gift of three hundred cannons sent outside an ambassadorial context reflected the Swedish king's keen military interests. This magnificent gift did not arrive until after Charles's death.

Charles XII (1682–1718), King of Sweden (r. 1697–1718)

Charles XII inherited the throne at the age of fourteen and only months later was declared to be of age to rule. Soon thereafter, Russia joined Denmark and Poland in making war against the young king of Sweden, and the "Great Northern War" (1699–1721) dominated his reign after 1700 when he left his capital, Stockholm, for the last time to campaign abroad. Charles's early victories in the Great Northern War (the battles of Narva, Dvina, Klissow, and Holovchyn) became legendary as he crossed eastern Europe with a small, well-trained, and devoted army. For this reason Voltaire later called him the "most remarkable man who ever lived." At first perceived as a potential conqueror of Russia, Charles was defeated by Tsar Peter I (q.v.) at the battle of Poltava in 1709, which ended all such hopes. This event marked the beginning of the end of Sweden's status as a major power, and Peter reattached Ingria and other Baltic territories to Russia. In reconquering the mouth of the Neva River from Sweden, Peter founded his new capital, St. Petersburg, at the site of the Swedish town of Nyen.

Charles sent a single embassy with an impressive quantity of 124 silver and gilded-silver objects to Russia in 1699 in a futile attempt to neutralize Russia in Sweden's potential conflicts with Denmark, Poland, and Saxony.

David von Krafft after Johan David Swartz, *Charles XII, King of Sweden*, 1706. Oil on canvas, 97 1/4 x 148 1/2 in. (249 x 380 cm). Nationalmuseum, Stockholm

Abraham Wuchters, *Christian IV, King of Denmark and Norway*, 1638. Oil on canvas, 79⁵/₈ x 42⁷/₈ in. (204 x 110 cm). Frederiksborg Castle, Hillerød, Denmark

Karel van Mander, *Valdemar Christian, Count of Denmark*, c. 1656. Oil on canvas, 85³/₄ x 44¹/₂ in. (220 x 114 cm.). Rosenborg Castle, Copenhagen

Frederick III, Duke of Schleswig-Holstein, Prince of the Holy Roman Empire, 1639. Oil on canvas, 78³/₄ x 44⁷/₈ in. (202 x 115 cm). Frederiksborg Castle, Hillerød, Denmark

DENMARK

Christian IV (1577–1648), King of Denmark and Norway (r. 1588–1648)

Christian's long reign of seventy-one years encompassed first a regency for the young king and then, after he began his personal rule in 1596, a substantial period of power and prosperity for his country, owing largely to Denmark's control of the entry to the Baltic Sea. Christian's efforts to stimulate the Danish economy by founding and supporting some industries are worthy of note. While the king had been an important leader of Protestant Europe against the great power of Catholic Austria, a series of military reverses, ending with the occupation of Jutland and much of his kingdom by the Austrians, produced a decline in his political fortunes and Danish power. Later, Sweden's invasions foretold the subsequent dominance of that country in Scandinavia, but Christian's gritty determination to hold on in the face of overwhelming adversity has made him a patriotic hero in Denmark.

The ill-defined frontier between Norway and Russia was the subject of a number of diplomatic exchanges during Christian's reign, while the complicated politics of his period and Denmark's rivalry with Sweden often suggested the desirability of Russian alliances. Christian's brother and his son by Kirsten Munk were both proposed as husbands for daughters of tsars, although these marriages never took place. Secret negotiations for the marriage of his niece to the tsar also did not work out, but all of these negotiations resulted in a number of embassies that produced numerous gifts of silver, guns, horses with trappings, and so on. The 1644 embassy in which Valdemar, Christian's son (1622–1656), sought the hand of Tsar Mikhail Romanov's daughter carried a variety of gifts and included about two hundred silver objects, notably German silver from Hamburg and Nuremberg (cat. no. 90). Christian's military problems after the invasion of Denmark by the Austrian army resulted in the sale of much of the king's royal plate to Tsar Mikhail Romanov in 1628.

SCHLESWIG-HOLSTEIN

Frederick III (1597–1659), Duke of Schleswig-Holstein-Gottorp, Prince of the Holy Roman Empire (r. 1616–59)

Frederick III was raised to the dukedom in 1616 by King Christian IV of Denmark (q.v.). Holstein was a German territory, but the duke was a vassal to the Danish throne. Frederick was both a shrewd diplomat and a ruler who cleverly avoided participating in the Thirty Years' War (1618–48), which devastated many other German provinces. Well educated and a patron of the arts, the duke sought in ingenious ways to increase the prosperity of Holstein and to make it a trading center. He hoped to exploit its location on the shores of the Baltic to his advantage, and he was persuaded by a Hamburg merchant, Otto Brügmann, to develop a shipping route to Persia by way of Swedish Livonia and Russia. Brügmann calculated that the cost of shipping Asian products through Holstein would be cheaper than by other routes, though ultimately his commercial scheme failed.

In 1632 Brügmann arrived in Moscow with a gift of twelve cannons, a supply of ammunition, and assurances that Russia, preparing to go to war with Poland, would be permitted to buy arms in Holstein. Brügmann's principal argument to Tsar Mikhail for commercial advantages equal or superior to those of other states soliciting Moscow's favor was precisely that Holstein was no great power, less of a potential threat than England, Holland, or Sweden. Negotiations in 1634 were successful, and a year later an expedition to Persia passing through Russia arrived in Moscow.

Duke Frederick's interests extended beyond trade, and so he sent with his trade embassy Adam Olearius, a graduate of Leipzig University, with a wide range of interests and considerable linguistic abilities. Olearius took profuse notes during his travels, which he carefully revised, edited, and published in 1647. (Many subsequent editions were published, and the book became a classic.) To support this scholarly enterprise, which comprised political and geographical details, as well as such ethnological studies as recipes, bathing habits, and much more, Duke Frederick placed Olearius in charge of his collection of curiosities, which Olearius organized into a museum.

Detail of cat. no. 39

BIBLIOGRAPHY

SOURCES

This is an abbreviated listing of references used in the essay notes and sources for each catalogue entry. A full version of the bibliography, with English translations of the Russian titles, is available from the Indianapolis Museum of Art, Department of Decorative Arts. Note that many of the early accounts written by foreign visitors to Russia exist in English versions; citations to original language editions and English translations may be found in Marshall Poe, *Foreign Descriptions of Muscovy, an Analytic Bibliography of Primary and Secondary Sources* (Columbus, Ohio: 1995). In earlier sources, where the citation reads "In Sukhman," the reader is referred to M.M. Sukhman, ed. *Inostrantsy o drevnei Moskve: Moskva XV–XII vekov* (Moscow, 1991). The dates given in brackets indicate date of original publication.

Citations in the catalogue entries of documents given as Ambassadorial Affairs, Ambassadorial Book, Ambassadorial Office, Book of Receipts, Brief Inventory, Diplomatic Section, Inventories, Pamiat' o *peredache*, Rolls and Stolbtsy refer to material in the Russian State Archive for Ancient Documents, Moscow (RGADA), or in the Department of Manuscript, Print, and Graphic Archives, Moscow Kremlin (ORPGF).

ABRAMOVA 1998. See *Treasures of the Moscow Kremlin* 1998.

ADAMS 1991 [1589]. Clement Adams. "Angliiskoe puteshestvie k moskovitam." In Sukhman 1991, pp. 38–42; Hakluyt 1589, p. 280–311; Poe 1995, p. 72.

ADELUNG 1846. Friedrich von Adelung. *Kritiko-literaturnoe obozrenie puteshestvennikov po Rossii do 1700 goda i ikh sochinenii.* Translated from the German *Kritisch-Literärische Übersicht der Reisenden in Russland bis 1700)* 2 vols., pt. 1. St. Petersburg.

ALPATOV 1966. M. A. Alpatov. "Chto znal Posol'skii prikaz o Zapadnoi Evrope vo vtoroi polovine XVII v." In *Istoriia i istoriki*, pp. 89–129. Moscow.

ANGLICHANE V MOSKVE 1997. "Anglichane v Moskve vremen Borisa Godunova (po dokumentam posol'stva T. Smita 1604–1605 godov)." In *Arkheograficheskii ezhegodnik za 1997 g*, pp. 439–55. Moscow.

APANOVYCH 1961. O. M. Apanovych. *Zaporiz'ka Sich u borot'bi proty turets'ko-tatars'koi agresii 50–70 roky XVII st.* Kiev.

AREL 1995. M. S. Arel. "The Moscovy Company in the First Half of the Seventeenth Century." Ph.D. diss. Yale University.

ARNOLD 2000. Lauren Arnold. *Princely Gifts and Paper Treasures.* San Francisco.

ARSENEV AND TRUTOVSKII 1914. Iu. V. Arsenev and V. K. Trutovskii, eds., *Putevoditel' po Oruzheinoi palate.* Moscow.

AUGSBURG 1968. *Augsburger Barock.* Exh. cat. Augsburg.

AUREA PORTA 1997. *Aurea Porta Rzeczypospolitej.* Exh. cat. Gdańsk.

BABELON 1924. Ernst Babelon. "Le tombeau de Childéric." *Mémoires de la Société des Antiquaires de France* 60–64, no. LX–XVI, pp. 60–66.

BAKLANOVA 1928. N. A. Baklanova. "Privoznye tovary v Moskovskom gosudarstve vo vtoroi polovine XVII veka." In *Trudy Gosudarstvennogo Istoricheskogo muzeia* 4, pp. 5–118. Moscow.

BARBER 1979. Peter Barber. *Diplomacy.* Exh. cat. London.

BARON 1967. Samuel H. Baron, Introduction to *The Travels of Olearius in 17th-Century Russia.* Stanford, California, pp. 3–30.

BARTENEV 1916. S. P. Bartenev. *Moskovskii Kreml' v starinu i teper'.* 2 vols. Moscow.

BAZILEVICH 1932. K. V. Bazilevich. "Kollektivnaia chelobitnaia torgovykh liudei i bor'ba za russkii rynok v pervoi polovine XVII v." *Izvestiia Akademii nauk*, no. 2, pp. 91–128.

BAZILEVICH 1940. K. V. Bazilevich. "Elementy merkantilizma v ekonomicheskoi politike pravitel'stva Alekseia Mikhailovicha." In *Uchenye zapiski Moskovskogo gosudarstvennogo universiteta*, vol. 41, pt. 1: History, pp. 3–34. Moscow.

BEDINI 2000. Silvio A. Bedini. *The Pope's Elephant.* London/New York.

BELIAEV 1852. I. D. Beliaev. "Perepisnaia kniga domovoi kazny patriarkha Nikona, sostavlennaia v 7166 godu po poveleniiu Tsaria Alekseia Mikhailovicha." *Vremennik Obshchestva istorii i drevnostei rossiiskikh*, bk. 15, pp. 1–136. Moscow.

BELOKUROV 1906. S. A. Belokurov. *O Posol'skom prikaze.* Moscow.

BENCARD 1990. Mogens Bencard. "Two 17th-century Eskimos . . ." in *Greenland, Man and Society*, pp. 47–55. Copenhagen.

BENCARD AND MARKOVA 1988. Mogens Bencard and Galina A. Markova. *Christian IV's Royal Plate and His Relations with Russia.* Exh. cat. Rosenborg.

BERTELA AND TOFANI 1969. Giovanna Gaeta Bertela and Anna Maria Petrioli Tofani. *Feste e Apparati Medicei da Cosimo I a Cosimo II.* Exh. cat. Florence.

BESSONE 1993. Silvana Bessone. *The National Coach Museum, Lisbon.* Lisbon.

BESSONE 1996. Silvana Bessone et al. *Marquês de Fontes' Embassy to Pope Clement XI.* Lisbon.

BIER AND BENCARD 1995. Carol Bier, with Mogens Bencard. *The Persian Velvets at Rosenborg.* Copenhagen.

BILLINGTON 1970. J. H. Billington. "Bell and Canon." In *The Icon and the Axe. An Interpretive History of Russian Culture.* pp. 37–43. New York.

BIMBENET-PRIVAT 1983. Michèle Bimbenet-Privat. "L'Orfèvrerie parisienne au XVIe siècle." *Revue de l'Art* 61, pp. 53–60.

BIMBENET-PRIVAT 1991. Michèle Bimbenet-Privat. "La Vérité sur l'origine de la 'coupe de Saint Michel,'" *Jahrbuch der Kunsthistorischen Sammlungen in Wien* 87, pp. 127–35.

BIMBENET-PRIVAT 1997. Michèle Bimbenet-Privat. "Pierre Fourfault and the Lennoxlove toilet service." *Burlington Magazine* 139 (Jan.), pp. 11–16.

BIMBENET-PRIVAT 1999. Michèle Bimbenet-Privat. "L'Orfèvrerie Flamande commandée par la Cour de France au XVIe siècle." In *European Royal Tables: International Symposium Acts*, pp. 58–71. Lisbon.

BIMBENET-PRIVAT 2000. Michèle Bimbenet-Privat. "L'Orfèvrerie d'Henriette-Marie de France, reine d'Angleterre." In *Mélanges offerts au Professeur Jacques Thirion.* Paris.

BIMBENET-PRIVAT AND DE FONTAINES 1995. Michèle Bimbenet-Privat and G. de Fontaines. *La Datation de l'orfèvrerie parisienne sous l'Ancien Régime.* Paris.

BIMBENET-PRIVAT AND KUGEL 1998. Michèle Bimbenet-Privat and Alexis Kugel. *La Collection d'Orfèvrerie du Cardinal Sfondrati au musée Chrétien de la Bibliothèque Vaticane.* Vatican City.

BLACKMORE 1985. H. L. Blackmore. *English Pistols.* London.

BLAIR 1965. Claude Blair. "The Emperor Maximilian's Gift of Armour to King Henry VIII and the Silvered and Engraved Armour at the Tower of London." *Archaeologia* 99, pp. 1–52.

BOBROVNITSKAIA 1988. I. A. Bobrovnitskaia. "Proizvedeniia kremlevskikh zlatokuznetsov XVI veka." In *Gosudarstvennaia Oruzheinaia palata*, pp. 60–70. Moscow.

BÖHM 1939. Ernst Böhm. *Hans Petzolt*, 1939. Munich.

BONDARENKO 1916. I. Bondarenko. "Zdaniia Posol'skogo prikaza." In *Sbornik statei v chest' grafini P. S. Uvarovoi, 1885–1915*, pp. 98–107. Moscow.

BONDARENKO 1997. I. A. Bondarenko. "Ansambl' stolichnogo Kremlia (XV–XVI vv.)." *Arkhitekturnoe nasledstvo*, no. 42, pp. 26–51.

BONDARENKO 1998. A. F. Bondarenko. *Moskovskie kolokola XVII v.* Moscow.

BRAMBACH 1991 [1603]. Johannes Brambach. "Otchet o poezdke Ganzeiskogo posol'stva iz Liubeka v Moskvu i Novgorod v 1603 godu" (From German ed. *Relatio. Was in der Erbarn von Lübeck*). In Sukhman 1991, pp. 159–61. See Poe 1995, p. 138.

BRANTL 1998. Mary Brantl. "Agency Studies: Art and Diplomacy in Northern European Protestant Courts of the Early 17th Century." Ph.D. diss., New York University.

BRASSAT 1989. Wolfgang Brassat. "Tapisserien und Politik an den europäischen Höfen." Ph.D. diss., Marburg.

BREMER-DAVID 1997. Charissa Bremer-David. *French Tapestries & Textiles in the J. Paul Getty Museum*. Los Angeles.

BRULON 1993. Dorothée Guillemé Brulon. "Les Services de porcelaine de Sèvres présents des Rois Louis XV et Louis XVI aux souvérains étrangers." In Jean-Pierre Babelon et al., eds., *Versailles et les tables royales en Europe, XVIIème–XVIIIème siècles*, pp. 184–87. Exh. cat. Paris.

BUCHAU 1991. Prince Daniel von Buchau. "Nachalo i vozvyshenie Moskovii." In Sukhman 1991, pp. 81–83.

BUCKLAND 1983. Frances Buckland. "Gobelins Tapestries and Paintings as a Source of Information about the Silver Furniture of Louis XIV." *Burlington Magazine* 75 (May), pp. 271–83.

BUCKLAND 1989. Frances Buckland. "Silver Furnishings at the Court of France 1643–1670." *Burlington Magazine* 131 (May), pp. 328–36.

BURGH 1991 [1630–31]. Albert Koenraad Burgh. "Donesenie niderlandskikh poslov Al'berta Kunratsa Burkha i Ioganna fon Feltdrilia o ikh posol'stve v Rossiiu v 1630 i 1631 godakh." In Sukhman 1991, pp. 310–14. See Poe 1995, p. 157.

BURSCHE 1974. Stefan Bursche. *Tafelzier des Barock*. Munich.

BUSHEV 1987. P. P. Bushev. *Istoriia posol'stv i diplomaticheskikh otnoshenii Russkogo i Iranskogo gosudarstv v 1613–1621 gg. (po russkim arkhivam)*. Moscow.

BUSSOW 1991. Konrad Bussow. "Smutnoe sostoianie Russkogo gosudarstva v gody pravleniia tsarei Fedora Ivanovicha, Borisa Godunova i, v osobennosti, Dimitriev i Vasiliia Shuiskogo" (from 1615 German ed. *Verwirrter Zustand des Russischen Reichs . . .*). In Sukhman 1991, pp. 186–99. See Poe 1995, p. 148.

CAMBRIDGE HISTORY 1922–1932. *The Cambridge History of India*. Cambridge.

CASTELLUCCIO 2000/1. Stéphane Castelluccio. "La Part de Philippe V d'Espagne . . ." *L'Estampille—L'Objet d'art* 347 (May), pp. 56–82, 87.

CASTELLUCCIO 2000/2. Stéphane Castelluccio. "La collection de vases en pierres dure du Grand Dauphin." *Versalia* 4, pp. 38–59.

CHANCELLOR 1991 [1589]. Richard Chancellor. "Kniga o velikom i mogushchestvennom tsare Rossii i kniaze Moskovskom . . ." From English *The voyage of Richard Chanceler . . . the first discoverer by sea of the kingdome of Muscovia. An. 1553.* In Sukhman 1991, pp. 28–38. See Hakluyt 1589, pp. 280–311; Poe 1995, pp. 72–73.

CITROEN 1975. K. A. Citroen. *Amsterdamse zilversmeden en hun merken*. Amsterdam.

COCKERELL 1927. Sydney C. Cockerell. Introduction to *A Book of Old Testament Illustrations of the Middle of the Thirteenth Century*. Cambridge.

COLLINS 1991 [1667]. Samuel Collins. "Nyneshnee sostoianie Rossii . . ." In Sukhman 1991, pp. 330–31. See Poe 1995, p. 173.

COMPAGNI 1991. Giovanni Paolo Compagni. "Moskovskoe posol'stvo." In Sukhman, pp. 86–91.

CONFORTI AND WALTON 1988. Michael Conforti and Guy Walton, eds. *Sweden: A Royal Treasury 1550–1700*. Exh. cat. Minneapolis/Washington, D.C.

CORNIDES 1967. Elisabeth Cornides. 1967. "Rose und Schwert im päpstlichem Zeremoniell, von den Anfängen bis zum Pontifikat Gregors XIII." Ph.D. diss., Vienna.

COURAL 1967. Jean Coural. "Notes et documents." In *Chefs-d'oeuvre de la tapisserie parisienne (1597–1662)*. Exh. cat. Paris.

COX-REARICK 1994. Janet Cox-Rearick. "Sacred and Profane, Diplomatic Gifts of the Medici to Francis I." *Journal of Medieval and Renaissance Studies* 24, pp. 239–58.

COX-REARICK 1995. Janet Cox-Rearick. *The Collection of Francis I: Royal Treasures*. New York/Antwerp.

CRIPPS 1903. W. J. Cripps. *Old English Plate: Ecclesiastical, Decorative and Domestic: Its Makers and Marks*. London.

CRUMMEY 1985. Robert O. Crummey. "Court Spectacles in Seventeenth-Century Russia: Illusion and Reality." In *Essays in Honor of A. A. Zimin*, pp. 130–58. Columbus, Ohio.

CZIHAK 1908. E. von Czihak. *Die Edelschmiedekunst früherer Zeiten in Preussen. Westpreussen*. Vol. 2. Leipzig.

DANILEVSKII 1991. N. Ia. Danilevski. *Rossiia i Evropa*. Moscow.

DAS GOLD 1989. *Das Gold aus dem Kreml . . .* Exh. cat. Munich.

DAS GOLD 1991. *Das Gold aus dem Kreml . . .* Exh. cat. Vienna.

DAVIS AND KASINEC 1991. Robert H. Davis, Jr. and Edward Kasinec. "Witness to the Crime: Two Little-Known Photographic Sources Relating to the Sale and Destruction of Antiquities in Soviet Russia During the 1920s." *Journal of the History of Collections* 3, no. 1, pp. 53–59.

DAVIS AND KASINEC 2000. Robert H. Davis, Jr. and Edward Kasinec. "Introduction." In *A Dark Mirror: Romanov and Imperial Palace Library Materials in the Holdings of The New York Public Library*, pp. 1–47. New York.

DEMKIN 1994. A. V. Demkin. *Zapadnoevropeiskoe kupechestvo v Rossii v XVII veke*, vols. 1–2. Moscow.

DENIS AND SAUNIER 1996. Isabelle Denis and Bruno Saunier. "Peinture et tapisserie." In *Lisses et delices*, pp. 31–39. Exh. cat. Paris.

DENISOV 1908. L. I. Denisov. *Pravoslavnye monastyri Rossiiskoi imperii*. Moscow.

DENISOVA 1954. M. M. Denisova. "Koniushennaia kazna: Paradnoe konskoe ubranstvo XVI–XVII vekov." In *Gosudarstvennaia Oruzheinaia palata Moskovskogo Kremlia*, pp. 247–304. Moscow.

DMITRIEV 1909. I. D. Dmitriev. *Moskovskii pervoklassnyi Novospasskii Stavropigial'nyi monastyr' v ego proshlom i nastoiashchem*. Moscow.

DOSIFEI 1836. Archimandrite Dosifei. *Geograficheskoe, istoricheskoe i statisticheskoe opisanie stavropigial'nogo pervoklassnogo Solovetskogo monastyria*, vol. 1. Moscow.

DREJHOLT 1996. Nils Drejholt. *Firearms of the Royal Armouries*. Stockholm.

DREVNOSTI 1849–53. *Drevnosti Rossiiskogo gosudarstva*, vols. 1–6. Moscow.

DRURY 1991. Martin Drury. "Diplomat's Prize." *Country Life* (October), pp. 54–55.

DUBON 1964. David T. Dubon. *Tapestries from the Samuel H. Kress Collection at the Philadelphia Museum of Art*. London.

DUNCAN 1968. David Douglas Duncan. *Great Treasures of the Kremlin*. New York.

DUTCH GUNS IN RUSSIA 1996. *Dutch Guns in Russia in the Moscow Kremlin Armoury, Moscow Historical Museum, Hermitage St. Petersburg, Gatchina Palace Museum*. Amsterdam.

EKHOLM 1974. L. Ekholm. "Rysk spannmål och svenska krigsfinanser 1629–1633." *Scandia*, no. 1, pp. 57–103.

ELAM 1988. Caroline Elam. "Art and Diplomacy in Renaissance Florence." *Royal Society of Art Journal* 136, pp. 813–26.

ENGLISH SILVER TREASURES 1991. *English Silver Treasures from the Kremlin*. Exh. cat. London.

ESPER 1967. Heinrich von Staden. *The Land and Government of Muscovy: a Sixteenth-century Account*. Stanford, Calif. See Poe 1995, p. 102.

ESTERLY 1998. David Esterly. *Grinling Gibbons and the Art of Carving*. New York.

FALKE 1919. O. von Falke. "Die Neugotik im deutschen Kunstgewerbe der Spätrenaissance." In *Jahrbuch der preussischen Kunstsammlungen* 40, pp. 75–92. Berlin.

FILIMONOV 1893. G. D. Filimonov. *Pol'nyi khronologicheskii ukazatel' vsekh marok na serebre Moskovskoi Oruzheinoi palaty*. Moscow.

FILLITZ 1964. Hermann Fillitz. *Die Schatzkammer in Wien*. Vienna.

FISCHINGER 1983. A. Fischinger. "Chrystian Paulsen i Jan Polmann, złotnicy gdańscy XVII wieku." *Biuletyn Historii Sztuki* (Warsaw), no. 3–4, pp. 317–26.

FISCHINGER 1990. A. Fischinger. *Srebrny orzeł w zbiorach Skarbka Koronnego na Wawelu*. Warsaw.

FLETCHER 1991 [1591]. Giles Fletcher. "O gosudarstve Russkom . . ." From English *Of the Russe Commonwealth*. In Sukhman 1991, pp. 132–33. See Poe 1995, p. 124.

FLORIA 1989. B. N. Floria. "K istorii peregovorov o russko-pol'skom antiosmanskom soiuze v seredine 40-x. godov XVII veka." In *Slaviane i ikh sosedi*, pp. 124–39. Moscow.

FLORIA 1990. B. N. Floria. "Russko-osmanskie otnosheniia i diplomaticheskaia podgotovka Smolenskoi voiny." *Sovetskoe slavianovedenie*, no. 1, pp. 17–27.

FLORIA 1991. B. N. Floria. "K istorii russko-osmanskikh otnoshenii v seredine 40-x godov XVII veka." *Etudes balkaniques*, no. 2, pp. 72–81.

FLORIA 1992. B. N. Floria. "Rossiia i stambul'skie greki v gody bor'by za Azov (1637–1642)." In *Slaviane i ikh sosedi*, vol. 4, pp. 111–22. Moscow.

FLORIA (In press). B. N. Floria. "Foma Kantakuzin i ego rol' v razvitii russko-osmanskikh otnoshenii v 20-x–30-x godakh XVII veka." In *Rossiia i Khristianskii Vostok*. Moscow.

FOSCARINI 1991 [1557]. Marco Foscarini. "Rassuzhdenie o Moskovii iz knigi." *Istoricheskoe skazanie o Moskovskom gosudarstve, sochinennoe venetsianskim poslom Foskarino.* In Sukhman 1991, pp. 50–57. See Poe 1995, p. 76.

FÜLEP 1989. Ferenc Fülep et al., "Hungarian National Museum," in *Museums in Budapest.* Budapest.

FUSCONI 1986. Giulia Fusconi. *Disegni decorativi del barocco romano.* Rome.

GALAKTIONOV 1960. I. V. Galaktionov. *Iz istorii russko-pol'skogo sblizheniia v 50–60–x godakh XVII veka.* Saratov.

GIUSTI 1992. Anna Maria Giusti. *Pietre Dure.* London.

GLANVILLE 1987. Philippa Glanville. *Silver in England.* New York.

GLANVILLE 1990. Philippa Glanville. *Silver in Tudor and Early Stuart England.* London.

GOLDBERG 1954. T. G. Goldberg. "Iz posol'skikh darov XVI–XVII vekov: angliiskoe serebro." In *Gosudarstvennaia Oruzheinaia palata Moskovskogo Kremlia,* pp. 435–506. Moscow.

GOLDSMITH 1992. Benjamin E. Goldsmith. *A Guide to Russian Illustrated Books and Photographic Albums in the Slavic and Baltic Division.* New York.

GOLLANDTSY I RUSSKIE 1989. *Gollandtsy i russkie 1600–1917.* Moscow.

GOLUBTSOV 1891. A. Golubtsov. *Preniia o vere, vyzvannyia delom korolevicha Val'demara i tsarevny Iriny Mikhailovny.* Moscow.

GOSUDARSTVENNAIA ORUZHEINAIA PALATA 1954. *Gosudarstvennaia Oruzheinaia palata Moskovskogo Kremlia.* Moscow.

GOULD 1994. Cecil Gould. "The Early History of Leonardo's Vièrge aux Rochers." *Gazette des Beaux Arts* 124 (December), pp. 215–22.

GRADOWSKI 1993. M. Gradowski. *Znaki na srebrze.* Warsaw.

GRALA 1994. Hieronim Grala. *Ivan Mikhailov Viskovatyi.* Moscow.

GREAT BRITAIN–USSR 1967. *Great Britain–USSR: An Historical Exhibition.* Exh. cat. London.

GRECHESKIE DOKUMENTY 1995. *Grecheskie dokumenty i rukopisi, ikony i pamiatniki prikladnogo iskusstva moskovskikh sobranii.* Exh. cat. Moscow.

GRIMALDI 1996. David A. Grimaldi. *Amber: Window to the Past.* New York.

GRZYBKOWSKA 1994. Teresa Grzybkowska. "Antykizacja w złotnictwie gdańskim: Sztuka XVII wieku w Polsce." In *Materiały Sesji Stowarzyszenia Historyków Sztuki. Kraków, grudzień 1993,* pp. 249–64. Warsaw.

GUALDO PRIORATO 1670–74. Count Galeazzo Gualdo Priorato. *Historia di Leopoldo Cesare.* 3 vols. Vienna.

GYLDENSTJERNE 1991. Axel von Gyldenstjerne. "Puteshestvie gertsoga Gansa Shlesving-Golshtinskogo v Rossiiu" (v 1602 godu)" (from 1814 Danish ed. *Udtog af Rigsraed Axel Gyldenstierna, holden paa hans Reise til og under hans Ophold in Moskow 1602–1603).* In Sukhman 1991, pp. 140–47. See Poe 1995, p. 136.

HABSBURG 1997. Géza von Habsburg. *Princely Treasures.* New York.

HAKLUYT 1589. Richard Hakluyt, ed. *The Principal navigations, voiages and discoveries of the English nation.* 2 vols. London. See Poe 1995, p. 105.

HAYDEN 1915. A. Hayden. *Chats on Old Silver.* London.

HEDIN 1992. Thomas Hedin. "Versailles and the *Mercure Galant.*" *Gazette des Beaux Arts* 119 (April), pp. 149–72.

HERBERSTEIN 1988 [1549]. Sigmund Freiherr von Herberstein. *Zapiski o Moskovii.* Moscow. See Poe 1995, p. 61.

HERING 1968. G. Hering. *Ökumenisches Patriarchat und Europäische Politik, 1620–1638.* Wiesbaden.

HERNMARCK 1951. C. Hernmarck. *Svenskt Silver 1580–1800, i Nationalmusei Samlingar.* Stockholm.

HERNMARCK 1977. C. Hernmarck. *The Art of the European Silversmith, 1430–1830.* London/New York.

HERNMARCK 1978. C. Hernmarck. *Die Kunst der Europäischen Gold- und Silberschmiede von 1450 bis 1830.* Munich.

HERTLINE 1965. E. Hertline. "Capolavori Francesi in San Francesco di Assisi." *Antiquità Viva* 4, pp. 54–70.

HEUSS 1991. Stephan Heuss. "Opisanie puteshestviia v Moskvu posla rimskogo imperatora Nikolaia Varkocha 22 iiunia 1593 goda." In Sukhman, pp. 133–337. See Poe 1995, p. 124.

HILL 1905–14. David Jayne Hill. *A History of Diplomacy,* 3 vols. London.

HOFF 1978. A. Hoff. *Dutch Firearms.* London.

HORSEY 1991 [1856]. Jerome Horsey. "Puteshestvie sera Dzheroma Gorseia." In Sukhman 1991, pp. 97–131. See Poe 1995, p. 117.

HÜSELER 1950. K. Hüseler. "Meisterliste der Hamburger Goldschmiede vom XIV bis XVII Jahrhundert." *Nordelbingen,* no. 19, pp. 136–68.

IABLONSKAIA 1988. E. A. Iablonskaia. "Zapadnoevropeiskoe vooruzhenie XV–XVII vekov." In *Gosudarstvennaia Oruzheinaia palata,* pp. 185–201. Moscow.

IABLONSKAIA 1988/1. E. A. Iablonskaia. "Proizvedeniia oruzheinogo iskusstva Irana i Turtsii XVI–XVII vekov" In *Gosudarstvennaia oruzheinaia palata,* pp. 202–20. Moscow.

IABLONSKAIA 1996. E. A. Iablonskaia. "Paradnoe vooruzhenie." In *Sokrovishcha Oruzheinoi palaty,* pp. 91–141. Moscow.

IKONNIKOVA 1914. A. Ikonnikova. *Tsaritsy i tsarevny iz doma Romanovykh (Istoricheskii ocherk),* repr. 1990. Moscow.

ISTORICHESKOE OPISANIE 1807. *Istoricheskoe opisanie drevnego Rossiiskogo muzeia, pod nazvaniem Masterskoi i Oruzheinoi palaty,* pt. 1. Moscow.

ISTORIIA SHVETSII 1974. *Istoriia Shvetsii.* Moscow.

ISTORIIA VNESHNEI POLITIKI 1999. *Istoriia vneshnei politiki Rossii: Konets XV–XVII vek (Ot sverzheniia ordynskogo iga do Severnoi voiny).* Moscow.

IUZEFOVICH 1977. L. A. Iuzefovich. "Iz istorii posol'skogo obychaia kontsa XV–nachala XVII veka (Stolovyi tseremonial Moskovskogo dvora)." In *Istoricheskie zapiski,* vol. 98 (Moscow), pp. 331–40.

IUZEFOVICH 1988. L. A. Iuzefovich. *Kak v posol'skikh obychaiakh vedetsia . . .* Moscow.

JACKSON 1921. C. J. Jackson. *English Goldsmiths and Their Marks.* London.

JACKSON 1989. *Jackson's Silver and Gold Marks of England, Scotland and Ireland.* Woodbridge.

JACKSON-STOPS 1985. Gervase Jackson-Stops, ed. *The Treasure Houses of Britain.* Exh. cat. Washington, D.C.

JACQ-HERGOUALC'H 1985. Michel Jacq-Hergoualc'h. "A propos des canons Siamois offerts à Louis XIV qui particérent à la prise de la Bastille." *Annales historiques de la Révolution française* 201, pp. 317–34.

JAFFÉ 1996. David Jaffé. "The Earl and Countess Arundel . . ." *Apollo* 144 (August), pp. 3–35.

JAHANGIR 1909. Jahangir, Emperor of Hindustan. *Memoirs of Jahangir,* vol. II. London.

JEDDING 1990. Herman Jedding. "Between Pomp and Politics." In *Flora Danica og der danske hof; Flora Danica and the Royal Danish Court,* pp. 142–73. Exh. cat. Copenhagen.

JENKINSON 1991 [1589]. Anthony Jenkinson. "Puteshestvie iz Londona v Moskvu." In Sukhman 1991, pp. 42–47. Hakluyt, 1589, pp. 333–49. See Poe 1995, p. 76.

JONES 1909. E. A. Jones. *The Old English Plate of the Emperor of Russia.* London.

JUAN DE PERSIA 1991. Urukh-Bek (Orudzh-Bek, Hussein of Persia). "Reliatsiia Khuana Persidskogo ispanskomu koroliu Filippu III: Posol'stvo Khuseina-Alibeka v Rossiiu v 1599–1600 godakh." In Sukhman 1991, pp. 138–40. See Poe 1995, p. 134.

KARGALOV 1998. V. V. Kargalov. *Na granitsakh stoiat' krepko. Velikaia Rus' i Dikoe pole. Protivostoianie XIII–XVIII vv."* pp. 164–328. Moscow.

KASINEC AND WORTMAN 1992. Edward Kasinec and Richard Wortman. "The Mythology of Empire: Imperial Russian Coronation Albums." *Biblion: The Bulletin of The New York Public Library* 1, pp. 77–100.

KEENAN 1971. Edward Keenan. *The Groznyi-Kurbskii Apocrypha.* Cambridge, Mass.

KERNER 1991. Thomas Kerner. "Dnevnik Livonskogo posol'stva k tsariu Ivanu Vasil'evichu." In Sukhman 1991, pp. 47–49. See Poe 1995, p. 75.

KHUDOZHESTVENNYE SOKROVISHCHA 1902. *Khudozhestvennye sokrovishcha Rossii.* St. Petersburg.

KIRILLOVA 1964. L. P. Kirillova. "Koniushennaia kazna." In *Oruzheinaia palata,* pp. 291–326. Moscow.

KIRILLOVA 1988. L. P. Kirillova. "Predmety paradnogo konskogo ubranstva XVI–XVII vv. In *Gosudarstvennaia oruzheinaia palata,* pp. 373–96. Moscow.

KIRILLOVA 1996. L. P. Kirillova. "Paradnoe konskoe ubranstvo evropeiskikh stran." In *Sokrovishcha Oruzheinoi palaty,* pp. 143–75. Moscow.

KOHLHAUSSEN 1968. H. Kohlhaussen. *Nürnberger Goldschmiedekunst des Mittelalters und der Dürerziet 1240 bis 1540.* Berlin.

KOLOGRIVOV 1911. S. A. Kologrivov. "Materialy dlia istorii snoshenii Rossii s inostrannymi derzhavami v 17 veke." *Vestnik arkheologii istorri,* no. 20. St. Petersburg.

KONDRIKOVA 1996. Zoia Kondrikova, ed. *Sokrovishcha Oruzheinoi palaty.* Moscow.

KORB 1991 [1698]. Johann Georg Korb. "Dnevnik puteshestviia v Moskoviiu." In Sukhman 1991, pp. 401–6. See Poe 1995, p. 189.

KOSTOMAROV 1905. N. I. Kostomarov. *Istoricheskie monografii i issledovaniia,* vol. 15. St. Petersburg.

KOSTOMAROV 1989. N. I. Kostomarov. *Istoricheskie monografii i issledovaniia.* 2 vols. Moscow.

KOTOSHIKHIN 1906. G. K. Kotoshikhin. *O Rossii v tsarstvovanie Alekseia Mikhailovicha* St. Petersburg. See also English trans. *O Rossii v carstvovanie Alekseja Mixajloviča.* Oxford/New York, 1980.

KOVÁCS AND LOVAG 1980. Éva Kovács and Zsuzsa Lovag. *The Hungarian Crown and Other Regalia.* Budapest.

KRATKII UKAZATEL' PATRIARSHEI RIZNITSY 1907. *Kratkii ukazatel' Patriarshei riznitsy v Moskve.* Moscow.

KUDRIAVTSEVA 1997. A. G. Kudriavtseva. "Luchshe s chest'iu domoi vorotit'sia." *Rodina,* no. 10, pp. 50–54.

KUDRIAVTSEVA 1998. A. G. Kudriavtseva. "Dary Severnoi Koronoi." *Mir muzeia,* no. 2, pp. 4–13.

KURZ 1969. Otto Kurz. "A Gold Helmet. . . ." *Gazette des Beaux Arts* 74 (November), pp. 249–58.

KURZ 1975. Otto Kurz. *European Clocks and Watches in the Near East.* London.

KWAŒNIEWICZ 1988. W. Kwaœniewicz. *Szabla Polska od XV do końca XVIII wieku.* Zielona Góra.

LAVIN 1992. James D. Lavin. "The Gift of James I to Felipe III of Spain." *The Journal of the Arms & Armour Society* 14 (September), pp. 64–88.

LAVRENTII 1805. Archimandrite Lavrentii. *Kratkoe izvestie o Krestnom nezhskom Arkhangel'skoi eparkhii monastyre.* Moscow.

LE XVI SIÈCLE EN EUROPE 1965–66. *Le XVI siècle en Europe.* Exh. cat. Paris.

LEIDS ZILVER 1977. *Leids Zilver.* Exh. cat. Leiden.

LEITHE-JASPER 1970. Manfred Leithe-Jasper. "Der Bergkristallpokal Herzog Philipps des Guten von Burgund—Das 'Vierte Stucke' der Geschenke König Karls IX. von Frankreich an Erzherzog Ferdinand II." *Jahrbuch der Kunsthistorischen Sammlungen in Wien* 66, pp. 227–42.

LEITHE-JASPER AND DISTELBERGER 1982. Manfred Leithe-Jasper and Rudolf Distelberger. *Vienna, The Kunsthistorische Museum.* Vienna. London.

LEONTEV 1961. A. K. Leontev. *Obrazovanie prikaznoi sistemy upravleniia v Russkom gosudarstve: Iz istorii sozdaniia tsentral'nogo gosudarstvennogo apparata v kontse XV-pervoi poloviny XVI veka.* Moscow.

LESSING 1883. I. Lessing. *Deutsche Kunstschau.* Berlin.

LEVINSON-NECHAEVA 1954. M. N. Levinson-Nechaeva. "Odezhda i tkani XVI–XVII vekov." In *Gosudarstvennaia Oruzheinaia palata Moskovskogo Kremlia,* pp. 305–86. Moscow.

LEVYKIN 1992. A. K. Levykin. "Oruzhnichie v XVI stoletii." In *Problemy izucheniia pamiatnikov dukhovnoi i material'noi kul'tury,* vol. 1, pp. 10–20. Moscow.

LEVYKIN 1997. A. K. Levykin. *Voinskie tseremonii i regalii russkikh tsarei.* Moscow.

LEVYKIN 1998. A. K. Levykin. "Oruzheinaia palata v XVI stoletii." In *Russkaia khudozhestvennaia kul'tura XV–XVI vekov,* vol. 11, pp. 240–54. Moscow.

LIGHTBOWN 1975. R. W. Lightbown. *Catalogue of Scandinavian and Baltic Silver.* London.

LIKHACHEV 1991. D. S. Likhachev. *Poeziia sadov: k semantike sadovo-parkovykh stilei: Sad kak tekst.* St. Petersburg.

LILEYKO 1987. J. Lileyko. *Regalia Polskie.* Warsaw.

LINK 1973. E. M. Link. *The Book of Silver.* New York.

LITVIN 1991. Mikhalon Litvin. "O nravakh tatar, litovtsev i moskvitian." In Sukhman 1991, pp. 91–96.

LIUBIMENKO 1912. I. I. Liubimenko. *Istoriia torgovykh snoshenii Rossii s Angliei.* Vol. 1. Yuriev (Tartu).

LIUBIMENKO 1923. I. I. Liubimenko. "Moskovskii rynok kak arena bor'by Gollandii s Angliei." In *Russkoe proshloe,* vol. 5, pp. 3–23. St. Petersburg-Moscow.

LIUBIMENKO 1933. I. I. Liubimenko. "Torgovye snosheniia Rossii s Angliei i Gollandiei s 1553 po 1649 god." *Izvestiia Akademii nauk SSSR, seriia 7,* no. 10, pp. 729–54.

LOUVRE 1999. *Les Bronzes de la couronne.* Exh. cat. Paris.

LUND AND WEBER 1991 [1604]. M. J. Lund and J. Weber. "Podlinnoe izvestie o russkom i moskovskom puteshestvii . . ." In Sukhman 1991, pp. 148–59. See Poe 1995, p. 135.

L'URSS ET LA FRANCE 1974. *L'URSS et la France: Les Grands moments d'une tradition.* Exh. cat. Paris.

LUTMAN 1978. Kh. Lutman. "Shvedskoe serebrianoe delo na protiazhenii trekh stoletii." In *Serebro Shvetsii: Iz sobraniia Korolevskoi sem'i i Natsional'nogo muzeia,* pp. 2–7. Moscow.

LYSECK 1991. Adolf Lyseck. "Skazaniia Adol'fa Lizeka o posol'stve ot imperatora Rimskogo Leopol'da k velikomu tsariu Moskovskogo Alek-

seiu Mikhailovichu v 1675 godu." In Sukhman 1991, pp. 363–68. See Poe 1995, p. 179.

MABILLE 1991. Gérard Mabille. "Germain, Durand, Auguste." In O. V. Krog, ed., *A King's Feast,* pp. 78–91. Exh. cat. Copenhagen.

MACHIAVELLI 1990. Niccolò Machiavelli. *Gosudar'.* Moscow.

MAHON 1949, 1950. Denis Mahon. "Note on the Dutch Gift to Charles II." *Burlington Magazine* 91 (Nov. 1949), pp. 303–5, 91 (Dec. 1949), pp. 349–50, and 92 (Jan. 1950), pp. 249–50.

MALEIN 1934. A. I. Malein, trans. of Albert Schlichting (fl. 16th cent.) *Novoe izvestie o Rossii vremeni Ivana Groznogo* (from "Nova ex Moscova per nobilem Albertum Schlicting . . . ," *Scriptoros rerum polonicarium,* vol. 1 [Cracow, 1872–1917]. Leningrad. See Poe 1995, p. 90.

MALININ 1901. V. E. Malinin. *Starets Eleazarova Monastyria Filofei i ego poslaniia.* Kiev.

MALITSKII 1954. G. L. Malitskii. "K istorii Oruzheinoi palaty Moskovskogo Kremlia." In *Gosudarstvennaia Oruzheinaia palata Moskovskogo Kremlia: Sbornik nauchnykh trudov,* pp. 507–60. Moscow.

MARGARET 1991 [1607]. Jacques Margaret. "Sostoianie Rossiiskoi imperii . . ." In Sukhman 1991, pp. 178–82. See Poe 1995, p. 143.

MARKOVA 1966. G. A. Markova. "Iantar' v Oruzheinoi palate." In *Iantar',* pp. 26–50. Kaliningrad.

MARKOVA 1969. G. A. Markova. "Pamiatniki diplomaticheskikh snoshenii Rossii i Avstrii v Oruzheinoi palate Moskovskogo Kremlia." In *Slaviano-germanskie kul'turnye sviazi i otnosheniia,* pp. 338–42. Moscow.

MARKOVA 1975. G. A. Markova. *Nemetskoe khudozhestvennoe serebro XVI–XVIII vekov v sobranii Gosudarstvennoi Oruzheinoi palaty.* . Moscow.

MARKOVA 1980. G. A. Markova. "Niurnbergskoe serebro v Oruzheinoi palate Moskovskogo Kremlia," pt. 1. In *Muzei,* 1: *Khudozhestvennye sobraniia,* pp. 90–135. Moscow.

MARKOVA 1988. G. A. Markova. "Posol'skie dary Gollandii i Danii." In *Gosudarstvennaia Oruzheinaia palata,* pp. 234–42. Moscow.

MARKOVA 1990. G. A. Markova. *Gollandskoe serebro v sobranii Gosudarstvennoi Oruzheinoi palaty.* Moscow.

MARKOVA 1996. G. A. Markova. "Pamiatniki evropeiskogo zolotogo i serebrianogo dela." In *Sokrovishcha Oruzheinoi palaty,* pp. 29–89. Moscow.

MARKOVA 1998. G. A. Markova. "Rasskazyvaet khudozhestvennoe serebro . . ." *Mir muzeia,* no. 2 (March–April), pp. 14–21.

MARTIN 1900/1. Fredrik Robert Martin. *Schwedische königliche Geschenke an russische Zaren 1647–1699.* Stockholm.

MARTIN 1900/2. Fredrik Robert Martin. *Dänische Silberschätze aus der Zeit Christians IV, auf bewahrt in der Kaiserlichen Schatzkammer zu Moskau.* Stockholm.

MARTYNOVA 1973. M. V. Martynova. *Dragotsennyi kamen' v russkom iuvelirnom iskusstve XII–XVIII vekov.* Moscow.

MARTYNOVA 1988. M. V. Martynova. "Moskva—krupneishii iuvelirnyi tsentr XVII veka." In *Gosudarstvennaia Oruzheinaia palata,* pp. 71–94. Moscow.

MASKIEWICZ 1991. Samuel Maskiewicz. "Dnevnik Maskevicha 1594–1621 godov" (from Polish). In Sukhman, pp. 258–70. See Poe 1995, p. 131.

MASSA 1874 [1612]. Isaac Massa. "Kratkoe povestvovanie o nachale i proiskhozhdenii sovremennykh voin i smut v Moskovii . . ." *Skazaniia Massy i Gerkmana o Smutnom vremeni v Rossii.* See Poe 1995, p. 146.

MAURICE 1968. Klaus Maurice. *Von Uhren und Automaten: Das Messen der Zeit.* Munich.

MCCABE c. 1999. Ina Baghdiantz McCabe. *The Shah's silk for Europe's silver.* University of Pennsylvania Armenian texts and studies, no. 15. Atlanta.

MELNIKOVA 1992. O. B. Melnikova. "Koniushennyi prikaz v XVI–XVII vekakh." In *Problemy izucheniia pamiatnikov dukhovnoi i material'noi kul'tury,* vol. 1, pp. 21–30. Moscow.

MELNIKOVA 1996. O. B. Melnikova. "Koniushennaia kazna Moskovskoi Oruzheinoi palaty: Novye atributsii." In *Iuvelirnoe iskusstvo i material'naia kul'tura,* pp. 41–43. St. Petersburg.

MENZHAUSEN 1968. Joachim Menzhausen. *Das Grüne Gewölbe.* Leipzig.

MENZHAUSEN 1977. Joachim Menzhausen. *Dresdener Kunstkammer und Grünes Gewölbe.* Vienna.

MEYERBERG 1903. Augustin von Meyerberg. *Al'bom Meierberga.* Moscow.

MIRONOVA 1996. O. Mironova. "Vostochnoe paradnoe ubranstvo." In *Sokrovishcha Oruzheinoi palaty*, pp. 176–97. Moscow.

MITCHELL 2000. David Mitchell. "'To Alderman Backwells for the candlesticks for Mr Coventy'. . ." *The Silver Society Journal* (Autumn), pp. 111–24.

MODERN 1901. Heinrich Modern. "Geweihte Schwerter und Hüte in den Kunsthistorischen Sammlungen des Allerhöchsten Kaiserhauses." *Jahrbuch der Kunsthistorischen Sammlungen des Allerhöchsten Kaiserhauses* 22, pp. 127–68.

MOLCHANOV 1984. N. N. Molchanov. *Diplomatiia Petra Pervogo*. Moscow.

MONCRIEFF 1991. Elspeth Moncrieff. "Politics and Plate: English Silver from the Kremlin." *Apollo* 133 (Jan.), pp. 50–52.

MOREL 1988. Bernard Morel. *Les Joyeaux de la couronne de France*. Anvers.

MORELLO AND KANTER 1999. Giovanni Morello and Laurence Kanter, eds. *The Treasury of Saint Francis of Assisi*. Exh. cat. Milan.

MÜLLER-JÜRGENS 1961. G. Müller-Jürgens. "Die Emdener Kanne von 1596 in der Moskauer Rustkammer." *Ostfriesland-Zeitschrift für Kultur Wirtschaft und Verkehr*, no. 1.

NARODZINY STOLICY 1996. *Narodziny Stolicy: Warszawa w latach 1596–1668*. Exh. cat. Warsaw.

NEUMANN 1957. Erwin Neumann. "Florentiner Mosaik aus Prag." *Jahrbuch der Kunsthistorischen Sammlungen in Wien* 53, pp. 157–202.

NICOLSON 1954. Harold Nicolson. *The Evolution of Diplomatic Method*. London.

NIKITINA 1995. V. M. Nikitina. *Orden sv. Georgiia*. Moscow.

NOVOSELSKII 1948. A. A. Novoselskii. *Bor'ba Moskovskogo gosudarstva s tatarami v pervoi polovine XVII veka*. Moscow.

NOWACKI 1995. D. Nowacki. "The Munich Exhibition of Augsburg Goldsmiths' Art." *Folia Historiae Artium*, n.s. 1, pp. 145–53.

OBUCHOWICZ 1991 [1660]. Michał Obuchowicz. "Dnevnik Mikhaila Obukhovicha, strazhnika velikogo kniazhestva Litovskogo, pisannyi v plenu v Moskve v 1660 godu." In Sukhman 1991, pp. 335–41. See Poe 1995, p. 168.

OKO VSEI VELIKOI ROSSII 1989. *"Oko vsei velikoi Rossii": Ob istorii russkoi diplomaticheskoi sluzhby XVI–XVII vekov*. Moscow.

OLEARIUS 1719 [1647]. Adam Olearius. *Voyages très curieux & très renommez, faits en Moscovie, Tartarie, et Perse*. Leiden. See Poe 1995, p. 159.

OLEARIUS 1906. Adam Olearius. *Opisanie puteshestviia v Moskoviiu i cherez Moskoviiu v Persiiu i obratno*. St. Petersburg. See Poe 1995, p. 159.

OLEARIUS 1967. See Baron 1967.

OLSEN 1903. B. Olsen. *Die Arbeiten der Hamburgischen Goldschmiede Jacob Mores, Vater und Sohn für die Dänischen Könige Frederik II und Christian IV*. Hamburg.

OMAN 1961. Charles Oman. *The English Silver in the Kremlin 1557–1663*. London.

OMAN 1970. Charles Oman. *Caroline Silver 1625–1688*. London.

OPIS' KELEINOI KAZNY 1630. *Opis' keleinoi kazny patriarkha Filareta Nikiticha 1630 g. avgusta 26*. St. Petersburg.

ORUZHEINAIA PALATA 1902. "Imperatorskaia Oruzheinaia palata v Moskve." *Khudozhestvennye sokrovishcha Rossii*, no. 9–10, pp. 211–68.

ORUZHEINAIA PALATA 1914. See Arsenov and Trutovskii 1914.

ORUZHEINAIA PALATA 1954. See Gosudarstvennaia Oruzheinaia palata 1954.

ORZEŁ BIAŁY 1995. *Orzeł Biały: 700-lat Herbu Państwa Polskiego*. Exh. cat. Warsaw.

OTTILLINGER 1988. Eva B. Ottillinger. *Kaiserliche Geschenke*. Exh. cat. Linz.

PAMIATNIKI DIPLOMATICHESKIKH I TORGOVYKH 1890. *Pamiatniki diplomaticheskikh i torgovykh snoshenii Moskovskoi Rusi s Persiei*. Vol. 1. St. Petersburg.

PAMIATNIKI DIPLOMATICHESKIKH SNOSHENII 1862. *Pamiatniki diplomaticheskikh snoshenii s Imperieiu Rimskoiu (s 1682 po 1685)*. In *Pamiatniki diplomaticheskikh snoshenii drevnei Rossii s derzhavami inostrannymi*, vol. 6. St. Petersburg.

PAUL OF ALEPPO 1896. Paul of Aleppo. *Puteshestvie antiokhiiskogo patriarkha Makariia v Rossiiu v polovine XVII veka . . .*, vol. 1. Moscow. In Sukhman 1991, pp. 321–29. See Poe 1995, pp. 163–64.

PECHSTEIN 1974. Klaus Pechstein. "Der Merkelsche Tafelaufsatz von Wenzel Jamnitzer." *Mitteilungen des Vereins für Geschichte der Stadt Nürnberg* 61, pp. 90–121.

PELKA 1920. O. Pelka. *Bernstein*. Berlin.

PEREPISNAIA KNIGA 1873. "Perepisnaia kniga moskovskogo Blagoveshchenskogo sobora XVII v." In *Sbornik na 1873 god, izdannyi Obshchestvom drevnerusskogo iskusstva*, pp. 1–49. Moscow.

PETR VELIKII I MOSKVA 1998. *Petr Velikii i Moskva: Katalog vystavki*. Exh. cat. Moscow.

PIACENTI 1986. Kirsten Aschengreen Piacenti. "Un Dono del Re Sole a Cosimo III: Due tappeti Savonnerie a Palazzo Pitti." *Antologia di Belle Arti* 29–30, pp. 17–20.

PICKFORD 1989. See Jackson 1989.

PIPONNIER 1970. Françoise Piponnier. *Costume et vie sociale*. Paris.

PISARSKAIA 1964. L. V. Pisarskaia. "Russkie zolotye i serebrianye izdeliia XII–XVII vekov." In *Oruzheinaia palata*, pp. 73–140.

PISARSKAIA, PLATONOVA, AND ULIANOVA 1974. L. V. Pisarskaia, N. G. Platonova, and B. L. Ulianova. *Russkie emali XI–XIX vv.* Moscow.

POE 1995. Marshall Poe. *Foreign Descriptions of Muscovy: An Analytic Bibliography of Primary and Secondary Sources*. Columbus, Ohio.

POKHLEBKIN 1992. V. V. Pokhlebkin. *Vneshiaia politika Rusi, Rossii i SSSR za 1000 let v imenakh, datakh, faktakh: Spravochnik*. Moscow.

POLYNINA AND RAKHMANOV 1994. Irina Polynina and Nicolai Rakhmanov. *The Regalia of the Russian Empire*. Moscow.

PORSHNEV 1945. B. F. Porshnev. "Russkie subsidii Shvetsii vo vremia 30-letnei voiny." *Izvestiia Akademii nauk SSSR: Seriia istorii i filosofii*, no. 5, pp. 319–40.

PORSHNEV 1964. B. F. Porshnev. "Na putiakh k Polianovskomu miru 1634 goda. In *Mezhdunarodnye otnosheniia . . .*, pp. 512–37. Moscow.

PORSHNEV 1970. B. F. Porshnev. *Frantsiia, angliiskaia revoliutsiia i evropeiskaia politika v seredine XVII veka*. Moscow.

PORSHNEV 1976. B. F. Porshnev. *Tridtsatiletniaia voina i vstuplenie v nee Shvetsii i Moskovskogo gosudarstva*. Moscow.

PORTNOV 1990. M. E. Portnov. *Tsar'-pushka i Tsar'-kolokol*. Moscow.

POSSEVINO 1586. Antonio Possevino. *Moscovia*. Vilnius. See Poe 1995, pp. 120–21.

POSTERNAK 1988. O. P. Posternak. "Ikonografiia 'Kiiskogo kresta' i ego povtorenie v XVIII veke." In *Original i povtoreniia v zhivopisi . . .*, pp. 44–62. Moscow.

POSTNIKOVA-LOSEVA 1954. M. M. Postnikova-Loseva. "Zolotye i serebrianye izdeliia masterov Oruzheinoi palaty XVI–XVII vekov." In *Gosudarstvennaia Oruzheinaia palata Moskovskogo Kremlia*, pp. 137–216. Moscow.

POTEMKIN 1959. V. P. Potemkin. *Istoriia diplomatii*. Moscow.

POVSIADNEVNYKH ZAPISOK 1769. *Povsiadnevnykh dvortsovykh vremeni Gosudarei, Tsarei i velikikh kniazei Mikhaila Fedorovicha i Alekseia Mikhailovicha, zapisok*, vol. 1, pts. 1–2. Moscow.

PRAG UM. 1988–89. *Prag um 1600: Kunst und Kultur am Hofe Rudolfs II*. Ausst. Exh. cat. Essen/Vienna.

PRÉAUD 1995. Maxime Préaud. *Les Effects du soleil, Almanachs du regne de Louis XIV*. Exh. cat. Paris.

PRIKLADNOE ISKUSSTVO FRANTSII 1995. *Prikladnoe iskusstvo Frantsii XVII–XX vekov ot barokko do suprematizma*. Moscow.

PUTESHESTVIIA RUSSKIKH 1954. *Puteshestviia russkikh poslov XVI–XVII vv.* Moscow/Leningrad.

PUTEVODITEL' PO VYSTAVKE 1960. *Putevoditel' po vystavke iranskogo i turetskogo iskusstva XVI–XVII vekov*. Moscow.

PYHRR AND GODOY 1998. Stuart W. Pyhrr and José-A. Godoy. *Heroic Armor of the Italian Renaissance. Filippo Negroli and his Contemporaries*. Exh. cat. New York.

RAEFF 1997. Marc Raeff. "The Romanovs and Their Books: Perspectives on Imperial Rule in Russia." *Biblion: The Bulletin of The New York Public Library* 6, no. 1, pp. 42–75.

RASHKOVAN 1988/1. N. V. Rashkovan. "Augsburgskoe serebro epokhi barokko." In *Gosudarstvennaia Oruzheinaia palata*, pp. 273–79. Moscow.

RASHKOVAN 1988/2. N. V. Rashkovan. "Kollektsiia izdelii iz naturalii i redkikh materialov." In *Gosudarstvennaia Oruzheinaia palata*, pp. 280–89. Moscow.

RASHKOVAN 1988/3. N. V. Rashkovan. "Pamiatniki diplomaticheskikh sviazei Rossii s Pol'shei i Shvetsiei." In *Gosudarstvennaia Oruzheinaia palata*, pp. 243–56. Moscow.

RASHKOVAN 1988/4. N. V. Rashkovan. "Iskusstvo frantsuzskikh masterov XVII–XVIII vekov." In *Gosudarstvennaia Oruzheinaia palata*, pp. 290–97. Moscow.

RECHMENSKII 1913. A. Rechmenskii. *Sobranie pamiatnikov tserkovnoi stariny v oznamenovanie trekhsotletiia tsarstvuiushchego doma Romanovykh*. Moscow.

REINEKING VON BOCK 1981. Gisela Reineking von Bock. *Bernstein: Das Gold der Ostsee*. Munich.

REMEKMÜVEK A CÁRI 1989. *Remekmüvek a cári Kunstarbol: Parade es vadászata XVII századi oroszagban.* Budapest.

RENOUVIN AND DUROSELLE 1997. Pierre Renouvin and Jean Baptiste Duroselle. *Introduction à l'histoire des relations internationales.* Paris.

REUTENFELS 1905–6 [1680]. Jacob Reutenfels. "Skazanie svetleishemu gertsogu Toskanskomu Koz'me Tret'emu o Moskovii." In *Chteniia v Obshchestve istorii i drevnostei rossiiskikh pri Moskovskom Universitete*, bk. 3, pp. 1–137; 1906, bk. 3, pp. 129–227. Moscow. See Poe 1995, p. 175.

RICCARDI-CUBITT 1992. Monique Riccardi-Cubitt. *The Art of the Cabinet.* New York.

RIJKSMUSEUM 1995. "Recent acquisitions at the Department of Sculpture and Decorative Arts, Rijksmuseum, Amsterdam," *Burlington Magazine* 137 (June), pp. 419–24.

ROGERS 1986. J. M. Rogers. *The Topkapi Saray Museum: The Albums and Illustrated Manuscripts.* Exh. cat. Boston.

ROGOZHIN 1994. N. M. Rogozhin. *Posol'skie knigi Rossii kontsa XV–nachala XVII vv.* Moscow.

ROGOZHIN AND CHISTIAKOVA 1988. N. M. Rogozhin and E. V. Chistiakova. "Posol'skii prikaz." *Voprosy istorii*, no. 7, pp. 113–23.

ROHDE 1942. Alfred Rohde. "Das Bernsteinzimmer Friedrichs I im Königsberger Schloss." *Pantheon* 30, pp. 200–3.

ROOSEN 1976. William James Roosen. *The Age of Louis XIV.* Cambridge, Mass.

ROSENBERG 1922–28. M. Rosenberg. *Der Goldschmiede Merkzeichen*, vols. 1–4. Frankfurt am Main.

RUSSEN EN NEDERLANDERS 1989. *Russen en nederlanders.* Exh. cat. The Hague.

RUSSISCHE SCHATZKUNST 1981. *Russische Schatzkunst aus dem Moskauer Kreml und Leningrader Ermitage.* Exh. cat. Main am Rhein.

RUSSKII BIOGRAFICHESKII SLOVAR' 1896–1918. *Russkii biograficheskii slovar'* 23 vols. Moscow/New York.

RUSSKOE SEREBRO 1984. *Russkoe serebro XIV–nachala XX veka iz fondov Gosudarstvennykh muzeev Moskovskogo Kremlia.* Moscow.

RUSSKOE ZOLOTO 1987. *Russkoe zoloto XIV–nachala XX veka iz fondov Gosudarstvennykh muzeev Moskovskogo Kremlia.* Moscow.

SÁENZ DE MIERA 1991. J. Saenz de Miera. "La Historia de El Escorial en sus objetos: las puertas taraceadas del palacio privado." *Reales Sitios*, no. 108, pp. 29–36.

SAKHAROV 1991. A. N. Sakharov. *Diplomatiia Sviatoslava.* Moscow.

SAMEK 1984. J. Samek. *Polskie rzemiosło artystyczne: Czasy nowofytne.* Warsaw.

SAMEK 1988. J. Samek. *Polskie złotnictwo.* Wrocław.

SANDIN 1998. Per Sandin, ed. *Peter den store och Karl XII i krig och fred.* Exh. cat. Stockholm.

SANDRART 1675–79. Joachim von Sandrart. *Teutsche Academie*, vol. II, bk. 3. Nuremberg.

SANIN 1979. G. A. Sanin. "Russko-pol'skie otnosheniia 1667–1672 godov i krymsko-turetskaia politika v Vostochnoi Evrope." In *Rossiia, Pol'sha i Prichernomorie v XV–XVIII vekakh*, pp. 276–86. Moscow.

SAPUNOV 1885. A. Sapunov. "Kratkii ocherk bor'by Moskovskogo gosudarstva s Litvoiu i Pol'shei v XVI–XVII vekakh." In *Vitebskaia starina*, vol. 4, pp. 3–71. Vitebsk.

SAVICH 1939. A. A. Savich. "Deulinskoe peremirie 1618." *Uchenye zapiski: Seriia istoricheskaia*, vol. 2. Moscow.

SAVVA 1883. Archbishop Savva (Tikhomirov). *Ukazatel' dlia obozreniia Moskovskoi Patriarshei. . . .* 5th ed. Moscow.

SBORNIK 1902. *Sbornik Imperatorskogo russkogo istoricheskogo obshchestva.* St. Petersburg.

SCHÄTZE 1987. *Schätze der Museen des Moskauer Kreml.* Exh. cat. Berlin.

SCHÄTZE 1991. *Schätze aus dem Kreml: Peter der Grosse in Westeuropa.* Munich. See also Seling 1991.

SCHEFFLER 1965. W. Scheffler. *Goldschmiede Niedersachsens*, vols. 1–2. Berlin.

SCHEURLEER 1980. Th. H. Lunsingh Scheurleer. "Pierre Gole, ébéniste du Roi Louis XIV." *Burlington Magazine* 112 (June), pp. 380–94.

SCHLIEMANN 1985. E. Schliemann, ed. *Die Goldschmiede Hamburgs*, vols. 1–3. Hamburg.

SCHUBNEL 1993. Henri-Jean Schubnel. *Trésor du Musée Revue de la Gemologie*, special no. (Sept.).

SCHÜRER 1985. R. Schürer. "Der Akeleypokal. Überlegungen zu einem Meisterstück." In *Wenzel Jamnitzer und die Nürnberger Goldschmiedekunst 1500–1700*, pp. 107–22. Munich.

SEELIG 1989. Lorenz Seelig. "Die Münchner Kunstkammer, Geschichte, Anlage, Ausstattung." *Jahrbuch der Bayerischen Denkmalpflege* (1986), 40, pp. 101–38.

SEELIG 1991. Lorenz Seelig. "Vier Jahrhunderte schwedisches Silber für Königshof und Bürgehaus." *Weltkunst*, no. 61 (Feb.), pp. 244–46.

SEELIG 1994. Lorenz Seelig. "Die Kunst der Augsburger Goldschmiede im Dienst höfischer Repräsentation." In *Silber und Gold 1994*, pp. 32–56. Munich.

SEELIG 1999. Lorenz Seelig. "German Silver Services at Foreign Courts: Foreign Silver Services at German Courts." In *European Royal Tables: International Symposium*, pp. 166–79. Lisbon.

SELING 1980. Helmut Seling. *Die Kunst der Augsburger Goldschmiede 1529–1868*, 3 vols. and suppl. Munich.

SELING 1991. See *Schätze 1991*.

SEREDONIN 1891/1. Sergei Mikhailovich Seredonin. *Izvestiia inostrantsev o vooruzhennykh silakh Moskovskago gosudarstva v kontse XVI veka.* St. Petersburg.

SEREDONIN 1891/2. Sergei Mikhailovich Seredonin. *Sochinenie Dzhil'sa Fletchera "Of the Russe Common Wealth" kak istoricheskii istochnik.* St. Petersburg.

SHAKUROVA 1984. E. V. Shakurova. "Russkie serebrianye izdeliia XIV–XVII vekov." In *Russkoe serebro XIV-nachala XX veka . . .*, pp. 9–66. Moscow.

SHASKOLSKII 1964. I. P. Shaskolskii. *Stolbovskii mir 1617 goda i torgovye otnosheniia Rossii so Shvedskim gosudarstvom.* Leningrad.

SHASKOLSKII 1998. I. P. Shaskolskii. *Ekonomicheskie otnosheniia Rossii i shvedskogo gosudarstva v XVII veke.* St. Petersburg.

SHPILEVSKII 1850. P. Shpilevskii. "Opisanie posol'stva Pavla Sapegi v Moskvu v 1600 godu." *Zhurnal Ministerstva narodnogo prosveshcheniia* 68, pp. 91–122.

SHUBINSKII 1995. S. N. Shubinskii. "Shvedskoe posol'stvo v Rossii v 1674 godu." In *Istoricheskie ocherki i rasskazy*, pp. 7–12. Moscow.

SILBER UND GOLD 1994. *Silber und Gold: Augsburger Goldschmiedekunst für die Höfe Europas.* Exh. cat. Munich.

SILVERSKATTER 1997. *Silverskatter från Kreml. Svenska regenters gåvor till tsaren under stormaktsiden. Silver Treasures from the Kremlin. Gifts from Swedish Monarchs.* Exh. cat. Stockholm.

SILVERSTOLPE 1996. S. Silverstolpe. "Shvedskie zolotykh del mastera v Sankt-Peterburge." In *Shvetsiia i Sankt-Peterburg: Vtoroi nauchnyi seminar*, pp. 50–52. St. Petersburg.

SKARBY KREMLA 1998. *Skarby Kremla: Dary Rzeczypospolitej obojga narodów.* Exh. cat. Warsaw.

SKRYNNIKOV 1991. R. G. Skrynnikov. *Gosudarstvo i tserkov' na Rusi XIV–XVI vv.* Novosibirsk.

SLOT 1990. B. J. Slot. *Osmanlilar ve Hollandalilar arasindaki 400 yillik iliskiler.* Exh. cat. Istanbul.

SMIRNOV 1946. N. A. Smirnov. "Rossiia i Turtsiia v XVI–XVII vekakh." In *Uchenye zapiski Moskovskogo Gosudarstvennogo Universiteta*, vol. 94, bks. 1–2. Moscow.

SMIRNOVA 1964. E. I. Smirnova. "Zapadnoe serebro XIII–XIX vekov." In *Oruzheinaia palata*, pp. 217–56. Moscow.

SMIRNOVA 1969. E. I. Smirnova. "Novye dannye o postuplenii v XVII veke nemetskogo khudozhestvennogo serebra v Kremlevskuiu sokrovishchnitsu." In *Slaviano-germanskie kul'turnye sviazi*, pp. 328–37. Moscow.

SMIRNOVA 1984. E. I. Smirnova. "Novye materialy o serebrianykh izdeliiakh, khranivshikhsia na Kazennom dvore v pervoi treti XVIII veka." In *Proizvedeniia russkogo i zarubezhnogo iskusstva XVI-nachala XVII veka (Materialy i issled.)*, vol. 4, pp. 221–25. Moscow.

SMIRNOWA 1985. J. I. Smirnowa [also E. I. Smirnova] 1985. "Hamburger Silberarbeiten des 16. und 17. Jahrhunderts." In *Schliemann 1985*, vol. 1, pp. 121–35. Hamburg.

SMIRNOWA AND HEITMANN 1986. J. I. Smirnowa and B. Heitmann. *Gold und Silber aus dem Moskauer Kreml.* Exh. cat. Hamburg.

SNEGIREV 1842–45. I. M. Snegirev. *Pamiatniki Moskovskoi drevnosti s prisovokupleniem ocherka monumental'noi istorii Moskvy i drevnikh vidov i planov drevnei stolitsy.* Moscow.

SNICKARE 1999. Mårten Snickare. "Enväldets Riter." Ph.D. diss. Stockholm.

SOBOLEV AND ERMOLAEV 1954. N. I. Sobolev and B. A. Ermolaev. "Ognestrel'noe privoznoe oruzhie XVI–XVII vekov." In *Gosudarstvennaia Oruzheinaia palata Moskovskogo Kremlia*, pp. 387–434. Moscow.

SOKROVISHCHA IRANA I TURTSII 1979. *Sokrovishcha prikladnogo iskusstva Irana i Turtsii XVI–XVIII vekov iz sobraniia Gosudarstvennykh muzeev Moskovskogo Kremlia*. Moscow.

SOKROVISHCHA KREMLIA 1997. *Sokrovishcha Kremlia: Khudozhestvennye chasy/Treasures of the Kremlin: Masterpieces of Horology*. Geneva.

SOLOVEV 1990. S. M. Solovev. *Sochineniia v 18 tomakh*. Moscow.

STADEN 1991 [1930]. Heinrich von Staden. "Strana i pravlenie moskovitov v opisanii Genrikha Shtadena." In Sukhman 1991, pp. 67–76. See Poe 1995, p. 102.

STAHR 1990. M. Stahr. *Medale Wazów w Polsce, 1587–1668*. Wrocław/Warsaw/Kraków.

STAREVISIER 1982. Adele Le Barre Starevisier. "The Byzantine Silk Industry." Ph.D. diss., Columbia University.

STAVROU AND WEISENSEL 1986. Theofanis G Stavrou and Peter R. Weisensel. *Russian Travelers to the Christian East from the Twelfth to the Twentieth Century*. Columbus, Ohio.

STEINMANN 1986. Linda Keehn Steinmann. "Shah Abbas I and the royal silk trade, 1599–1629." Ph.D. diss., New York University.

SUKHMAN 1991. M. M. Sukhman, ed. *Inostrantsy o drevnei Moskve: Moskva XV–XVII vekov*. Moscow.

SVENSKT SILVER 1990. *Svenskt Silver från Renässans till Rokoko*. Stockholm.

SVENSKT SILVERSMIDE 1941–63. E. Andrén, O. Källström and C. Hernmarck. *Svenskt Silversmide 1520–1850*. 3 vols. Stockholm.

SVIAZI 1990. *Sviazi Rossii s narodami Balkanskogo poluostrova: pervaia polovina XVII v*. Moscow.

SYNDRAM 1994. Dirk Syndram. *Prunkstücke des Grünen Gewölbes zu Dresden*. Munich.

SYNDRAM 1999. Dirk Syndram. *Die Schatzkammer Augusts des Starken: von de Pretiosensammlung zum Grünen Gewöble*. Leipzig.

SZMYTKI 1995. R. Szmytki. *Vente du mobilier de Jean Casimir en 1673/Wyprzedaæ mienia po Janie Kazimierzu w roku 1673*. Warsaw.

TANANAEVA 1996. L. I. Tananaeva. *Rudol'fintsy: Prazhskii khudozhestvennyi tsentr na rubezhe XVI–XVII vekov*. Moscow.

TANNER 1991 [1680 or 1689]. B. L. F. Tanner. "Posol'stvo pol'sko-litovskoe v Moskoviiu v 1678 godu." In Sukhman 1991, pp. 385–401. Nuremburg. See Poe 1995, p. 180.

TEREKHOVA 1988. A. M. Terekhova, "Zapadnoevropeiskie tkani XVI–XVIII stoletiia." In *Gosudarstvennaia oruzheinaia palata*, pp. 313–16. Moscow.

TESORI DEL CREMLINO 1982. *Tesori del Cremlino*. Exh. cat. Venice.

TESORI DEL CREMLINO 1993. *Tesori del Cremlino: L'arte e la storia: Catalogo della Mostra, Castello di Torre Canavese, Torino, Italia*. Exh. cat. Moscow/Vienna.

TESOROS 1982. *Tesoros del Kremlin: Museo de San Carlos*. Exh. cat. Mexico City.

TESOROS 1988. *Tesoros del Kremlin*. Exh. cat. Buenos Aires.

TESOROS DEL KREMLIN 1990. *Tesoros del Kremlin: Ceremonial de gala en la Rusia del siglo XVII*. Exh. cat. Munich.

TESOUROS 1988. *Tesouros do Kremlin*. Exh. cat. São Paulo.

THE GOLD 1991. *The Gold of the Kremlin: Russian Gold and Silverworking and Jewellery from the 12th to the 20th Century*. Exh. cat. Moscow.

THE ILLUSTRATED BARTSCH 1980–81. *The Illustrated Bartsch*, vols. 2–3. New York.

THOMAS, GAMBER, AND SCHEDELMANN 1964. Bruno Thomas, Ortwin Gamber, and Hans Schedelmann. *Arms and Armour of the Western World*. New York.

TREASURES 1979. *Treasures from the Kremlin*. Exh. cat. New York.

TREASURES FROM THE MUSEUMS 1988. *Treasures from the Museums of the Moscow Kremlin*. Exh. cat. New Delhi.

TREASURES OF THE CZARS 1995. *Treasures of the Czars from the State Museums of the Moscow Kremlin*. London.

TREASURES OF THE MOSCOW KREMLIN 1998. *Treasures of the Moscow Kremlin: Arsenal of the Russian Tsars: A Royal Armouries Exhibition*. Exh. cat. Leeds.

TREASURES OF THE TSAR 1995. *Treasures of the Tsar: Court Culture of Peter the Great from the Kremlin*. Rotterdam.

TRÉSORS 1979. *Trésors des Musées du Kremlin*. Paris.

TREZORI 1985. *Trezori museja moskovskog Kremlija: Nardni muzej-Beograd*. Moscow.

TRIUMPH OF SIMPLICITY 1988. *The Triumph of Simplicity*. Exh. cat. Stockholm.

TRUSTED 1985. Marjorie Trusted. *Catalogue of European Ambers in the Victoria and Albert Museum*. London.

TRUTOVSKII 1913. V. K. Trutovskii. "'Romanovskaia' tserkovno-arkheologicheskaia vystavka v Moskve." *Starye gody*, no. 6 (June), pp. 36–43.

TSAARIEN AJAN AARTEITA 1996. *Tsaarien ajan aarteita Moskovan Kremlin museoista ja Trejakovin galleriasta*. Näyttelyn suojelija Rouva Eeva Ahtisaari.

TSGADA GUIDE 1991. *Tsentral'nyi gosudarstvennyi arkhiv drevnikh aktov: Putevoditel'*, 4 vols. Moscow.

TUTOVA 1997. T.A. Tutova. "K istorii opisanii kollektsii Oruzheinoi palaty v XIX v." In *Sokrovishcha Rossii. Muzei "Moskovskii Kreml" vchera, segodnia, zavtra.*, pp. 12–14. Moscow.

TYDÉN-JORDAN 1997. Astrid Tydén-Jordan. "Praktsilver och makt." In *Silverskatter 1997*, pp. 13–22. Stockholm.

ULUÇ 1987–88. Lale Uluç. "Ottoman Book Collectors and Illustrated 16th Century Shiraz Manuscripts." *Revue des Mondes Musulmans et de la Méditerranée*, pp. 85–107.

USPENSKII 1907. A. I. Uspenskii. "Tsarskii zhivopisets dvorianin Ivan Ievlevich Saltanov." *Starye gody*, no. 3 (March), pp. 75–86.

USPENSKII 1912. A. I. Uspenskii. *Stolbtsy byvshego arkhiva Oruzheinoi palaty*, vol. 2. Moscow.

USPENSKII 1958. A. I. Uspenskii. *Zapisnye knigi i bumagi starinnykh dvortsovykh prikazov: Dokumenty XVIII–XIX vekov byvshego Arkhiva Oruzheinoi palaty*. Moscow.

VAHLNE 1986. Bo Vahlne, ed. *Möbelhistoria, på Gripsholm*. Stockholm.

VAINSHTEIN 1947. O. A. Vainshtein. *Rossiia i tridtsatiletniaia voina*. Leningrad.

VALERIO BELLI VICENTINO 2000. *Valerio Belli Vicentino, 1468–1546*. Vicenza.

VAN KLENCK 1677. Koenraad van Klenck. *Historisch verhael, of beschryving van de voyagie, gedaen onder de suite van den heere Koenraad van Klenck*. Amsterdam.

VAN DER CRUYSSE 1991. Dirk van der Cruysse. *Louis XIV et le Siam*. Paris.

VELTMAN 1844. A. F. Veltman. *Moskovskaia Oruzheinaia palata*. Moscow.

VERLET 1982. Pierre Verlet. *The Savonnerie: Its History. The Waddesdon Collection*. Fribourg.

VERSAILLES ET LES TABLES ROYALES 1993. *Versailles et les tables royales en Europe XVIIème–XIXème siècles*. Exh. cat. Paris.

VIER JAHRHUNDERTE SCHWEDISCHES SILBER 1991. *Vier Jahrhunderte Schwedisches Silber für Königshof und Bürgerhaus*. Exh. cat. Munich.

VIKTOROV 1877–83. A. E. Viktorov. *Opisanie zapisnykh knig i bumag starinnykh dvortsovykh prikazov v 1584–1725gg.*, vols. 1–2. Moscow.

VISHNEVSKAIA 1993. I. I. Vishnevskaia. "Iranskie tkani na Rusi XVII veka: K probleme vzaimodeistviia russkogo iskusstva i khudozhestvennoi kul'tury sosednikh narodov." In *Dekorativno-prikladnoe iskusstvo*, vol. 9, pp. 155–61. Moscow.

VISHNEVSKAIA 1996/1. I. I. Vishnevskaia. "Dragotsennye tkani." In *Sokrovishcha Oruzheinoi palaty*, pp. 229–65. Moscow.

VISHNEVSKAIA 1996/2. I. I. Vishnevskaia. "Iuvelirnye izdeliia i torevtika Vostoka." In *Sokrovishcha Oruzheinoi palaty*, pp. 199–227. Moscow.

VISHNEVSKAIA 1999. I. I. Vishnevskaia. "Dragotsennye tkani na Rusi v XVI–XVII vekakh." In *Iskusstvo srednevekovoi Rusi*, vol. 12, pp. 276–86. Moscow.

VLADIMIRSKAIA 1998. See *Petr Velikii i Moskva* 1998.

VOET 1912. E. Voet. *Merken van amsterdamsche goud- en zilversmeden*. The Hague, repr. 1966.

VOET 1963. E. Voet. *Nederlandse goud- en zilvermerken, 1445–1951*. The Hague.

VOET AND GELDER 1941. E. Voet and H. E. von Gelder. *Merken van haagsche goud- en zilversmeden*. The Hague.

VON SANSSOUCI 1994. *Von Sanssouci nach Europa: Geschenke Friedrich des Grossen an europäische Höfe*. Exh. cat. Potsdam.

VYKHODY GOSUDAREI 1844. *Vykhody Gosudarei tsarei i velikikh kniazei, Mikhaila Fedorovicha, Alekseia Mikhailovicha, Fedora Alekseevicha, vseia Rusi samoderzhetsev (s 1632 po 1682 god)*. Moscow.

VZDORNOV 1986. G. I. Vzdornov. *Istoriia otkrytiia i izucheniia russkoi srednevekovoi zhivopisi. XIX vek*. Moscow.

WALKER AND HAMMOND 1999. Stefanie Walker and Frederick Hammond, eds. *Life and the Arts in the Baroque Palaces of Rome*. Exh. cat. New Haven.

WALTON 1992. Guy Walton. "The Era of Louis XIV: A Turning Point in the History of Diplomatic Gifts." In *Versailles: French Court Style and Its Influence*, pp. 199–213. Toronto.

WASILKOWSKA 1974. A. Wasilkowska. "O złotnikach wyszkolonych w Krakowie, a działajacych w Poznaniu w XVII wieku." *Biuletyn historii sztuki*, no. 3, pp. 351–55.

WATSON AND WHITEHEAD 1991. Francis Watson and John Whitehead. "An Inventory Dated 1689 of the Chinese Porcelain in the Collection of the Grand Dauphin at Versailles." *Journal of the History of Collections*, no. 3, pp. 13–52.

WEBER 1975. J. Weber. *Deutsche, niederländische und französische Renaissance plaketten 1500–1650*, vols. 1–2. Munich.

WEIGERT 1962. Roger Armand Weigert. *French Tapestry*. London.

WEIGERT AND HERNMARCK 1964. Roger Armand Weigert and Carl Hernmarck. *L'Art en France et en Suède*. Stockholm.

WELCH 1978. Stuart Cary Welch. *Imperial Mughal Painting*. New York.

WENZEL JAMNITZER 1985. *Wenzel Jamnitzer und die Nürnberger Goldschmiedekunst 1500–1700*. Exh. cat. Nuremberg.

WILKINS 1991 [1605]. George Wilkins. "Sera Tomasa Smita puteshestvie i prebyvanie v Rossii . . ." In Sukhman 1991, pp. 164–67. See Poe 1995, p. 139.

WILLIAMS 1985. E. V. Williams. *The Bells of Russia*. Princeton.

WITSEN 1666–67. Nicolaas Witsen, *Moscovische reyse, 1664–1665*. The Hague.

WITSEN 1996. Nicolaas Witsen. *Puteshestvie v Moskoviiu 1664–1665* (from the 1671 Antwerp ed. *Noord en Oost Tartarye . . .*). [St. Petersburg]. See Poe 1995, p. 172.

WÓJCIK 1968. Z. Wójcik. *Miïdzy traktatem Andrusowskim a wojn tureck. Stosunki polsko-roszjskie 1667–1672*. Warsaw.

WORTMAN 1995, 2000. R. S. Wortman. *Scenarios of Power: Myth and Ceremony in Russian Monarchy*. 2 vols. Princeton.

YABLONSKAYA. See Iablonskaia.

ZABELIN 1853. I. E. Zabelin. *Istoricheskoe obozrenie finiftiannogo i tseninnogo dela v Rossii*. St. Petersburg.

ZABELIN 1915–18. I. E. Zabelin. *Domashnii byt russkikh tsarits v XVI i XVII stoletiiakh*. Novosibirsk.

ZABOROVSKII 1981. L. V. Zaborovskii. *Rossiia, Rech' Pospolitaia i Shvetsiia v seredine XVII veka*. Moscow.

ZAGORODNIAIA 1998. I. A. Zagorodniaia. "Dary poselskie z Litwy i Polski od schyłku XV do końca XVII wieku." In *Skarby Kremla* 1988.

ZILVER UIT DE GOUDEN 1988. *Zilver uit de gouden eeuw van Antwerpen*. Exh. cat. Antwerp.

ZOLOTO KREMLIA 1989. *Zoloto Kremlia: Russkoe iuvelirnoe iskusstvo XII–XX vekov*. Exh. cat. Munich.

INDEX